OXFORD HISTORICAL MONOGRAPHS

A Patriot Press

NATIONAL POLITICS
AND THE LONDON PRESS
IN THE 1740s

ROBERT HARRIS

CLARENDON PRESS · OXFORD
1993

Oxford University Press, Walton Street, Oxford OX2 6DP
Oxford New York Toronto
Delhi Bombay Calcutta Madras Karachi
Petaling Jaya Singapore Hong Kong Tokyo
Nairobi Dar es Salaam Cape Town
Melbourne Auckland
and associated companies in
Berlin Ibadan

Oxford is a trade mark of Oxford University Press

Published in the United States
by Oxford University Press, New York

British Library Cataloguing in Publication Data

Data available

Library of Congress Cataloging in Publication Data

Harris, Robert.
A patriot press: national politics and the London press in the
1740s/Robert Harris.
p. cm.
Includes bibliographical references and index.
1. Press and politics—England—London—History—18th century.
2. Great Britain—Politics and government—1727–1760. I. Title.
PN5116.H37 1993
072'.1—dc20   92–24882
ISBN 0–19–820378–0

Typeset by Graphicraft Typesetters Ltd., Hong Kong
Printed and bound in
Great Britain by Biddles Ltd.,
Guildford and King's Lynn

PREFACE

SINCE J. B. Owen wrote his account of the ministerial and parliamentary dimensions to the politics of the 1740s, *The Rise of the Pelhams* (1957), political historians have tended to ignore the period. Studies of the 1730s and 1750s continue to grow, but work on the intervening decade has generally been limited to selected episodes, notably the Jacobite Rebellion of 1745–6. This neglect has been unfortunate. As this book aims to show, close examination of the confusing and fragmented politics of the 1740s sheds important light on patterns of change and continuity in the political culture of mid-eighteenth-century English politics. The book also represents an attempt to build on Owen's work by illuminating an aspect of the political scene to which he devoted almost no attention: the press.

Thanks are due to the staffs of the Bodleian Library, Oxford, the British Library, British Museum, and the Public Record Office, Chancery Lane. I am also grateful to the Governing Body of Lincoln College, Oxford, for electing me to a Senior Scholarship and for generous financial assistance from the Graduates Research Fund.

In the course of researching and writing this book, I have benefited from discussions with many people, and any list of acknowledgements would undoubtedly be incomplete. However, I would like to mention the help and stimulation provided by members of the Oxford Eighteenth-Century History Seminar. Amongst those who have helped me on my research on the eighteenth century, a particular debt must be recorded to Jeremy Black, who read certain chapters in early drafts and whose encouragement and generosity have been unfailing.

Particular mention must also be made of Paul Langford and Joanna Innes. Paul Langford supervised the thesis on which this book is based. He did this with characteristic tact and sagacity, and his contribution has been invaluable. Joanna Innes was kind enough to read the thesis after it had been completed and offer her invariably helpful comments.

This book is dedicated to my parents, who have never failed to give me their support, and to my friends.

BOB HARRIS

May 1992

CONTENTS

LIST OF PLATES

ABBREVIATIONS

GM	*Gentleman's Magazine*
HMC	Historical Manuscripts Commission
LEP	*London Evening Post*
Lewis, *Walpole*	*The Yale Edition of Horace Walpole's Correspondence*, 34 vols., ed. W. S. Lewis et al. (New Haven, Conn., 1937–70)
LM	*London Magazine*
OEJ	*Old England, or, the Constitutional Journal*
Parl. Hist.	*The Parliamentary History of England from the Earliest Period to the Year 1803*, 36 vols., ed. W. Cobbett (1806–20)
Richmond–Newcastle Correspondence	*The Correspondence of the Dukes of Richmond and Newcastle, 1724–1750*, ed. T. J. McCann (Sussex Record Society, 73; 1982–3)
Rose, *Marchmont Papers*	*A Selection of Papers of the Earls of Marchmont in the Possession of the Right Honourable Sir George Rose*, 3 vols., ed. G. H. Rose (1831)
Walpole, *Memoirs of King George II*	Horace Walpole, *Memoirs of the Reign of King George II*, 3 vols., ed. J. Brooke (New Haven, Conn., 1985)
WJ	*Westminster Journal, or, the New Weekly Miscellany*

NOTE ON CONVENTIONS

Dates are Old Style, unless otherwise indicated, with the year always commencing on 1 January. Place of publication is London, unless otherwise stated.

A major source for the book was pamphlets. Eighteenth-century authors and printers were not scrupulous about consistency with respect to titles, especially capitalization. A decision has been taken, therefore, to impose some consistency. Nouns, verbs, and adverbs have been capitalized in all pamphlet titles. In quotations, however, spelling and punctuation has not been modernized.

INTRODUCTION

THE relations between the press, public opinion, and politics in eighteenth-century Britain have long attracted the attention of historians. Yet no consensus has emerged about their nature and significance. How far did the press reflect popular opinion? How easily was the press able to mobilize this opinion on political issues? How capable and how willing was the press to follow closely events in Parliament and at court? In what ways and to what extent did the press and popular opinion enter the world of ministers and MPs? These questions have divided historians ever since Sir Lewis Namier sought to demonstrate their alleged irrelevance to an accurate understanding of eighteenth-century political life. In the last few years the divisions have, if anything, only widened. Thus, whereas some historians have emphasized recently what they see as the vigour and influence of the Hanoverian press, others have emphasized instead what they insist was, variously, its political 'shallowness', the 'lack of real information' on politics in its pages, its distant relationship to public opinion, and its even more distant relationship to events at court and in Parliament.[1] Which of these views represents a better portrayal of press involvement at least in mid-century Hanoverian politics is a question that this book attempts to answer. But it is not just with the nature of the contribution that the press made to politics that this book is concerned.

It is at least as much concerned with the patterns of change and development in early Hanoverian politics during the middle decades of the eighteenth century. Until comparatively recently, these decades attracted only limited attention. According to the account of early Hanoverian political development that became entrenched between the 1930s and 1960s, and which was to be influentially reformulated by J. H. Plumb in his 1967 Ford Lectures, these years represented the Whig oligarchy's finest hour.[2] Sir Robert Walpole had guided the

---

[1] The quotations are from *The Memoirs and Speeches of James, 2nd Earl Waldegrave, 1742–1763*, ed. J. C. D. Clark (Cambridge, 1988), 33. The current state of debate about the political role of the 18th-century press is summarized in M. Peters, 'Historians and the Eighteenth-Century Press: A Review of Possibilities and Problems', *Australian Journal of Politics and History*, 24 (1988), 37–50.

[2] J. H. Plumb, *The Growth of Political Stability in England, 1675–1725* (1967).

nation into a state of political torpor. Party rivalry had finally fizzled out
in the later 1720s, and Jacobitism had long since collapsed as a serious
threat to the Hanoverian regime. Only occasional squalls of popular and
press outrage remained to disturb the tranquil scene; but even these
were characterized by their transience and their failure to stimulate
significant innovations in extra-parliamentary politics. In sum, politics
was almost devoid of serious issues and controversy; there was little of
great interest for historians to explore.

Since the late 1970s, revisionist historians have challenged key
elements of this interpretation. Linda Colley has argued that the Tory
party—motivated by hopes of office under the Hanoverians—retained a
distinctive organizational and ideological identity for most of the early
Hanoverian period.[3] Only in the later 1750s did the two-party alignment of politics that had prevailed since about 1700 begin to unravel.
This view, that the 1750s marked a crucial turning-point in the role of
party, has been put forward even more strongly by J. C. D. Clark and
Eveline Cruickshanks.[4] Yet, for Clark and Cruickshanks, the persistence
of the Whig and Tory parties into the 1750s had nothing to do with
prospects of office; rather, it was a function of the central importance of
dynastic questions throughout most of the early Hanoverian period.
The Tories, they have argued, were predominantly a Jacobite party,
engaged in seeking the overthrow of the Hanoverian dynasty by means
of an armed rising supported by foreign powers. Nor were their hopes
without any basis in reality. Jacobitism, Clark and Cruickshanks have
also argued, remained a vital force in politics, and a potent threat to
political stability, until Culloden, and perhaps until 1759.[5] Several other
historians have argued that many of the tactics and the platform
traditionally associated with the Wilkite movement were substantially
foreshadowed in earlier episodes.[6] According to this account, the

[3] L. Colley, *In Defiance of Oligarchy: The Tory Party, 1714–60* (Cambridge, 1982).

[4] J. C. D. Clark, *The Dynamics of Change: The Crisis of the 1750s and English Party
Systems* (Cambridge, 1982); E. Cruickshanks, *Political Untouchables: The Tories and the
'45* (Edinburgh, 1979).

[5] An exhaustive and even more recent examination of Jacobitism in all its guises,
which is generally supportive of this assessment of the Jacobite threat, is provided by P.
Monod, *Jacobitism and the English People, 1688–1788* (Cambridge, 1989).

[6] L. Colley, 'Eighteenth-Century Radicalism before Wilkes', *Transactions of the Royal
Historical Society*, 5th ser. 31 (1981), 1–19; N. Rogers, *Whigs and Cities: Popular Politics
in the Age of Walpole and Pitt* (Oxford, 1989); M. Peters, 'The "Monitor" on the Constitution, 1755–65: New Light on the Ideological Origins of English Radicalism', *English
Historical Review*, 86 (1971), 706–25: K. Wilson, 'Empire, Trade, and Popular Politics in
Mid-Hanoverian Britain: The Case of Admiral Vernon', *Past and Present*, 121 (1988), 74–
109.

foundations for John Wilkes's explosion on to the political scene in 1763 had been firmly laid in the previous two decades or so. This book takes up many of the questions raised by the revisionist scholarship of recent decades, and in particular the view that the 1750s was a watershed separating two political systems. It also seeks to fill a major gap in the current historiography: the relative neglect of the 1740s. Recent studies of mid-century politics have concentrated very largely on the 1750s. As well as the new studies of party, there has been a wave of recent work on various aspects of politics during the Seven Years War (1756–63).[7] By comparison, sustained interest in the preceding decade has been conspicuously lacking. Apart from Nicholas Rogers's survey of London politics, the only other work in the last few decades on aspects of politics in the 1740s has concentrated almost exclusively on one episode: the '45.[8] The neglect of the press of the 1740s has been even greater. It found no place in the only detailed modern examination of parliamentary and court politics in this period, J. B. Owen's classic study *The Rise of the Pelhams* (1957). More recent work on the eighteenth-century English press has done little to fill the gap that this left. Michael Harris's investigation of the London press in the Walpolian period, although purporting to include developments up until 1746, provides only a sketchy account of the period after about 1740.[9] Certain individual newspapers and pamphlets of the decade, as well as a number of incidents relating to the press, have been explored in a series of articles by Jeremy Black.[10] But major elements of the picture remain unclear or simply unexamined. Most obviously, for

[7] M. Peters, *Pitt and Popularity: The Patriot Minister and London Opinion during the Seven Years War* (Oxford, 1980); R. Middleton, *The Bells of Victory: The Pitt–Newcastle Ministry and the Conduct of the Seven Years War* (Cambridge, 1985); E. J. S. Fraser, 'The Pitt–Newcastle Coalition and the Conduct of the Seven Years War, 1757–1760', D.Phil. thesis (Oxford, 1976).

[8] Rogers, *Whigs and Cities*; Cruickshanks, *Political Untouchables*; W. A. Speck, *The Butcher: The Duke of Cumberland and the Suppression of the '45* (Oxford, 1981); F. J. McLynn, *The Jacobite Army in England: The Final Campaign* (Edinburgh, 1983); J. Black, *Culloden and the '45* (Stroud, 1990).

[9] M. Harris, *London Newspapers in the Age of Walpole: A Study in the Origins of the Modern English Press* (1987).

[10] J. Black, 'A Short-Lived Jacobite Newspaper: The National Journal of 1746', in K. Schweizer and J. Black (eds.), *Politics and the Press in Hanoverian Britain* (Lewiston, 1990), 77–88; id., 'Parliamentary Reporting in England in the Early Eighteenth Century: An Abortive Attempt to Influence the Magazines in 1744', *Parliaments, Estates, and Representations*, 7 (1987), 61–9; id., 'Whig Propaganda in the Early Eighteenth Century: A Yorkshire Example', *York Historian*, 7 (1986), 40–5; id., 'Falsely Attributed to Lord Bolingbroke', *Publishing History*, 17 (1985), 81–9; id., 'A Genoese Gentleman', *Factotum*, 19 (1984), 16–17.

example, no work comparable to that done on the *Craftsman* or the *Monitor*, the influential essay paper established by the Beckfords in 1755, has hitherto been undertaken on the two leading essay papers of the 1740s, *Old England, or, the Constitutional Journal* and the *Westminster Journal, or, the New Weekly Miscellany.*

It is not difficult to suggest reasons why the 1740s have failed to attract the same degree of attention as the subsequent decade. Not the least of these is the quality of J. B. Owen's *The Rise of the Pelhams*. This was Namierite history at its most convincing; and, as an analysis of political manoeuvre at court and in Parliament between 1742 and 1748, it is unlikely to be bettered. But it is not just the shadow cast by *The Rise of the Pelhams* that has deterred further enquiry. Only marginally less important is the character of politics in the 1740s. As far as politics at home was concerned, and as Owen was able to demonstrate so clearly, the fall of Walpole in February 1742 was followed by four years of confused factional struggles. Negotiations were continually started and broken off as various politicians attempted to force their way into the administration on favourable terms. Ministries were unstable and divided, their personnel subject to repeated reshuffles. Only in 1746 was a degree of domestic political stability obtained. Nor did any politicians obviously emerge to fill the substantial gaps left in the political landscape when Walpole was finally forced from office, and his long-time opponent, William Pulteney, was elevated to the Lords in July 1742. Henry Pelham, who eventually emerged as Walpole's successor, was a leader in a very different mould. He never imposed himself on the Commons or his fellow ministers to the degree that Walpole had done at the height of his rule; and, like Lord Liverpool in the early nineteenth century, his unobtrusive style of leadership has made it very easy to underestimate his considerable political skills. Amongst the opposition, it was William Pitt who shone most brightly, his thundering anti-Hanoverian philippics of 1742–4 earning him the soubriquet of the 'Great Orator'. But even he was quickly dimmed following admission to the ministry in 1746.

Internationally, the picture was no clearer, and the personalities no more commanding. The War of the Austrian Succession had many faces, undergoing a series of dramatic shifts in character over its eight-year course.[11] As should become very clear in the second part of this

---

[11] The fullest and most recent narrative account of the war is contained in R. Butler, *Choiseul: Father and Son, 1719–1754* (Oxford 1980).

book, this only accentuated the discontinuities in domestic politics as positions and arguments had to be adjusted to accommodate abrupt changes in the war. Militarily it was a war of manœuvre and attrition; great and significant military actions were extremely rare (Dettingen, Fontenoy, the capture of Cape Breton, and, to a lesser extent, Rocoux, Laffeldt, and the naval battles off Belle-Isle and Cape Finistère). No great military reputations were forged. The Duke of Cumberland may have achieved considerable stature as a result of the crushing of the Jacobite army at Culloden; but this was significantly eroded during the remainder of the war by, first, the controversies created by his treatment of the defeated Jacobites and the Highland population after the battle, and, then, his failure to arrest the advance of the French in the Low Countries in the final stages of the war. The war also ended in a military stalemate, with the Peace of Aix-la-Chapelle being accurately perceived by contemporaries as marking only the beginning of a brief hiatus before conflict between the two principal participants, Britain and France, would be rejoined. The major issue that the war raised— Anglo-French rivalry for commercial and imperial supremacy— appeared to have been simply left to re-emerge more vividly in the next decade.

One of the principal themes of this book is that a failure to examine closely the press and politics of the 1740s has led some historians to underestimate the strands of continuity in mid-century politics. On questions of war and empire, in terms of the political forces underpinning press activity, and, perhaps most strikingly, on the debate about patriotism, the shape of developments and events in the 1750s can be very clearly discerned in the preceding decade. Patriotism was the mid-century variant of country ideology. It embraced all the traditional arguments of the country tradition, the concern about the encroachment of the executive on traditional liberties, and the need to defend the independence of Parliament from the court. But it was also taking on new meanings and emphases. Britain's identity as a trading power, and the desirability of popular involvement in politics were, for example, becoming more prominent themes. As several historians have recently emphasized, patriotism's malleability, its capacity to expand its significance and constituency, made it a very vital force in early Hanoverian politics.[12] It was also, as I shall attempt to argue, a force that, by the 1740s at the very least, was blurring the edges of traditional

---

[12] See esp. Rogers, *Whigs and Cities, passim.*

party rivalry. Patriotism's adherents in the press and beyond the walls of Parliament appear to have cared little whether their parliamentary champions were opposition Whigs or Tories. What did concern them was seeing their creed accepted at the heart of government. Nor was this, as some historians have sought to argue, without relevance to, or influence on, Whig and Tory behaviour in Parliament. High politics, as it is sometimes called, was never hermetically sealed off from low, or popular, politics; neither was the latter simply a pallid reflection of the former. Rather, the two spheres of politics—both of which possessed its own dynamic—overlapped and interacted at many points; their relationship was a two-way one. The intrusion of the press into most aspects of politics, its willingness to trespass on subjects allegedly outside its competence, was for the most part something that ministers and MPs could only either exploit or fulminate against: it could not be prevented.

To argue that patriotism overshadowed much of the contemporary political terrain is not the same as arguing that Whig and Tory had no place in politics in the 1740s. What is being argued, however, is that there were important aspects of contemporary political life from which the two-party alignment was already in full retreat. In these same areas the grounds for the Tory absorption in the Whig consensus in the 1750s had, as Ian Christie has recently commented, 'long been prepared'.[13] Such a conclusion is reinforced, as I will attempt to show in Chapter 2, by consideration of the Tory contribution to press debate in this period. The confused politics of the 1740s and, in particular, the fall of Walpole and the initial Tory participation in the Broad-Bottom ministry in late 1744 provoked a number of identifiably Tory pamphleteers to defend and explain the nature of their party's role in contemporary politics. As will be carefully demonstrated, their efforts further reveal the extent to which Toryism had become subsumed in the politics of patriotism. Tories may have had some sense of identity distinct from that of the Whigs, but this was less important than their assertions of a strict Tory identification with patriotism, and the greater importance in contemporary politics of the patriot–ministerial division.

If the degree of continuity in mid-century politics has been underestimated, so has the vigour and influence of press debate during the War of the Austrian Succession. Traditionally, perceptions of the

---

[13] I. Christie, 'The Changing Nature of Parliamentary Politics, 1741–1789', in J. Black (ed.), *British Politics and Society from Walpole to Pitt, 1742–1789* (1990), 108.

intervention of the press in politics have been much influenced by the change that took place in the relationship between politics and literary activity between the 1730s and 1740s. Under Walpole, the literary giants Swift, Gay, Pope, and Fielding all sooner or later wrote about politics or directly participated in the anti-Walpolian press campaign. By the 1740s writers were giving politics far less attention. Questions of a more general moral nature occupied the attention of the decade's major writers. Thus, if Gay's *Beggar's Opera* is typical of the advance of politics into literature under Walpole, Richardson's *Pamela* is typical of its retreat after Walpole's fall. The impact that this shift has had on historians has only been amplified by a recognition that ministerial intervention in the press declined sharply following Walpole's departure from office. But, as I shall argue, the change in ministerial behaviour towards the press cannot be attributed to an abrupt diminution in the press coverage of politics after 1742. Equally, it is necessary to be careful about not pre-dating the sharp retraction of public involvement and interest in politics that undoubtedly occurred in the course of the decade.

This only became very apparent after 1746. Before then press intervention in politics was extremely vigorous. Fuelled by the combination of instability in domestic politics and Britain's growing entanglement in a major war—so often the motors of press involvement in eighteenth-century politics—press debate about politics raged, reaching the peak of its influence in the winter of 1743–4, when it stimulated a popular outcry against the alleged subordination of Britain's role in the war to Hanoverian ends. As I shall attempt to show, the vigour and range of the anti-Hanoverian press campaign between late 1742 and early 1744 is hard to exaggerate, and almost certainly matched anything seen in the Walpolian era. Examination of this campaign also reveals a little-regarded aspect of the role in mid-century politics of the Grenvilles and their close allies. Towards the end of the 1750s Horace Walpole was to write of the Grenvilles' contribution to politics in the early part of the preceding decade: 'These men, who, if they had any talents, had the greatest art that ever I knew of decrying those they wanted to undo, soon kindled such a flame in the nation, that the King was forced to part with his favourite [Lord Carteret], and all his airy schemes of Germany glory.'[14] As I shall show, substantial and sustained intervention

---

[14] Walpole, *Memoirs of King George II*, i. 112.

in the press by these politicians was the means by which the flame was kindled.

If the popular anti-Hanoverian outcry of the winter of 1743–4 provides a good example of the political possibilities opened up by a relatively unfettered press, it also serves to highlight a further major concern of this book; namely, the press and popular debate of issues arising out of the government's conduct of foreign affairs. As Jeremy Black and others have recently emphasized elsewhere, the importance of these issues in mid-eighteenth-century public and press debate is hard to exaggerate.[15] Information and opinion about foreign affairs dominated the press coverage of politics to a degree that would be inconceivable in today's press. Yet, in contrast to argument on patriotism, party, and the role of the people in politics, this aspect of press debate has often been passed over quickly or even ignored completely by historians of the extra-parliamentary dimension of eighteenth-century politics. Moreover, with a few notable exceptions, when it has been examined, it has been dismissed either as simplistic or as simply evidence of the force of popular prejudices—for example, isolationism —in the popular debate of politics.[16] Assessing the extent to which the debate about foreign policy corresponded to contemporary diplomatic and international realities, however, is not necessarily the best way of treating the subject. As John Brewer has demonstrated in another context, a more illuminating approach to political argument can be to explore why certain arguments acquired a contemporary force and plausibility.[17] This is the approach that is adopted in this book, with the underlying intention of showing why particular arguments were put forward and how events and developments in the War of the Austrian Succession interacted with these arguments to, in some cases, give them weight and, in others, to erode their plausibility. Only by doing this is it possible to understand fully the progress of press debate during the war, and the shifts in popular mood that it helped to stimulate.

One of the very few periods in mid-century when foreign policy was not at the forefront of press and public debate was during the height of the Jacobite Rebellion. The intense anti-Hanoverianism of the early

---

[15] J. Black, *The English Press in the Eighteenth Century* (1987), 197–243.

[16] See e.g. G. C. Gibbs, 'English Attitudes towards Hanover and the Hanoverian Succession in the First Half of the Eighteenth Century', in Adolph M. Birke and Kurt Kluxen (eds.), *England and Hanover* (Munich, 1986), 33–50.

[17] J. Brewer, *Party, Ideology and Popular Politics at the Accession of George III* (Cambridge, 1976).

1740s led to considerable optimism amongst Jacobites about the prospects of overthrowing the Hanoverian regime. In the event, as is well known, their hopes were to be shattered by the failure of the '45. For most people it seemed, anti-Hanoverianism, did not signify support for the Stuart cause. But what role did the London press play in thwarting the Jacobite Rebellion? Despite the marked revival of interest in recent years in the '45 and, in particular, in the domestic response to the rebellion, the role of the press in the crisis has never been examined systematically. Yet, as I shall show in Chapter 6, the same press that had done so much to create popular alienation from the politics and personnel of the Hanoverian regime in the preceding three years had an influential contribution to make in rousing popular resistance to the Jacobite challenge. As Richard Finch, a London tradesman, reported to a business partner on 22 October 1745: 'the newspapers [are] every day full of pathetic incitements to fight for our king and our liberties; and the pamphlet shops crowded with entire new books on the same important subjects.'[18] With some justification, I shall argue, the London press could claim to have been one of the principal bulwarks of defensive loyalism during the Hanoverian regime's darkest hour.

Although the influence of the press appears to have diminished markedly after the '45, this does not mean that the press debate of the later years of the war was without significance. The final stages of the War of the Austrian Succession gave a decisive impetus to popular and press attitudes towards foreign affairs and, in particular, towards the contemporary international rivalry for commercial supremacy. Before the war a central focus of debate about foreign policy was the possibilities for imperial and commercial aggrandizement represented by Spain's American empire. When the war ended, it was the French threat to Britain's trade and empire, and French rivalry for control of North America that dominated public and press discussion of Britain's relations with foreign powers. Concern about French commercial and colonial ambition was nothing new. What was new, however, was the prominence that the issue was accorded, and the identification of North America as a crucial area in the competition between Britain and France for 'power and plenty'. As will be shown, absolutely central to this shift in popular perceptions was the capture of Cape Breton in July 1745. It was Cape Breton that provided the stimulus to the expression of concern about French commercial advances since the Peace of

---

[18] Quoted in Black, *Culloden and the '45*, 91.

Utrecht, and the impetus behind the explosion of excitement and interest regarding the commercial advantages to be gained by control of North America. The final stages of the war also provided a fillip to those who saw Britain's navy as the crucial instrument of her international aims and influence. With the growing evidence of Britain's naval supremacy, particularly after 1747, destruction of French trade and colonial power seemed not only a desirable goal, but also a feasible one. In this area of press debate, just as in the debate about patriotism and in a number of other areas, the press of the 1740s looks forward to the 1750s and the rise of the Elder Pitt. Pitt, patriotism, and empire may have represented the future, but the fact that this was so was due in no small part to longer-term trends in early Hanoverian politics.

The following account is divided into two parts. The first part is thematically organized, and examines those factors which strongly shaped the basic contours of the relationship between national politics and the press between 1740 and 1748: the intervention of politicians in the press; the ability and willingness of the press to comment on events in Parliament and at court; the relationship between the press and patriotism. An attempt is also made to assess the influence of the press on different elements of the contemporary political nation. The second part consists of a narrative account of the press debate created by the War of the Austrian Succession.

Throughout this book 'the press' is understood to comprise all forms of contemporary printed political polemic published in London: political essay papers, pamphlets, prints, newspapers, periodicals, ballads and odes. Eighteenth-century newspapers and periodicals are often studied in isolation from other forms of printed material. The validity of this approach, particularly for the mid-century period, can be questioned. Contemporaries accepted that all forms of polemic were part of a chain of communication and propaganda; overlap between the various forms was very marked. Only by adopting an inclusive approach is the full picture of press involvement in politics revealed. The omission of the provincial press from this study was dictated primarily by limitations of time; it was also done in the knowledge that provincial papers at this time were totally dependent on the London press for their political comment.

Part I

National Politics and the London Press

THE PRESS, PARLIAMENT, AND POPULAR OPINION

THE basic aim of this and the following chapter is to describe a number of the most important factors shaping the intervention of the press in politics between 1740 and 1748. The present chapter is concerned principally with three areas of the relationship between the press and national politics. The first part examines how far the political opinions expressed in the London press of the period matched the views of a substantial section of the political nation 'without doors'. The second part seeks to show the various ways in which the early Hanoverian press sought (and was used) to extend the ambit of national politics beyond the confines of Westminster and St James. And the third and last part investigates various aspects of the relationship between the press and the politicians. By looking at each of these in turn, one of the things that it is hoped to show is that the press was influential at most levels of politics. The mid-century press may not have governed the fortunes of ministries (or individual politicians), but it deserves to be taken seriously as one of the principal ways in which views about national politics were circulated among the extra-parliamentary nation, and, partly but not solely because of this, as an important element of politics in Parliament and at court.

Since the early 1970s a reasonably full picture has emerged of how, and in what quantities, elements of the press were circulated amongst a broad social and geographical cross-section of early Hanoverian society. Yet this has not prevented a marked tendency in the last few years to question the closeness of any correspondence between the political opinions expressed in the press, particularly in the newspaper and periodical press, and public opinion (however defined). Of those factors to which a number of historians have drawn attention as justification for this scepticism, two stand out. The first is the economic considerations that affected the selection of a paper's content. In this context, prominence has been accorded to the role of the booksellers who financed a significant proportion of the newspaper press. These individuals were more concerned about profit than politics. In many instances this led them to establish papers that avoided political controversy. Such ventures were, moreover—as Jeremy Black has recently observed—the most consistently successful elements of the London press throughout the eighteenth century.[1] Bookseller interests also, it is argued, significantly affected the content of those papers which did devote space and attention to politics. The most detailed exposition of this position has been the work of Michael Harris.[2] Put very simply, Harris has argued that after the 1720s the booksellers established a growing stranglehold on the London press. Their business and economic interests, Harris further argues, led them to pursue political respectability. Under their control, and with the additional influence of the law and the political system, the press tended towards the 'predominantly routine and business-like content' that allegedly characterizes the press of the mid-century. In other words, it was the commercial interests of newspaper proprietors, and not the political interests of readers, which were paramount in shaping the political content of the press.

The second principal factor employed to justify scepticism regarding the value of the press as a guide to popular opinion is the observation that political comment was generally written for, rather than by, public opinion.[3] According to this view, political opinion in the press represented the views of various interested parties such as politicians and mercantile lobbies, and not the views of the public, whoever they may have been.

It would be perverse to deny the validity of much of the case for scepticism. There can be no doubt, for example, that financial and business incentives motivated bookseller investments in the press, and that such investments were expected to provide a good rate of return. It is also undeniable that politicians and special interest groups were behind a substantial proportion of the political comment carried in the press. The use of the press by such groups, as John Brewer has recently

---

[1] J. Black, *The English Press in the Eighteenth Century* (1987), 118–19.

[2] See esp. M. Harris, *London Newspapers in the Age of Walpole* (1987). For a convincing discussion of some of the problems raised by Harris's account, see K. T. Winkler, 'The Forces of the Market and the London Newspaper in the First Half of the Eighteenth Century', *Journal of Newspaper and Periodical History*, 4 (1988), 22–35.

[3] See e.g. J. C. D. Clark's comments on the press as evidence for 'popularity', in 'The Politics of the Excluded: Tories, Jacobites, and Whig-Patriots, 1715–1760', *Parliamentary History*, 2 (1983), 209–22.

emphasized, intensified from the 1730s.[4] Spurred on by the success of the campaign against Walpole's Excise Bill of 1733, systematic exploitation of the press and 'popular clamour' became a staple element of lobbying activity. Political factions were, as we shall see later, equally ready to intervene in the press at this time. Indeed, such was the scale of this intervention in the mid-century that James Ralph—one of the leading journalists of the period—was to be provoked into complaining in the 1750s: 'as to the community . . . they have never thought of taking it [the press] out of the Hands of Faction, and, by special warrant, transferring it to some able Hands to be made use of, not for their Amusement, but their service, not to inflame their Resentments, but to bring their Grievances, if any, to a fair, full, and effectual audit'.[5] Yet it is arguable that the relationship between the political views and concerns of readers and the content of the political press was closer than the above remarks would suggest. Pressures were placed on London's booksellers, printers, and Grub Street hacks to follow closely the political views of readers. The evidence of the newspaper and periodical press itself suggests, moreover, that these pressures were far from negligible.

The first point to be made in this context is that the market for newspapers and periodicals published in London during the central decades of the eighteenth century was limited in extent, and thus only capable of absorbing a relatively small number of new titles. Competition between papers for readership was correspondingly intense, with many more new titles failing than succeeded. In this competition, politics often had a not insignificant role to play. The political stance or content of a paper or periodical was, in many cases, a key factor in determining whether a particular paper either secured or lost a foothold in the market. It is far from accidental, for example, that one of the two leading opposition essay papers of the 1740s, the *Westminster Journal, or, the New Weekly Miscellany*, was successfully established during the crisis that surrounded Walpole's fall in the winter of 1741–2, when popular interest in politics was unusually intense. Alienating readers through the political views expressed in a paper was equally possible, and something that papers took steps to avoid. The veteran essay paper

[4] J. Brewer, *The Sinews of Power: War, Money, and the English State, 1688–1783* (1989), 242–3.
[5] J. Ralph, *The Case of the Authors, by Profession or Trade, Stated with Regard to Booksellers, the State, and the Public* (1758), 20.

the *Craftsman* was forced to change political direction in the summer of 1742. For a number of issues in early July 1742 it attempted to defend the conduct of its former patron, William Pulteney, in the political settlement that followed Walpole's fall. This, however, was to underestimate the strength of popular revulsion created by Pulteney's alleged betrayal of the opposition cause. The political line of the paper was swiftly adjusted, and the defence of Pulteney was dropped almost as soon as it had begun.[6]

Similarly pragmatic in the face of popular opinion was the most influential opposition paper of the early 1740s, *Old England, or, the Constitutional Journal*. Having identified itself very closely with the so-called Broad-Bottom opposition of 1742–4, the paper attempted to induce its readers to support the ministry when most of the leaders of that opposition were admitted to it in late 1744. But it recognized that its ability to achieve this aim was entirely dependent on evidence being forthcoming that the admission of leading opposition politicians represented a change of measures as well as men. On 2 February 1745 the paper employed the analogy of the fate of Actaeon to clarify its position: should no change of measures occur, the paper avowed, and its former heroes prove themselves to be turncoats, then the *Old England Journal* would attack them with the ferocity that had characterized the dismemberment of the metamorphosed Actaeon by his dogs. In the event, there was no substantial change of measures, and the *Old England Journal* became the Broad-Bottom ministry's most outspoken critic in the first half of 1745, with one particularly noteworthy issue provoking the ministry to take action against the paper.[7] These examples of papers adapting their political content in reaction to the views of their readers could be multiplied many times. Their significance is, of course, that they illustrate just how closely the views of readers impinged on the content of the political papers of the 1740s.

The closeness of the relationship between political content, the views of readers, and demand in the press can also be illustrated in a number of other ways. There is no doubt that the attraction of certain issues of papers could be increased by a particularly noteworthy essay or other political item. It was not unknown for a paper to increase its print-run in anticipation of this happening. In the late 1720s this was a practice adopted by both the *Craftsman* and the popular Tory paper *Mist's Weekly Journal*, and it seems probable that it was also followed by

---

[6] See below, Ch. 4, for a detailed discussion of this.   [7] See below, Ch. 6.

the most successful political papers of the 1740s.[8] Another response to increased demand was to reprint the relevant essay or series of remarks in a subsequent issue. On 5 January 1742, for example, the influential tri-weekly *London Evening Post* published a letter on the attendance of MPs at the forthcoming session of Parliament. On 9 January the paper reprinted the same letter, remarking: 'there having been great Demand for our letter of Thursday last, relating to Attendance in Parliament'. Yet another possibility was to reproduce the successful essays in pamphlet form. This is what happened to many of the early issues of the *Old England Journal*, with some of the resulting pamphlets going through a number of editions.[9]

A much broader feature of the coverage of politics in the press that also reveals sensitivity to readers' opinions was the effect on the amount of space devoted to politics of the successive betrayals of the opposition in 1742 and 1744, and of the '45. As the following chapter will discuss in detail, these factors combined to produce a substantial reduction in popular interest in national politics, a fact that, significantly, was reflected in an equally marked reduction in the volume of political comment printed across the gamut of the press after 1746. In a number of cases it actually precipitated the collapse of opposition papers. As the *Gentleman's Magazine* observed in 1747, the vigorous opposition of the 1730s and early 1740s had been 'communicated' to all elements of the press, and had 'multiplied essay papers'. But politics had now retreated from its position as the 'universal topick' of interest, thereby providing scope at last for science and literature to flourish.[10] In the present context it is also worth noting that, contra Michael Harris, the view that political quietism had overtaken the press by the early 1740s would have been the source of much surprise to contemporaries. Rather, had there been a general consensus on this issue, it would probably have been that at least between 1742 and 1744 the violence of the political comment expressed in the leading opposition papers surpassed anything that had been seen during the famous press wars of the Walpolian era.[11]

It seems, then, that the relationship between the political content of

[8] See Winkler, 'The Forces of the Market', 24.

[9] See e.g. *A Collection of Letters Published in Old England, or, the Constitutional Journal* (1743) (this pamphlet contained the essays published in the first 12 issues of the paper); *Four Letters Published in the Old England Journal* (8, 22, 29 Oct., 5 Nov. 1743); *Four Letters Published in Old England, or, the Constitutional Journal* (25 Feb., 2, 10, 17 Mar. 1744).

[10] *GM* 16 (1747), preface.   [11] See below, Ch. 5.

those newspapers which were predominantly concerned with politics, the 'papers of faction' as pro-ministerial writers often called them, and the views of readers needed to be sufficiently close if a paper was to stand a reasonable chance of success or even survival. A very similar view of the significance and influence of the political opinion expressed in the press also emerges from the remarks of contemporaries. A number of polemicists even commented directly on the relationship between the search for profit and political writing. Thus, in 1744 one pamphleteer attacked the 'common writers', who were, it was asserted, 'little known' and 'little knowing', and whose activities were 'guided by the common maxim of writing, *what will most take and what will best sell*' (my italics).[12] A similar degree of conviction is evident in relation to the influence of the press. Indeed, for supporters of the ministry (or individual ministers), it was the perceived servitude of popular opinion to the press that gave cause for alarm. Few expressed this alarm more vehemently than Lord Carteret and his supporters, a fact that is perhaps unsurprising in view of the volume of press abuse directed at Carteret (which is examined in a later chapter) for his supposed subordination of British interests to Hanover in his conduct of the war between 1742 and 1744. In Parliament in early 1744 Carteret denounced the fact that news-writers were, as he put it, the 'oracles' of the people.[13] In early 1745, following Carteret's dismissal from office at the end of the previous year, a pro-Carteret pamphleteer expressed even greater outrage at the apparent influence of the press: 'O England! O England! Into what a state of Degeneracy art thou fallen: The Manners of thy sons govern'd by the Dictates of scriblers, and thy Honour ass-rid by Hirelings, who earn their Bread at the Expence of thy shame and infamy.'[14] Various explanations were also put forward in the pro-ministerial press to account for the allegedly biddable nature of popular opinion. The most favoured were the general lack of knowledge among the people, and the attraction for the 'lowest sort' of the scurrilous and defamatory style of writing that was said to predominate in the contemporary political press.[15]

The level of hostility expressed towards the role of the press by vari-

---

[12] *A Warning to the Whigs, and to Well-Affected Tories* (1744), 3.

[13] *Parl. Hist.*, xiii. 326. See also below, Ch. 5, for Carteret's attitude towards the press in the winter of 1743–4.

[14] *The Plain Reasoner* (1745), 40. See also *A Continuation of the Plain Reasoner* (1745), 23.

[15] See esp. *A Letter to a Friend in the Country, upon Occasion of the Many Scurrilous Libels, which Have Been Lately Published* (1743), 2–32.

ous supporters of the ministry in this period is only fully understandable in terms of at least three factors. First, there is no doubt that by the later 1730s and early 1740s the press battle for popular support had been comprehensively won by the opposition. In fact, a number of pro-ministerial polemicists were only too ready to concede the greater popularity of the opposition. Thus, in 1740 one pro-ministerial pamphleteer offered the following explanation of the behaviour and loyalties of the 'people':

> You are to know, therefore, sir, that in *England* it is presumption enough that a man is a man of Honour and sense if he opposes the court. This opens the way for him into the Affections of the people, and the same person who they before (while perhaps he was deep in the measures of the ministry) look'd upon with Aversion, or at least cold indifference, becomes then the Darling, and is regarded with Affection, nay with Rapture.[16]

Secondly, there was a concern that the press, by alienating a broad section of the nation from the personnel and policies of Hanoverian Britain, was providing succour to the Jacobite cause. Much of the time ministerial comment on this subject was deliberately alarmist. Nevertheless, as will be shown elsewhere in the present work, at least in the early 1740s their fears were an entirely reasonable response, given that Britain was at war with both France and Spain, to the attacks of the opposition press on the Anglo-Hanoverian union. Thirdly, the press also seems to have been perceived by many supporters of the ministry as threatening that most holy of eighteenth-century holies, the relationship between property and government. In this respect, not only was the allegedly low social standing of the majority of political writers the object of much comment, so were the political pretensions of the urban middling ranks who constituted such a substantial proportion of press readership. The degree of class animus that informed some of this comment is evident in the very terms that were employed to describe (or denigrate) this element of press readership: the 'vulgar' or the 'mob'.

The fiercest attack that the press of the 1740s made on the political aspirations of such groups was contained in Lord Perceval's hugely influential pamphlet, *Faction Detected by the Evidence of Facts*, published in September 1743. Perceval, it will be recalled, had had

---

[16] *An Historical View of the Principles, Characters, Persons, &c. of the Political Writers of Great Britain* (1740), 22.

first-hand experience of the political behaviour of the popular opposition in Westminster in 1741–2, when he had gained selection as one of their candidates at the by-election caused by Parliament's nullification of the return made for the constituency at the 1741 general election.[17] Significantly, he identified the press as the Broad-Bottom opposition's single most important means of expediting its political goals. He also made a series of heated remarks about the penetration of the press far into and across the middling ranks of metropolitan society. At one point he referred to the activities of what he called 'a wretched set of people'. These individuals, he inveighed, 'who with Education just sufficient to enable them to read, spend all their leisure Time . . . in some blind coffee house, and thence retiring to their Tavern Assemblies, retail it [opposition polemic] out again to men still below them in this great Qualification'. According to Perceval, these same individuals also affected to be 'consummate politicians', 'judging of the interests of all states and kingdoms, all ministers and Princes'.[18] Elsewhere Perceval demanded, thus echoing a relatively frequent refrain in comment hostile to the role of the press, 'Shall every Cobbler in his stall pretend a knowledge of political Affairs, superior to that of the best . . . the greatest men of this and all former Ages, who their whole Turn of Life have adapted and dedicated wholly to the study of Politicks and Government?' It was also, Perceval continued, 'ridiculous vanity' to suppose that 'men who have not interest in the state, but the profits of their Daily labour' should have a greater concern for their country than 'those who have vast properties to take care of'.[19] Perceval, it is perhaps worth pointing out, was biting the hand that fed him, in more ways than one. He first brought the possibility of his candidature to public notice by placing an advertisement declaring his readiness to stand in a number of papers; and, as his account of the election makes clear, this advertisement played a crucial role in securing his long-coveted seat in Parliament.[20]

If, therefore, there would seem to be convincing grounds for believing that the press articulated the political views held by a substantial section of the political nation, in what ways was the press used to open

---

[17] For this, see N. Rogers, *Whigs and Cities: Popular Politics in the Age of Walpole and Pitt* (Oxford, 1989), 170–1.

[18] *Faction Detected*, 65, 94–5.   [19] Ibid., 105.

[20] For Perceval's own account of the circumstances that led to his election for Westminster in 1741, see BL Add. MS 47093 (Egmont Papers), fos. 1–4. See also *An Enquiry into the Independency of a Dependent Lord* (1743), *passim*.

up various aspects of national politics to popular scrutiny? As far as providing information about activities in Parliament was concerned, a very significant contribution was made by the two leading monthly magazines, the *Gentleman's Magazine* and the *London Magazine*. It is well known that a notable feature of both periodicals was their accounts of parliamentary debates, which after 1738 were disguised by transparent subterfuges to circumvent the renewed efforts of the Commons in that year to enforce and extend the parliamentary privilege of prohibiting the printing of the proceedings of either House without permission.[21] Less often emphasized is how far this aspect of the magazines' activities was driven by the fierce rivalry between them and by the popular interest in the debates. In the first place, this is disclosed by the respective advertisements for the two magazines, and by the protracted arguments carried on between them regarding the authenticity and origin of their reports. In this context, it is also significant that when a short-lived rival to both magazines, the *Publick Register, or, Weekly Magazine*, announced its establishment in 1741, its principal claim was to provide the earliest and most complete account of debates.[22] In the second place, the history of the rivalry between the *Gentleman's Magazine* and the *London Magazine* with regard to their accounts of debates, and its effect on the content of the latter magazine, were actually described in an editorial letter published in the 1747 edition of the *London Magazine*.[23] The letter was prompted by the punishment of both magazines by the Lords in August 1747 for their reporting of Lord Lovat's trial. This had angered the printers appointed by Parliament to print such items as addresses, who saw the coverage of the trial as an illegal infringement of their privileges, and duly instigated action against the magazines.[24] In the letter to his readers the editor of the *London Magazine* defended the utility of the publication of the debates. He also remarked that it had been rivalry with the *Gentleman's Magazine* that had compelled the *London Magazine* to commence the publication of individual parliamentary speeches in 1739. Up until then, as the editor noted, the magazine had only provided the 'substance of several debates, by way of argument, answer,

[21] See L. Hanson, *The Government and the Press, 1695–1763* (Oxford, 1967), 76–82.

[22] For the *Publick Register*, see the advertisement for the magazine in the *Daily Post*, 1 May 1741. For the claims and counter-claims between the *GM* and the *LM* regarding the quality of their parliamentary reporting, see e.g. *GM* 9 (1739), 111–13, 223–4; *LM* 11 (1742), preface.   [23] *LM* 16 (1747), 353–4.

[24] Hanson, *Government and the Press*, 79.

and reply'. Following the 'heavy expence' incurred as a result of the Lords punitive action, the editor announced his intention of returning to the earlier format. However, if any Member of Parliament should choose to send him a speech, that would be published in full. The *Gentleman's Magazine* confined its reportage of debates in the later 1740s to this last alternative. In May 1748, for example, it reprinted a speech made by the Leicester House MP Thomas Potter during the Commons debate on the petition against the election return for Seaford at the 1747 general election.[25] Other politicians who seem to have supplied the same magazine with copies of a parliamentary speech earlier in the 1740s include George Selwyn and the ubiquitous Lord Perceval.[26]

Interestingly, in 1744 Lord Chancellor Hardwicke made an unsuccessful attempt to restrain the reporting of parliamentary debates by the magazines.[27] The catalyst was an account published in the *London Magazine* of a speech made by Hardwicke's eldest son, Philip Yorke, in one of the great Hanoverian troop debates of the beginning of the same year. As correspondence between Philip Yorke and the biographer and historian Thomas Birch makes clear, the impact of the printed account of the speech was the source of considerable concern. On 15 July Yorke was driven to remark: 'I did not expect that Messrs Cave [Edward Cave, printer-owner of the *Gentleman's Magazine*] & Astley [Thomas Astley, the major bookseller-proprietor of the *London Magazine*] had been of such influence as I find them to be.'[28] Hardwicke's response to the incident seems to have been to use an agent, a certain Thomas Harris, to try and persuade a number of papers—the *General Evening Post*, the *Daily Post*, the *Daily Advertiser*, the *Champion*, the *Daily Gazetteer*, and the *London Gazette*—to publish a letter attacking what were dubbed the 'scandalous' accounts of debates that appeared in the magazines, and warning of the determination of 'several members of the first distinction' to get the legislature to suppress the practice at the next session of Parliament. All the papers refused to reprint the letter, all except the *Gazette* on the grounds that they did not wish to incur the displeasure of the magazines, and the *Gazette* because it was not its usual practice to print controversial items. Confronted with such a

---

[25] *GM* 17 (1748), 195–8.   [26] Ibid. 15 (1746), 622–3; ibid. 14 (1745), 7–23.

[27] For a recent discussion of this, see J. Black, 'Parliamentary Reporting in the Early Eighteenth Century: An Abortive Attempt to Influence the Magazines in 1744', *Parliaments, Estates, and Representations*, 7 (1987), 61–9. The origins of the attempt appear to have been unknown to Black.

[28] BL Add. MS 35396 (Hardwicke Papers) fo. 223: Yorke to Birch, 15 July 1744.

uniform (and negative) response, Hardwicke appears to have dropped the matter.

The monthly magazines were not the only elements of the political press that made efforts to extend the audience of parliamentary debates. Both the opposition essay papers and various occasional pamphlets also 'echoed forth', as James Ralph put it, the basic lines of argument deployed at Westminster.[29] Here, as in so many areas of the relationship between the political press of the early Hanoverian period and politics at the centre, it was the willingness of certain opposition politicians to intervene in the press that was often vital. In 1740, for example, one pro-ministerial observed of the short-lived *Englishman's Evening Post*: 'Some of the papers in it were wrote so much in the spirit of the speeches that were made in P——t, that it was soon discover'd that they came from the same Hands that Spoke them.'[30] Similarly, it was political connections that were almost certainly behind a number of noteworthy issues of the *Old England Journal* and another of the leading opposition essay papers of the 1740s, the *Remembrancer*, which was founded in 1747. In early 1748 the *Remembrancer* referred, over a number of issues, to divisions in the ministry on the question of the desirability of concluding peace with France in the War of the Austrian Succession. To support its contention that Pelham was an advocate of peace, the paper referred explicitly to an intervention that Pelham had made in Parliament in early 1748 warning of the dangerous level of the present fiscal commitments created by Britain's role in the war. The paper also referred to speeches in a similar vein made by two of Pelham's 'lieutenants' in the same debate.[31] Given that none of these speeches was reported elsewhere, it seems highly probable that the paper was, in this instance, exploiting its very close links with the Leicester House opposition of the later 1740s.[32]

As far as occasional pamphlets are concerned, it was a common tactic to publish a substantial pamphlet at the end of a parliamentary session, drawing together and summarizing opposition argument as it had been expressed in the major debates of that session. An important example of this was the pamphlet entitled *A Review of a Late Motion*, which was published in May 1741. This defended the famous *motion* of 13 February 1741, and summarized the case against Walpole as articulated

[29] [Ralph] *A Critical History of the Late Administration of Sir Robert Walpole* (1743), 1.

[30] *An Historical View . . . of the Political Writers of Great Britain*, 47.

[31] *Remembrancer*, 4 Jan., 5 Mar. 1748.   [32] For these links, see below.

by leading opposition speakers in both Houses. On occasion, the opposition did not wait for the end of the session before disseminating similar pamphlets, a practice that was condemned by the pro-ministerial *Daily Gazetteer* as representing a 'manifest' invasion of the freedom of Parliament, and therefore unconstitutional.[33] There were also pamphlets—although they were much less common—which provided a narrative account of a parliamentary session that had just ended. In fact, during the 1740s only one such pamphlet seems to have appeared, and, in that instance, it was only the very high level of interest in the parliamentary session that followed Walpole's fall which accounts for its appearance.[34] As was usual with the more substantial political pamphlets of the period, most of the pamphlets that fell into the categories referred to above were extracted by the essay papers and one or other of the monthly magazines.

Another notable way in which the press attempted to stimulate (or satisfy) popular interest in Parliament and its membership was by publishing lists either of MPs who had just been returned at a general election or which indicated voting behaviour in specific parliamentary divisions. The most sophisticated list of the 1740s was an election return list published in the *Gentleman's Magazine* following the general election of 1741. This appeared in the May issue of the magazine for that year, and used italic type to distinguish MPs in the 'Country Interest' from those in the 'Court Interest'.[35] In addition, together with less controversial information, the list also indicated the voting behaviour of MPs, where it was relevant, on the Excise Bill of 1733, the 1734 attempt to repeal the Septennial Act, and the Spanish Convention of 1739. Appended to this list was a subsidiary list of MPs who had voted against the *motion* of 13 February 1741, and a complete account of the voting in the Lords on the same occasion. Other election return lists in 1741 were published in the *London Evening Post* and the *Craftsman*.[36] Like the *Gentleman's Magazine*, both distinguished MPs in the 'country' interest from those in the 'court' interest. In the case of the *Craftsman*, it also repeated the practice that it had pioneered in 1734—rearranging the constituencies in relation to the size of their contribution to the land-tax, in order to support opposition claims that, despite the numerical superiority of the ministry in the Commons, the

---

[33] *Daily Gazetteer*, 25 May 1741.
[34] *The Critical History of the Last Important Sessions of Parliament, which Probably Put a Period to British Liberty* (1742).   [35] *GM* 11 (1741), 311–16.
[36] *LEP* 2 July 1741; *Craftsman*, 25 July 1741.

elections were a popular defeat for Walpole. The pro-ministerial paper the *Daily Gazetteer* immediately attacked the *Craftsman* for allegedly inciting mob rule by distinguishing between MPs on the basis of their parliamentary conduct.[37] It is a good measure of a much changed political climate that no similar election return lists accompanied the general election of 1747. In fact, there were no lists at all in the *Gentleman's Magazine* or any of the contemporary political papers; and the only distinction that the *London Magazine* made in the election return list that it carried was between those MPs who had, and those who had not, sat in the last Parliament.[38]

Of the lists indicating voting behaviour in specific parliamentary divisions published during the 1740s, the majority were occasioned by the crucial debates on the employment of the Hanoverian troops of 1742 and 1744.[39] Details of the voting behaviour of MPs on 10 December 1742, the division that followed the first great debate of the early 1740s on this question, appeared in pamphlet form, in the *London Magazine*, and in the *Westminster Journal*.[40] That they were not without effect is suggested by remarks regarding their widespread dissemination and impact made by a number of contemporary polemicists. One of these, the author of the pamphlet *A Compleat View of the Present Politicks of Great Britain* (1743), referred to the lists as a 'gross insult' to Parliament, and commented that they were 'in common use and in every Body's Hands'.[41] In a number of instances the division lists were published together with a Lords protest on the same issue. The propaganda potential of these protests had been firmly established by their systematic use and reprinting by the group known as 'Cowper's cabal' between 1721 and 1723.[42] Thus, when Carteret was informed in 1741 of proposals for a motion in the Lords on 13 February to address the King to remove Walpole from his councils, he responded with the comment that the attempt could have no utility but 'to make a noise and enter

[37] *Daily Gazetteer*, 30 July 1741.

[38] *LM* 16 (1747), 369–76. The magazine had printed a similar list in 1741 (ibid. 10 (1741), 521–9).

[39] The only other lists that were published in the 1740s described the voting in either the Lords or the Commons on the *motion*. For this, see above.

[40] *LM* 11 (1742), 80–2; *WJ* 12 Feb. 1743: *A List of the Members of Parliament who voted for and against taking the Hanover Troops into British Pay, December 10, 1742. To which is added, The Lords Protest on that Occasion, &c.*

[41] *A Compleat View of the Present Politicks*, 22.

[42] For this, see Clyve Jones, 'The House of Lords and the Growth of Parliamentary Stability', in Clyve Jones (ed.), *Britain in the First Age of Party, 1680–1750: Essays Presented to Geoffrey Holmes* (1987), 103–4.

a Protest'.[43] It was also usual for protests to be entered in significant numbers during the last session of a Parliament. In April 1741 the *Gentleman's Magazine* reprinted all the protests of the previous parliamentary session, remarking: 'It has been observ'd, that in the last sessions of a parliament generally more Protests are entered than in any other: In the late sessions no less than 11 Questions occasion'd Protests, which, we doubt not, our Readers will expect.'[44] In 1747 the early dissolution of Parliament prevented, amongst other things, any 'popular' questions being raised in the Lords, and thus forestalled any concerted campaign of protesting.[45]

A more controversial aspect of the intervention of the press in national politics than either the publishing of division lists or protests in the Lords—which also had the effect of fixing popular attention on parliamentary activity—was the championing and reprinting of constituency instructions to MPs. Two aspects of the role of the press in this context are of particular relevance. The first is that, whatever the origins and representativeness of the instructions, readers of the opposition press were encouraged to view them as a legitimate means of impressing popular demands on Parliament. They were also encouraged to view the instructions as expressing the 'sense of the people' on certain issues, and instructed to measure the performance of Parliament and their MPs against them. In 1739, for example, one opposition pamphleteer advocated that the 'people' use their MP's response to the campaign of instruction, then in its initial stages, demanding the enactment of a place bill as the litmus test of his suitability (or unsuitability) for re-election at the forthcoming general election.[46] The second is the prominence that was accorded to instructions by most opposition papers. In 1742 the two waves of instructions that were produced in the months that followed Walpole's fall were published across the gamut of the opposition press, appearing in the *Champion*, the *Craftsman*, the *London Evening Post*, the *Daily Post*, and the *Universal Spectator*. They were also published, along with a number of letters of thanks in reply from MPs, in both the monthly magazines, the *Gentleman's Magazine* and the *London Magazine*, and were collected together and published

    [43] Jones, 'House of Lords', 105.   [44] *GM* 11 (1741), 200.

    [45] On 21 June the *WJ* claimed that the early dissolution had also prevented a campaign, similar to the one that took place in 1734, to repeal the Septennial Act.

    [46] *An Address to the Electors and Other Free Subjects of Great Britain, Occasioned by the Late Secession* (1739). See also [Marchmont] *A Serious Exhortation to the Electors of Great Britain*, (1740), 16–17.

in pamphlet form.[47] As has been recently emphasized elsewhere, the importance that was attached to the instructions in the opposition press ensured that they provoked a vigorous debate about their legitimacy, and that they also provided a powerful focus for the discussion of the related issue of the proper role of the 'people' in the political process.[48]

On 26 November 1748 the opposition essay paper the *Westminster Journal* observed that it was during a parliamentary session that its office of 'political watchman' was of 'most importance'. Apart from the reprinting of material from the *Votes*, and, occasionally, the King's address to Parliament at the beginning of the session, and, even less commonly, the Commons and Lords addresses of thanks in response, the press possessed a number of means of commenting on the parliamentary session in progress. The process actually began in the weeks before the session commenced, when a series of essays were printed in most of the leading opposition papers and, in certain instances, in pamphlet form, emphasizing the duty of attendance of MPs.[49] A major function of these essays was to relate directly current issues of opposition and opposition press concern to the forthcoming parliamentary campaign. As such, they formed a crucial element in the wave of political polemic, pamphlets, ballads, and essays that usually heralded the return of the parliamentary classes to London for a new parliamentary session.[50]

Two examples of these essays, published in successive issues of the leading opposition essay paper, the *Old England Journal*, on 5 and 12 November 1743, show very clearly how they were designed to work. Both identified one specific parliamentary objective or issue: in this case, the dismissal of the 16,000 Hanoverian troops from British pay. Both also sought to establish the necessity and, equally important, the legitimacy of this goal. As far as the former was concerned, the essays

---

[47] The pamphlet was entitled *Great Britain's Memorial: A Collection of Instructions, etc. to the Members of Parliament, Part, II* (1742).

[48] See esp. Rogers, *Whigs and Cities*, 246–50; Kathleen Wilson, 'Inventing Revolution: 1688 and Eighteenth-Century Popular Politics', *Journal of British Studies*, 28 (1989), 349–86.

[49] Probably the best example of a pamphlet on the subject of the attendance of MPs in this period is *A Key to the Business of the Present Sessions*, published in advance of the crucial 1741–2 session of Parliament.

[50] On 4 Oct. 1743 Philip Yorke observed of this feature of press activity: 'I have long observed that particular art & industry is employed to infuse a large dose of uneasiness & jealousy amongst the people, upon some favourite, or perhaps plausible, point, within a competent distance of the meeting of parliament.' (BL Add. MS 35396, fos. 164–6: Yorke to Birch.)

provided a summary of the case against the Hanoverian troops that had been articulated more fully in other essays and pamphlets during the preceding weeks. In support of the latter, the paper referred its readers to the precedent of the Parliament of the 1690s, which had forced William III to dismiss his Dutch guards. As the *Old England Journal* declared: 'Such were the sentiments of that truly *British* parliament, which refused to King *William* the continuance of his *Dutch* Blue Guards, which he so earnestly solicited, and ardently wish'd.' If, then, the dismissal of the Hanoverians was both necessary and justified by recent precedent, it was also, the paper further argued, a realizable goal. In this context, it was alleged in one of the essays that the majority of the 'old court party' (the term by which the paper referred to the supporters of the Pelhams, more usually known as the 'old corps') would, now, unlike in 1742, support their dismissal.[51] In the other essay, the paper referred to the 'great crisis' that was allegedly confronting Britain, and remarked: 'that none but the worst of Hanoverians, I mean such recreant *Englishmen* as wear the livery of the *Electorate*, can or will give a vote in their [the Hanoverian troops] favour'.[52]

In certain cases, essays in the opposition press on the attendance of MPs may have been one important factor in creating popular pressure on opposition MPs to appear at Westminster. Certainly, in 1742 Lord Egmont reported in his diary that Sir William Courtenay, the Tory MP for Devon, had ben mobbed at Exeter for 'not being up at parliament to attend his duty'.[53] It is also likely that the care with which they were composed, and the prominence that they were accorded, in many instances reflect the scale of the problem that absenteeism among MPs, particularly before Christmas, represented for leading opposition politicians seeking to mount an effective challenge to the ministry.[54]

Once the parliamentary session had started, the press possessed two principal means of circumventing the parliamentary prohibition on the reporting of its proceedings. The first, and most obvious, was the insertion of a short and often cryptic paragraph, verse, or ballad. The resourcefulness with which the press exploited this device can be seen very clearly in the weeks that followed Walpole's fall in February 1742. On 11 March, for example, the *London Evening Post* responded to the

[51] *OEJ* 5 Nov. 1743.   [52] Ibid. 12 Nov. 1743.
[53] HMC, *Diary of Viscount Percival, Afterwards first Earl of Egmont*, 3 vols. (1920–3), iii. 243.
[54] See A. Foord, *His Majesty's Opposition, 1714–1830* (Oxford 1964), 171–5.

unexpected defeat of Lord Limerick's first Commons motion to appoint a committee of inquiry into the conduct of Walpole—a result of the defection to the ministerial side of a number of opposition Whigs who had been admitted to the ministry following Walpole's fall—by printing a ballad entitled 'The Screen—a Simile', an obvious reference to a growing conviction that Walpole was still managing affairs at court. In its next issue (13 March) the same paper included a report of a meeting of 200 opposition MPs to 'consult about matters of the utmost import-ance in the present crisis of affairs', which took place on 12 March at the Fountain Tavern. On the subject of Walpole's apparent evasion of justice, the paper commented elsewhere in the same issue:

But notwithstanding these bare-faced countenanced proceedings 'tis our comfort to find we have some worthy patriots left of such *stubborn virtue* that they are resolutely determin'd not to be discourag'd by the *highest* opposition [presumably George II], but to pursue their country's Enemies thro' all their secret mazes, and by bringing them to justice, save the sinking s[tat]e.

On 16 March the *London Evening Post* was again hounding the apos-tate patriots, juxtaposing the rectitude of the Duke of Argyll's resig-nation on 10 March with the alleged perfidy of those opposition Whigs who remained in office. Underneath another ballad entitled 'A Contrast Resignation', the paper bluntly exclaimed: 'Notwithstanding their boasted pretensions, we find the Path of virtue too rugged for some clamorous votaries of St S[tephen]'s.' Another paper that was also assiduously following the events of this period was the essay paper the *Champion*. On 1 July, for example, it commented: 'Yesterday a hopeful Babe of which the whole Three Kingdoms had conceived the highest Expectations was STRANGLED in the BIRTH, at a certain GREAT HOUSE at Westminster, and 'tis believed the Grand Inquest will find it wilfull murder.' The day before, the Commons had rejected a motion to authorize the printing of the report of the secret commitee that had eventually been established to investigate the last ten years of Walpolian domestic administration.

The second of the means employed by the opposition papers to respond and comment on the parliamentary session in progress was the publication of essays obliquely related to proceedings in Parliament. In the first half of 1742 the most obvious of these were the widely reprinted essays expounding the desirability and necessity of a parlia-mentary inquiry into alleged maladministration and corruption under

Walpole, and defending Parliament's right to impeach the 'Grand Corrupter'.[55] A much more interesting example from the same period, however, is two essays that were printed in the *Craftsman* in May, both of which were entitled 'Considerations upon the Nature and Expediency of Tacking'. The first appeared on 8 May, and the second on 29 May. Both addressed the possibility that an effective inquiry into Walpole's administration might be blocked either by the Crown or the Upper House. It was argued that the Commons control of the purse was the only leverage that could be used to overcome obstacles originating from either, or both, of these sources. The essays were an accurate commentary on the reality of the political situation. There is little doubt that George II deeply resented being compelled to part with Walpole, and that he was anxious to protect Walpole from any form of prosecution.[56] The House of Lords was an essential tool in ministerial control of the Commons. In the parliamentary session of 1741–2, for example, ministerial superiority in the Upper House was used to block the passage of place and pension bills, a tactic frequently employed to obstruct popular measures likely to embarrass the ministry in the Lower House.[57] Furthermore, the issue of using the Commons control of the purse in such a way had actually been raised in Parliament on 19 February 1742, when the Tory leader, Sir Watkin Williams Wynn, moved a motion in the Commons on granting supply only after the redress of grievances. It was, however, the matter of the bill to indemnify evidence against Walpole that projected the relationship between the two Houses into real prominence in early 1742.

The committee of inquiry into Walpolian maladministration, which was finally established in May, quickly encountered difficulties.[58] It failed to uncover any important evidence against Walpole through the scrutiny of written records. This compelled an almost exclusive reliance on oral testimony. But this merely produced a new set of problems. The key witness, the Solicitor to the Treasury, Nicholas Paxton, refused to answer questions regarding allegations of electoral corruption at the borough of Wendover in 1735 on the grounds that he might incriminate himself. The Commons, following a report from the committee's chairman, Lord Limerick, debated Paxton's refusal, and

[55] See e.g. *Craftsman*, 6 Mar., 10 Apr. 1742; *Champion*, 6, 8 May, 26 June 1742.

[56] See J. B. Owen, *The Rise of the Pelhams* (1957), 93.

[57] Eveline Cruickshanks, 'The Political Management of Sir Robert Walpole, 1720–42', in J. Black (ed.), *Britain in the Age of Walpole* (1984), 24.

[58] For the progress of the inquiry, see Owen, *Rise of the Pelhams*, 106–10.

voted, first, to commit him to the custody of the Serjeant-at-Arms, and subsequently, when confronted with Paxton's continued obduracy, to Newgate. In order to overcome the problem raised by the grounds of Paxton's refusal to testify, a bill of indemnity was introduced into the Commons and passed on 19 May. Even before the bill had reached the Lords, the opposition foresaw its rejection. On 21 May a meeting was held at the Fountain Tavern to discuss how to proceed. On 25 May the bill was debated in the Upper House and rejected. The Lords rejection of the bill came close to precipitating an interesting breach in relations between the two Houses. In the event, however, a motion of censure on the Lords was defeated in the Commons on 29 May. It is only by placing the publication of the second essay in the *Craftsman* in this precise political context that the vigour of the press in evading the stringent legal restraints on the reportage of parliamentary proceedings is fully revealed. As the editor remarked on 29 May, by way of a prefix to the essay in the paper: 'I was in Hopes that no incident, as to public Transactions, should have call'd upon a further *Disquisition* of this self evident maxim, far less did I think that the application would be *necessary at this juncture*.'

Alongside the practical efforts to expose the activities of the politicians at court and in Parliament, the opposition press also articulated a variety of arguments defending the role of a free press in the political process. A near commonplace was the claim that the press was vital to the exercise of the people's alleged right to examine 'the measures of every administration'. This view was forcefully expressed by the Earl of Marchmont in his election pamphlet, *A Serious Exhortation to the Electors of Great Britain*, published in 1740. As Marchmont explained:

Tho' the complaisance of Parliament's have furnish'd the Crown with both wealth and power whenever it has been desir'd, yet it has still remain'd a Privilege of the subject to pass his publick judgement on measures, to point out where he thinks they may have been carried on wrong, to shew mankind the dangerous tendency of them, to exhort them to lawful means of obtaining a Remedy, and to apprise them against any future Inconveniences they may be brought under; all this the Freedom of the Press allows us . . .[59]

A broadly similar view was also developed in an essay entitled 'An Apology for the Liberty of the Press', which appeared in the *Old*

[59] [Marchmont] *A Serious Exhortation*, 19–20.

England Journal on 2 April 1743. The essay began with two sweeping claims, neither of which could have stood much serious historical scrutiny. First, it was asserted that both the present ministry and the constitution owed their existence to the 'Freedom of writing'. Secondly, this same freedom was also alleged to be essential to, and coeval with, all free governments. The fact that, under the present constitution, the essay continued, the power of the people was 'actively confined to *Deliberative* and *prudential* considerations, and to a periodical Election of those who are to judge for them', made the freedom of the press proportionately more important. As the *Old England Journal* declared:

The *executive* power of the Government here, being absolutely independant [*sic*] of the people in every sense, and the *legislative* power being but partially and mediately dependant [*sic*] on them, the people of *England* without the *Liberty of the Press* to inform them of the *Fitness* and *Unfitness* of measures, approv'd or condemn'd by those whom they have *trusted*, and *whom they may trust again*, would be in as blind a state of subjection, as if they lived under the most arbitrary and inquisitorial Government.

It is worth noting briefly that, in discussing the role of the press and the closely related issue of the people's right to scrutinize and express their views on the government of the day, a number of opposition polemicists were prepared to advance unusually radical claims. Particularly striking in this respect is the relationship that at least three pamphleteers of the 1740s attempted to forge between taxation and the right to know. As one of them remarked:

as Government *concerns* every man, so it seems but natural that every man should *concern* himself about *Government*, and as the *Lowest Fellow* in the kingdom contributes out of what he *gets* to the *public service*, so it seems but *just* that he should, if he has a mind, know *what he pays* for, and *see*, if he *can see*, whether the public is *well served* or *not*.[60]

There is not an enormous gulf between the right to know and the right to participate more fully in the political process through the exercise of the franchise, and here in the 1740s is an argument that thus foreshadows (albeit in a weak form) the attempt by certain elements of the political nation in the early years of George III's reign to relate, in part

---

[60] *The New Opposition Compared with the Old in Point of Principles and Practice* (1744), 51. The same pamphleteer seems to have made almost identical claims in *The Case of the Opposition Impartially Stated*, published in 1742. See also *The Desertion Discussed, or, the Last and Present Oppositions Placed in their True Light* (1743), 1–2; *The Livery-Man, or, Plain Thoughts on Publick Affairs* (1740), *passim*.

under the stimulus of events in America, taxation and the right to vote. It would, of course, be wrong to suggest that such arguments were anything other than atypical: the vast bulk of opinion expressed in the opposition press of the 1740s was notably conservative in its implications. Nevertheless, their presence shows how the political possibilities created by the early Hanoverian press were an important impetus to ideological development at the same time as they were invigorating politics 'without doors'.

So far, the political role of the press has been considered primarily from the perspective of its constituting an important link between politics at the centre and the political nation 'without doors'. But what of the relationship between the politicians and the press? This question can perhaps most usefully be approached from two slightly different angles. The first of these is from the point of view of the influence that the political press had on the world of politics at court and in Parliament. Studies of the episodic popular outcries of the early Hanoverian period, such as the Excise Crisis of 1733, the outcries created by the Jew Bill in 1753, and the fall of Minorca in 1756, have convincingly shown that the press could have a marked impact on the actions of ministers.[61] It has recently been argued, however, that such outcries give a misleading picture of the influence of the press. Most of the time, the argument continues, the press had a negligible impact on political decisions and relationships at Westminster.[62] That the role of the press was more important in certain conjunctures than in others is, of course, undeniable. But this should not be used to obscure the less dramatic, but nevertheless significant, interactions that regularly took place between the press and politics at the centre. As sporadic comments in contemporary correspondence make very clear, most politicians, whether ministers or back-bench MPs, paid some degree of attention to the political press. Thus, as far as the very heart of the court is concerned, Lord Chancellor Hardwicke and George II could hold a conversation in early January 1745 in which both animadverted on the virulence of the opposition press during the past two years.[63]

[61] See esp. P. Langford, *The Excise Crisis* (Oxford, 1975); T. W. Perry, *Public Opinion, Propaganda and Politics in Eighteenth-Century England* (Cambridge, Mass., 1962); L. Sutherland, 'The City of London and the Devonshire–Pitt Administration, 1756–7', in Lucy Sutherland, *Politics and Finance in the Eighteenth Century*, ed. Aubrey Newman (1984), 67–107; Rogers, *Whigs and Cities*, esp. 95–105.

[62] *The Memoirs and Speeches of James, 2nd Earl Waldegrave, 1742–1763*, ed. J. C. D. Clark (Cambridge, 1988), 33.

[63] W. Coxe, *Memoirs of the Administration of the Right Honourable Henry Pelham*, 2 vols. (1827), i. 199–201.

One minister whose sensitivity to adverse comment in the press seems to have been particularly pronounced was the Duke of Newcastle. In 1742, for example, he was apparently aggrieved by a ballad written by Lord Hervey that accused the new ministry of forcing measures and personnel on a reluctant George II.[64] In 1748 he was complaining to the Earl of Sandwich of 'being pelted with pamphlets, and papers every day'.[65] Even Newcastle's brother, Henry Pelham, who, as is discussed below, maintained a position of determined indifference towards press comment, found himself writing to another member of the ministry in late 1743 regarding two recently published pamphlets.[66] In the case of back-bench MPs, it is likely that Philip Yorke and Sir Charles Hanbury Williams, for both of whom extensive correspondence survives documenting their interest in the press, were unusual only in the assiduity with which they followed press debate.[67] Both ensured that they were forwarded the latest pamphlets and essay papers, when they were away from London. In late 1743, for example, Philip Yorke was pestering his regular correspondent, Thomas Birch, to send him a copy of Perceval's *Faction Detected by the Evidence of Facts.* He also relayed a similar demand from his brother and the future MP Joseph Yorke.[68]

On occasion, the press seems to have done more than simply arouse the interest of back-bench opinion. In late 1742 the granting of British pay to 16,000 Hanoverian troops the previous August provoked a small wave of opposition pamphlets, the most influential of which was the Earl of Chesterfield's well-known *The Case of the Hanover Forces in the Pay of Great Britain.* On 12 December 1742, two days after the first great debate on the issue, referred to earlier, an anonymous correspondent wrote to the Earl of Morton (Morton was a supporter of the ministry in the Lords): 'We had generally the justice of the debate on our side yet pamphlets and popular declamations made several good

---

[64] BL Add. MS 51390 (Holland House Papers), fos. 45–6: Hanbury Williams to Fox, 27 Sept, 1742.

[65] Quoted in Black, *The English Press,* 171.

[66] See *Letters to Henry Fox Lord Holland, with a Few Addressed to his Brother Stephen, Earl of Ilchester,* ed. Earl of Ilchester (1915), 3: Pelham to Fox, 27 Sept. 1743.

[67] Both Yorke and Hanbury Williams had a personal interest in the printing trade, Yorke in his capacity as an enthusiastic historian, and Hanbury Williams as the author of a succession of popular odes.

[68] BL Add. MS 35396, fos. 150–3: Yorke to Birch, 13 Sept. 1743. Joseph Yorke was at this time serving in the army, rising to the position of aide-de-camp to Cumberland in 1745. He did not gain election to Parliament until 1751.

friends leave us.'[69] During the actual debate both Sir William Yonge and Horatio Walpole attacked *The Case of the Hanover Forces*, with the latter inveighing against the alleged influence of the pamphlet on the exchanges in the House.[70] Such examples, together with the evidence that press debate was followed by a broad section of the political élite, provide a good indication of the pervasiveness of the press as an element of the environment in which mid-eighteenth-century politics was conducted.

The second of the angles from which the relationship between politicians and the press can usefully be approached is in terms of the intervention of certain political groups in the press. One of the more interesting aspects of this question in the 1740s is the relative lack of press activity by the ministry. The contrast with the height of Walpolian rule, when Walpole retained a panoply of writers at his beck and call, is very striking. Following the disbandment of the 'Gazetteer Legion' (the pro-ministerial writers of the *Daily Gazetteer*) at the time of Walpole's fall, there are notably few instances of ministerial sponsorship of press activity. Allegations were periodically made in the opposition press that the ministry had links with the *Daily Advertiser*, the *General Advertiser*, and the revamped *Daily Gazetteer*,[71] but no independent evidence survives to corroborate these claims, and, in any case, none of these papers regularly printed political comment. Almost the only writer who successfully attracted the favour of the ministry in this period was Henry Fielding. That even this occurred, however, undoubtedly owed much to Fielding's connections with a number of leading opposition figures who were admitted to the ministry in late 1744.[72] Nor was ministerial support for Fielding automatically forthcoming. No ministerial subventions seem to have eased the way of his anti-Jacobite paper published during the '45, the *True Patriot*.[73] And it was not until 1747–8 that Fielding received ministerial support, first, for his lengthy election pamphlet, *A Dialogue between a Gentleman of London and an Honest Alderman of the Country Party* (1747), and then

---

[69] Quoted in J. Black, 'The Crown, Hanover, and the Shift in British Foreign Policy', in J. Black (ed.), *Knights Errant and True Englishmen: British Foreign Policy, 1600–1800* (Edinburgh, 1989), 115.

[70] *Parl. Hist.*, xiii. 941, 1036–7.

[71] See [Walpole] *Three Letters to the Whigs* (1748), 2; *Champion*, 1 Oct., 19 Nov. 1741.

[72] Fielding had particular connections with Lyttleton and Chesterfield.

[73] Henry Fielding, *The 'True Patriot' and Related Writings*, ed. W. B. Coley (Oxford, 1987), pp. lxviii–lxix; M. C. Battestin, *Henry Fielding: A Life* (1989), 401–3.

for the weekly essay paper the *Jacobite's Journal*, first published on 5 December 1747.[74] During the earlier 1740s the general absence of intervention in the press by the ministry is made more surprising by the volume and influence of the anti-Hanoverian press campaign of 1742–4. The non-appearance of a ministerial 'antidote' to this press onslaught seems to have caused a certain degree of concern at the time among various supporters of the ministry.[75] Yet the response to this concern was extremely equivocal. In April 1743 Horatio Walpole wrote in a letter to Robert Trevor, Britain's diplomatic representative at The Hague, that 'friends' had 'called loudly' for a reply to Chesterfield's *The Case of the Hanover Forces.*[76] The ministers, Walpole continued, 'were uneasy'. Nevertheless, according to him, they had unsuccessfully solicited the support of Stephen Poyntz and Francis Hare, Bishop of Salisbury.[77] They also, Walpole alleged, 'even hinted coolly to Lord Orford to take the pen'. All three refused; Lord Orford allegedly because 'he was not *au fait* with respect to foreign affairs'. Walpole's interest in these matters was in large part a result of his own unsolicited efforts to rebut Chesterfield's pamphlet with one of his own, entitled *The Interest of Great Britain Steadily Pursued.* This was planned as a two-part work, but only the first part actually appeared. The peculiar fate of the second section was described in Walpole's letter to Trevor: 'everybody called for *part second*, but the ministers would give it no countenance, read it with uneasiness, and discouraged the vent of it'. It seems that Walpole instructed the printer to inform Edward Weston, one of the Under-Secretaries of State in the northern department, of the plans for the second part.[78] Weston's response was to deliver a lecture to the printer regarding the presumption of writing 'anything' that related to the affairs of the Secretary of State without prior consultation. In the event, under the stimulus of this outburst, the second section was never published.

[74] Henry Fielding, *The 'Jacobite's Journal' and Related Writings*, ed. W. B. Coley (Oxford, 1974), pp. xxxv, liii; Battestin, *Henry Fielding*, 419–20, 425–6.

[75] See below; see also *A Vindication of our Present Royal Family* (1744), 1.

[76] HMC, Fourteenth Report, Appendix 9 (1895), 87–8: Walpole to Trevor, 25 Apr. 1743.

[77] Poyntz was presumably asked because of his diplomatic experience, which had included a period as British envoy in Paris, Hare because of his role in the 1710s and 1720s as a notable Whig apologist.

[78] According to Walpole, Weston had been ordered, along with another of the Under-Secretaries, Andrew Stone, to collect facts for a reply to *The Case of the Hanover Forces*.

How is the general lack of ministerial intervention in the press of the 1740s to be accounted for? The shift in attitude towards the press among ministers between the 1730s and 1740s has recently been the subject of comment elsewhere. Attention has been drawn in this context to changes in personnel and, in particular, to the downfall in 1742 of two men who had been at the heart of the Walpolian press empire, namely Nicholas Paxton and Joseph Bell (Bell had been the Comptroller of the Post Office under Walpole).[79] Jeremy Black has also suggested that the shift in ministerial attitudes actually represented a hardening of a trend that had been apparent since the mid-1730s. On this account, the consolidation of Walpole's newspaper activity into one paper (the *Daily Gazetteer*) in 1735 is viewed as a reflection in part of a growing feeling among ministers, following the weathering of the storm created by Walpole's Excise Bill and the disintegration of the parliamentary opposition after the 1734 general election, that the press was not so much of a threat to their political fortunes.[80] Another important factor may well have been the increasing political influence of Henry Pelham. By contrast to Walpole, Pelham seems to have been little disturbed by press comment. In 1753 he summarized his attitude to the press in a letter to Newcastle, which had been prompted by the latter's desire to take action against James Ralph for material contained in an issue of the opposition essay paper the *Protestor*:

I have been abused in every paper he [Ralph] has wrote, and you may expect your turn. It gives me not the least concern; though sometimes the fellow hits upon truths, which you know I would rather have never given an opportunity for him to do. I am satisfied, the less notice is taken of him the better: it has been my doctrine always, and I think experience shews I am in the right.[81]

Significantly, in 1746 Fielding identified Pelham's low estimation of the press as one of the reasons why he and others had not received direct ministerial support for their anti-Jacobite writing during the '45.[82]

There were also two political reasons why, after 1742, the ministry may have been less inclined to intervene in the press. The first of these

[79] See Harris, *London Newspapers*, 127–9; Black, *The English Press*, 166–7.

[80] See Black, *The English Press*, 142–3, 168–9. But for an interpretation of the establishment of the *Daily Gazetteer* that emphasizes possible organizational causes, see Harris, *London Newspapers*, 123–4.

[81] Coxe, *Memoirs of the Administration of Pelham*, ii. 484–5: Pelham to Newcastle, 20 July 1753. See also Thomas Davies, *Memoirs of the Life of David Garrick* (1780), 230–1.

[82] See below, Ch. 5, for this and the wider question of ministerial press activity during the '45.

is the prominence that was accorded to the exposure by the secret Commons committee inquiry into Walpole's administration of the level of ministerial press subsidies during the last ten years of his rule.[83] It was precisely because the inquiry achieved so little that disproportionate significance was attached to this aspect of its findings. No doubt there were those who saw this reaction as yet further grounds for keeping press activity to a minimum after Walpole's fall. The second reason only has relevance to the period between 1742 and 1744. Pro-Carteret polemicists were to claim after 1745 that the Pelhams had actually connived with the opposition in promoting the anti-Hanoverian press campaign during Carteret's period of office as Secretary of State for the northern department.[84] Although there is no evidence to substantiate such claims, there is little doubt that there were considerable undercurrents of antagonism between the new Whigs—that is, Carteret and his fellow opposition Whigs admitted to the ministry in 1742—and the Pelhams and their supporters.[85] This antagonism, and the feeling that Carteret and the new Whigs were attempting to gain a monopoly of political power by submitting to George II's Hanoverian interests, may well have reinforced the determination of many ministerial supporters and of the Pelhams not to defend Carteret's policies in the press. That this was in fact so is suggested by a report of comments made by the Earl of Bath (as William Pulteney was known following elevation to the peerage in July 1742) in early January 1743. According to the report, Bath, at this stage on good terms with the Pelhams, had responded to a question as to why no pamphlets had been forthcoming in response to the anti-Hanoverian pamphlets of the winter of 1742–3 by remarking '[that] they could not be answered—the facts were *true*—it was not his *business*—let the minister [Carteret] answer it—the measure was *managed* not to be defended'.[86]

If the occasional nature of ministerial sponsorship of press activity suggests, therefore, that the general attitude among ministers towards the press in this period was characterized by a high degree of pragmatism and by a conviction that keeping one's head down was probably the

[83] See Hanson, *Government and the Press*, 118.

[84] See e.g. *The Plain Reasoner* (1745), 5; [Egmont] *An Examination of the Principles, and an Enquiry into the Conduct of the Two B——rs* (1749), 3–6.

[85] For the rivalry between the new Whigs and the old corps, see P. A. Luff, 'Henry Fox, The Duke of Cumberland, and Pelhamite Politics, 1748–1757', D.Phil. thesis (Oxford, 1981), 13–14.

[86] BL Add. MS 51437, fo. 32: Political Journal of Dr Francis Ayscough.

most prudent policy, this is a conclusion that is also suggested by the ministry's contemporaneous efforts at policing the press. Here again it is what did not happen that is most significant. Between 1742 and 1745 a concerted attempt was made, with little success, to disrupt publication of the leading vehicle of anti-Hanoverianism in the press in these years, the *Old England Journal*.[87] This attempt was limited to issuing warrants for the arrest of the personnel of the paper, and imposing recognizances on the printer and various booksellers against their appearance in front of the Court of King's Bench at the beginning of the next legal term, from which the court usually released them at the end of the same or the following term. This process was also used against those responsible for the printing and dissemination of two popular anti-Hanoverian tracts published in late 1743.[88] At no stage, however, was a prosecution attempted. In the case of the *Old England Journal*, it seems to have been recognized that the support for the paper, particularly among the parliamentary opposition, meant that such a course of action was likely to prove counter-productive.[89] There was a contemporary recognition that antipathy to such action was very widely based, even amongst those usually inclined to support the ministry.[90] It was easy, therefore, for the opposition to turn press prosecutions into a cause célèbre, as had in fact occurred in 1731, when Walpole had prosecuted the *Craftsman*.[91] Another difficulty facing any ministry wanting to proceed with a prosecution was that of finding a jury in London, despite the Select Juries Act of 1730, which would convict for libel.[92] In this situation, the ministry unsurprisingly confined themselves to exploiting the capacity for harassment that the power of issuing general warrants conferred upon them.

There was also the time-honoured alternative of paying certain writers to lay down their pens. In late 1744 the admission into the ministry of various leading opposition politicians, some of whom, as shall be shown below, had close links with the *Old England Journal*, provided the opportunity to silence the paper's joint editors, William

[87] See Harris, *London Newspapers*, 147–8.   [88] PRO, TS 11/982.

[89] For this, see Coxe, *Memoirs of the Administration of Pelham*, i. 203.

[90] See esp. J. Black, 'George II and the Juries Act: Royal Concern about the Control of the Press', *Bulletin of the Institute of Historical Research*, 61 (1988), 359–62. See also L'Abbé le Blanc, *Letters on the English and French Nations* (1747), ii. 25–6.

[91] See Harris, *London Newspapers*, 150.

[92] See esp. T. A. Green, *Verdict According to Conscience: Perspectives on the English Criminal Trial Jury, 1200–1800* (Chicago, 1985), 322–3.

Guthrie and James Ralph, with pensions.[93] Successful action against the printer of the *Old England Journal*, John Purser, had to wait until 1746, and then it was Purser's connection with the crypto-Jacobite paper the *National Journal, or, the Country Gazette* that got him into trouble. On 10 June the paper printed an openly Jacobite letter. With the Habeas Corpus Act suspended following the '45, Purser was held in Newgate on a charge of treason.[94] Having agreed to cease printing the *National Journal*, Purser was eventually discharged on 26 February 1747, when the act suspending habeas corpus expired. As a later chapter will amplify, the conclusion that should perhaps be drawn from these instances of ministerial action against the press is that, despite the array of powers available to police press comment on politics, the ministry's ability to moderate the vigour of the opposition press was, at least in the first half of the decade, very closely circumscribed.

What of press activity among opposition groups? Throughout the 1740s it was various groups of opposition Whigs who were easily the most active in the press. Following Walpole's fall, this activity was heavily concentrated in two periods, 1743–4 and after 1747. In the first period it was certain of the opposition Whigs who had been excluded from the political settlement that followed Walpole's fall who intervened in the press. These included, most notably, Edmund Waller, George Bubb Dodington, and, the most active of them all, the Earl of Chesterfield.[95] That they should have chosen to exploit the press is perhaps unsurprising. Most had been involved in this area of opposition activity in the latter part of Walpole's ministry. Chesterfield, for example, had been involved, with George Lyttleton, on the opposition essay paper *Common Sense*, first published in 1737. The importance of this experience is underlined by the probable organizational links between *Common Sense* and the principal vehicle for opposition Whig press activity between 1743 and 1744, the *Old England Journal*, first published on 5 February 1743. As Michael Harris has noted elsewhere, this organizational link is suggested by William Guthrie's arrest in March 1743 for an essay published in both papers on the same day.[96] It is also suggested by the fact that the opposition politician who seems to have been most closely linked to the *Old England Journal* was Chesterfield. It was he who wrote the essays that appeared in the first

---

[93] For Guthrie's pension, see Harris, *London Newspapers*, 131. The case for Ralph having received a pension at the same time is convincingly argued in J. B. Shipley, 'James Ralph: Pretender to Genius', Ph.D. thesis (Columbia, NY, 1963), 419.
[94] See PRO, SP 44 and 36.　　[95] See also below, Ch. 4, for this.
[96] Harris, *London Newspapers*, 130.

and third issues of the paper at least.[97] Whether he wrote any others is unclear. That he continued, however, to exercise a close influence on the paper is suggested by a number of factors. The first is an attack made on Chesterfield's polemical activities by a hostile pamphleteer in 1744. In the course of this attack the pamphleteer referred to Chesterfield's authorship of '*Saturday*'s lectures' to the 'coffee-house politicians'.[98] In the same year another pamphleteer remarked of the *Old England Journal*: 'Those concern'd in this weekly packet of scandal and sedition affect to have it thought to come from the Pen of one of high Rank and consequence.'[99] Chesterfield's continued super-intendence of the paper would also seem to be suggested by an exchange that took place between, on the one hand, Lord Bolingbroke and, on the other, the Earl of Marchmont and Alexander Hume Campbell (Marchmont's brother) in late 1744. During the protracted negotiations that preceded the formation of the Broad-Bottom ministry, Lord Hardwicke informed Bolingbroke that the Pelhams—who by this stage had steeled themselves sufficiently for the attempt to dislodge Carteret from office—resented the attack levelled against them in a current issue of the *Old England Journal*. When Bolingbroke broached the subject with Chesterfield, the latter seems to have accepted full responsibility for the paper's political indelicacy, saying only with reference to the negotiations 'that he thought all was over'.[100]

Significantly, the relationship between the opposition Whigs and the *Old England Journal* does not seem to have represented the totality of the paper's political connections. Important, albeit fragmentary, evidence survives of a link with the Westminster Society of Independent Electors, the extra-parliamentary body formed during the struggle to overturn the ministerial candidates at the general election of 1741, whose ringleaders were, as Lord Egmont (as Perceval was known following the death of his father in 1746) put it, 'not so much entitled to vote in any Election, being Tradesmen or . . . the low attorneys & solicitors in the force of the Inns of Court'.[101] Two of the most

---

[97] See R. Coxon, *Chesterfield and his Critics* (1935), 213–18.
[98] *An Apology for the Conduct of the Present Administration* (1744), 7.
[99] *A Vindication of our Present Royal Family*, p. v.
[100] Rose, *Marchmont Papers*, i. 78, 80.
[101] BL Add. MS 47159, fos. 114–17. The political complexion of the Independent Electors is a matter of debate, although it seems fairly clear that they were a mongrel body encompassing those excluded from power—Jacobites, patriots, and Tory-patriots—under Whig oligarchy. It also seems clear that the relative importance of its constituent elements and its overall strength changed during the decade. But for a convenient summary of the debate, see Rogers, *Whigs and Cities*, 193–5.

important pieces of evidence for this connection are an anonymous memorandum in the State Papers Domestic, and MacNamara Morgan's polemical poem *The Triumvirade, or, Broad-Bottomry*, published in 1745.[102] In his poem Morgan alleged that both Ralph and Guthrie were 'Independent Electors of Westminster Both!' Guthrie's association with the Independent Electors is confirmed by a letter that Thomas Birch wrote to Philip Yorke in July 1747, after the general election of that year. Birch noted of the Independent Electors that 'their leaders have now abandon'd them'. In this context, he also observed that Guthrie was now affecting 'the character of a most zealous subject'.[103]

Another claim that Morgan made in his poem was that one 'Little Broadbottom P-l-n', 'A Hoop-Petticoat maker for Folks', was providing the financial support for his son's third-share in the *Old England Journal*. It is the memorandum referred to above that gives substance to this particular allegation. It reads: 'Mr Paulin called upon me in Scotland Yard on Friday the 2 March 1743–4 before noon to offer— [me] Half of the Con. Jour, to sales. Told me a great deal about being ill used by the people agreeably to his principles wanted to get rid of it.'[104] Almost certainly, the Mr Paulin of the memorandum (and the 'Little Broadbottom P-l-n' of Morgan's poem) was one Thomas Paulin, coal-merchant, mercer, and vestryman of the parish of St Paul's, Covent Garden.[105] Personal testimony of Paulin's politics survives in the form of an appeal to Lord Perceval on 24 November 1742 for the

---

[102] See also [Morgan] *The Sequel, Containing what Was Omitted in the Triumvirade or Broad-Bottomry, at the Asterisks* (1745). The connection with the Westminster Independents may also have been behind the reference to the 'hired hacks of greedy tradesmen' associated with the *Old England Journal* in *A Vindication of our Present Royal Family*.

[103] BL Add. MS 35397, fos. 53–5: Birch to Yorke, 11 July 1747.

[104] PRO, SP 36/63, fo. 217.

[105] Paulin's identity can be inferred from two pieces of evidence. A vital clue is a reference in Morgan's poem to his role as a vestryman. Inspection of vestry minutes for the various parishes that made up Westminster reveals that the only possible candidate is one Thomas Paulin of Tavistock Street, Covent Garden. An entry in a trade directory published in the 1760s suggests that this is, in fact, the Paulin we are looking for. The entry reads: 'Paulin & Cotes, Lace, Warehousemen, and Haberdashers, Tavistock Street, Covent Garden' (*The London Directory for the Year 1769* (1769)). In 1746 Paulin seems to have clashed with Samuel Johns, one of the leading members of the Westminster Independents of the later 1740s and early 1750s. The cause was a bill promoted by Lord Perceval to tighten up the regulations surrounding the import of coal into Westminster. For this, see L. Colley, *In Defiance of Oligarchy: The Tory Party, 1714–60* (Cambridge, 1982), 165. For Paulin's role in the affair, see *Journals of the House of Commons*, xxv. 148; BL Add. MS 47014a, fos. 93–7.

latter's help in securing the lucrative right to supply coal to the King's household. Paulin prefaced his request with a heavily drawn reminder of his endeavours at the heart of the Westminster opposition of 1741–2:

> As your lordship cannot but be sensible of the great pains I have taken to serve your lordship and consequently the cause of Liberty against the late minister [Walpole], as you know that I have lost a great part of my Business and had almost lost Life on that Account, as that my interest is perhaps stronger and my Endeavours have been more strenuous than those of any other men in Westminster.[106]

The alliance between the opposition Whigs and the Independent Electors on the *Old England Journal* during 1743–4 is made all the more probable by the fact that the same opposition Whigs were prominent amongst those members of the parliamentary opposition who patronized the Independent Electors between 1743 and 1745 as stewards at the annual anniversary dinners of the society.[107] An interesting footnote to this relationship was the parliamentary inquiry which took place after the 1747 anniversary dinner, when the landlord of the White Hart, Piccadilly, had apparently been assaulted for harbouring a leading witness at the Jacobite Lord Lovat's trial.[108] Nothing came of the inquiry. But, as Horace Walpole wrote to Sir Horace Mann on 10 April 1747, it provided a source of embarrassment for various of the opposition Whigs who had taken advantage of the political resource represented by the Independent Electors earlier in the decade. As Walpole noted of the inquiry and of the toasts that accompanied the annual dinners of the society:

> Had it extended to three years ago, Lord Sandwich and Grenville of the Admiralty would have made an admirable figure as dictators of some of the most Jacobite Healths that were ever invented. Lord Doneraile, who is made Comptroller to the Prince, went to the committee . . . and plagued Lyttleton to death, with pressing him to inquire into the healths of the year '43.[109]

It is also worth noting that, by bringing together an important section of the metropolitan opposition and the prominent members of the parliamentary opposition, the *Old England Journal* looks forward to

---

[106] BL Add. MS 47013B, fo. 94: Paulin to Perceval, 24 Nov. 1742.

[107] The stewards chosen at the 1743 dinner for the following year included George Dodington and George Grenville. For this and the toasts drunk at the dinner, see *Daily Post*, 24 Dec. 1743.

[108] See Rogers, *Whigs and Cities*, 82.   [109] Lewis, *Walpole*, xix. 386–90.

some of the better known essay papers of the 1750s and, in particular, to the *Monitor*, founded in 1755.[110]

The formation of the Broad-Bottom ministry in late 1744 brought to an end the involvement of Chesterfield and his colleagues in the press. In the later 1740s it was Lord Granville (as Carteret was known following the inheritance of the family title on the death of his mother in December 1744) and the Leicester House politicians who together were responsible for nearly all the most significant opposition polemic. In the final years of the War of the Austrian Succession, as is discussed in a later chapter, Granville and his supporters produced a series of substantial pamphlets attacking the Pelhams' conduct of the war, and calling for more vigorous exploitation of the possibilities allegedly created by Britain's naval supremacy after 1747. The most important contribution of Leicester House was the essay paper the *Remembrancer*. Its editor was James Ralph, who, it seems, was prepared to forgo the security of the government pension with which he had been provided at the time of the formation of the Broad-Bottom ministry, and a prominent contributor may well have been Lord Egmont. Horace Walpole later noted that the *Remembrancer* had been 'more than once emboldened' by 'Egmont and others'.[111] Walpole's recollection is likely to be accurate, given that Egmont was certainly the author of most of the more influential pamphlets emanating from Leicester House in the late 1740s.[112]

By contrast to various groups of opposition Whig politicians, the Tories and the Jacobites were notably inactive in the press during the 1740s. One pro-ministerial pamphleteer reflected in early 1744 that, without the intervention of the opposition Whigs after 1742, 'the Efforts of the disaffected *Tories*, would have been like the Bulk of the Faction, absurd, gross, and contemptible'.[113] As for the period of Walpole's rule, there is no evidence that Tory parliamentarians were active in the newspaper and periodical press of the 1740s, and, as is discussed in detail in Chapter 2, Tory pamphlets in the 1740s are conspicuous by their rarity. As for Jacobite involvement in the press, the exiled Stuart court placed very little value on propaganda activities, as Paul Chapman has recently shown. When, therefore, indigenous Jacobite publishing largely collapsed in the aftermath of the débâcle of the Atterbury Plot in 1722–3, distinctive Jacobite argument was only

---

[110] M. Peters, *Pitt and Popularity: The Patriot Minister and London Opinion during the Seven Years War* (Oxford, 1980), 13–14.

[111] Walpole, *Memoirs of King George II*, i. 237.   [112] See below, Ch. 6.

[113] *A Warning to the Whigs, and to Well-Affected Tories*, 12–13.

very occasionally intruded into press debate.[114] Interestingly, in 1743 Thomas Carte wrote to Rome recommending that a paper be established to exploit the bitter anti-Hanoverianism of the early 1740s.[115] Nothing seems to have come of this. However, in 1746 the man whom he put forward as a suitable candidate to organize such a venture, George Gordon, was responsible for the short-lived crypto-Jacobite *National Journal, or, the Country Gazette*. All that the early issues contained to alert the unsuspecting reader to the Jacobite inclination of the paper was a series of items criticizing, on the one hand, the allegedly brutal treatment of the Jacobite army at Culloden and the subsequent raids into the Highlands, and extolling, on the other, the heroism in adversity of the Young Pretender. However, as noted above, on 10 June (the Pretender's birthday) the paper printed a letter that put its Jacobitism beyond dispute and also made government action against the paper inevitable. The offending letter was basically a sentimental reflection of the condition of a monarch in exile. It emphasized that it was his father's 'misdemeanours' that were the cause of the Pretender's exile; he himself, it was argued, could not be held responsible for the 'least wrong'. The letter also referred to the 'fatal issue of the late glorious, but unsuccessful struggle in the present

[114] P. Chapman, 'Jacobite Political Argument, 1714–1766', Ph.D. thesis (Cambridge, 1983). In his recent book, *English Society, 1688–1832* (Cambridge, 1985), Jonathan Clark inaccurately characterizes the fate of Jacobite argument in the press under the first two Georges as 'a story of ideological resilience in adversity' (144–6). For the period after 1722–3 the evidence he cites in support of his contention suggests that a better characterization would be a story of ideological capitulation to Whiggism. In the case of the Jacobite printer Nathaniel Mist's papers, *Mist's Weekly Journal* and *Fog's Weekly Journal*, and the weekly essay paper *Common Sense, or, the Englishman's Journal*, which are described by Clark as Jacobite, the nature of their relationship to the Stuart cause, and the effects of government vigilance are much more accurately encapsulated by remarks made by James Ralph in 1743. Ralph noted that *Mist's Weekly Journal* 'seem'd not to be directed merely against the Administration. It was sometimes interpreted to go Higher, and the printers were so prosecuted on Account of a letter sent from France by the late Duke of Wharton [the famous Persian letter of 1728], that it was thought proper to change the title, and new model the principles of the journal; staunch whiggism, and a firm Adherence to the Revolution Constitution, were now propagated in it against those in power, tho' now and then with a little Deviation into what were supposed to be the Author's real sentiments. In a word, Mr Molloy [Charles Molloy], both in *Fog* and afterwards in *Common Sense* has been a useful coadjutor to Mr Amhurst [Nicholas Amhurst, editor of the *Craftsman*] and his patrons.' (*A Critical History of the Late Administration of Sir Robert Walpole*, 516.) For a recent account of Jacobite argument under the first two Georges that correctly emphasizes the accommodation with Whiggism, see P. Monod, *Jacobitism and the English People, 1688–1788* (Cambridge, 1989), 5–44.

[115] Harris, *London Newspapers*, 131.

Rebellion'. Those who had rebelled had only been 'so weak', the letter continued, to attribute the 'calamities' in which the country found itself to the 'Exclusion of him, who they call the *right* and *lawful* king'. The letter and the ministerial action that it provoked prompted one correspondent to write to the Earl of Marchmont on 17 June: 'The printer of the National Journal is cast into Newgate for the paper of the 10 June which is so silly a Jacobite paper that it is wonderful how it came out. Gordon is also taken up and in a messenger's house. I wonder he could be so ignorant and let it be publish'd.'[116] Among the papers belonging to Gordon that were seized by the King's Messengers was a manuscript version of a pamphlet entitled *Britain the Ship, Hanover the Rudder*. Under examination, Gordon stated that he had intended to publish it when Granville had been a Secretary of State, but because, as he put it, 'some business' had intruded, it had never been published.[117]

On 14 October 1743 Philip Yorke wrote that his was an 'idle age, w[hi]ch cares for nothing but a party pamphlet, a Broad-Bottom journal, or a satyre filled with spleen & ill Nature'.[118] It has been the aim of this chapter to illustrate some of the more important features of the role that party pamphlets and Broad-Bottom journals were capable of playing under the politics of oligarchy. It is commonly observed that the early Hanoverian press had a diversified audience. One important corollary of this was the diverse nature of its political impact. For different parts of the political nation, the press had a different political significance. 'Without doors' it succeeded in providing, for much of the time, a vigorous and potentially influential commentary on the political world of Westminster and St James. But perhaps equally important was its role 'within doors', where it was one factor that shaped the political behaviour and perceptions of ministers and Members of Parliament. For both of the above reasons, it provided significant political opportunities that were successively exploited by certain groups of opposition Whigs. As will be shown in a later chapter, between 1743 and 1744 this opposition activity was to have great impact and importance.

Finally, the failure of the Tories to intervene to any significant extent in the press deserves brief comment. As part of her recent influential attempt to rescue the early Hanoverian Tory party from the condescen-

---

[116] HMC, Polwarth Papers, v (1961), 180.   [117] PRO, SP 36/84, fos. 136–7.
[118] BL Add. MS 35396, fos. 172–3: Yorke to Birch, 14 Oct. 1743.

sion of generations of Whigs and eighteenth-century historians, one of the many challenging claims that Linda Colley has made is that the Tories were a vital and innovating anti-oligarchical force in the politics of the reigns of the first two Georges.[119] Given that, as has rightly been emphasized elsewhere, the press was one of the principal vehicles of flexibility in the early Hanoverian political system, the Tories' failure to make any sustained effort to exploit this potential is at least one of the factors that suggests that Colley's attempt to portray the dynamics of politics 'without doors' as closely dependent on Tory initiative is not supported by the facts. A similar conclusion is also reached, as it is the major purpose of the next chapter to show, by an examination of the influence of the ideology of patriotism on the political role of the press of the 1740s.

[119] See esp. L. Colley, 'Eighteenth-Century Radicalism before Wilkes', *Transactions of the Royal Historical Society*, 5th ser. 31 (1981), 1–19.

2

PATRIOTS, OLD WHIGS, AND NOMINAL TORIES

ONE of the principal aims of the last chapter was to illustrate the various linkages that the press of the 1740s formed between Parliament, the politicians, and the political nation 'without doors'. The purpose of the present chapter is to examine the influence on the intervention of the press in politics (and on this series of relationships) of the mid-century variant of country ideology—patriotism.

About many aspects of patriotism there is substantial agreement among historians. That it was an anti-political language, a language of philosophical and moral absolutes, of virtue against corruption, national interest against self-interest; that it was never a static language, but one that evolved over time; that it was embraced by a diverse coalition of political outsiders and malcontents; and that its major themes were, as far as politics at home were concerned, liberty and independence, and, as far as foreign affairs were concerned, the desirability of pursuing blue-water policies—on these points there exists a strong consensus.[1] Where this consensus dissolves, however, is on the question of how far, under the first two Georges, patriotism cut across and weakened the Whig and Tory party rivalry that had pervaded all aspects of politics in the Augustan era.[2]

---

[1] More recent studies of country or patriot ideology include H. T. Dickinson, *Liberty and Property: Political Ideology in Eighteenth-Century Britain* (2nd edn., 1979); J. G. A. Pocock, 'The Varieties of Whiggism from Exclusion to Reform: A History of Ideology and Discourse', in J. G. A. Pocock (ed.), *Virtue, Commerce, and History* (Cambridge, 1985), 215–310; M. Peters, 'The "Monitor" on the Constitution, 1755–65: New Light on the Ideological Origins of English Radicalism', *English Historical Review*, 86 (1971), 706–25; L. Colley, 'Radical Patriotism in Eighteenth-Century England', in Raphael Samuel (ed.), *Patriotism: The Making and Unmaking of British National Identity* (1989), i. 168–88; H. Cunningham, 'The Language of Patriotism, 1750–1914', *History Workshop*, 12 (1981), 8–33.

[2] See esp. L. Colley, *In Defiance of Oligarchy: The Tory Party, 1714–60* (Cambridge, 1982); E. Cruickshanks, *Political Untouchables: The Tories and the '45* (1979); B. W. Hill, *The Growth of Parliamentary Parties, 1689–1742* (1976); J. C. D. Clark, *The Dynamics of Change: The Crisis of the 1750s and English Party Systems* (Cambridge, 1982); W. A.

It will be argued here that the extent to which the conflict between patriotism and the court had, at least by the 1740s, superseded and blurred Whig–Tory rivalry should not be underestimated. As the political essay papers and occasional pamphlets of the decade reveal, the dominance of patriotism over press debate was near-total. These sources also show how far the Whig–Tory polarity had become submerged in the patriot–ministerial division, with all elements of opposition opinion—Whig, Tory, or other—seeking to identify themselves with the patriot cause. The full extent of the Tory identification with patriotism is—as will be demonstrated below—brought into especially sharp focus by examination of the limited Tory press activity in this period. A handful of Tory pamphleteers were provoked into defending the conduct of Tory MPs in the early 1740s by, first, the recriminations and arguments that accompanied the political settlement following Walpole's fall in 1742, and, then, by the participation of prominent Tories in the so-called Broad-Bottom ministry in the winter of 1744–5. Tory conduct, these pamphleteers basically argued, was proof that Toryism and patriotism were one and the same. Tories may have retained a distinctive sense of identity, but more significant was their acknowledgement of the overriding importance in contemporary politics of the patriot–ministerial division, and their assertions that Toryism had no meaning independent of patriotism.[3]

One other prominent feature of the conflict between patriotism and the court in the 1740s that had important repercussions for the political role of the press was the diminishing force of patriotism as the decade proceeded. As has long been recognized, patriotism's decline in this period was primarily a consequence of Pulteney's 'great betrayal' of the patriot cause following Walpole's fall. Less closely examined, however, have been the respective contributions of the failure of the admission of most of the Broad-Bottom opposition leadership of 1742–4 into the administration in late 1744 to bring about the long-awaited patriot reform of government, and the impact of the '45. The combined effect

Speck, *The Butcher: The Duke of Cumberland and the Suppression of the '45* (Oxford, 1981); Dickinson, *Liberty and Property*, esp. 163–92; P. D. G. Thomas, 'Party Politics in Eighteenth-Century Britain: Some Myths and a Touch of Reality', *British Journal for Eighteenth-Century Studies*, 10 (1987), 201–11; N. Rogers, *Whigs and Cities: Popular Politics in the Age of Walpole and Pitt* (Oxford, 1989), esp. 393.

[3] For a different view of the significance of mid-century Tory-patriot polemic, which seeks to demonstrate the alleged importance of the Whig–Tory division at least until 1757, see M. Peters, ' "Names and Cant": Party Labels in English Political Propaganda c.1753–1763', *Parliamentary History*, 7 (1984), 103–27.

of all three factors, and of patriotism's decline, on press debate is examined in the last part of the chapter.

Among the essay papers of the 1740s, by far the most influential were *Old England, or, the Constitutional Journal* and the *Westminster Journal, or, the New Weekly Miscellany*. The *Old England Journal*, as we saw in the last chapter, was first published in February 1743, and was the product of the direct intervention in the press of a group of opposition Whig politicians, led by the Earl of Chesterfield, and their metropolitan allies, the Westminster Society of Independent Electors. Between 1743–4, in large part because of its status as the principal press organ of the Broad-Bottom opposition of those years, its pre-eminence in the London press was unrivalled.[4] Exactly what happened to the paper after the admission of Chesterfield and most of his colleagues into the ministry in late 1744 is unclear. One thing that seems certain, however, is that support for the paper from these politicians ceased at this point, with the *Old England Journal* becoming, as noted in the last chapter, the most violent critic of the Broad-Bottom ministry in the first half of 1745. In late 1746 a change in the paper's editorship seems to have occurred, and the title was altered to *Old England, or the Broad-Bottom Journal*.[5] For the rest of the 1740s the paper lent its support to the Leicester House opposition, with the anomalous consequence that it found itself defending the conduct of the politician who had been the target of its most bitter invective between 1743 and 1744, namely, Lord Carteret. There is no evidence, however, that the support for Leicester House was prompted by subventions or direction from that source. Such a realignment, moreover, seems not to have unduly damaged the profitability of the paper, as a notice that the paper carried soon after the change of title and direction suggests: 'Old England having lately increased in the sale, encourages the Gentlemen concerned to give it, for the future, better paper, and in order to make Room for other Advertisements . . . the medicinal Advertisements shall be, occasionally, confined to the last page.'[6]

By contrast to the *Old England Journal*, the *Westminster Journal* does not appear to have received direct political support at any stage. It was first published, in the form that it was to retain throughout the 1740s,

---

[4] See below, Ch. 5.

[5] The change occurred in the issue for 4 Oct. 1746. The title was altered again on 11 July 1747, to simply *Old England*. The reason for this further change seems to have been a desire to distance itself from its role and patrons between 1743 and 1744.

[6] *OEJ* 13 Dec. 1746.

OLD ENGLAND: Or, The Conftitutional Journal.

EXTRAORDINARY.

By JEFFREY BROADBOTTOM, of Covent-Garden, Eſq; [Thurſday, May 19, 1743.]

HAD one Day the Map of *Europe* open before me, and, not without many a painful Reflection, was computing the Route taken by the Confederate Army to *Blanheim*, and from thence into *Bavaria* in the triumphant Year 1704, with that of our *Britiſh* and mercenary Troops now marching, as 'tis ſaid, to the Affiſtance of the Queen of *Hungary*, when a Friend came in, who is apter to ſee Things in a ridiculous, than a melancholy Light, and took the Hint to entertain me pretty much to the following Purpoſe.

So, Mr. *Broadbottom*, you are amuſing yourſelf with the Theatre of War, and, no doubt, feaſt your Imagination glow, with the illuſtrious Proſpect opening before us, of Victories Abroad and Triumphs at Home: Of *France* repuls'd, *Auſtria* retou'd, *Bavaria* chaſtis'd, and *Britain* once more elevated to the higheſt Pinacle of Worldly Glory?

I think my Head only by way of Reply, and he went on.

I am then miſtaken, it ſeems, and you remain as much an Infidel as ever: Why, I muſt acknowledge a March of 5 or 600 Miles is much eaſier perform'd by a Pair of Compaſſes, than an Army: In the Map, every Paſs is open, every River fordable, every Fortreſs acceſſible; no Defiles embarraſs us, no bad Roads weary us, no croſs-grain'd Peaſants provoke us. We proceed at our Leiſure, we halt where we pleaſe, we want no Neceſſary, we lament no Inconvenience, we ſtand in Awe of no Enemy.—Whereas, you will ſay, the Caſe is widely different, when we come to meaſure, in *Earneſt*, the Ground we thus ſkim over, as it were in a Dream. That Armies, eſpecially, with their Baggage, Ammunition, and Artillery, are unweildy Things; where a thouſand Difficulties where there were none before, and double ten-fold all they find. All which is true for the general,—But then you know a happy *Raſhneſs* ſometimes works Wonders: Beſides our Army is of a peculiar Kind, and our Conduct in every Inſtance ſo exquiſite, that Obſtacles, one would think, riſe only that we may have the Honour to ſurmount them.

But, as our Divines ſay, firſt of the Firſt; the peculiar Kind of our Army: It is, near upon, Half-national, Half-mercenary, Half-catholic, Half-heretic, a *as* *Chriſtian*; a Characteriſtic which it better deſerves than any Body of Troops ſince the famous *ſtanding Legion*: For, though they wear Swords, good Men, they are not in haſt to uſe them: On the contrary, their Cry is a Goſpel-Cry, *Peace on Earth and good Will towards Men*: They covet no Man's Poſſeſſions, they thirſt after no Man's Blood, and 'tis plain they ſteer their Neighbours better than themſelves: For, tho' we had an Enemy of our own to deal with, who had inſur'd us almoſt beyond Forgiveneſs, we left our own Cauſe to the Care of Providence, and, in Contempt of all Perils whether by Land or Water, becauſe devoted *Knights-errant* in the Cauſe of the diſtreſſed Queen of *Hungary*, and arm'd Mediators to re-eſtabliſh the Peace of *Germany*; not only without Money, and without Price, but with a noble Reſolution to expend *our laſt Guinea*, rather than her Dominions ſhould undergo any farther Diminution. A mediating Army, a peace-making Army, a diſintereſted Army, a ſelf-denying Army, and, therefore, be held a very peculiar Kind of Army; what never, perhaps, had a Precedent, nor ever will be made ſo.

And now Mr. *Broadbottom*, as to our Conduct; tho' we, the People of *England*, are at the whole Expence of this amazing Expedition, and have nothing either to hope or fear from the Emperor; though be the ſad Emperor firſt kindled the War, and *France* takes the Field only as his *friend*, yet ſuch is the extreme Delicacy of our Complaiſance and good Breeding, that we give his Imperial Majeſty to underſtand, that we are his Friends and Humble Servants as well as the Queen of *Hungary's*, and that it will not be *our Faults*, if a Hair of his Head fall to the Ground. It is true, that by this Management we can ſerve the Houſe of *Auſtria* by Halves only: But then we ſhall have but one Enemy to deal with inſtead of Two (for ſurely the *Imperialiſts* will ſtorm to fall upon thoſe, who refuſe to fall upon them) and whether we get the better of Oppoſition by rough or ſmooth Methods, the Advantage is the ſame.

Nor, my old Friend, is even this all: If we lead Peace in one Hand, we ſcatter Plenty with the other. For with ſuch Exactneſs and Punctuality do our good Friends the REMITTERS fulfil their late *extraordinary* and *advantageous* Bargain, that we are able to bribe to the Right and Left, as we go; and purchaſe the Good-will, of the Nations, we undertake to ſave, with our *own ready Money*. Thus if our Landlubbers plant, and our Merchants water, *Germany* hath the Increaſe.

Again, caſt your Eye upon the Map before you, and obſerve the Train-row-order of our Forces? What a noble Contempt doth it ſhew of our Enemies? What a Dependance on our own Bravery and Reſolution? and what a ſuperiour Wiſdom in our Councils? Rather than ſtarve in a Body, we chuſe to expoſe our Troops in Detachments, and perſuade ourſelves, no doubt, that if a few bold *Britons* in the Van ſhould be cut off, the Rear would be ſafe.

Indeed, I have heard of a Greyhound at a Boarding-School, who, if ſharp-ſet, when the little *Miſſes* were ſet at Dinner in two long Rows, us'd to ſpring boldly upon the Table, and working a Traverſe, as the Seamen call it, would clear every Plate from Side to Side, and make off almoſt before it could be ſaid that he had been there.

But the *French*, for Reaſons beſt known to themſelves, have not hitherto thought fit to make a Puſh of this Nature, and on the contrary, content themſelves with obſerving (the Duſt we raiſe) as if once more confident, that *the more we came over, the more they ſhould kill*.

At all Hazards and Adventures, we make a bouncing *Tintamarre*, our Drums and Trumpets echo to every Corner of *Europe*: *Dunkirk*, tho' compleatly reſtory'd, firſt takes the Alarm, and from thence thro' *Lorrain* and *Champagne*, it reaches *Paris* itſelf: On the News that our Troops were making their Approaches, his Imperial Majeſty, notwithſtanding the Compliments paid him, as Head of the Empire, by our polite General, withdraws in a Panic: The King of the Two *Sicilies* trembles for his Capital: The *Dutch* think it high Time to provide for the Security of the *Auſtrian Netherlands*: and the Court of *Pruſſia* holds it more adviſeable to *conſult* with us on the Means to retrive the Tranquillity of *Europe*, than to co-operate once more with *France* againſt us.

It may be urg'd, Indeed, that, under all this Shew, there appears to be little Subſtance: That the Gilding is worth more than the Work: That the *French* continue to pour freſh Troops into the Empire, and that, thereby, they will at once be able, if they pleaſe, to diſpute our Progreſs, and to carry the War a ſecond Time into *Bohemia*.

But, then again, to this it is reply'd, that our Army is only a *covering Army*, and that if we can make a Shift to cover the Enemy, we aſpire to no more.

And here, Mr. *Broadbottom*, I fancy we may join Iſſue with our Courtiers very ſafely: That we ſhall affect the Enemy *Diverſion* enough, I believe no body makes any

Doubt: and that our Army is a *covering* Army, is evident even to Demonſtration; for, whether it covers us the kindneſs of our Ally or not, I am ſure it covers an almoſt immeaſurable Extent of Ground: I queſtion, whether that famous Army of *Xerxes*, which level'd Mountains, and drunk up Rivers in its March, cover'd more: For while the *forlorn Hope* is on the other Side of the *Rhine*, our Artillery is ſcarce on the Road, our Cavalry have not quitted *Flanders*, we ſee Reinforcements diſemburſh from *Iceland*, and even the very Highlands of *Scotland* ſend forth their Heroes to vie with the *Huſſars*, *Croats*, *Pandours*, and other Military Monſters, in the Service of the Queen of *Hungary*.

And this brings into our Head a Device or Conceit, Mr. *Broadbottom*, which ſhall be at your Service to make what Uſe of you pleaſe.

You know it is a common Saying, that *every one hath his Play-thing*; indeed, therefore, of aſcribing every great Event, ſuch as the declaring War, aſſembling ſuch Armies, and embroiling half the World, to a Cauſe equally great, we ought rather to ſuppoſe that it led to Riſe from the Artifice of ſome deſigning *Miniſter*, who found a *political Toy* neceſſary to keep his Maſter in Humour, and himſelf *in Place*: Nothing being more certain, than that the light Cloud which numbers, the thin Vapour which is almoſt imperceptible, as often forebodes a Hurricane, as the ſolid Darkneſs, which the Mighty fly to the Mountains, and bolder Horror ſtikes upon whole Nations.

I am, therefore, led to conſider the preſent *Expedition* to *Germany*, as a Toy of this Nature, as a KITE let fly to amuſe that Spirit *abroad*, which might prove unmanageable at *home*; and with this Image, I am ſo much the more pleas'd, as it ſeems to exemplify every decent Idea that *we* ever upon the Subject.

For Inſtance: If any ruſticated Politician deſired *to know* the general Route and Diſpoſition of our Army, what Map could give him better Information than might be contained in the *Body* of our Kite? If he ſhould enquire the Uſe of our Mercenaries, the *Hanoverians* and *Huſſians*, would not the two Taſſels, that ſerve as Wings to the Kite, afford him all the Satisfaction he can hope for? And as to the String of Corps, of which the Reinforcements are to be form'd, could he be furniſhed with a more clear and ſimilar Explanation, than may be gathered from the different Tuſts which compoſe its Tail? If we ſhould fix a Lanthorn to the End of it, would it not very aptly repreſent the new *Light*, which ſo many *wife Men* have ſo implicitly followed, as an infallible Guide to the *Power* they reſolv'd to worſhip? When can think of G――――! C―――― and his Miſſion, without recollecting the Id. of a *Meſſenger* ſent up to keep the KITE STEDY? Would not the *Kite-flyer* already think it high Time to taking himſelf of that enterpriſing Genius, who both undertaken, by his own Strength, on his own Bottom, at his own Peril, to give the Syſtem of *Europe* what Turn he pleaſed? Should it be aſk'd once of whole Bowels the Thread was ſpun, and that *Button* wound up, by which this *Paper-Meteor* became to near a Neighbour to the Clouds, would not the whole Kingdom ſpeak forth on Anſwer? Should it be aſk'd for whole *Amuſement* this notable *Frolick* was play'd—

Here I thought it high Time to interrupt my Friend, by crying out, Hold! hold, Sir! my Apprehenſion is become ſtronger than my Curioſity—Suppoſe ſome *Buſy-Body* ſhould cut the String?

Of her our ſoaring Genius looks to that, reply'd my Friend; 'tis none of our *Buſineſs*—and ſo Mr. *Broadbottom*, your Servant.

LONDON: Printed (according to Act of Parliament) for J. PURSER in *Red-Lyon Court, Fleetſtreet.*

PL. 1. The *Old England Journal* was unrivalled in influence amongst the opposition press for much of the 1740s. The Kite here symbolizes Britain's alleged subservience to Hanoverian interests.

in November 1741, and represented the culmination of a process of transformation that had commenced at the beginning of the year, when William Webster brought to an end his High Church periodical, the *Weekly Miscellany*.[7] As regards its political role, one particularly noteworthy issue reprinted the Commons division list of 10 December 1742 and the Lords protest of 1 February 1743, both pertaining to the retention in British pay of the 16,000 Hanoverian troops for the coming year.[8] Its success, however, seems to have been founded not only on its political coverage, but also on the breadth and sophistication of its foreign and domestic news content. Thus, unusually for a paper of any kind in the mid-eighteenth century, the foreign news was digested into narrative form under the heading 'The Present History of Europe'. And, whereas the *Old England Journal* was prepared to sacrifice its news coverage in order to accommodate an increased volume of advertising in the winter of 1743–4—when both papers were probably at the summit of their influence—the *Westminster Journal* resisted this temptation.[9] After 1745, in part the beneficiary of the fact that it had never been closely identified with a particular parliamentary faction, the *Westminster Journal* seems to have overtaken the *Old England Journal* as the leading contemporary essay paper. On 20 November 1748 the former paper declared that it was in 'as healthy and thriving a state as ever', a claim that is lent substance by the frequency with which, to the exclusion of almost all other political papers, it was extracted after 1746 by the two monthly magazines, the *Gentleman's Magazine* and the *London Magazine*.

If the pre-eminence during the 1740s of the *Old England Journal* and the *Westminster Journal* seems indisputable, their patriot identity is equally certain. This was disclosed most obviously by their identification of ministerial attempts to subvert the constitutional goals and achievements of the Revolution (which were held to include the Act of Settlement of 1701) as the principal threat confronting the country. As the *Old England Journal* declared of its function:

It is intended to vindicate the Honour of the Crown of Great Britain, and to assert the Interest of her people against all Foreign considerations [a reference to the alleged impact of Hanover on the politics of the Whig regime]; to keep up the spirit of virtuous opposition to wicked power, to point out the means of

---

[7] For a more detailed account of the establishment of the *WJ*, see M. Harris, *London Newspapers in the Age of Walpole*, (1987), 126.

[8] *WJ* 12 Feb. 1743.   [9] For this, see below, Ch. 5.

compleating the great End of Revolution; and, in short, to give the Alarm upon any future Attacks that may be made, either open or secret, of the Government upon the constitution.[10]

Similarly, the *Westminster Journal* declared in 1744, two and a half years after its establishment: 'The Original Design of this paper was to combat vice, chiefly political and ministerial, it set out with a Declaration of war against all Invaders of our constitutional Freedom, and has never yet suspended Hostilities.'[11]

In the present context, two other features of the patriotism of both papers are also worth emphasizing. The first is the depth of their commitment to libertarian principles, and, in particular, their insistency on the contractual basis of government. As the *Westminster Journal* remarked on 5 May 1744: 'the civil and Religious Liberty of the subject, the Independency of Parliament, the Accountableness of a Crown receiv'd by compact, and upon oath, have ever been favourite Topics in the Westminster Journal.' On another occasion the same paper quoted from Locke to defend its commitment to principles of liberty. It was Locke, the paper declared, 'who hath so clearly stated the terms of *command* and *submission*, as they ought to be understood by every subject of *Great Britain*'. Meanwhile, the first issue of the *Old England Journal* included the contractualist warning that the 'people' had never given up their right to cashier their monarch should the Crown attempt to infringe 'English Liberties'.[12] The second feature is the emphasis that was placed, particularly in the *Westminster Journal*, on the related themes of trade and empire. One measure of the importance that was attached to these themes in the *Westminster Journal* was the interest that the paper showed between 1743 and 1744 in the possibility of expelling the French from North America. Elsewhere in the opposition press there were very few polemicists who addressed this prospect before the capture of Cape Breton in 1745. By 1747 the *Westminster Journal* was able to boast, with some justification, that it was a particular friend to the British colonies in North America.[13]

What, then, of the attitudes towards the labels of Whig and Tory expressed in the *Old England Journal* and the *Westminster Journal*? Between 1742 and 1744—not surprisingly, given the paper's identification with the Broad-Bottom opposition coalition—the *Old England Journal* maintained that the Whig–Tory division had no contemporary

---

[10] *OEJ* 5 Feb. 1743.   [11] *WJ* 5 May 1744.
[12] Ibid. 14 Apr. 1744; *OEJ* 5 Feb. 1743.   [13] *WJ* 31 Jan. 1747.

meaning or relevance. On 19 February 1743 the paper declared: 'As to Whig and Tory I know no real Distinction between them; I look upon them as two Brothers, who, in truth, mean the same Thing, tho' they pursue it differently; and therefore ... I declare myself for neither, yet for both.' The same message was repeated on 1 October, at the height of the anti-Hanoverian outcry of the winter of 1743–4. Referring to George II's decision to wear the yellow sash of Hanover at the Battle of Dettingen, the paper counselled: 'The scarlet sash is neither Whig or Tory. Let us unite in it at home ... against our Enemies. Scarlet or yellow is now our sole Distinction; and it is a real one.' If anything, the insistence in the *Old England Journal* on the irrelevance of traditional Whig and Tory identities increased after the formation of the Broad-Bottom ministry in late 1744. On 16 February 1745 the paper argued that the 'chief Article of an old whig's political creed' was that the people of England should, as the paper put it, 'be safe'. This same goal, the paper continued, was shared by a 'sensible Tory'. The only difference, recalling the statement that the paper had made in February 1743, was about means. But, it concluded, 'This Difference at last, was found to consist more in words than Things till common Danger had took away the Distinctions ministerial craft had form'd.' There was no essential change in the position of the paper in the later 1740s, with the labels of Whig and Tory continuing to be eschewed in favour of ministerial and patriot or opposition.[14]

This position, that the Whig–Tory division had no application to present political reality, was fundamentally similar to that maintained by the *Westminster Journal*. In the case of the *Westminster Journal*, however, its repudiation of party and party labels was even more pronounced. This is most strikingly demonstrated by its attitude towards the conduct of foreign policy. During the War of the Austrian Succession the paper basically advocated the blue-water strategy favoured by patriot opinion. It was, however, prepared to deviate from this stance on a number of occasions. The first of these followed the arrival of the news in June 1743 of the Allied army's victory over the French at Dettingen.[15] Responding to the widespread hopes of a successful invasion of French territory fuelled by the battle, the *Westminster Journal* articulated its support, over a number of issues, for a bellicose interventionist strategy. Defending its apparent support

---

[14] See e.g. *OEJ* 4 Oct. 1746, 11 July 1747.

[15] See below, Ch. 5, for a detailed examination of the press reaction to news of the victory.

for the ministry's conduct of the war, on 20 August 1743 the paper declared:

I conclude what I have to say at present concerning the *French* war, with declaring, that if any Thing I have advanced in these papers, seems to fall in more with some present ministerial views that could be expected from a professed *Anti-ministerial writer*, it only shews that my Design in it was *honest*, and dictated by a spirit of *Liberty*, without Regard either to *parties* or *men*.

The *Westminster Journal* was again supporting interventionist policies in the final stages of the war. The basic reason for this was its desire to see Britain exploit the opportunities for securing a favourable peace settlement allegedly ·opened up by her naval supremacy, particularly after 1747. This supremacy, the paper argued, enabled Britain to avoid repeating the mistakes of the end of the War of the Spanish Succession, when the Tory ministry of 1710–14 had allegedly sacrificed Britain's military superiority for the disastrous peace settlement of Utrecht.[16] Yet, if the *Westminster Journal* thus condemned the Tory conduct of foreign policy in the early 1710s, it was equally condemnatory about Whig policies during the early stages of the same conflict and during the earlier Nine Years War. In both wars, the paper argued, Whig ministries had imprudently committed Britain to a principal role in a conflict on the European mainland, thereby contravening one of the cardinal tenets of the blue-water strategy, namely, the necessity of restricting Britain's role in a land war to that of an auxiliary.[17]

Both the *Old England Journal* and the *Westminster Journal*, therefore, provide important evidence of the meaning and influence of mid-century patriot ideology, and the relative unimportance of the Whig–Tory division. Less influential opposition papers of the 1740s underline the dominance of patriotism in the opposition press. Thus, the long-standing tri-weekly evening paper the *London Evening Post* and its sister paper, the *Daily Post*, also eschewed the old party labels in favour of those of patriot or 'country interest'. The same was true of the other opposition essay papers of the period: the *Champion* (1739–43); *Common Sense* (1737–); the *Craftsman* (1736–); the short-lived crypto-Jacobite *National Journal, or, the Country Gazette* (22 March–10 June 1746); and the Leicester House-sponsored paper, the *Remembrancer* (1747–51). On 21 May 1748 the last of these, the *Remembrancer*,

---

[16] See *WJ* 23 Apr., 23 July, 6 Aug. 1748.
[17] Ibid. 16, 23 June 1744. See below, Ch. 3, for a discussion of various aspects of the opposition press advocacy of blue-water policies.

declared that nothing less than 'a general confederacy of all parties and Factions will be able to rescue the constitution out of their [the ministry's] Hands'. Five months later the same paper proposed a threefold division in contemporary politics: first, the ministerial party; secondly, the Jacobite party; and thirdly, 'those who are equally apprehensive of Ruin from these Quarters, without any purpose to fortify themselves against either'.[18] Perhaps the most prominent feature of the *Remembrancer*'s political stance, however, was not its declaration of indifference towards traditional party identities, but the frequency with which its editor, James Ralph, drew on or quoted from the country polemicist Charles Davenant. As Ralph explained on 23 January 1748, Davenant deserves to be 'consulted as the oracle of this country'. The recurring influence of Davenant throughout the political polemic of the 1730s and 1740s has recently been noted elsewhere.[19] The extent of this influence is itself another measure of patriotism's ascendancy in mid-century public debate.

It has already been suggested that the contemporary importance of patriotism can also be illustrated by examining the numerous occasional pamphlets published during the 1740s. Significantly, the vast majority of these tend to divide simply into pro-ministerial or opposition pamphlets, particularly in the case of those devoted to issues of foreign policy. It was only comparatively infrequently that the pamphleteers either employed the old party labels or discussed the relevance (or irrelevance) of traditional party identities. As their predecessors had done throughout the period of Walpolian rule, a small number of pro-ministerial polemicists attempted to assert the continuing existence and importance of the Whig–Tory division, often also alleging Tory support for the Jacobite cause.[20] When they were made, such claims were forcefully rejected by opposition pamphleteers. In late 1742 one of these pamphleteers argued that the present opposition was not designed to 'recommend the Designs of any party'. Rather, the opposition had 'united the free-thinking of the whigs, with the publick spirit of the Tories', and had 'shewn that a rational opposition comprehends all that is good and rejects all that is evil in every party'.[21]

[18] *Remembrancer*, 8 Oct. 1748.
[19] J. A. W. Gunn, *Beyond Liberty and Property: The Process of Self-Recognition in Eighteenth-Century Political Thought* (Kingston and Montreal, 1983), 27–8.
[20] See e.g. *A Letter from a By-Stander to a Member of Parliament* (1742); *A Warning to the Whigs, and to Well-Affected Tories* (1744).
[21] *The Case of the Opposition Impartially Stated* (1742), 54.

Perhaps the most robust attack on the pro-ministerial 'revival of party names', however, was the pamphlet *A Proper Answer to the By-Stander* (1742), a rebuttal of Corbyn Morris's well-known apologetic for Walpolian rule, *A Letter from a By-Stander to a Member of Parliament* (1742).[22] Party, Morris's critic argued, was a calculated deception. Its only purpose was to lead others 'into or prevent their opposing something, that is inconsistent with, or, dangerous to the constitution and liberties of their country'. The principal threat to British liberties was, it was further argued, ministerial ambition, of which party was simply an extension. Thus far the argument was unremarkable and merely a reiteration of the standard country or patriot critique of party. But where the author of *A Proper Answer* diverged from most other patriot writers was in applying this explanation of the role of party to the Augustan period. The Tory ministers of 1689–1714 were portrayed as having endeavoured to establish arbitrary power 'by means of that ridiculous principle called *Passive Obedience* and *Non-Resistance*'. To disguise their aim, they had concealed themselves under 'the mask of loyalty' and 'a true Regard for our constitution in church and state'. The Whig ministers of the same era were also alleged to have been pursuing arbitrary power, but through different means. To disguise their schemes, they had employed the much more dangerous 'mask of liberty itself'. The choice that faced the British people, therefore, was not Whig or Tory, but liberty or slavery. This choice was made all the more pressing under the contemporary conditions of politics. As the author concluded:

The Crown, and consequently our *ministers*, are now possessed of a most numerous *Standing Army*, and an infinite Fund for *Corruption*. These have been the chief causes, these are the sole supports of arbitrary power in all countries where it is established . . . we ought not, therefore, to think of who are *Whigs*, or who are *Tories*, or of the Behaviour of any amongst us, we ought now to think only of who are *Friends*, and who are *Enemies* to *Corruption*, and a *Standing Army*.[23]

---

[22] *A Letter from a By-Stander* was published in Feb. 1742, that is, almost contemporaneously with Walpole's resignation, and was widely (and incorrectly) regarded as having been written under Walpole's guidance. It also provoked a pamphlet controversy about the nature of the Stuart government. For this, see [T. Carte] *A Full Answer to a Letter from a By-Stander* (1742); [T. Birch?] *A Letter to the Rev. Mr T. Carte, Author of the Full Answer to the By-Stander* (1743); *A Full and Clear Vindication of the Full Answer from a By-Stander* (1743).

[23] *A Proper Answer to the By-Stander*, 39–42.

It was thus the conflict between the court and patriotism that preoccupied all levels of the opposition press in the 1740s. But what evidence is there that the Tories themselves identified with (and were identified with) patriotism? In the first place, there are the hostile comments of a number of pro-ministerial pamphleteers. In 1744, for example, the author of *A Warning to the Whigs, and to Well-Affected Tories* observed: 'The latter [the Tories] may well disguise themselves, be ashamed of the Name of their own principles, and conduct under that Name, and confidently usurp the Name of old whigs, men who they persecuted . . .'[24] The same anomaly, that of Tory espousal of the principles of the seventeenth-century Whigs, was also remarked on by Samuel Squire in his pamphlet *A Letter to a Tory Friend* (1746). As Squire put it, the Tories had seemingly adopted the principles of the 'patriots' that had been killed by the Tories' fathers.[25] Henry Fielding, meanwhile, noted in his pro-ministerial paper the *Jacobite's Journal* that 'Liberty in Danger' had replaced 'Church in Danger' as the 'cant-phrase' of what he alleged was a Tory–Jacobite opposition.[26]

In the second place, there are the declarations of various patriot and Whig-patriot polemicists. As has already been illustrated, the denial of the existence of a traditional or even a distinctive Toryism was a feature of much patriot polemic. On this point, certain other patriot writers could not have been more explicit. Representative in this respect were the Earl of Chesterfield and James Ralph in the pamphlet *A Defence of the People* (1743). As Chesterfield and Ralph demanded: 'how . . . shall we prove, that there either is, or can be any such Thing as a Tory remaining? The Church is in no Danger, the Prerogative is no Distress; both are safe . . . In a word, hath any Tory-motion been made in either House, for almost these thirty years pass'd?' Furthermore, they also demanded, was not ministerial Whiggism, with its measures allegedly to increase the power of the Crown, more characteristic of traditional Tory conduct than that of so-called Tories?[27] Another pamphleteer evoked the memory of one of the heroes of the struggle against Charles I's personal rule, John Hampden, to underline the same basic point, remarking: 'We have proof that the malignant Tories, together with many worthy whigs, have acted, not only like men of Honour, by

---

[24] *A Warning to the Whigs, and to Well-Affected Tories*, 5–6.
[25] *A Letter to a Tory Friend*, 27–30. Squire reiterated his view of Tory conduct two years later in *An Historical Essay upon the Ballance of Civil Power in England* (1748), pp. xxvi–xvii.
[26] *Jacobite's Journal*, 16 Jan. 1748.   [27] *A Defence of the People*, 95–6.

keeping upon such principles as Old Hampden himself would not be ashamed of.'[28] It is, however, the contemporary Tory-patriot pamphlets that can confidently be identified that, as suggested at the beginning of this chapter, provide the strongest evidence of Tory identification with patriotism.[29]

Significantly, it seems to have taken the political crisis that followed Walpole's fall to provoke the first intervention of certain Tories in the press in the 1740s. In order fully to understand both the nature and timing of this intervention it is worth looking in some detail at the impact on press and popular opinion of the political settlement that emerged in the months after Walpole's fall. Exaggeration of the importance and scale of this impact would be almost impossible. The final defeat of the Robinarch in February 1742 created widespread expectations of the reform of government along patriot lines, and of the prosecution of Walpole for twenty years of alleged misrule and graft. In this respect, what was expected was no less than the dismantling of the apparatus of Walpolian rule, and the triumph of patriotism over the Whig establishment. In addition to the opposition press, the principal vehicle for the expression of popular demands for the substantial reform of government were forty-nine constituency instructions to MPs—a significant number of which were from Tory-represented constituencies —which were forwarded to London between February and April.[30] Typically, these called for the repeal of the Septennial Act, the passage of place and pension bills, and the establishment of a far-reaching inquiry into Walpolian rule. Other prominent demands included measures to arrest the alleged 'general Decay of trade', and an end to 'all party Distinctions'. With regard to the latter, the grand jury of Hereford observed, in terms that recall almost exactly those employed by the author of *A Proper Answer to the By-Stander*, that they were 'invented and encouraged by wicked ministers, to divert the general attention from their pilfering practices and treacherous designs'.[31]

When these popular demands met with the less inspiring reality of the ineffectual Commons inquiry into the last ten years of Walpole's rule, and a very limited place bill, the opposition press launched a

[28] *National Unanimity Recommended* (1742), 26.

[29] See below, Appendix, on identifying Tory-patriot polemic in this period.

[30] 26 instructions were from English constituencies; 15 from Scottish counties and burghs; and 7 from Welsh constituencies. Of the 26 English constituencies, Tories either monopolized or shared the parliamentary representation of 22. All 7 Welsh constituencies were represented by Tories. But for different figures, see Colley, *In Defiance of Oligarchy*, 242.   [31] *LEP* 3 Apr. 1742.

campaign of vituperation against Pulteney and the new Whigs, which only began to subside in the spring of the following year. As Thomas Birch, a supporter of the ministerial Whigs, observed on 23 October: 'The Abuse of my Lord of Bath [as Pulteney was known following his elevation to the peerage in July] both in prose and verse fills our daily as well as weekly papers.'[32] The period between August and November 1742 also saw a second wave of instructions to MPs. Although considerably fewer in number than the instructions of the first half of the year, these provided another means of articulating the widespread detestation of Pulteney.[33] In its instruction to its representatives, the City of London expressed satisfaction at the level of popular outrage created by Pulteney's apostacy. It also expressed incredulity that politicians could be found 'who, under the mask of integrity, and by dissembling a zeal for their country, had long acquired the largest share of confidence, should, without the least hesitation or seeming remorse, greedily embrace the first occasion to disgrace all their former conduct'.[34]

As important as the volume and intensity of the press and popular vilification of Pulteney is the impact that his apostacy had on popular and press attitudes towards patriotism. As M. M. Goldsmith has argued elsewhere, an important ideological consequence of the failure of Walpole's fall to produce substantial political change was the crystallization of more cynical attitudes towards national politics.[35] Throughout the Walpolian period pro-ministerial polemicists had argued that patriotism was merely a mask adopted by place-hunting opposition politicians. Pulteney's betrayal of the patriot cause only seemed to confirm this view. The depth of the disillusionment with national politics and patriotism created thereby was commensurate with the intensity of the expectations that had been raised in early 1742.

Among the newspaper press, it is the *Westminster Journal* that illustrates this most clearly. In issue after issue in the latter part of 1742, and, indeed, throughout the following two years, the paper condemned what it called the 'down-right farce' of February to July 1742, and the mercenary nature of what was dubbed 'modern patriotism'.[36] In both the *Westminster Journal* and other opposition papers the

---

[32] BL Add. MS 35396 (Hardwicke Papers), fos. 77–8: Birch to Yorke, 23 Oct. 1743.

[33] There were 19 instructions in late 1742; there were also 3 counter-instructions in favour of the ministry, from Bristol, Nottingham, and Worcester.

[34] Quoted in Rogers, *Whigs and Cities*, 68.

[35] M. M. Goldsmith, 'Faction Detected: Ideological Consequences of Robert Walpole's Decline and Fall', *History*, 64 (1979), 1–19.

[36] See *WJ* 23, 30 Oct., 6, 20 Nov., 25 Dec. 1742.

worst possible construction was also placed upon the alleged obstruction of 'national justice'—that is, the failure to prosecute Walpole.
This, it was argued, had been motivated by the fear of the new Whigs
that the same fate might await them at a future date.[37] A number of
opposition polemicists even argued that Walpole had been controlling
events all along, and remained as the minister 'behind the curtain'.[38]
It was, however, left to another form of printed polemic, the contemporary political print, to convey most forcefully the alienation from
national politics that was widely felt in late 1742. In this respect, no one
could have failed to understand the print entitled *Magna Farta, or,
The Raree Show at St J———'s* (1742).[39] The print depicts a raree show
displaying the tricks and dispensing the rewards of modern politics
to an enthralled crowd of patriot politicians. A new opposition, significantly labelled a 'modern opposition', is being led into the fray
by a two-faced master of ceremonies. A character in the background
exclaims: 'knaves all'. Meanwhile, George II, positioned in a window
overlooking the scene, defecates on the crowd below, and wipes his
backside with the second of the two reports of the Commons committee
established to investigate Walpole's domestic administration. The message was self-evident: contemporary politics was governed by chicanery
and self-interest.

Pulteney's betrayal of the patriot cause, therefore, in addition to
creating intense popular outrage, led many who were naturally disin-
clined to support the ministry to question the nature both of opposition
and patriotism. It was in these circumstances that the first identifiable
Tory-patriot pamphlet of the 1740s, entitled *Opposition More Necessary
than Ever* and published in September 1742, appeared, along with a
number of other vindications of the patriot cause and the opposition to
both Walpole and the new ministry.[40] The immediate cause of their
publication, however, was the polemical attempts to portray new Whig
conduct in 1742 as consistent with a continued commitment to patriotism.[41] These polemicists also argued that, given the alleged patriotism

---

[37] See e.g. ibid. 27 Nov. 1742.
[38] See e.g. *A Letter to the Secret Committee* (1742), 7.
[39] See Pl. 2.
[40] See esp. *The Case of the Opposition Impartially Stated* (1742); *National Unanimity
Recommended, or, the Necessity of a Constitutional Resistance to the Sinister Designs of False
Brethren* (1742).
[41] See esp. *An Enquiry into the Present State of our Domestick Affairs* (1742);
Observations on the Conduct of Great Britain in Respect of Foreign Affairs (1742). See also
below, Ch. 4, for the new Whig defence in 1742 of their conduct.

Pl. 2. Magna Farta, or, The Raree Show at St J——'s.

of the new Whigs and the new ministry, opposition should now cease. It further followed from this, they declared, that all that was motivating continued opposition in the present conjuncture was the ambition for places of those who had found themselves excluded from the political settlement that had emerged following Walpole's fall.[42] In short, patriotism was safe in new Whig hands, and the present wave of revulsion against Pulteney and his colleagues, and the opposition to the new ministry, were being incited by factious politicians dissatisfied with their failure to gain places in the political changes of 1742.

Two related features distinguish the response of the Tory-patriot author of *Opposition More Necessary than Ever* to the challenges to patriotism and opposition of, on the one hand, the events of 1742 and, on the other, of the new Whig polemicists from that of other patriot writers in late 1742. The first of these was hostility towards, or at least a sense of separateness from, Whiggism. The case against Whiggism was twofold. First, there was the conduct of post-Revolution ministerial Whigs. When in office, all Whigs, it was alleged, had sought to extend Crown and ministerial power. In support of this view, a list of measures supposedly designed to achieve this end, and enacted under the aegis of Whig ministers, was reproduced. This list included, among other things, the Septennial Act, the Riot Act, the Black Act, and the proliferation of penal laws under Whig rule.[43] Secondly, as was deemed to have been conclusively demonstrated by the apostacy of Pulteney, Whiggism was identifiable with self-interest. In contrast, and this was the second of the Tory-patriot pamphlet's distinguishing features, it was claimed that it was the Tories who were the true custodians of patriotism and public virtue. This had been evident, it was argued, since the Revolution. As the author declared:

View their [the Tories] *Resistance* at the *Revolution*; view their Abhorrence of a *Standing Army* in all King William's Reign; see the same virtuous, steady Dislike of it in the latter part of *Queen Anne's* Reign; when they had the power to continue a *Standing Force*; and when it would have been their *Interest*; if they were capable of an interest separate from that of the community.[44]

In short, the Tories had been the 'warmest Asserters of the people's liberties for half a century past'.

In the more recent past this was asserted to have been disclosed by the Tory opposition to the famous *motion* of 13 February 1741. The

---

[42] *An Enquiry into the Present State of our Domestick Affairs*, 54.
[43] *Opposition More Necessary than Ever*, 52–5.   [44] Ibid. 52–53.

opposition Whigs had, it was alleged, only sought to use this device to force themselves into office. Even more recent was the Tory conduct after Walpole's resignation, when the Tories had struggled to secure the patriot reforms so long promised. Given their conduct both before and after Walpole's fall, the pamphlet concluded:

> If there be any such Thing as public virtue remaining amongst us, 'tis certainly with those whom the whigs have branded with non-resisting principles. The Tories, if ever they gave room for the imputation, which I think they have not, have taken up the whiggish principles; and the whigs have constantly acted, whenever in power, on those slavish principles they would invidiously impute to the Tories.[45]

A number of other features of *Opposition More Necessary than Ever* are also worthy of notice, as well as its articulation of a sense of a distinctive 'Tory' contribution to patriotism. First, as was common to all patriot polemicists in this period, the Tory-patriot pamphleteer also expressed opposition to 'party Distinctions'. As the pamphlet reiterated, such divisions 'were first set on Foot and continued ever since by bad men for bad purposes'. It was only, it was further declared, for 'method sake' that the author had been obliged to use 'the old Appelations of Tories and Whigs'.[46] Secondly, it also needs to be emphasized that many, if not the majority, of the arguments put forward in the pamphlet were virtually identical to those employed by many of patriotism's other defenders in the 1740s, defenders, moreover, who made no, or at most only the slightest, reference to Tory or Whig labels. Thus, in late 1742 a lengthy 'black' list of the ministerial Whig 'Tory' measures of the last thirty years was included by at least one other patriot polemicist.[47] Similarly, the failure of many members of the opposition to support the *motion* of 13 February 1741 was also defended, in terms almost identical to those used by the Tory-patriot pamphleteer, by the author of the patriot pamphlet *The Case of the Opposition Impartially Stated* (1742). It was, this latter pamphlet argued, the opposition Whig pursuit of self-interest on that occasion, and thus their failure to adhere to the principles upon which the opposition (which, interestingly, was alleged to have been founded in the aftermath

---

[45] *Opposition More Necessary than Ever*, 58.   [46] Ibid. 48.

[47] *National Unanimity Recommended*, 52–3. For other black lists of ministerial measures printed during the 1740s, see e.g. *Opposition not Faction, or, the Rectitude of the Present Parliamentary Opposition to the Present Expensive Measures, Justified by Reason and Facts* (1743), 55–6; *The Measures of the Late Administration Examin'd* (1745), *passim*; *WJ* 15 Aug. 1747.

of the South Sea affair of the early 1720s) was based, which had ensured that the motion gained less than unanimous support amongst the opposition.[48]

If the publication of *Opposition More Necessary than Ever* needs to be set against the background of the peculiar conditions of politics following Walpole's fall, the same is true of two further Tory-patriot pamphlets of the early 1740s—*The Opposition Rescued from the Insolent Attacks of Faction Detected* (1744), and *Public Discontent Accounted for, from the Conduct of our Ministers in the Cabinet, and of our Generals in the Field* (1743). What provided the stimulus for both pamphlets was the publication, in September 1743, of Lord Perceval's famous defence of new Whig conduct in 1742, *Faction Detected by the Evidence of Facts*. That it should have provoked a Tory response causes no real surprise. No other pamphlet that appeared during the 1740s remotely rivalled its influence. Signs of its impact in the winter of 1743–4 can be found almost everywhere: in the opposition essay papers; in the two monthly magazines; in various widely reprinted odes and ballads; and in contemporary political correspondence.[49] Still more impressive is the large number of editions that it rapidly went through: despite its enormous length of over 170 pages, and its relatively high cost of 2s., by the end of 1743 it was already in its sixth edition, and a seventh was published in early 1744. Yet another measure of its influence is the unprecedented number of pamphlet rebuttals that it provoked. During the next few months, in addition to the two Tory-patriot rebuttals, at least seven other pamphlets were published in direct response to *Faction Detected*, one of which—a satirical attack on the Earl of Bath's failure to succeed the Earl of Wilmington as First Lord of the Treasury during the previous summer—itself went through six editions, and two of which went through two editions.[50]

---

[48] *The Case of the Opposition Impartially Stated*, 19–20.

[49] See e.g. *Common Sense*, 15 Oct. 1743, 7 Jan. 1744; *OEJ* 1, 8 Oct. 1743; *WJ* 1 Oct., 12 Nov. 1743; *GM* 12 (1743), 537; Lewis, *Walpole*, xviii. 315–21: Walpole to Mann, 3 Oct. 1743; BL Add. MS 35396, fos. 150–3, 154–5, 159–60, 172–3, 179–80; [Hanbury Williams] 'To the Earl of Bath, Occasioned by a Late Pamphlet, Entitled Faction Detected' (*LM* 12 (1743), 462). In a note in his *Memoirs of the Reign of George II*, i. 24, Horace Walpole later referred to *Faction Detected* as 'that masterly pamphlet . . . a work which the Pitts and Lyttletons have never forgiven him [Perceval], . . . and which made him quite unpopular during all the last Parliament'.

[50] (1) *The New Opposition Compared with the Old in Point of Principles and Practice* (1744); (2) *A Letter to the Rev. Dr Zachary Pearce, Occasion'd by his Advertisement in the Daily Advertiser of Oct. 28, 1743, in which the Secret History and Real Tendency of a Late Pamphlet, Intitled Faction Detected . . . Are Clear'd Up* (1743); (3) *Opposition not Faction,*

Apart from the particular political circumstances in which the pamphlet appeared, which are discussed in detail elswhere in the present work, two factors seem to have been primarily responsible for the scale of the reaction that it provoked. First, it was widely believed to have been directly inspired by the Earl of Bath.[51] Secondly, and more directly relevant to the Tory response, Perceval succeeded in offending almost the entire spectrum of contemporary political opinion. Not only did he brand the opposition Whigs and, more particularly, the Tories as Jacobite fellow-travellers, he also displayed total indifference to the sensibilities of the old corps (the supporters of Walpole and then the Pelhams) by vigorously castigating the Walpolian regime for twenty years of alleged deviation from 'Whig' principles. As Henry Pelham wrote to Henry Fox: 'The laborious inconsistent pamphlet *Faction Detected* bids defiance of the Torys, and att [*sic*] the same time provokes the resentment of two-thirds of the whigs.'[52]

Like the new Whig polemic of late 1742, discussed above, a major aim of *Faction Detected* was to expose the allegedly spurious patriotism of the Broad-Bottom opposition that had emerged in the second half of 1742. The means by which Perceval attempted to achieve this end, however, differed. Thus, it was argued that what was motivating the present opposition was not the desire for places, but disloyalty. The Whiggish declarations of what was, in reality, a disaffected 'Tory opposition and Jacobite Faction' represented a dangerous deception in this respect. It was explained that 'In fact, every Faction will without scruple, assume any appellation to impose upon mankind; and the most inveterate Jacobite Faction, to carry its view, will profess to act upon a whig principle, when that becomes a *favourite principle*, as it is this time.'[53] To support this contention, Perceval advanced an extremely narrow criterion of Whig conduct. Having dismissed self-classification as an unreliable guide to political identity, he insisted that the true nature of political commitment was

or, the Rectitude of the Present Parliamentary Opposition to the Present Expensive Measures (1743); (4) *The Desertion Discussed* (1743, 2 editions); (5) *The Detector Detected, or, the Danger to which our Constitution Now Lies Exposed* (1743); (6) [Chesterfield and Ralph] *A Defence of the People* (1743, 2 editions); (7) *A Congratulatory Letter to a Certain Right Honourable Person upon his Late Disappointment* (1743, 6 editions); (8?) *A Review of the Whole Political Conduct of a Late Eminent Patriot* (1743).

[51] For Perceval's difficulty in persuading others that he was the author of *Faction Detected*, see BL Add. MS 35396, fos. 176–7: Birch to Yorke, 15 Oct. 1743.

[52] *Letters to Henry Fox Lord Holland*, ed. Earl of Ilchester (1915), 3: Pelham to Fox, 27 Sept. 1743.   [53] *Faction Detected*, 6.

only revealed by actions and, in particular, by responses to the external threat posed by the French. Thus, according to Perceval, the primary component of Whiggism was active and persistent opposition to French diplomatic objectives. This was the 'grand point' that had motivated opposition Whig divergence from the old corps under Walpole—his foreign policy having allegedly failed to adhere to this essential tenet of Whiggism. The purpose of the opposition to Walpole, a 'whig-opposition', had been, it was further maintained, to remove Walpole from office, and thereby to force Britain to resume its true interest of 'resisting and reducing the power of France'. As for new Whig support for the so-called 'popular laws' (the repeal of the Septennial Act, place and pension bills), this had only been conceded for the sake of opposition union. By contrast to the Whig opposition, the 'Jacobite or Tory Faction' was identifiable by its efforts, 'directly or indirectly, to assist, encourage, and support the interests of France'. This was the policy that the Tories had assiduously pursued, or so Perceval alleged, during Britain's wars against Louis XIV's France, conduct that had culminated in the notorious Peace of Utrecht.[54]

Not surprisingly, a prominent feature of the patriot response to *Faction Detected*, including that of the two Tory-patriot pamphleteers, was attacks on Perceval's remarks regarding the alleged relationship between attitudes towards foreign policy and party identity. The view that hostility towards France was the only reliable guide to Whig identity was derisively rejected. As the author of *Opposition Rescued from the Insolent Attacks of Faction Detected* declared: 'Antipathy to France, the grand criterion as they call it, and contend for, no more denominates a whig, than a mahometan.'[55] A number of patriot pamphleteers, including the author of *Public Discontent Accounted For*, offered alternative definitions of the principles of a 'true Whig'. All these definitions sought to identify 'true Whiggism' with, most notably, supporting the liberties of the people and opposing the encroachments of the Crown, preventing and punishing corruption, and opposing the growth of the national debt and additional taxation; or, in other words, with country or patriot principles.[56] Common to all the pamphlet responses to *Faction Detected* was also a declared repugnance towards Perceval's attempt to 'revive party names'.

Where the two Tory-patriot pamphleteers diverged from their fellow

---

[54] Ibid. 6, 13, 73, 9.
[55] *The Opposition Rescued from the Insolent Attacks of Faction Detected*, 29–30.
[56] See e.g. *A Defence of the People*, 10; *Public Discontent Acounted For*, 16.

pamphleteers, however, was in their partisan defence of past Tory conduct. In the case of the author of *Public Discontent Accounted For*, this involved maintaining, and thereby echoing *Opposition More Necessary than Ever*, that the Tories had the greatest right to identify themselves as patriots. Thus it was argued that 'nominal tories' had been 'whigs and patriots' since 1689, whilst the so-called 'whigs', who, when in office, had been advocates of standing armies and the extension of penal laws, were 'tories in principle'. Unlike the Whig-patriots, it was also remarked, again as it had been in *Opposition More Necessary than Ever*, the 'nominal tories' had never betrayed the 'people'. Given this fact, the author of *Public Discontent Accounted For* exclaimed:

What I contend for is that, for above half a century, those improperly called *Tories* have, in general, been the warmest Asserters of the People's *Liberties* in every shape; and those, improperly called *whigs*, have constantly, when in power been the boldest invaders of the people's liberties, and properties in every instance and every Reign.[57]

It is worth noting that, in defence of this proposition, the pamphlet also included a novel vindication of the Tory peace policy of 1710–14, which, as we have seen, was one of the many butts of Perceval's pen. As a counter to Perceval's censure of the Peace of Utrecht, the Tory-patriot pamphleteer portrayed Robert Harley as guiding the country on Whig principles, safeguarding the Protestant succession, and securing the welfare and freedom of the people by negotiating the much-misrepresented peace settlement of 1713.[58]

In the early 1740s, then, or, more specifically, in the bitter political atmosphere created by the new Whig betrayal of the patriot cause following Walpole's fall, a small number of Tory-patriot pamphlets were published. These pamphlets underline how little meaning the Whig–Tory division was felt to have, at least by those opposing the Whig establishment, at the level of press debate and politics 'without doors'. While Tory-patriot pamphleteers were prepared to provide a partisan defence of Tory conduct since 1689, this was designed to reinforce the Tory identification with patriotism. Perhaps even more significantly, they also eschewed the label of Tory, preferring old Whig, true Whig, or patriot. Equally significant is the fact that, apart from a partisan portrayal of past Tory conduct, there is almost nothing to distinguish Tory-patriot argument from patriot and Whig-patriot argu-

---

[57] *Public Discontent Accounted For*, 42–3.   [58] Ibid. 47.

ment. Examination of three other Tory-patriot pamphlets published in the early 1740s that were concerned almost exclusively with issues of foreign policy would provide further support for this conclusion.[59] But it is by examining the press reaction in the winter of 1744–5 to the formation of the Broad-Bottom ministry that, as referred to above, the extent to which Tory identity was submerged in the broader patriot–ministerial division in this period (and the importance of the patriot–ministerial division) can best be further illustrated.

What is most immediately striking about the response of all elements of the opposition press to the admission of various opposition politicians, including a number of leading Tories, into the ministry in late 1744 is the comparisons that were widely made between the formation of the Broad-Bottom ministry and the admission and subsequent conduct of Pulteney and the new Whigs in 1742. Overshadowing almost all comment in the press about the formation of the Broad-Bottom ministry was the possibility of a second betrayal of the patriot cause. Typical in this respect was the query that appeared in the *Daily Post* on 14 January 1745: 'Whether there is not, at this time, a moral certainty of obtaining the *benefits* by that change [the formation of the Broad-Bottom ministry] which were then [in 1742] lost by the Treachery of a very few?' A number of opposition polemicists, having already witnessed Pulteney's apostacy in 1742, were very pessimistic about the chances of any substantial patriot reforms being enacted in early 1745. It was also recognized that a second betrayal of the patriot cause could only increase the alienation and disillusionment of the extra-parliamentary nation.

One pamphleteer who suggested that the prospects for both the achievement of any of the patriot demands and the future of patriotism were virtually nil was the author of the pamphlet *Christmas Chat, or, Observations on the Late Change at Court*, published at the beginning of 1745. Even if the opposition leaders had stipulated the passage of country or patriot measures as a condition of their entering the administration, the overwhelming dominance of the Pelhams in the Broad-Bottom ministry suggested, it was argued, that they would not be secured. As the pamphleteer demanded: 'Supposing the few of your party that are brought *in*, were to continue as honest and sincere, as those Deserters, who are made room for them, were disingenuous and

[59] The three pamphlets are *Seventeen Hundred and Forty-Two* (1743), *A Plain Answer to the Plain Reasoner* (1745), and *The English Nation Vindicated from the Calumnies of Foreigners* (1744). For these, see below, Appendix.

self-interested; what can you do against Numbers? What success can poor *England* expect from the Endeavours of so few?' The probable consequence of the failure of the Pelhams to submit to such guidance, and, therefore, of successive betrayals of the patriot cause, would be, it was further argued, the extinction of patriotism.[60] The possibility that the opposition leaders had been admitted to the ministry with the sole aim of buttressing the power of the Pelhams was also addressed in another pamphlet published in early 1745, *Miscellaneous Thoughts, Moral and Political, upon the Vices and Follies of the Present Age.* Should the people be confronted with a second betrayal in two years, the author of this pamphlet argued, they would 'be brought to despair of ever meeting with Redress from Parliament'.[61]

The significance of such remarks is, of course, that they disclose very clearly the criteria by which the Broad-Bottom experiment was to be judged in the opposition press. In short, the issue at stake was how far the opposition leaders succeeded, where Pulteney had failed in 1742, in achieving the enactment of patriot measures of political reform and the instigation of patriot policies in foreign and domestic affairs. Thus, as the measures and character of the Broad-Bottom administration increasingly diverged from the path of patriot purity during the first half of 1745, the opposition leaders who had been admitted to the ministry, like Pulteney in 1742, were subjected to a wave of outrage and criticism from the opposition press.

In the case of the pamphlet *An Address of Thanks to the Broad-Bottoms* (1745), this criticism seems to have been of Tory provenance.[62] The pamphlet listed twelve 'Broad-Bottom promises' that were said to have been made between 1725 and 1744. These included the standard trinity of country reform measures (the repeal of the Septennial Act, and the passage of place and pension bills); the traditional Tory demand that new commissions of the peace be established across the country, 'admitting all Gentlemen of fortune without Distinction'; the disfranchisement of revenue officers; and the appointment of secret committees to inspect the public accounts.[63] Having compiled this list, the pamphlet then went on to illustrate the extent to which the Broad-Bottom leaders had failed even to emulate the very limited concessions to popular demands made by the 'deserters' of 1742. Patriotism, the

---

[60] *Christmas Chat*, 6, 43.   [61] *Miscellaneous Thoughts*, 35–6.
[62] See below, Appendix.
[63] *An Address of Thanks*, 33–5: 8 of the Broad-Bottom promises were identical to the so-called Broad-Bottom propositions submitted to Lord Gower in early 1745. See below.

pamphlet concluded, thus providing support for the prognostications of the patriot pamphleteers referred to above, was now extinguished; the people will 'necessarily abjure all patriots and patriotism for the future'.[64]

Another notable source of polemical attacks on the failure of the Broad-Bottom ministry to realize expectations of patriot reform came from supporters of the Earl of Granville. Between December 1744 and the summer of 1745 pro-Granville pamphleteers robustly defended Granville's conduct of the war between 1742 and 1744, and condemned the opposition leaders who had co-operated in forcing him from office for allegedly conniving at the entrenchment in power of the Pelhams.[65] As the author of a pro-Granville pamphlet significantly entitled *The Modern Patriot, or, Broad-Bottom Principles* exclaimed: 'They charg'd a M——st-r [Walpole] with all the most violent and flagrant Things that could have been done against a free country, they even drove his successor [Granville] out of pow-r for protecting him: And what is now the case? they have join'd that very detested p——ty [the old corps], and now support it.'[66]

The opposition leadership who had entered the Broad-Bottom ministry were thus vigorously attacked in the early months of 1745 by patriots, Tory-patriots, and supporters of Granville for an alleged second betrayal of the patriot cause. One leading opposition politician who was singled out for particular criticism in the press was the Tory leader, Sir Watkin Williams Wynn. Thus, it was Wynn who was the target of the pamphlet *An Expostulatory Epistle to the Welch Knight*, published in February 1745. What had stimulated this attack was his conduct in the early stages of the parliamentary session that had recommenced, after a brief Christmas adjournment, in early January. In a Committee of Supply on 23 January Wynn had given his vote and spoken in support of a motion to increase the number of British troops to be deployed in Flanders for the coming year. As Philip Yorke remarked of the incident in his parliamentary journal: 'Sir Watkin Williams Wynn, to the surprise of the generality, spoke for the question, and as he said himself, agreed with the court for the first time of his life.'[67] The condemnation of Wynn's conduct began with the warning that his intervention in the Committee of Supply threatened to

[64] *An Address of Thanks*, 52.
[65] See esp. *A Plain Reasoner* (1745); *A Continuation of the Plain Reasoner* (1745); *The Modern Patriot, or, Broad-Bottom Principles* (1745).
[66] *The Modern Patriot*, 59–60.   [67] *Parl. Hist.*, xiii. 1054.

undermine his reputation as an incorruptible supporter of the patriot cause. The pamphleteer then proceeded to hound Wynn with the alleged parallels between his and his fellow opposition leaders' conduct in the winter of 1744–5 and the conduct of another 'Band of Auxiliaries'—as it was put—in 1742. Added significance is given to *An Expostulatory Epistle to the Welch Knight* by the fact that, according to the then Solicitor-General, Sir Dudley Ryder, it was the criticisms levelled against Wynn in this pamphlet that caused his reversion to opposition towards the end of the 1744–5 session of Parliament.[68]

Significantly, Wynn and the other Tory leaders who participated in the early stages of the Broad-Bottom ministry did not go undefended in the press in early 1745. Attempts to rebut allegations that Wynn had submitted to the favours of the court were made in both the *Old England Journal* and in the pamphlet *An Apology for a Welch Knight* (1745).[69] A much more detailed and important attempt to exonerate both Wynn and the Tory leadership, however, was a pamphlet entitled *The Case Fairly Stated*, published in May 1745. A number of factors suggest that this represented a desperate attempt to arrest the alienation of the Tories' natural support. First, as should be apparent by now, identifiable Tory interventions in the press in this period were comparatively rare. In fact, between 1740 and 1748 there seem to have been fewer than ten Tory-patriot pamphlets published.[70] Secondly, and perhaps more importantly, the pamphlet was unique in this period for its close attention to the minutiae of high political manœuvre. In this respect, great efforts were made to provide a detailed and closely argued account of the role of the Tory leadership in the negotiations that immediately preceded the formation of the Broad-Bottom ministry. An important element of this aspect of the pamphlet was the reproduction of the nine-point plan (the so-called Broad-Bottom propositions) submitted by Lord Noel Somerset and Wynn to Lord Gower in early 1745.[71] On the basis of this internal evidence, Linda Colley has argued that the author of *The Case Fairly Stated* 'must have been a Tory M.P.,

---

[68] See Colley, *In Defiance of Oligarchy*, 246. Tory sensitivity to the attacks made in *An Expostulatory Epistle* and *An Address of Thanks to the Broad-Bottoms* was also remarked on in *An Apology for the Welch Knight* (1745). Thus, one of the characters (the pamphlet was in the form of a dialogue), Broad-Bum (Sir John Hynde-Cotton), was made to remark of the 'Duns of our own Party', that 'Ever since the publication of that damn'd *Epistle*, and *Address*, they are become intolerably impatient, and not a little troublesome and impertinent.' (*An Apology*, 1.)

[69] See esp. *OEJ* 30 Mar. 1745.   [70] See below, Appendix.

[71] For these propositions see Colley, *In Defiance of Oligarchy*, 247–8.

or supplied by leading Tories to compose their apologies'.[72] An entry in the ledger of Charles Ackers, best known as the printer of the *London Magazine*, of which Colley seems to have been unaware, attributes the authorship of the pamphlet to the crypto-Jacobite Thomas Carte.[73] Whether Carte was the author or not, the importance of *The Case Fairly Stated* as a declaration of 'Tory' principles is undoubted. As the Tory peer Lord Oxford, for one, remarked, it provided a 'full and clear' account.[74]

As might be expected from the reaction of patriot and Tory-patriot polemicists to the formation of the Broad-Bottom ministry, to which *The Case Fairly Stated* was a response, and as has already been suggested, what it very forcefully emphasizes is the extent to which a separate Tory identity was submerged in the broader patriot–ministerial division. In the first place, this is disclosed by the full title of the pamphlet: *The Case Fairly Stated in a Letter from a Member of Parliament in the COUNTRY INTEREST to One of his Constituents* (my emphasis). In the second place, there are the strained attempts of the author of the pamphlet to demonstrate that the conduct of the Tory leaders in the winter of 1744–5 was consistent with their continued commitment to patriotism. With this end in view, the comparisons being made with the conduct of the new Whigs in 1742 caused the author to remark: 'But I must confess, we little imagined our conduct would have been compared with that of the Gentlemen who so shamefully deserted us three years ago.'[75] Attempts were also made to show how Tory support in early 1745 for the Broad-Bottom ministry's conduct of the war did not constitute reneging on their former advocacy of blue-water policies. Thus it was argued that support for the extrication of Britain from

[72] Ibid. 38.

[73] *A Ledger of Charles Ackers, Printer of the 'London Magazine'*, ed. D. F. McKenzie and J. C. Ross (Oxford, 1968), 201. *The Case Fairly Stated* carries the imprint of the leading trade publisher Mary Cooper, and usually she, and not the author or anyone else closely connected with the pamphlet, would have dealt directly with the printer. But fortunately in this case normal practice was not followed, and the entry in Ackers's ledger, dated 4 May 1745, supplies additional information. Thus, the entry debits the cost of printing a run of 1,000 pamphlets to Mr George Gordon, later editor of the crypto-Jacobite *National Journal, or, the Country Gazette*, and attributes the authorship to Carte. Although there is no corroborative evidence, as far as I am aware, for Carte's authorship in his papers, Ackers's entry seems plausible. As was noted in the last chapter, in 1743 Carte contacted the exiled Stuart court regarding a project to set up a paper to exploit the favourable political conditions of the early 1740s, suggesting that Gordon was the man to organize this venture.

[74] See Colley, *In Defiance of Oligarchy*, 351 n. 27.

[75] *The Case Fairly Stated*, 7.

a European land war, even if this involved an increased commitment of men and money to the Continent in the short term, was entirely consistent with a continued commitment to a naval-based strategy. One particular triumph in the area of foreign policy, it was alleged, was the dismissal of the 16,000 Hanoverian troops that had been in British pay between 1742 and 1744.[76] As regards the enactment of measures of domestic reform, the pamphlet protested that the Tories had shown undivided attention to the aim of 'obtaining constitutional points'. All that could be offered in support of this claim, however, was the passage of a heavily amended bill to tighten up the property qualifications for JPs.[77] Nevertheless, the pamphlet concluded its efforts to bolster the Tories' continued identification with patriotism by arguing, in the face of the formidable array of evidence to the contrary, that their role in the Broad-Bottom ministry represented the glorious culmination of thirty years of assiduous guardianship of the 'people's interests'. As the author boasted:

We have this thirty years persevered in a constant opposition against all incroachments of power:—we have the same English hearts we ever had; and we are resolved by a strict and regular Attendance upon Duty in Parliament, to profit of every occasion that may appear favourable for restoring the constitution to its former vigour:—without taking too much merit to ourselves, we may venture to say, this is the first session in *Thirty Years*, wherein any Thing has been done towards a reformation of abuses.[78]

A significant postscript to the publication of *The Case Fairly Stated* was the publication in June of a formidable rebuttal of Carte's central assertion—namely, that Tory actions in early 1745 were consistent with a patriot stance—in the form of the pamphlet *A Letter to the Author of the Case Fairly Stated, from an Old Whig*. According to the author of this pamphlet, the so-called Broad-Bottom propositions, around which the bulk of the defence of the Tory leaders had been constructed, had played no actual role in the negotiations that preceded their admission into the administration. They had, it was alleged, never even been submitted to the Pelhams. As for the propositions themselves, they were portrayed as falling into either of two categories: the 'vague and general', or the 'trifling and minute'. Included in the former category

---

[76] See below, Ch. 6, for a detailed examination of the opposition press attacks on the Broad-Bottom ministry's conduct of the war in early 1745, and the response of *The Case Fairly Stated*.

[77] For this, see J. B. Owen, *The Rise of the Pelhams* (1957), 260–1.

[78] *The Case Fairly Stated*, 38.

was the demand 'That such measures only be pursued as shall be consistent with the interest of Great Britain'. Without any attempt to identify in explicit terms which measures were inconsistent with national interest, and which measures were to be approved, this demand was, or so the author of *A Letter to the Author* declared, meaningless. This and the other demands had only served, the hostile pamphleteer continued, as 'plausible Excuses' for the Tory acceptance of places.[79]

There was also no difficulty in showing how far removed from the hyperbolic rhetoric of *The Case Fairly Stated* the reforming record of the Tories and the Broad-Bottom ministry actually was. In the area of domestic reform, it was pointed out that no substantial 'popular bills' had even been proposed. Similarly, no attempts had been made to instigate inquiries into alleged abuses in civil and military administration. The only inquiry of this nature to be pursued in early 1745, the parliamentary inquiry into the naval miscarriage at Toulon of the spring of 1744, was the result, it was observed, of an MP who was described as an 'old courtier'.[80] In short, the Tories had proved themselves to be a 'party of swiss', merely selling themselves to the highest bidder, which in this case happened to be the Pelhams. In this context, the parallels with 1742 were again raised. In particular, the failure to hold a meeting equivalent to that at the Fountain Tavern of 12 February 1742, when Pulteney had attempted publicly to defend his conduct in negotiations with the ministry to an audience of his former allies (both opposition Whigs and Tories), provoked the demand: 'How happened it that there was not one meeting at your beloved *Fountain-Tavern*? Were not your *leaders* frequently called upon to summon one, in order to submit their Actions to Publick Censure? Did they not all constantly decline it?'[81]

Despite the jeremiads of opposition polemicists in early 1745, the failure of the Broad-Bottom ministry to undertake significant changes in government measures did not mark an end of patriotism. There is no doubt, however, that, by reinforcing the even greater effects of the political settlement of 1742, it was one of the more important causes of the substantial reductions in the vitality of politics 'without doors' and

---

[79] *A Letter to the Author*, 17–18.
[80] Ibid. 24–6. The motion for the inquiry was in fact proposed by Charles Selwyn, an MP who defies easy political categorization, but who was generally in opposition during the early 1740s. It was seconded by Velters Cornwall, Tory MP for Herefordshire, who had a personal interest in the affair, his brother having been killed in the action.
[81] Ibid. 37–8. For the Fountain Tavern meeting, see Owen, *Rise of the Pelhams*, 97–8.

in the political influence of the press during the later 1740s. As far as the press was concerned, the effects of successive betrayals of the patriot cause were manifested in at least two important ways. First, there was a significant reduction, particularly discernible after 1746, in the overall volume of political comment that was reprinted across the London press. Not surprisingly, of the longer-standing papers, it was certain of the opposition papers that were most affected. In 1746 the sister paper of the *London Evening Post*, the *Daily Post*, ceased publication. In addition, both the *Craftsman* and *Common Sense* seem to have finally disappeared into total obscurity. In the case of the former paper, in 1748 its current editor, Thomas Cooke, was notifying the ministry of his readiness to transform the paper into a non-political miscellany.[82] The *Champion*, meanwhile, had changed its character as early as 1743, concentrating from October of that year on material of purely literary interest. This, however, seems to have been a far from successful transformation, with the paper ceasing publication some time in 1745.[83]

Other elements of the press to reflect the general drift away from politics were new papers that were founded in the later 1740s, and the monthly magazines. Thus, the newly established papers often advertised themselves on the basis of their strict avoidance of political controversy.[84] Among the monthly magazines, it was Thomas Cave's *Gentleman's Magazine* that seems to have adapted most successfully to the change in political climate. The change in editorial strategy was the subject of the preface to the 1747 edition, which declared:

While a determin'd spirit of opposition in the national assemblies communicated itself to almost every individual, multiplied, and invigorated periodical papers, and render'd politics the chief, if not the only object of curiosity, we acted a secure and easy part, having an ample field for our collections, which, as they were faithfully and impartially made, had a ready and extensive reception. Hence some imagined, and not without reason, that when this resource should fail us, our work would meet with less regard, at the same time it would be attended with greater difficulty. But as a fondness for politicks, tho' general, was never universal, we have happily substituted other subjects, not indeed, equally adapted to excite the passions, but more useful and permanent; so that instead of a diminished, we have experienced an increasing sale.

One other factor that reinforced the tendency towards a more miscellaneous content in the *Gentleman's Magazine* was the Lords decision in

---

[82] L. Hanson, *The Government and the Press 1695–1763* (Oxford, 1967), 120.
[83] See Harris, *London Newspapers*, 132.   [84] See below, Ch. 6.

1747 to take action against the monthly magazines for their reports of Lord Lovat's trial, which was discussed in the last chapter. Unlike the effect on his major competitor, the *London Magazine*, this seems to have induced Cave largely to cease the attempt to provide accounts of parliamentary debates.[85]

Secondly, and even more directly a consequence of the successive betrayals of the patriot cause, there was a prevailing tone of disillusionment among the remaining political papers regarding the possibilities of reviving widespread popular support for a patriot opposition. Perhaps unsurprisingly, it was the Leicester House paper established at the end of 1747, the *Remembrancer*, which expressed the most concern about popular indifference. A continual theme in the paper's early issues was the dissolution of confidence in patriotism and in patriot politicians caused by the betrayals of the first half of the decade. Representative in this respect were the remarks made in the paper on 26 December 1747:

All agree, that we are gasping at Life; and yet so peculiarly alarming is the crisis, that we have almost as much Reason to dread the Doctor [i.e. the patriot opposition] as the Disease: For as Abuse of power hurried us almost to the last stage of Existence, so Abuse of confidence has broke all the connections between man and man, which are necessary for our preservation.

That the Prince of Wales and his allies were not vastly exaggerating the popular disillusionment with patriotism in the later 1740s is suggested by the many scathing remarks on the factitious nature of patriotism that can be found in all forms of printed political polemic published at that time. In view of the Elder Pitt's later reputation as a patriot hero, particularly striking in this context is the volume of acerbic reflection on patriotism that was provoked by his speech in favour of the employment of the 18,000 Hanoverian troops in February 1746. As is well known, Pitt's anti-Hanoverian philippics of 1742–4 had been a major feature of the Broad-Bottom opposition of those years. His volte-face in 1746, which followed his admission to the ministry as joint Vice-Treasurer of Ireland, was seen by a good many opposition polemicists, and in particular by the *Old England Journal*, the *London Evening Post*, and the crypto-Jacobite *National Journal*, as further proof, if any were needed, of the mercenary nature of 'modern patriot-

---

[85] See above, Ch. 1.

ism'.[86] As the *London Evening Post* remarked on 17 April 1746, comparing Pitt's conduct to that of Admiral Vernon, who had recently resigned as Admiral of the White following disagreements with the Board of Admiralty,

> That Patriotism's a Joke, we must allow
> For P——T, the last professor, owns it now.
> But rigid V——N keeps his steady Plan,
> And claims not Title—but of *Honest man.*

It would, of course, be wrong to attribute patriotism's languishing condition in the later 1740s to just the effects of the apostacies of various opposition politicians, starting with Pulteney in 1742 and ending with Pitt in 1746, although this must form a major part of the explanation. As was suggested at the beginning of this chapter, another very influential factor was the impact of the Jacobite Rebellion of 1745–6. To review all the effects of the '45 on patriotism and opposition 'without doors' is beyond the scope of this work; the majority of these, in any case, have been more than adequately dealt with by other historians.[87] In the present context, only two of the more important effects require particular emphasis. The first is the fact that the '45 rendered the opposition vulnerable to the charge of disloyalty. Particularly damaging in this respect was, as Nicholas Rogers has very convincingly shown in his work on London politics in this period, the failure of a section of the metropolitan opposition to identify themselves unconditionally with the court-sponsored loyalist schemes of the winter of 1745–6.[88] There was also the embarrassment of the Westminster Society of Independent Electors. Not only was one of its members, David Morgan, executed in 1746 for having joined the Young Pretender's army, but, as was discussed in the last chapter, an incident at the Society's 1747 anniversary dinner provoked a parliamentary inquiry into the organization. The case of the opposition was not helped either by revelations made at Lord Lovat's trial. As part of his testimony, one of the leading witnesses against Lovat, John Murray of Broughton, divulged, amongst other things, that a number of leading Tories had been engaged in negotiations with a Jacobite agent in 1743.[89]

---

[86] See e.g. *OEJ* 20 Dec. 1746 (this essay was reprinted in the same paper on 27 Dec. 1746 and 3 Jan. 1747, and a further 3 times as a broadsheet; it was also reproduced as a pirate pamphlet, with the title *A Comparison between Orator H and Orator P*); *LEP* 15, 19 Apr. 1746; *National Journal*, 17, 23 Apr., 17 May 1746.

[87] See esp. Rogers, *Whigs and Cities*, 70–86; Cruickshanks, *Political Untouchables*, 104–9.   [88] Rogers, *Whigs and Cities*, 70–86.

[89] Ibid. 82; Cruickshanks, *Political Untouctables*, 104–5.

Such incidents, skilfully exploited by the ministry and its supporters, exposed the opposition to the full force of the widespread and powerful pro-Hanoverian feeling created by the rebellion. One of the consequences of this was the successes of the ministry, especially in London and the neighbouring constituencies of Westminster and Middlesex, at the 1747 general election.[90] The second of the effects, and one that is closely related to the vulnerability of the opposition to accusations of disloyalty, is the fact that the '45 also enabled the ministry to reclaim much of the traditional terrain of patriotism from the opposition. After 1745 pro-ministerial polemic echoes with declarations of the ministry's defence against the Franco-Jacobite threat to English liberties and the Revolution settlement.[91] Just how far the '45 transformed the debate about patriotism, however, can be seen most clearly by comparing the attitudes towards Jacobitism expressed in the press before and after the Jacobite invasion. Both under Walpole and during the early 1740s a prominent strand of the patriot platform was the denial that domestic disaffection constituted a serious threat to the Hanoverian succession. The degree to which opposition writers were prepared to defend this position—forced upon them not least because of ministerial allegations that the opposition press was either motivated by, or the unwitting aid of, Jacobitism —was starkly revealed by the French invasion attempt of 1744. Throughout February and March 1744 patriot polemicists, including both the *Westminster Journal* and the *Old England Journal*, were scathing in their rejection of ministerial claims that the invasion scheme had been contrived with the support of disloyal individuals in England. Such allegations, it was argued, were merely a device, or, in contemporary parlance, 'a plot', designed to enable the ministry to suppress domestic criticism, most notably by means of the suspension of habeas corpus. It is worth noting that the *Old England Journal* even portrayed the taking-up of Lord Barrymore, William Cecil, and Thomas Carte, and their subsequent release without charge, as demonstrations of the proof of this contention.[92] The same paper, together with a number of

---

[90] Rogers, *Whigs and Cities*, 84–5.

[91] *General Advertiser* 15, 19 June 1747; *True Patriot*, 6 May 1746; *Jacobite's Journal*, 26 Dec. 1747.

[92] *WJ* 25 Feb. 1744; *OEJ* 3, 17 Mar., 14 Apr. 1744. That the belief that the invasion attempt was 'a plot' gained significant ground, at least initially, is suggested by Lord Orrery's remarks in a letter dated 18 Feb. 1744 that 'It is imagined a Plot is necessary for the ministers, and therefore our Dangers (if any) are treated as proceeding from the ministerial Quarter.' (*The Orrery Papers*, ed. E. C. Boyle, Countess of Cork and Orrery, 2 vols. (1903), i. 184–5.)

other patriot polemicists, was also prepared to deny the reality of the attempt itself; the French preparations, it was alleged, had been a 'feint', intended to divert British attention from the French military designs in the Low Countries.[93] After the '45 such arguments appeared, at the very least, irresponsible.

Thus, even while the rebellion was in progress, various polemicists were remarking that the Jacobite declarations that were published and disseminated by the Jacobites during the '45—a number of which had actually been originally drawn up for the 1744 invasion attempt— proved the genuineness of the French invasion schemes of the previous year.[94] Perhaps even more damaging was the appropriation by the same Jacobite declarations of large areas of the programme and rhetoric of the patriot press of the early 1740s. This, it was argued, was incontrovertible evidence of the succour that the opposition 'without doors' and the opposition press had provided the Jacobites. The claim was even made that the anti-Hanoverian press campaign of 1742–4, which will be examined in a later chapter, was a major cause of the Jacobite Rebellion.[95]

If, then, the '45 was exploited by pro-ministerial writers retrospectively to attack the irresponsibility (or worse) of the patriot opposition of the early 1740s, it also seems to have been held to have discredited the view that Jacobitism was no longer a potent force in Britain. As one ministerial writer wrote in the *Whitehall Evening Post*:

> The mention of Jacobitism within these few years was treated in the most August assemblies, and upon the most important occasions, like the story of a stalking ghost, after a Bloody murder; and I am sorry to say, that nothing but dear bought experience could have dispelled the enchantment of speeches and writings, which long locked up the senses of the public. We were at last awakened; but danger had like a Torrent broken into our enclosure, before we had broken off the fatal delusion.

The same paper also averred that, despite the extremely limited active support for the Young Pretender south of the Scottish border during

---

[93] *OEJ* 10 Mar. 1744; *A Letter from Flanders, Giving an Account of the Present State of the War in the Netherlands* (1745), 6.

[94] *Remarks on the Pretender's Declaration and Commission* (1745), 5.

[95] [Squire] *A Letter to a Tory Friend*, 5–13, 72–3; *True Patriot*, 17 June 1746; *General Advertiser*, 8 May 1747; *GM* 15 (1745), 657–60. The allegation that opposition attacks on the personnel and politics of Hanoverian Britain were responsible for the '45 was rejected by the author of *An Enquiry into the Causes of our Late and Present National Calamities* (1745).

the '45, English Jacobitism was far from dead.[96] Significantly, it was not necessary to be a ministerial supporter to acknowledge the existence of domestic disaffection in the later 1740s. In 1748, as we have seen in an earlier part of this chapter, the *Remembrancer* included a 'Jacobite party' in its tripartite portrayal of contemporary politics. In the previous year a similar admission had been implicitly made by the *Westminster Journal*, when it warned its readers to avoid candidates who were either Jacobites or corrupt supporters of the ministry at the 1747 general election.[97] To what extent, by thus attempting to distance themselves from disaffection, the opposition press succeeded in freeing opposition from the taint of disloyalty is doubtful. At one stage during 1748 the *Remembrancer* directly urged its readers not to be any longer 'bugbear'd ... out of their senses ... by the shameless Endeavours of those who would resolve all opposition into Jacobitism'.[98] There is little doubt that the 'shameless Endeavours' to which the paper was principally referring were those of Henry Fielding in his pro-ministerial essay paper the *Jacobite's Journal*. In issue after issue of the *Jacobite's Journal* Fielding reiterated one claim: namely, that opposition in the present circumstances could only be motivated by disloyalty. Unfortunately for the opposition, a wave of crypto-Jacobite demonstrations and revelry, most notably in Staffordshire in 1747 and at Oxford in 1747 and 1748, only provided Fielding with more evidence with which to elaborate his allegations.[99]

In his *Letters on the English and French Nations*, first published in Paris in 1746 and in translation in London the following year, the Frenchman the Abbé le Blanc remarked:

> The odious Names of whig and Tory, which you mention in your letter, and which made so much noise in the reign of Queen Anne, are now almost entirely forgot in England; but the same parties still subsist under different denominations. Corruption and opposition, are the same terms at present made use of, to distinguish those who are for and against the ministry.[100]

---

[96] *GM* 17 (1747), 257–8. See also ibid. 12 (1746), 414; *True Patriot*, 15, 29 Apr., 20 May, 3 June 1746.

[97] *WJ* 11 July 1747.   [98] *Remembrancer*, 8 Oct. 1748.

[99] For Fielding's exploitation of what Pelham called 'a lurking Jacobite spirit', see *The 'Jacobite's Journal'*, ed. Coley, esp. Introduction. For the most recent discussion of crypto-Jacobite activity in the later 1740s, see P. Monod, *Jacobitism and the English People, 1688–1788* (Cambridge, 1989). The incidents at Oxford are discussed in P. Langford, 'Tories and Jacobites, 1714–51', in L. S. Sutherland and L. G. Mitchell (eds.), *The History of the University of Oxford: The Eighteenth Century* (1986), 99–127.

[100] Le Blanc, *Letters on the English and French Nations*, i. 352.

As it has been the major aim of this chapter to show, remarks such as Le Blanc's cannot be dismissed as the ill-informed comments of a foreigner. The London press of the period demonstrates, particularly the *Old England Journal* and the *Westminster Journal*, that, for a substantial body of opinion 'without doors', it was patriotism that gave meaning to their political viewpoint. In this view of politics, moreover, there was, by the 1740s, little or no room for the old Whig–Tory division. About the only thing that could possibly have reactivated this division—namely, parliamentary attacks by Erastian, anticlerical Whigs on the prerogatives of the Established Church—was, significantly, not even contemplated during the decade. As a result, religious questions were noticeably absent from political discussion in the press. As Horace Walpole wrote of a slightly later period: 'religious animosities were out of date'.[101] Thus, when the *Westminster Journal* briefly attempted in 1748 to promote a correspondence on the question of ministerial laxity regarding the execution of laws against Catholics, this quickly brought criticism from a number of the paper's readers. Referring to this criticism on 3 December 1748, the paper's editor remarked that he had been 'roasted in letters very smartly written . . . for what I printed . . . on the subject of popery, merely because the Dispute seemed to favour of Religion'.

As the press response to the formation of the Broad-Bottom ministry starkly illustrates, amongst the supporters of patriotism it mattered little whether it was Pulteney, other opposition Whigs, or the Tories who were admitted to the ministry: what did matter was proof that patriotism had conquered the court. In both 1742 and the winter of 1744–5 this was not forthcoming, a fact that substantially undermined the capacity of patriotism and the opposition press to command widespread popular support thereafter. In the debate about patriotism, as both this chapter and Chapter 1 have attempted to indicate, and as is further illustrated elsewhere in the present work, the Tory contribution seems to have been notably limited. This contribution was also, in most instances, defensive in character. The majority of Tory-patriot polemicists of the 1740s only intervened in the press to defend or reassert the Tory identification with patriotism at moments when it was under severe strain. After 1745 there seem to have been no further identifiable Tory pamphlets published in London in the 1740s, an absence that is most likely explained by the confusion and introspection

---

[101] Walpole, *Memoirs of the Reign of George II*, i. 97.

that seems to have overtaken the Tories in the aftermath of the failure of the Broad-Bottom experiment and the '45.[102]

Ironically, patriotism's greatest beneficiaries in the 1740s were perhaps neither the Tories nor the opposition Whigs, but the Pelhams. The decline of patriotism, under the stimulus of successive betrayals and the '45, was largely the ministry's gain. Thus, apart from the outcry over the Jew Bill in 1753, Pelham's ministry was confronted with a comparatively quiescent wider political nation. Indeed, Horace Walpole was evidently surprised as late as 1755 when patriotism was revived by the early stages of the Seven Years War and by the parliamentary opposition of 1755–6 led by Pitt. As Walpole remarked in August 1755: 'There is not a mob in England now capable of being the dupe of patriotism; the late body of that denomination have really so discredited it, that a minister must go great lengths indeed before the people would dread him half so much as a patriot.'[103]

---

[102] For the Tories in the later 1740s, see Colley, *In Defiance of Oligarchy*, 251–60.

[103] Quoted in P. Langford, *A Polite and Commercial People: England, 1727–1783* (Oxford, 1989), 230.

Part II

The London Press and the War of
the Austrian Succession

3

INTRODUCTION: THE PRESS AND THE CONDUCT OF FOREIGN POLICY

THE first part of this book has been devoted to exploring various important features of the relationship between the press of the 1740s and politics at Westminster and St James. Some of the points that have already been made will be amplified in the course of the second part, which examines the response of the press to what was by far the most controversial area of ministerial activity in the same period: the conduct of the War of the Austrian Succession.

Recent discussions of the public debate about foreign policy in the early Hanoverian period have tended to concentrate on three areas: first, the quantity and accuracy of the information and comment about foreign affairs disseminated by the press; secondly, the social and geographical range of popular interest in foreign affairs; and thirdly, the material and economic factors that underpinned this interest.[1] Much less notice has been given to the attitudes and assumptions that largely determined the way in which the press and a substantial section of the wider political nation viewed Britain's relations with foreign powers.[2] The major purpose of this chapter is to provide a brief outline of the most important of these. It is also hoped to show that any explanation of the vigour and intensity with which, particularly before 1746, the press responded to major developments in the war needs to take their influence into account.

[1] See esp. J. Black, *The English Press in the Eighteenth Century* (1987), 197–243; J. Brewer, 'Commercialisation and Politics', in Neil McKendrick, John Brewer, and J. H. Plumb (eds.), *The Birth of a Consumer Society: The Commercialisation of Eighteenth-Century England* (1982), 197–262; K. Wilson, 'Empire, Trade, and Popular Politics in Mid-Hanoverian Britain: The Case of Admiral Vernon', *Past & Present*, 121 (1988), 74–109.

[2] The following discussion concentrates on those assumptions which were most important in shaping the mid-century press responses to foreign affairs. The focus is, therefore, on opposition views. The best examination of the wider debate about foreign policy, of which these were one aspect, is still R. Pares, 'American versus Continental Warfare, 1739–63', *English Historical Review*, 51 (1936), 420–65. But see also J. Black, *British Foreign Policy in the Age of Walpole* (Edinburgh, 1985), 173–84.

Undoubtedly the most important contemporary popular assumption about foreign affairs was the conviction that Britain's island position and her indifference towards territorial acquisition in Europe allowed her to pursue an influential international role independent from continental rivalries. As one opposition pamphleteer declared in early 1745, Britain 'need only to seriously consult their own interest, and heartily pursue it, to become the happiest and most powerful Nation in Europe'.[3] Closely related to this view was the belief that this interest was both easily established and unchanging.[4] First, as a 'trading power', British interests (basically identifiable with her commercial interests) could only be served by a foreign policy that both protected and extended her trade. As far as the opposition press and popular opinion were concerned, this meant a foreign policy based firmly on Britain's naval power. Secondly, Britain should also avoid pursuing a foreign policy that had adverse domestic effects. In many respects, this was simply one aspect of the broader country or patriot suspicion regarding deficit finance and the opportunities for parasitism allegedly created by an expanding national debt.[5] Thus, a number of opposition polemicists even argued, following Charles Davenant, that Britain's annual expenditure should not exceed her annual revenue.[6] It was also a position informed by a recognition that the high level of wartime expenditure necessitated heavy taxation in the specific form of excises, which, it was claimed, both reduced the competitiveness of British manufactures in overseas markets and placed an unreasonable burden on the poor by inflating the prices of basic necessities.[7]

A policy within such constraints, however, would not (as the remarks of the opposition polemicist quoted above reveal) consign Britain to the margins of European affairs. Rather, her ability to dominate the seas, a consequence of her allegedly unrivalled naval mastery, not only rendered Britain invulnerable to invasion, but also enabled her to exercise a decisive influence over European affairs. As the Abbé le Blanc wrote some time in the decade 1737–47: 'If you credit the English, both the empire of seas, and the right of holding the Ballance of Europe equally belong to them; and in their pretensions at

---

[3] *A Modest Enquiry into the Present State of Foreign Affairs* (1745), 9.

[4] Ibid.

[5] See H. T. Dickinson, *Liberty and Property: Political Ideology in Eighteenth-Century Britain* (2nd edn., 1979), 191–2.

[6] See e.g. *The Criterion of the Reason and Necessity of the Present War* (1745), 36–7.

[7] See e.g. *Britons Awake and Look Around You, or, Ruin the Inevitable Consequence of a Land-War* (1743), 5–6.

least you find a proof of their power.'[8] The key to English pretensions, or so a number of opposition polemicists argued, was the possibility of using Britain's navy to destroy and capture Bourbon trade and colonies respectively, thereby depriving France and Spain of the means to upset the balance of power in Europe. Such a strategy—combined with financial subsidies (the so-called blue-water policy)—allegedly constituted a more effectual means of supporting the anti-Bourbon powers on the Continent than the commitment of British land forces to a European war.[9] It also, it was argued, avoided the escalating costs and fiscal strain of deploying British troops on the European mainland.

In retrospect, it is difficult not to regard (as many other historians have done) opposition press and popular attitudes towards foreign affairs as, at best, simplistic. Such an assessment is, moreover, only reinforced by the prevalence of an equally exaggerated view of the extent of Britain's independence from events on the Continent. Representative in this respect was the author of the pamphlet *The Free and Impartial Examiner* (1745), who argued:

> It is certain that Nature has not been sparing in her Bounties to render us a free Independent and happy people, and we can boast of more Advantages of that sort, than any people on the Face of the Earth. She has seated us on an *Island*, invironed with seas capacious enough to prevent any Anxiety from the ambitious views or mercenary Quarrels of her Neighbours on the continent.[10]

Another measure of the degree to which a sizeable body of opinion (probably a majority) was convinced that Britain was able to maintain an Olympian detachment from the squabbles of European powers was the willingness of a number of opposition polemicists openly to question Britain's need to enter into treaties of alliance with foreign powers. One of these polemicists claimed that the only treaties that Britain could conceivably want to negotiate were commercial treaties.[11] The wish of most Englishmen to isolate themselves from European rivalries was also an extremely important factor behind the sensitivity of the political nation to the possibility that Hanoverian ends were controlling British foreign policy. In this context, it was widely argued that union with Hanover, by entangling Britain in Hanover's rivalries with various Baltic and German states, was negating all the advantages inherent in Britain's island situation. The opposition peer Lord Barrington was

---

[8] L'Abbé Blanc, *Letters on the English and French Nations*, 2 vols. (1747), i. 3–4.
[9] See e.g. *The Question Stated with Regard to our Army in Flanders* (1742), *passim*.
[10] *The Free and Impartial Examiner*, 3.   [11] *A Modest Enquiry*, 30.

undoubtedly speaking for many when he purportedly remarked during one of the great debates on the employment of the 16,000 Hanoverian troops in 1744: 'if an Angel could come and tell us, I will separate you from Hanover, I will make you an island again'.[12]

Why did these arguments retain such an attraction for the bulk of the English people? No doubt, as others have maintained, part of the explanation lies in the advantages offered to various economic interests by pursuing blue-water policies. In this respect, those involved in the Atlantic economy and particularly in the sugar trade could be expected to support the use of Britain's naval power to remove the threat posed to their commercial position by the competition of French merchants.[13] Nor is it difficult to appreciate that other important elements of the political nation would have been extremely receptive to a set of foreign policy prescriptions that substituted quick profits, in the form of new and expanded markets, for heavy taxation on both land and trade. Thus, in early 1745 embittered pro-Carteret pamphleteers argued that those opposed to his conduct of the war between 1742 and 1744 had gained the support of the landed interest by stressing the fiscal strain created by fighting the French on the European mainland.[14]

Another factor that helps to explain the enduring attractiveness of blue-water policies is the belief that most Englishmen had in the possibilities and efficacy of naval action. If, as is increasingly becoming clear, the reality was one of difficulties concerning manning, climate, keeping ships seaworthy, co-ordination between different branches of the armed forces in combined operations, conflicting strategic objectives, and limited influence over events on the Continent, then the opposition press and popular opinion showed few (or no) signs of acknowledging these problems.[15] It was not, however, solely economic self-interest or a misplaced confidence in the efficacy of Britain's naval strength as a lever on the international stage that recommended blue-water policies. Their attraction can also be related to the most important preoccupation of foreign policy debate not yet discussed: namely, the French threat to European stability.

Significantly, although pro-ministerial and opposition supporters

---

[12] Walpole, *Memoirs of King George II*, i. 102.

[13] See Wilson, 'Empire, Trade and Popular Politics'; P. Jenkins, 'Tory Industrialism and Town Politics: Swansea in the Eighteenth Century', *Historical Journal*, 28 (1985), 102–23.   [14] See e.g. *The Plain Reasoner* (1745), esp. 5–6.

[15] See esp. Philip Woodfine, 'Ideas of Naval Power and the Conflict with Spain, 1737–1742', in Jeremy Black and Philip Woodfine (eds.), *The British Navy and the Use of Naval Power in the Eighteenth Century* (Leicester, 1988), 71–90.

may have been divided on the question of how best to combat this threat, there was an almost universal consensus regarding its nature. Just as hostility to French politics and culture negatively defined English national identity in the eighteenth century, the same antithetical relationship was also seen as defining the role and identity of the two countries in international affairs. Thus, where Britain, it was alleged, only aimed to preserve the territorial integrity of her European neighbours, France's historic and constant aim was the subversion of European independence and liberty. Closely related to this view of France as the principal threat to European peace was the assumption that the interests of the rest of Europe were broadly conterminous with Britain's own interests on the Continent. Thus, Britain's guardianship of European liberty, it was further assumed, could only induce support throughout the Continent. As the author of the pamphlet *Considerations on the Politics of France* (1744) declared: 'We pursue our own Advantage most when we contribute most to maintaining the Liberty and Independency of other powers; and the sense of this while we continue to act upon so generous a maxim, will always render them the natural Guaranties of ours.'[16] Certain elements of the opposition took this line of reasoning one stage further, and maintained that the depth of the opposition to French aims in Europe was such that Britain would never need to assume more than an auxiliary role in a continental war. Should French schemes proceed too far, it was argued, this would only provoke the rest of Europe into forming a powerful anti-Bourbon coalition.[17]

Such arguments reveal a curious myopia regarding other powers' perceptions of Britain's role in foreign affairs. While Britain pursued, largely unheeded, the ultimate prize of commercial supremacy, the rest of Europe was expected to exhaust itself in the struggle for territorial and national aggrandizement. The widespread failure to accept the depth of the international hostility aroused by British naval and commercial assertion was yet one more factor behind the confidence of opposition opinion regarding blue-water policies. It also discloses a failure—much commented on by pro-ministerial polemicists at the time —to appreciate the closeness of the relationship between Britain's commercial position and her international reputation. The latter, as pro-ministerial polemicists were fond of pointing out (and with

---

[16] *Considerations on the Politics of France* (1744), 56.

[17] *A Detection of the Views of those who Would, in the Present Crisis, Engage an Incumber'd Trading Nation . . . in a Ruinous Expensive Land-War* (1746), 41; *Ministerial Artifice Detected* (1749), 20.

justification), required a more active role in continental affairs than that stipulated by supporters of isolationism and blue-water policies.[18]

Interestingly, an important element of the opposition press onslaught on Carteret's conduct of the war, especially in 1743, was an attempt to play down the French threat to European stability, arguing that France was actively seeking a settlement of the War of the Austrian Succession on the basis of the territorial status quo. Significantly, however, the power and plausibility of this position were much eroded in early 1744, when the traditional attitudes towards France were widely revived as a result of the French invasion attempt at the end of February. Furthermore, their continued hold on popular and press opinion had in fact been disclosed in 1743, following the military defeat of the French by the British and Allied army (the so-called Pragmatic army) at Dettingen in June. The military opportunities created by the victory were, as will be shown later, the cause of a brief wave of enthusiasm for the war amongst a majority of the political nation. At the heart of this outburst of pro-war feeling was the hope that the allied forces might be able to impose a peace settlement on France that would permanently disable her from attempting to overturn the balance of power in Europe. The attraction of this goal was also evident during the final stages of the war, when the press was absorbed with the question of the nature of the peace that Britain could expect from the conflict. As Pitt was to argue at the beginning of the 1760s, the opposition press held that Britain should continue to fight until French power could be finally shackled, a possibility allegedly created by Britain's naval dominance in the war after 1747. When the news of the peace preliminaries that were signed at Aix-la-Chapelle emerged in the spring of 1748, they were duly condemned for sacrificing Britain's interests and security. Peace on these terms, it was argued, merely held out the prospect of the renewal of war in Europe and the Americas, and in circumstances that would inevitably be far more favourable to France and her allies than those of the recently ended war.

One last feature of the press debate of foreign affairs between 1740 and 1748 that requires brief comment here—and one which was very closely related to the views of the French role in Europe discussed above—is the importance that many elements of the press attached to the 'old system' (the Grand Alliance of Britain, Austria, and the Dutch

[18] *The Important Question Discussed, or, a Serious and Impartial Enquiry into the True Interest of England with Respect to the Continent* (1746), *passim.*

Republic) and to the wars against Louis XIV's France. This is perhaps unsurprising. After all, the War of the Spanish Succession was not only the last experience of British military involvement on the European mainland to which the politicians and public had to turn for guidance, it had also stimulated a number of great contributions to the debate regarding the prudence (or imprudence) of intervention in European rivalries. One particular contribution to this debate that was disinterred on a number of occasions was Swift's famous pamphlet *The Conduct of the Allies*, first published in 1711. Finally, in early 1748, Swift's great defence of Harley's peace policy, and his dissection of the domestic costs of intervention in Europe, was republished in its entirety and went through two editions.[19]

Another factor that undoubtedly encouraged contemporaries to look to the debates and wars of 1689–1714 was the influence of historic Whig and Tory divisions. The depth and significance of this influence was examined in the previous chapter. In the present context, all that it is necessary to emphasize is that—apart from the shadow that they cast over political debate in general—certain elements of the ministry on occasion sought political advantage either by identifying themselves with or by recalling the foreign policy stances of the Augustan Whig and Tory parties. By far the most important example of this between 1740 and 1748 was the attempt of the new Whigs to defend their role in the political settlement that followed Walpole's fall by claiming to have revived the Whig measures in foreign affairs associated with William III and Marlborough. This claim forced the patriot polemicists of 1742–4, including a small number of Tory-patriots, into attempting to demonstrate the imprudence of interventionist policies as manifested in both the present conflict and in the earlier Nine Years War and the War of the Spanish Succession. In this context, it was also the assumptions upon which the policy of intervention was based that were the objects of opposition press attacks. These assumptions, notably the 'balance of power' and the 'Protestant interest', it was argued, were merely devices to deceive the credulous into supporting ill-judged and often inconsistent measures (as demonstrated by Walpole's foreign policy), or worse. As Chesterfield exclaimed in his pamphlet *Natural Reflexions on the Present Conduct of his Prussian Majesty* (1744): 'The *Balance of Power*

---

[19] *The Conduct of the Allies* was republished under the new title *Good Queen Anne Vindicated*. It was also advertised as having been written by the author of *A Dissertation upon Parties*, that is, Lord Bolingbroke.

is an ideal chimera, introduced among us by corrupt and designing ministers, to subject and fleece their deluded countrymen.'[20]

Given the ease with which the bulk of the political nation seemed to think that Britain could impose its own priorities in Europe and beyond, it is tempting to suggest that it was beyond the capacity of any mid-eighteenth-century ministry to have gained popular support for its conduct of foreign affairs for any length of time. As recent studies have emphasized, that the Elder Pitt succeeded in doing so for the two-year period 1759–60 owed a great deal to circumstances beyond his control.[21] The difficulties confronting a ministry attempting to defend its foreign policy were, moreover, multiplied many times when it was faced with a determined parliamentary opposition. As one pro-ministerial pamphleteer summed up in 1742: 'There is a wide, there is a manifest Difference between the conduct necessary to gain the Applause of the mob, and that which is fit to be pursued for the service of the Nation. The former are intirely governed by sounds; and nothing is easier than to promise them mountains to obtain power.'[22] As the events of the late 1750s were to show, only repeated success could shield a ministry from popular dissatisfaction and adverse press criticism, and then only for so long as the English people forgot the fiscal and economic burdens imposed by war. However, military victories during the War of the Austrian Succession were limited to Dettingen, the capture of Cape Breton in 1745, Cumberland's defeat of the Jacobites at Culloden, and the naval victories of the penultimate year of the war; for the rest, it was continuing military failure and inefficacy, and mounting annual expenditure. This situation, together with the level of extra-parliamentary interest in foreign affairs, was at least one important factor ensuring that the ministry's conduct of the war created a heated and, especially during the winter of 1743–4, influential press debate.

[20] *Natural Reflexions*, 93.
[21] R. Middleton, *The Bells of Victory: The Pitt–Newcastle Ministry and the Conduct of the Seven Years War, 1757–1762* (Cambridge, 1985).
[22] *Considerations on the War* (1742), 23.

4

THE FALL OF WALPOLE AND THE
OUTBREAK OF THE WAR, 1740–1742

THE impact on domestic politics of the early stages of the War of the Austrian Succession has not generally received the attention that it merits. This neglect is unfortunate for at least two important reasons. The first is the role that the war played in forcing Walpole from power. Traditionally, it has been the effects of failure and apparent misman-agement in the war against Spain, which had broken out in October 1739, which have been emphasized in this context—often to the exclusion of events on the Continent. Yet, when Walpole was finally compelled to resign from office, Britain was facing a crisis in her relations with Europe, the gravity of which was almost certainly comparable (if not worse) than those the country faced in 1756–7 and 1778–9.[1] By the end of 1741 Belle-Isle's ambitious schemes to establish France's mastery of Europe—by parcelling out Austria's dominions among various lesser powers, and placing the Wittelsbach Elector of Bavaria on the imperial throne—seemed to be on the point of realization. Louis XV had scaled the heights of diplomatic ambition that had eluded his more illustrious great-grandfather, Louis XIV; 'universal monarchy', that historic French goal, was in his grasp. Scarcely less significantly, the measures taken by the ministry in 1741 to support Austria, hitherto the mainstay of the anti-French cause on the Continent, were completely undermined in October by the Hanoverian neutrality convention, concluded by George II when the French army under Maillebois threatened to invade Hanover. Not surprisingly, as the first part of this chapter aims to show, in these circumstances it was the question of British (and Hanoverian) respons-ibility for Austria's plight that increasingly came to dominate press debate as 1741 progressed. By the eve of Walpole's fall, concern about

---

[1] For the British and Hanoverian roles in the early stages of the war, see Uriel Dann, *Hanover and Great Britain, 1740–60: Diplomacy and Survival* (Leicester, 1991), 15–44.

the crisis on the Continent was threatening completely to overshadow concern with events in the Americas.

The second significant consequence for domestic politics of the early stages of the war was the intrusion into press debate, under the stimulus of the Hanoverian neutrality, of the alleged Hanoverian control of British foreign policy. At the end of 1742 the award of British pay to 16,000 Hanoverian troops was to unleash a torrent of bitter anti-Hanoverianism, culminating in the popular outcry against Hanoverian influence in the winter of 1743–4. As the latter part, in particular, of this chapter attempts to show, the fact that the issue had already been firmly raised by the neutrality was an important factor in shaping the popular and press response to the war over the next two years. Some idea of this importance can be gained from an outburst as late as 1745 by a rare polemical apologist for the Anglo-Hanoverian union, who declared of the neutrality: '[it] has been more exaggerated, if possible, and represented in more odious colours than the taking of the 16,000 Hanoverians into British pay'.[2]

One other aspect of the press debate stimulated by Britain's role in the war between 1740 and 1742 that also needs to be considered is the impact on that debate of Walpole's fall and the political settlement that followed it. What will be revealed is how closely the political recriminations and popular indignation created by the events that surrounded the defeat of the Robinarch shaped the press reaction to the new ministry's conduct of the war as it developed in the second half of 1742.

The first significant signs that concern about developments on the Continent was beginning to assume an important position in press debate occurred in the spring of 1741. The crucial impetus was the famous attempt from both Houses of Parliament on 13 February to call on the King to dismiss Walpole from his councils.[3] Although the importance of the *motion*, as it was referred to, in the context of parliamentary politics is well known, less well known is the prominence that

[2] *The Advantages of the Hanover Succession and English Gratitude Freely and Impartially Considered* (1745), 68–9.

[3] For the *motion*, see L. Colley, *In Defiance of Oligarchy: The Tory Party, 1714–60* (Cambridge, 1982), 228; I. Doolittle, 'A First-Hand Account of the Commons Debate on the Removal of Sir Robert Walpole, 13 Feb. 1741', *Bulletin of the Institute of Historical Research*, 53 (1980), 125–40; A. Foord, *His Majesty's Opposition, 1714–1830* (Oxford, 1964), 140; Eveline Cruickshanks, 'The Political Management of Sir Robert Walpole, 1720–42', in J. Black (ed.), *Britain in the Age of Walpole* (1984), 40–1.

it was accorded in the press in the period immediately preceding the general election.[4] During the spring of 1741 a wave of pamphlets, essays, ballads, and an unusually large number of prints all addressed themselves directly to the *motion* and to the various questions that it was held to raise.[5] Of the opposition contributions to this polemical activity, the most influential was the opposition Whig pamphlet *A Review of a Late Motion*, published in May.[6] This seems to have been the principal opposition pamphlet of the general election, being extensively publicized in both leading opposition essay papers, the *Craftsman* and *Common Sense*.[7] The pro-ministerial *Daily Gazetteer* also alleged that it had been 'spread with the utmost diligence all over the nation'.[8]

As well as defending the legitimacy of the *motion* as a device to remove Walpole from power, the pamphlet also delineated the major charges that had been levelled against Walpole in Parliament on 13 February. These fell into three broad areas: first, attacks on British foreign policy since 1725; secondly, attacks on the allegedly inept direction of the current war against Spain; and thirdly, attacks on supposed domestic maladministration and corruption. The emphasis that the opposition press placed on the pamphlet provoked the *Daily Gazetteer* into printing a series of essays in response, entitled 'The Review Reviewed'.[9] It is a good measure of the growing concern regarding the situation on the Continent that the only area that the *Daily Gazetteer* chose to contest was the attacks on Walpole's conduct of foreign policy.

The assertion that the pro-ministerial writers were anxious to refute was that the alleged anti-Austrian direction of Walpole's foreign policy was the origin of the present troubles in Europe. The great betrayal of British interests and of Austria, or so the author of *A Review of the Late Motion* argued, was British participation in the Treaty of Hanover in 1725. It was this 'fatal source of French power' that had signalled Britain's departure, under Walpole, from the Grand Alliance strategy

---

[4] But see M. M. Goldsmith, 'Faction Detected: Ideological Consequences of Robert Walpole's Decline and Fall', *History*, 64 (1979), 1–19, which emphasizes the unusual interest in the *motion* displayed by the *London Magazine*.

[5] For the prints on the *motion*, see M. Dorothy George, *English Political Caricature to 1792: A Study of Opinion and Propaganda* (Oxford, 1959), i. 89–91.

[6] The other major pamphlets on the *motion* were *The Sense of the Nation, in Regard to the Late Motion in Parliament* and *The Sentiments of a Tory, in Respect to a Late Important Transaction* (1741).

[7] *Craftsman*, 21 Feb., 25 Apr. 1741; *Common Sense*, 11 July 1741.

[8] *Daily Gazetteer*, 25 May 1741.   [9] Ibid. 8, 16, 20, 23, 27 June.

that had successfully guided British foreign policy between 1714 and 1725. It was further alleged that Walpole (unfairly identified here with Townshend's interventionist diplomacy of the 1720s) had ignored the opportunity to effect a lasting division between the two branches of the House of Bourbon created by the Austro-Spanish alliance of the same year. In forming a counter-alliance, he had instead embarked upon a long series of measures unified by their contribution to the 'absolute Depression of the Austrian Family, and the Elevation of the House of Bourbon'. In the 1730s the most important manifestation of the anti-Austrian direction of British foreign policy had ben British neutrality in the War of the Polish Succession. The failure to support Austria in that war was portrayed as the most immediate cause of France's present diplomatic and military supremacy in Europe. Had Britain acted to prevent Austria's defeat, it was argued, the rest of Europe would not now be either acquiescing in or supporting the French-led onslaught against the Habsburg dominions. In short, responsibility for Austria's present plight was clearly assignable. As the author of *A Review of a Late Motion* concluded: 'It was not, therefore, the Death of the late Emperor, that destroy'd the house of Austria, *for it was in a manner undone before.*'[10]

Before the *Daily Gazetteer* undertook its defence of Walpole's foreign policy, at least two pro-ministerial pamphlets had already appeared that were devoted to the same task—the most influential being *The False Accusers Accused, or, the Undeceived Englishman.*[11] Viewed as a whole, this body of pro-ministerial polemic constituted a closely argued and vigorous attack on the opposition critique of Walpole's foreign policy and, in particular, on the allegation that Walpole had sacrificed British interests to France. Not least of the weaknesses of the opposition position, and one that was emphasized by the *Daily Gazetteer*, was its failure to recognize the role played by circumstance in foreign affairs. As the *Daily Gazetteer* observed: 'The circumstances of Things will always regulate the councils of wise men.'[12] The Treaty of Hanover, it was argued—as it had been at the time—was a prudent response to the circumstances in which Britain had found herself following the forma-tion of the first Treaty of Vienna. Confronted with an Austro-Spanish threat to Britain's trade and navigation and the balance of power in

---

[10] *A Review of a Late Motion* (1741), 10.
[11] The other pamphlet was entitled *The Present Influence and Conduct of Great Britain Impartially Considered* (1741). [12] *Daily Gazetteer*, 20 June 1741.

Europe, the British ministry had exploited French power to extinguish this threat.[13]

As for Britain's role in the War of the Polish Succession, three factors were emphasized. The first was the fiscal and commercial advantages that had accrued to Britain as a result of her non-intervention in a continental war. As the author of *The False Accusers Accused* remarked, by following the policy that had been advocated by Walpole, Britain had not only avoided 'the miseries of a consuming war both by sea and land', she had also enjoyed 'a free and uninterrupted commerce with all parts of the world'.[14] The second was the impossibility of intervening effectively on the Continent without the full support of the Dutch Republic.[15] Had Britain entered the war without this support, it was further observed, the ministry would also have had to contend with intense domestic criticism:

Should we not have been called the *Tools* and *Dupes* of the *Dutch* for exhausting our Treasure, and spilling our Blood in a cause which so *immediately* affected them, and so *remotely* ourselves, while they reap'd the Advantage of the most beneficial Branches by remaining *Neuter*, which we should have lost by engaging in what might more properly be called their cause than our own?[16]

That such remarks were justified was demonstrated after 1742 by the prominence that the opposition press accorded to the Dutch Republic's failure to commit itself fully to support the measures in the War of the Austrian Succession of, first, Lord Carteret and, then, the Pelhams.

The third factor was the failure of the War of the Polish Succession, or so it was argued, to alter fundamentally the balance of power on the Continent. In this context, the opposition was alleged to be magnifying the 'exorbitant Encrease of power to France from the reversionary Acquisition of Lorrain'.[17] The same was true of the situation in Italy. One of the pro-ministerial pamphleteers even argued that the loss of Naples and Sicily in the war had in fact strengthened Austria's position. Austria's territories in Italy, the pamphleteer argued, were, as a result of the loss of the two kingdoms (and the acquisition of the Tuscan succession by Maria Theresa's husband, Francis Stephen,

---

[13] *The False Accusers Accused* (1741), 6–8; *The Present Influence and Conduct of Great Britain*, 10–13; *Daily Gazetteer*, 8, 16, 20 June 1741. The pro-ministerial defence of the Treaty of Hanover owed a great deal to Benjamin Hoadly's famous pamphlet *An Enquiry into the Reasons of the Conduct of Great Britain with Relation to the Present State of Affairs in Europe* (1726).   [14] *The False Accusers Accused*, 35.

[15] See below, Ch. 5, for the debate on this question.   [16] *The False Accusers Accused*, 35.   [17] Ibid. 39.

Duke of Lorraine), more compact and, therefore, more defensible. Rather less plausibly, the same pamphleteer was also confident that, under Walpole, Britain had retained sufficient influence abroad to preserve the balance of power in Europe at little cost to herself. Thus it was asserted: 'If *France*, without unsheathing the sword may be supposed to be able to embroil *all Europe*, so, in my poor opinion, will *Great-Britain* be able without Expence or spilling of any Blood or very Little Blood.'[18]

In the months preceding the general election of 1741, then, a vigorous debate had already commenced in the press concerning the issue of Walpole's responsibility for the deteriorating situation in Europe. One other feature of this debate that, in view of the contrast with the situation that obtained after Walpole's fall, is worth further comment is the degree to which Walpole's pacific foreign policy of the 1730s had confused the traditional lines of division regarding Britain's relationship to the Continent. Thus, Walpole was being charged with having destroyed the very foundations of the traditional Whig policy towards Britain's role on the Continent. As the author of *A Review of a Late Motion* declared: 'The *Protestant Interest* in Europe is broke to pieces, and the *Grand Alliance* seems not to be in a possibility of being restored; at least not by *those*, who have thus destroyed it.'[19] Meanwhile, defenders of Walpole's conduct of foreign affairs were employing language and terms more usually associated with the patriot or country opposition. Perhaps the most obvious example of this was the emphasis that pro-ministerial polemicists placed on the fiscal and domestic strains imposed by more interventionist policies. The only argument of the pro-ministerial polemicists that recalled traditional Whig prejudices was the proposition that the pattern of foreign policy over the previous twenty years was attributable primarily to the Tory Peace of Utrecht. This peace, the author of *The False Accusers Accused* alleged, had been 'So little comprehensive of the various Interests of *Europe*, that nothing but the unwearied labours of the ablest ministers could rectify as occasion offer'd . . .'[20] In 1742 Carteret's interventionist policies ensured that the traditional lines of division in the debate of foreign policy were reasserted.

If the issues raised by the outbreak of the war in Europe had already intruded into press debate in the early months of 1741, there is no

---

[18] *The Present Influence and Conduct of Great Britain*, 28, 15–16.
[19] *A Review of a Late Motion*, 7.   [20] *The False Accusers Accused*, 4.

direct evidence to indicate that they had any significant impact on the general election, which took place in May. Rather, as has recently been emphasized, and as was acknowledged by an opposition pamphleteer in 1742, the successes of the opposition, where they were not due to the electoral influence of the Prince of Wales or of the Duke of Argyll, were largely the result of the successful exploitation of Vernon's popularity as a focus for the alienation of a broad cross-section of middling and mercantile opinion from the Whig establishment and from the conduct of the war against Spain.[21] (Vernon had achieved the only military successes of the war against Spain, at Porto Bello in 1739 and Fort Chagre in 1740.) So great was the importance of the attachment to Vernon during the election that Pulteney wrote to him on 16 June: 'You are certainly, at this Time, the most popular and best beloved man in *England*: All places that send members to Parliament have been struggling to have you for their Representative, and, I dare say, you might have been chosen in twenty more places than you are at present.'[22] Vernon had, in fact, been nominated as a candidate in a total of five constituencies, with the opposition forces in Westminster distinguishing themselves by the title 'Vernonians'. In the vital constituency of London, moreover, his candidature had actually been sponsored by the ministry, albeit unsuccessfully, in an attempt to exploit his popularity in order to disrupt the metropolitan opposition.[23] In the event, he was returned for three constituencies, a number that was unmatched by any other politician in the eighteenth century.[24]

It was, then, Vernon's popularity and the conduct of the war against Spain that overshadowed the general election. What is far less clear, however, is the extent to which they continued to remain at the forefront of press and popular attention in the period between the end of the general election and the fall of Walpole. This is not to say that issues arising from the war with Spain ceased to occupy a prominent position in the final press assault against Walpole. At least two factors

[21] See Gerald Jordan and Nicholas Rogers, 'Admirals as Heroes: Patriotism and Liberty in Hanoverian England', *Journal of British Studies*, 28 (1989), 201–24; Kathleen Wilson, 'Empire, Trade and Popular Politics in Mid-Hanoverian Britain: The Case of Admiral Vernon', *Past and Present*, 121 (1988), *passim*; *The Conduct of the Last and Present M——ry Compar'd* (1742), 6.

[22] [Vernon] *Original Letters to an Honest Sailor* (1746), 43–4.

[23] N. Rogers, *Whigs and Cities: Popular Politics in the Age of Walpole and Pitt* (Oxford, 1989), 66.

[24] See Wilson, 'Empire, Trade and Popular Politics', 90–1; Jordan and Rogers, 'Admirals as Heroes', 204.

prevented this occurring. The first was the arrival in July of the news of another set-back in the West Indies: the failure of the great combined expedition under Vernon and Wentworth to capture Cartagena. This news undoubtedly reinvigorated the opposition press campaign against Walpole's alleged misconduct and treachery in the war.[25] The failure at Cartagena also provoked a developing controversy about the respective responsibilities of the navy and army for the disaster, a dispute stimulated not least by Vernon's own attempts, aided by an admiring opposition press, to foist the blame for the poor military showing in the West Indies on to Wentworth and the army.[26]

The second factor was the prominence accorded by the press in late 1741 to the issue of the alleged failure of the ministry to ensure that British commercial shipping was provided with adequate naval protection against the attacks of Spanish privateers. As ministerial supporters were not slow to point out, the vulnerability of British trade to Spanish attacks in the war had been a fact continually laboured in the defence of Walpole's search for a diplomatic solution to the Anglo-Spanish disputes.[27] Towards the end of 1741 the precise volume of trade and shipping captured by the Spanish since 1739 was contested in two pamphlets, an argument that was followed closely in the *Craftsman* and the monthly magazines.[28] The *Craftsman* was also one of a number of opposition papers that lent their support to a successful attempt by a group of London merchants to organize a petition to protest at the level of attacks on British commercial shipping and to call for better naval support.[29] Yet, despite the concern expressed about these raids on shipping and about the failure at Cartagena, there seems, nevertheless, to

---

[25] It was claimed throughout the opposition press that Walpole had aimed to sacrifice Vernon as part of a broader scheme to disable the effective prosecution of the war, thereby vindicating his pacific stance in 1738–9.

[26] For a recent examination of the war against Spain that argues that most of the allegations made by Vernon and the opposition regarding the conduct of the war against Spain between 1739 and 1741 were misplaced, see R. R. Harding, 'Sir Robert Walpole's Ministry and the Conduct of the War with Spain, 1739–41', *Bulletin of the Institute of Historical Research*, 60 (1987), 299–320.

[27] See e.g. *Considerations on the War* (1742), 12.

[28] *The Profit and Loss of Great Britain in the Present War with Spain* (1741); *Hireling Artifice Detected on the Profit and Loss of Great Britain in the Present War with Spain* (1742); *Craftsman*, 12 Dec. 1741; *GM* 11 (1741), 644; *LM* 10 (1741), 600–2; ibid. 11 (1742), 73–9, 122–6.

[29] *Craftsman*, 12 Dec. 1741; *Champion*, 10 Nov. 1741; *Daily Post*, 16 Dec. 1741. The merchants' petition, together with a supporting petition from the Corporation of London, was presented to Parliament at the beginning of 1742.

have been a reduction in the intensity of press interest in the war against Spain in the latter part of 1741. That this was in fact the case is suggested most obviously by the relative neglect of the popular celebrations that took place on Vernon's birthday in November. Similar celebrations in 1740 had been widely and prominently reported throughout the opposition press, often in considerable detail. In 1741 they merited only one very general paragraph noting their occurrence in London and Westminster.[30]

What of the impact on press debate in the same period (between the general election and the fall of Walpole) of developments in the war on the Continent? As far as politics at home was concerned, and as was emphasized at the beginning of the chapter, these developments were twofold: first, the collapse of Austria; and secondly, the Hanoverian neutrality. Of the immediate impact of the latter there can be no doubt. Confirmation that the neutrality had been concluded reached the London press in the second week of October. By the beginning of November Horace Walpole was writing: 'The Neutrality begins to break out and threatens to be an excise or convention. The newspapers are full of it, and the press teems.'[31] It is not difficult to account for the scale of the press reaction. First, as has been emphasized elsewhere, the neutrality was the first demonstration since the accession of the Hanoverians that France might exploit Hanover's vulnerability as a lever against Britain.[32] Secondly, it was not just British interests on the Continent that appeared to be affected. It was widely believed that the neutrality included provision for French mediation in the Anglo-Spanish war. The origin of this belief was the French communication of the neutrality convention to the States General at The Hague, which declared that George II was 'disposed' to accept a French peace settlement in Britain's war with Spain.[33] Any impact that ministerial denials of the inclusion of Britain within the terms of the neutrality may have had was nullified towards the end of November, when news arrived that the Mediterranean squadron under Admiral Haddock had failed to oppose a Spanish expedition to Italy. In the opinion of the opposition press, there was no military reason, despite the protection of the

---

[30] See Jordan and Rogers, 'Admirals as Heroes', 210–11.

[31] Lewis, *Walpole*, xvii. 183–9: Walpole to Mann, 2 Nov. 1741.

[32] See D. McKay and H. M. Scott, *The Rise of the Great Powers: 1648–1815* (1983), 166.

[33] In fact, George II resisted French attempts to extend the terms of the neutrality to cover the war with Spain.

Spanish expedition by the French fleet based at Toulon, for Haddock's inactivity; it could only be explained in terms of the neutrality.[34]

The belief that the terms of the neutrality would force Britain to accept a French-brokered peace settlement in its war with Spain provoked some of the most extreme outbursts in the press during the winter of 1741–2. The two elements of the opposition press that illustrate this most clearly are the essay paper the *Champion*, and the pamphlet *A Letter from a Member of the Last Parliament to a New Member of the Present, Concerning the Conduct of the War with Spain, and with Some Observations on the Hanoverian Neutrality, as far as it May Relate to or Affect Great Britain*, which was published in January 1742 and went through three editions. On 19 January 1742 the *Champion* referred its readers to the Act of Settlement and, in particular, to the clause that declared that Britain was not obliged to defend territories that did not belong to the Crown of England without the consent of Parliament. In the view of the paper, this last condition had rendered the clause worthless as a bar to the subordination of British foreign policy to Hanoverian ends: 'But alas! these fatal words, *without the consent of Parliament*, what use has already been made of them? What use, from past Examples, may we not expect will be made of them?' In the same issue the paper also dismissed the argument, favoured by supporters of the ministry, that Hanover's vulnerability was a consequence of union with Britain.[35] As the *Champion* exclaimed:

If . . . it should be argued that *Hanover* is like to suffer on our Account, and a Diversion may be made there to put a stop to our Attempts in the *West-Indies*; I answer, the Argument concludes too much; it argues that we can never draw the sword in our own Defence, or use the means which God has put into our Hands [i.e. maritime supremacy] to be aveng'd on our Enemies for fear of our Half-Brothers, the *Hanoverians*, should be made to pay the Forfeit of our Transgression; it argued that, therefore, the interests of two such divided sovereignties are incompatible and consequently that *********.

The same point was put differently in *A Letter from a Member of the Last Parliament*. The pamphlet alleged that Hanover was entirely dependent on Britain for both its defence and its ability to expedite its aim of territorial aggrandizement. Recognition of this fact by France and other powers, it was argued, had deprived Britain of the 'great Benefit of being an Island'. Union with Hanover, as the neutrality had

---

[34] See *Champion*, 26 Dec. 1741; *A Letter from a Member of the Last Parliament* (1742), 39, 64–5.   [35] For this argument, see below.

fully revealed, meant that Britain had 'come to be placed, and design'd to be attacked as if it were part of the continent'.[36] What is perhaps most significant about these arguments is how closely they foreshadow essential elements of the anti-Hanoverian press outcry of 1742–4. If the response of the press to the Hanoverian neutrality owed much to its supposed consequences for Britain's war with Spain, it also, of course, owed an increasing amount, as Austria's position rapidly deteriorated in the final months of 1741, to its effects on Britain's efforts to support Maria Theresa. It was all too easy to demonstrate in this context not only that the neutrality had deprived Austria of Hanover's support, but that it had also undermined Britain's measures in aid of Austria. The most obvious way in which it had done this, as at least one opposition polemicist pointed out at the time, was by immobilizing in Hanover the 12,000 Hessian and Danish troops in British pay that had been promised to Austria as part of the Anglo-Austrian alliance of June 1741.[37] Interestingly, the pro-ministerial paper the *Daily Gazetteer* attempted to minimize the significance of the neutrality by arguing that, under certain circumstances, a temporary neutrality constituted a prudent measure. To buttress this claim, and presumably to suggest that such an agreement did not preclude the future and effective deployment of British and Hanoverian resources on Austria's behalf, the paper also made a comparison between the Hanoverian neutrality and Louis XIV's negotiation of the Peace of Ryswick in 1697.[38] (The Peace of Ryswick was commonly (and not unreasonably) regarded as having been entered into by Louis XIV with the aim of maximizing France's ability to exploit the issue of the Spanish succession.[39]) The forced arguments articulated in the *Daily Gazetteer* were an easy target for both the *Craftsman* and the *Daily Post*.[40] But they were undermined even more effectively by Austria's collapse in late 1741.

Given the extent of this collapse—by the end of the year anti-Habsburg forces had occupied Bohemia and Upper Austria—it is unsurprising that the opposition press did considerably more than just attack the Hanoverian neutrality's influence on Britain's efforts to

[36] *A Letter from a Member of the Last Parliament*, 50.
[37] Ibid. 51.   [38] *Daily Gazetteer*, 25 Nov. 1741.
[39] For this view of the Peace of Ryswick, see *An Address to the People of Great Britain by a Country Clergyman* (1744), 16–17. The peace of 1697 was also viewed as an important example of the dangers of accepting moderate peace terms from the French.
[40] *Craftsman*, 14 Nov. 1741; *Daily Post*, 25 Nov. 1741.

support Austria. The final months of 1741 and the early part of 1742 also saw an intensification of the attacks in the opposition press against the alleged underlying causes of the crisis that was confronting Britain, and the emergence of a detailed critique of the British and Hanoverian response to events in Europe following the death of Charles VI in October 1740. Perhaps the most influential contributions to these areas of press debate were two pamphlets published in October and the following February respectively.[41] The first was entitled *The Groans of Germany*. Its immediate impact caused Thomas Birch to observe on 27 October: 'There is just publish'd here a pamphlet call'd The Groans of Germany, which has already been thro' three Editions . . . some ascribe it to Lord Bolingbroke, but I cannot think it at all Equal to such a hand. It abounds with such free strokes, as even in the present licentiousness of the press, are not commonly met with.'[42] Its impact also impressed Anton von Zöhrern, Austria's diplomatic representative in London. In a letter to the Austrian Chancellor, Count Philip von Sinzendorff, Zöhrern informed his superior of the high level of interest created by *The Groans of Germany*. He also reiterated the contemporary (and probably inaccurate) speculation that its author was the arch-political intriguer Bolingbroke.[43]

The second pamphlet was entitled *The Affecting Case of the Queen of Hungary*, and purported to share the same author as *The Groans of Germany*. Both pamphlets, as their titles suggest, were concerned solely with the seemingly imminent dismemberment of Austria's dominions and the French achievement of hegemony in Europe. As *The Affecting Case of the Queen of Hungary* declared of France's apparent power and influence:

So broad a bottom has spread the *Pyramid* of her power, so deep has she sunk the Foundation, so high has she raised the point, from whence enthron'd like the mother of Gods, she demands and receives the Homage of her Fellow-Princes at her Foot-stool and issues out the commands, which are to be listen'd to, and obey'd like those of Fate.[44]

---

[41] But see also *A Letter to a Right Honourable Member of Parliament, Demonstrating the Absolute Necessity of Britain's Assisting the House of Austria* (1742); *Britannia in Mourning, or, a Review of the Politicks and Conduct of Great Britain with Regard to France* (1742); *A Letter to a Member of this New Parliament from a True Lover of the Liberties of the People* (1742).

[42] BL Add. MS 35396 (Hardwicke Papers), fos. 35–6: Birch to Yorke, 27 Oct. 1741.

[43] For Zöhrern's letter, which was intercepted by the British ministry, see J. Black, 'Falsely Attributed to Lord Bolingbroke', *Publishing History*, 17 (1985), 87–9.

[44] *The Affecting Case of the Queen of Hungary* (1742), 20. The question of the authorship of *The Affecting Case* and *The Groans of Germany* (1741) is discussed in J. B. Shipley, 'James Ralph: Pretender to Genius', Ph.D. thesis (Columbia, NY, 1963), 351.

The significance of *The Groans of Germany* lies not only in its concentration on the crisis on the Continent, but also in the prominence that it accorded to the question of Hanover's role in Austria's collapse. As with the arguments concerning the influence of Hanover on Britain's international position articulated in the *Champion* and *A Letter from a Member of the Last Parliament, The Groans of Germany* was also foreshadowing an important line of argument in the anti-Hanoverian press campaign of 1742–4. Thus, the central thrust of the pamphlet was to attribute France's present mastery of Europe to the alleged Hanoverian control of British foreign policy since 1714. In what is a very striking piece of polemical simplification, most likely aimed at the accommodation of historic Whig and Tory divisions, the Peace of Utrecht was portrayed as the culmination of a post-1688 foreign policy that had been informed by a 'glorious spirit' and had 'animated Europe to a confederacy against this dictating Crown [France]'. It was alleged that, since 1714, rather than guarding the supposed achievement of the Peace of Utrecht, namely, the establishment of Austria as a counter-poise to French power in Europe, Britain had sacrificed the 'Liberties of Europe' to the goals of aggrandizing and defending Hanover. It was these goals, or, more specifically, Austria's opposition to them, which had motivated Britain's allegedly anti-Austrian foreign policy under Walpole. In this context, the critique of Walpole's foreign policy that had been expressed earlier in the year, most notably in *A Review of a Late Motion*, was reiterated in its entirety. The roots of Austro-Hanoverian antagonism, again anticipating what was to occur between 1742 and 1744, were traced back to disagreements between the two powers regarding the imperial investiture of the Electors of Hanover with the duchies of Bremen and Verden, and the control of the duchy of Mecklenburg.[45] Much less plausibly, George II's agreement, as part of the Hanoverian neutrality, to give his vote in the forthcoming imperial election to the French candidate (Charles VII of Bavaria) was portrayed as simply the latest manifestation of Hanover's alleged aim of weakening Austria.[46]

Many of the arguments expressed in *The Groans of Germany* were far from original. In particular, most of the specific allegations regarding Hanover's control of British foreign policy, such as the charge that Townshend's anti-Austrian schemes of the later 1720s had been designed to protect Hanover, had been made both at the time of the

[45] For these disagreements, see J. Black, *British Foreign Policy in the Age of Walpole* (Edinburgh, 1985), 27–48.
[46] Charles VII of Bavaria was elected King of the Romans on 24 Jan. 1742.

relevant measures and on a number of subsequent occasions. In the early 1730s, for example, an important focus for the expression of this concern had been the payment of subsidies to the Landgrave of Hesse-Kassel.[47] What lent them weight in late 1741 was the Hanoverian neutrality. As has already been emphasized, this agreement seemed to provide incontrovertible evidence of the subversion of British interests by Hanoverian ends. Confronted with this evidence, other opposition polemicists declared that one of the consequences of the neutrality had been to confirm 'beyond contradiction', as one of them put it, the validity of long-standing criticisms of Hanover's influence on the conduct of British foreign policy.[48]

The major contribution of *The Affecting Case of the Queen of Hungary* was twofold. First, it was the principal vehicle for the detailed attack against the British and Hanoverian responses to events on the Continent following the death of Charles VI. The central feature of this attack was the emphasis that was placed upon an alleged failure to compel Austria to accede to terms of accommodation said to have been offered by Prussia in late 1740. It was argued that, rather than encouraging Austrian acceptance, the parliamentary grant in April 1741 of £300,000 for the support of the House of Austria and the mobilization of the Hanoverian army and the 12,000 Hessian and Danish troops at Hanover, Britain and George II had induced Austria to adopt a belligerent stance. The result was well known: the entry of the French into the war, and the rapid collapse of Austria. What needs emphasizing in this context, given the importance that was attached to these events later on in the war, is the degree to which George II was already being portrayed as primarily responsible for the outbreak of a general war in Europe in 1741. Thus, the author of the pamphlet maintained that George II's personal antipathy towards Frederick II, and his jealousy of the latter's power, had been a major factor behind the defeat of Frederick II's proposals.[49] George II had, it was further alleged, responded to Prussia's overtures to Maria Theresa by attempting to incite Russia to march against Prussia to prevent Frederick II's invasion of Silesia. It is perhaps worth noting that this allegation anticipated the opposition claims in 1743 that in the winter of 1740–1 George II had attempted to put in motion a plan to dismember Prussia.[50]

[47] See J. Black, 'Parliament and Foreign Policy in the Age of Walpole: The case of the Hessians', in J. Black (ed.), *Knights Errant and True Englishmen: British Foreign Policy, 1600–1800* (Edinburgh, 1989), 41–54.
[48] *A Letter from a Member of the Last Parliament*, 50.
[49] *The Affecting Case*, 6.   [50] See below, Ch. 5.

The second major contribution was the pamphlet's exploitation of the cult of Maria Theresa created by the onslaught against Austria in 1741. Faced with a young female ruler beset by the most formidable bellicose alliance of European powers in thirty years, it was easy for the opposition to introduce a moral coloration into their arguments during the winter of 1741–2. Thus, the author of *The Affecting Case of the Queen of Hungary* declared of the present consequences of the intoxication of most of Europe's rulers with the goals of power and dominion:

That these purple Homicides [France and her allies], therefore, can with such wanton prodigality, offer such whole Hecatombs of their fellow creatures to the state idols of theirs [power and dominion] is not so much to be wondered at, as that so delicate a Flower [Maria Theresa] should bear up, against so many storms, tho' shook so rudely, and tho' so often bent to the very Earth on which it grew.[51]

In the six months preceding Walpole's fall, therefore, issues arising from the War of the Austrian Succession had been intruded into the forefront of press debate. By the winter of 1741–2, moreover, the response in the press was already displaying many of the characteristic features of press debate for much of the rest of the war. Perhaps the most important of these was the failure, very clearly disclosed in *The Affecting Case of the Queen of Hungary*, to appreciate the depth and significance of Austro-Prussian rivalry after 1740. As with so many other aspects of mid-century foreign policy debate, this failure had its roots in the ill-founded belief that the rest of Europe shared Britain's view of the threat posed by the French.[52] As a result of this belief, both ministerial and opposition supporters assumed too readily that both powers would subordinate their rivalry to an alleged common interest in opposing French aims in Europe. There was little understanding here of the determination that underpinned Austria's opposition to Prussian aggression in 1741, and of the subsequent Austrian desire to compensate herself for the eventual cession of Silesia to Frederick II at the Peace of Breslau in June 1742.[53] It was also the tenacity with which most Englishmen held to the view that Austrian and Prussian war aims were easily reconcilable that, as *The Affecting Case of the Queen of Hungary* also shows, partly explains the remarkable propensity of the opposition press to see the influence and war aims of Hanover and

---

[51] *The Affecting Case*, 19. [52] See above, Ch. 3.
[53] See also below, Ch. 5.

George II as the mainspring of the troubles in the empire between 1740 and 1745.

One other interesting feature of the press debate created by the War of the Austrian Succession in the winter of 1741–2 is the divisions among the opposition that it reveals regarding the possibility of committing British resources to a land war on the Continent. Significantly, the views expressed on this issue did not split the opposition along simple Whig–Tory lines. Rather, they closely followed the divisions within the opposition caused by the widely held belief that William Pulteney and Lord Carteret were seeking an accommodation with Walpole. As J. B. Owen has shown elsewhere, it was this belief that was the most serious obstacle to opposition unity on the eve of Walpole's fall.[54] What Owen overlooked, however, was how closely this belief seems to have become intertwined in 1741 with conflicting views about how Britain should respond to the deteriorating situation on the Continent. Both the suspicions regarding the aims of Carteret and Pulteney and the corresponding division among the opposition regarding Britain's response to the war were revealed in Parliament by the motion of 13 April 1741, referred to earlier, which granted £300,000 'for preventing the subversion of the House of Austria, and for maintaining the Pragmatic sanction, and supporting the liberties and balance of power in Europe'. Carteret and Pulteney both seem to have supported the grant, or at least the necessity of providing immediate and effective aid to Austria.[55] The support of other leading opposition Whigs and of the Tories, however, was less enthusiastic. In the Lords, Chesterfield and the Duke of Argyll refused Carteret's admonition to support the grant. In the Commons, as Chesterfield later explained to the Earl of Marchmont, he had been compelled to urge acquiescence: 'I plainly saw that it would be almost a Tory opposition, and that Pulteney would have carried Two Thirds of the Whigs present along with him; a triumph I thought it better he should not have had at the end of this Parliament.'[56]

The divisions exposed by the vote of 13 April were the subject of a pamphlet, published in June, entitled *The Plain Truth: A Dialogue*

[54] J. B. Owen, *The Rise of the Pelhams* (1957), 15–18.
[55] For Pulteney, see *Parl. Hist.*, xii. 178–83. Pulteney did, however, express opposition to the practice of granting votes of credit. He also called for an alliance to be negotiated with Prussia and for the formation of a grand anti-French alliance. For Carteret, see below.
[56] Rose, *Marchmont Papers*, ii. 249: Chesterfield to Marchmont, 24 Apr. 1741.

*between Sir Courtly Jobber, Candidate for the Borough of Guzzledown,
and Tom TellTruth, Schoolmaster and Freeman in the Said Borough.* In
addition to attacking the false 'patriotism' of Carteret and Pulteney and
'the H——r vote of credit' (the grant of 13 April), this pamphlet also
included a strident defence of a basically isolationist stance towards the
war in Europe:

> Don't talk to me of preserving the Balance of power in *Europe*, when the
> balance of our c-nst——n at home is destroy'd, and all the weight thrown into
> the C——n scale: Besides I don't see that any thing has been done to preserve
> the balance of power in *Europe*; but I see a great deal that has been done to
> destroy it. We pull'd down the Emperor's power so low, that we can't set it up
> again; and we set up the power of *France* so high, that we can't pull it down
> again . . .[57]

The probable author of *The Plain Truth* was James Ralph.[58] As is
described elsewhere in the present work, Ralph had close links with the
opposition Whig faction of which Chesterfield was a leading member.
The case for Ralph's authorship is strengthened by the fact that almost
the only other element of the opposition press to advocate an isolationist position between 1741 and early 1742 was the essay paper edited by
Ralph—the *Champion*. On 19 January 1742 the *Champion* offered a
similar justification for avoiding intervention in a land war to that
which had been articulated in *The Plain Truth*. Thus the paper argued
that Britain needed to apply 'the Remainder of our wealth, strength,
and vigour, agreeable to the Dictates of *self-preservation*'. As for support
for Austria: 'The *Austrian* Interest has already cost us more than 'tis
worth; and if it had not . . . *Time is pass'd*.'

The full extent of the divisions among the opposition in late 1741
regarding the prospect of British intervention in Europe is revealed by
The Groans of Germany and the *Craftsman*, the opposition essay paper
that had the closest links with Pulteney. On 7 November the *Craftsman*
outlined a broadly similar position on the war on the Continent to that
held by leading members of the ministry.[59] It was stated that British
intervention in Europe was impractical in the present circumstances.
The reason, although not stated by the paper, was the impossibility

[57] *The Plain Truth*, 19.

[58] W. B. Coley, 'The "Remarkable Queries" in the Champion', *Philological Quarterly*,
41 (1962), 426–36.

[59] See esp. Newcastle's retrospective discussion of ministerial attitudes towards the
opening stages of the war drawn up in 1743 (*The Life and Correspondence of Philip Yorke,
Earl of Hardwicke*, ed. Philip Yorke, 3 vols. (Cambridge, 1913): i. 318–19).

of intervening effectively without detaching Prussia from the anti-Habsburg alliance system. Yet, if immediate intervention was precluded, preparation for the occasion when it was practicable was not. As the *Craftsman* declared: 'It may be true that, in our present situation we must be content to vindicate our own Rights, and wait for *fresh opportunities* to aid our neighbours in the Recovery of theirs.' Britain should, the paper further argued, continue vigorously to pursue the war against Spain in order to demonstrate to the rest of Europe the recovery of 'true British Firmness and Intrepidity', the effects of which, it was asserted, might animate other powers to join Britain in an anti-Bourbon alliance. *The Groans of Germany*, meanwhile, sketched large areas of the policy that Britain would eventually pursue following the admission of Carteret and the new Whigs into the ministry in 1742. Perhaps the most significant element of the pamphlet's recommendations in this respect was its suggestion that, following the death of Charles VI, Britain should have encouraged the Dutch to join with them in mobilizing an army in the Austrian Netherlands.[60] In May 1742 the mobilization of the so-called Pragmatic army commenced with the dispatch of 16,000 British troops to Flanders.

How significant was the difference in attitude towards continental entanglements expressed in the opposition press in the winter of 1741–2 during the period surrounding Walpole's fall? Given the near silence of the opposition press and, in particular, of the essay papers on any issue relevant to the war between Walpole's fall and the last quarter of 1742, it is impossible to answer this with any degree of certainty. However, two observations are worth making in this context. First, the conflicting positions articulated in, most importantly, the *Craftsman* and the *Champion* closely anticipate the very clear line of division on this issue that emerges towards the end of 1742. Secondly, it seems likely that most Englishmen, in the face of the obvious French threat to the balance of power in Europe in the winter of 1741–2, were prepared to overcome their natural aversion to interventionist measures aimed at countering this threat and supporting Austria. In this respect, it is significant that the new ministry's foreign measures, which included the formation of a British army for deployment abroad and a subsidy of £500,000 (£200,000 was designed for Sardinia, and the remainder for Austria), received the unanimous support of Parliament in the spring

---

[60] *The Groans of Germany*, 28. Another proponent of intervention in Europe in early 1742 was the author of *A Letter to a Member of this New Parliament*.

of 1742. As J. B. Owen has emphasized, the unanimity in Parliament regarding foreign affairs at this stage is underlined by Pulteney's ability to persuade Sir John Barnard, the leading City and independent MP, to move the grant of supply for the subsidy referred to above.[61] It is also worth noting that between 1742 and 1745 a prominent feature of the polemical defence of Carteret's conduct of the war was the claim that, at the time of Walpole's fall, both parliamentary and popular opinion had been united in their demands for vigorous measures to be taken in aid of Austria.[62] This claim, moreover, was never directly challenged by Carteret's many detractors.[63]

Whatever the extent of the unanimity on foreign affairs in the early part of 1742, there is no doubting that the principal cause of its breakdown was the political settlement that followed Walpole's fall, the nature of which was finally confirmed in July 1742, when Pulteney was elevated to the peerage. That it should have been this, and not events in Europe, although they were a contributory factor, is no surprise. As has been demonstrated in an earlier chapter, the frustration between February and July 1742 of the widespread expectations of fundamental political change created by Walpole's fall was felt at almost all levels and aspects of press debate and politics 'without doors' throughout the 1740s. It was also, as Lucy Sutherland has noted elsewhere, still overshadowing press debate during the mid-1750s.[64] More immediately, the intensity and scale of the popular and press outrage that followed the betrayal of the patriot cause by Pulteney and his fellow new Whigs was such that it could not but influence closely the emerging debate in the second half of 1742 about the new ministry's conduct of the war. However, what brought the relationship between the issues of, on the one hand, political reform and, on the other, Britain's role in the War of the Austrian Succession sharply into focus in this period was the attempts of the new Whigs to defend both their conduct and the political settlement that followed Walpole's fall.

---

[61] Owen, *Rise of the Pelhams*, 132–3.

[62] See e.g. *A Letter to a Great Man in France* (1743); *A Compleat View of the Present Politicks of Great Britain* (1743); *An Apology for the Conduct of the Present Administration* (1744).

[63] It was usually claimed by the opposition press that their support for assistance to Austria in the winter of 1741–2 had only been for measures 'according to the British sense of Treaties'.

[64] L. Sutherland, 'The City of London in Eighteenth-Century Politics', in *Politics and Finance in the Eighteenth Century*, ed. A. Newman (1984), 55.

The most prominent elements of the new Whig polemical offensive
in 1742 were the two pamphlets *An Enquiry into the Present State of our
Domestick Affairs* and *Observations on the Conduct of Great Britain in
Respect of Foreign Affairs.*[65] That their publication had a greater impact than most occasional pamphlets is suggested by the fact that in
early 1743 it was alleged (probably inaccurately) that they had been
disseminated throughout the nation by the new ministry.[66] Their basic
line of argument was, perhaps unsurprisingly, that Pulteney and his
fellow new Whigs had fully and triumphantly demonstrated their
continued commitment to the patriot cause, given, and this was the
crucial condition, the limitations that had been imposed upon their
conduct by the 'nature and circumstances of Things'. The most
significant of these circumstances had been, it was argued, the crisis
on the Continent at the time of Walpole's fall. All their actions had
proceeded from the necessity of doing nothing in that situation to
weaken Britain's capacity to support her interests in Europe. As the
author of *Observations on the Conduct of Great Britain* declared of the
international crisis that had faced Britain in early 1742: '[it] demanded
all our Attention, and Respect to our Interests abroad ought to have
superceded all such concerns (as were incompatible with them) at
home'.[67] With this end in view, the new Whigs had acted in such a
manner as to 'quiet Fears and stifle Animosities', a reference primarily
to the failure to prosecute Walpole.[68] Another new Whig polemicist
was less conciliatory, demanding of the opposition call for Walpole's
prosecution: 'Will it reduce the exorbitant power of *France,* and secure
the *Austrian* Interest in *Germany?*'[69] As for political reform, enough had
been achieved between February and July 1742 to indicate that, under
more propitious circumstances, a 'thorough reformation' could be
expected.[70]

Undoubtedly a vital stimulus to this vigorous defence of the new
Whigs was the very marked improvement in the military and diplomatic
outlook that took place in the months that immediately followed
Walpole's fall. In this, as a number of opposition polemicists claimed

---

[65] See also *A Vindication of the Conduct of a Certain Eminent Patriot* (1742); *Seasonable
Expostulations with the Worthy Citizens of London* (1742); *Considerations on the War*
(1743).
[66] *Seventeen Hundred and Forty Two* (1743), 9–10.
[67] *Observations on the Conduct of Great Britain* (1742), 25.
[68] Ibid. 29.   [69] *Seasonable Expostulations,* 9.
[70] *Observations on the Conduct of Great Britain,* 30.

at the time, there was a great deal of good fortune.[71] Its effect, nevertheless, was to enable the pamphleteers to claim that the new Whigs' policies and conduct since their admission to the ministry had been completely vindicated by events. The most celebrated achievement of the new ministry in this respect was Britain's role in detaching Prussia from the French-led anti-Habsburg alliance system at the Peace of Breslau. What principally allowed the new Whigs to magnify the significance of this achievement was its apparent consequences, the most important of which was the rapid collapse of France's military position in the empire in the latter part of 1742. Against this background, it was argued that the Peace of Breslau had laid the basis for 'every step that has been taken since towards the establishing the peace and independency of *Europe*'.

There were, moreover, other areas of Europe, such as the Mediterranean and the Baltic, to which new Whig polemicists could turn for further evidence of the efficacy of the new ministry's conduct of the war. In the Mediterranean Britain's increasing naval control had forced Naples to negotiate a neutrality and was preventing the Spanish from sending reinforcements to the Bourbon forces in Italy; in the Baltic Russia seemed to be about to conclude a peace settlement with Sweden, independently of the French.[72] Meanwhile, the deployment of the British forces in Flanders had, it was alleged, prevented France from sending reinforcements to either Italy or Germany.[73] In short, the new ministry's 'well-concerted' measures had 'in so short a space of time raised Great Britain to her proper station, and once more put the balance of power in Her Hands'.[74] The aim was now to 'form a new confederacy as powerful as the old one [i.e. the Grand Alliance]', which would 'effectually reduce the exorbitant power of *France*, and settle the Balance of Power in Europe, in such a manner, as it shall not be shaken again for some Ages'.[75]

That either the arguments of the new Whig polemicists or the dramatic change in the character of the war in the second half of 1742 succeeded in weakening the popular outrage created by the political settlement that followed Walpole's fall is unlikely. In the first place, the

---

[71] See e.g. *The Conduct of the Last and Present M——ry Compar'd*, 40–1. See also Owen, *Rise of the Pelhams*, 129–31.

[72] See e.g. *Seasonable Expostulations*, 6–9.   [73] Ibid. 7.

[74] *An Enquiry into the Present State of our Domestick Affairs* (1742), 23.

[75] *Observations on the Conduct of Great Britain*, 45.

new Whig pamphlets, or rather the claim that, given the alleged patriotism of Pulteney and the new ministry, opposition was no longer necessary, merely provoked a number of vigorous pamphlet rebuttals.[76] It is, furthermore, not necessary to view these rebuttals, as one historian has done recently, as a crucial stage in 'tory radicalisation' in order to appreciate their importance as a measure of the discontent among opposition and popular opinion in late 1742.[77] Thus, they all emphasized their apprehensions in the present conjuncture for the future of 'British liberty'. They also rehearsed the full array of patriot grievances and demands for reform that had emerged under Whig oligarchy, including demands for the repeal of the Black and the Riot Acts, measures of fiscal retrenchment, and what was later to be called 'Economical Reform' (the retrenchment of salaries and pensions, the abolition of sinecures, the regulation of the civil list). The only demand directly relevant to foreign affairs (a demand that further reflects the impact of the Hanoverian neutrality) was that 'they would have the Act of Settlement observed with Regard to *Foreign concerns*'.[78]

In the second place, the continued depth of popular exasperation in late 1742 is further disclosed by the second wave, since Walpole's fall, of constituency instructions to MPs, which took place between September and November.[79] The violence of the language of these instructions caused a young Charles Pratt (later Lord Camden) to remark: 'The last Instructions are so outrageous, that I am ashamed of calling them Liberty; for to me they appear to mean the coarse and brutal fierceness of misrule and anarchy.'[80] In making these remarks, Pratt probably had in mind the instruction drawn up on 2 November by the Westminster Society of Independent Electors. Admittedly, the Independent Electors constituted a collection of the more extreme and malcontent elements of the metropolitan opposition.[81] Nevertheless,

---

[76] See esp. *Opposition More Necessary than Ever* (1742); *The Case of the Opposition Impartially Stated* (1742); *National Unanimity Recommended, or, the Necessity of a Constitutional Resistance to the Sinister Designs of False Brethren* (1742).

[77] L. Colley, 'Eighteenth-Century Radicalism before Wilkes', *Transactions of the Royal Historical Society*, 5th ser., 31 (1981), 8. One of the alleged Tory pamphlets cited by Colley in support of her view of a post-Walpole Tory radicalization, *A Key to the Business of the Present Session*, was actually published before Walpole's resignation (Colley, 'Eighteenth-Century Radicalism', 8 n. 21).

[78] *National Unanimity Recommended*, 52.

[79] See also above, Ch. 2, for this wave of instructions.

[80] *Biographical Memoirs of the Rev. Sneyd Davies, DD, Canon Residentiary of Lichfield*, ed. G. Hardinge (1846), 140–1: Pratt to Davies, 29 Nov. 1742.

[81] See above, Ch. 1, for the Westminster Independents.

the radical terms and language that it employed in drawing up its instruction are still very striking. Representative in this respect is the contractualist warning with which the instruction commenced:

> Nor does this Application flow from any mistaken notion of our own importance, or from the least distrust of your virtue and liberties; but that the Supreme Councils and legislature of this Kingdom may be justly informed of what we conceive to be the voice of the People, to which, whenever Government perverts the End of its institution, the last Appeal must Lye.

Not surprisingly, given the populist implications of such real Whig rhetoric, the Westminster instruction was singled out by at least one pro-ministerial pamphleteer for vigorous condemnation.[82]

As well as being a vehicle for articulating outrage at the betrayal of the patriot cause by the new Whigs, the instructions of late 1742 also expressed the view, in contradiction to that put forward by the new Whigs, that foreign affairs should not divert Parliament from the essential tasks of political reform (the passage of place and pension bills, the repeal of the Septennial Act) and the revival of the secret committee that had been established in the previous parliamentary session to investigate the last ten years of Walpole's domestic administration. As the Westminster instruction urged its MPs:

> We hope you will not suffer any Foreign Affairs to divert your Attention from our Domestick Interests; nor the Pretence of restoring the Balance of power abroad betray you into a loss of that Equilibrium of our constitution at home, on which the mutual Advantage both of the Crown and People depends, the Glory of the most successful war will we apprehend be too dearly purchased at the Expence of our *Liberties*.

To ensure that this did not occur, the instructions called for the vote of supplies to be postponed until the programme of reform that they advocated had secured a passage through Parliament. As was usual with such campaigns of the early Hanoverian period, the instructions of late 1742 were widely reprinted throughout the opposition press. This same element of the press also reinforced their message regarding the dangers of being diverted from expediting essential measures of political reform by, as one opposition pamphleteer put it, 'the flattering prospect of success and Glory abroad'.[83]

One other interesting measure of how closely the two issues, the

---

[82] *Seasonable Expostulations*, 15.
[83] *Address to the Electors of Great Britain* (1742), 7.

recovery of 'British liberty' and the conduct of the war, had become intertwined in the second half of 1742, and of the strength of popular indignation with the new Whigs, is provided by the *Craftsman*. In July the paper reprinted two leading articles that emphasized the prospects of an effective assertion of Britain's international power created by the Peace of Breslau. This attempt to defend, albeit obliquely, the conduct of its former patrons provoked a vigorous attack from at least one patriot pamphleteer in late 1742.[84] More significantly, it also seems to have alienated the paper's readership. This at least is the most likely explanation for its abandonment of its defence of their conduct at the end of July, and of its joining in the hue and cry against the new Whigs thereafter.

In the area of foreign affairs, the extent to which the *Craftsman* altered its position is very strikingly illustrated by the leading articles reprinted in the paper on 11 September and 6 November respectively. On the former occasion the paper quoted from a speech that had been made by the high Tory Lord Rochester at the outbreak of the War of the Spanish Succession, in which he had expressed his opposition to any step that might have led to British intervention on the Continent. The purpose of quoting from this speech in late 1742 was to provide support for the view that intervention in continental rivalries entailed disproportionate domestic costs. On the latter occasion the paper defended the position that political reform was of greater importance than the situation on the Continent. As the paper declared: 'till our Grievances are redress'd we shall ever be a divided people; nor shall we ever come heartily into LAND-wars Abroad, till we are at Ease at home. What concern I have for the Queen of Hungary, I have much more for the people of *Great Britain*.'

Between July 1742 and the opening of the new parliamentary session in December, therefore, the opposition press, together with the instructions to MPs, argued that political reform at home was of more pressing concern than intervention in the war in Europe. Towards the end of the year more specific criticisms of the new ministry's conduct of the war, and opposition to the principle of intervention itself, also became increasingly common features of press debate. Somewhat ironically, it was the most prominent old corps Whig victim of the political changes that had followed Walpole's fall, namely, Lord Hervey, who was the author of what was perhaps the most powerful attack against

<hr />

[84] *National Unanimity Recommended*, 5–6.

the interventionist schemes of the new ministry, the pamphlet *Miscellaneous Thoughts on the Present Posture of our Foreign and Domestick Affairs*, published in November.[85] Most of the arguments articulated by Hervey and a number of other opposition polemicists in late 1742 were to be much repeated and amplified in the following two years, and are discussed in detail in the following chapter. In the present context, it is worth briefly drawing attention to two aspects of the developing press campaign against the conduct of the war.

The first of these comprised the questions that were already being raised in the latter part of 1742 regarding the military purpose of the mobilization of the Pragmatic army in the Low Countries. Confronted with the failure of the forces in Flanders to attempt any positive military action in 1742, opposition polemicists, perhaps unsurprisingly, displayed a remarkable willingness to speculate about more sinister and undeclared reasons for the mobilization. Few, however, were as explicit as one opposition polemicist, who declared that it was one aspect of 'the general scheme of securing the new ministry, enlarging the power of the court, and preventing an effectual Enquiry into the conduct of the *late Minister*'.[86] The second aspect of the press campaign was the prominence that was accorded to the issue of Hanover's alleged influence on Britain's role in the war. Two pamphlets published during the early part of the summer disclose how close to the surface of press debate this issue had remained following the Hanoverian neutrality.

The first, published in April, was a retrospective defence of Walpole's foreign policy, entitled *The Conduct of the Late Administration with Regard to Foreign Affairs from 1722 to 1742*. The second, published in June, was a direct riposte entitled *The Late Minister Unmask'd*. A central feature of both pamphlets was the attention and industry that they devoted respectively to attacking and defending the allegation that Walpole had sacrificed British interests to Hanoverian ends. Given the small volume of pro-ministerial polemic produced in the 1740s, it is the position expressed by Walpole's apologist that is the more interesting. This was twofold. First, as part of the 'Protestant interest' in Germany, Hanover's defence, and even the extension of the electorate's dominions were compatible with British interests. As Walpole's defender declared: 'A minister can never act up to the spirit

---

[85] Hervey was removed from office as Lord Privy Seal to make way for Lord Gower. He was also the author of a number of ballads attacking the new ministry. The most influential was entitled *The Patriots Are Come, or, a Doctor for a Crazy Constitution* (1742).   [86] *An Important Secret Come to Light* (1743), 48.

of the *Revolution*, nor answer the Ends of it, unless he have a constant Eye to the defeating all secret as well as open Attempts in favour of the *Pretender*, and the supporting, and even extending the power and influence of our present Royal Family in *Germany*.' Secondly, Hanover's vulnerability was a consequence of dynastic union with Britain. Reasons of justice and self-interest, therefore, dictated that Britain provide support for George II as Elector against 'all infringements and invasions of his Rights and Dominions'.[87]

In the latter part of 1742 a further stimulus to press discussion of alleged Hanoverian influence on Britain's international position was the news from Holland that the Earl of Stair had attempted (unsuccessfully) to induce the Dutch Republic to conclude a defensive alliance with Hanover. This news provoked the publication of at least two pamphlets that concentrated almost exclusively on attacking Hanover's role in the early stages of the war in Europe.[88] One of these amplified the allegations that had been developed earlier in the year in *The Affecting Case of the Queen of Hungary*, regarding the role of George II's Hanoverian interests in preventing an Austro-Prussian accommodation in 1740. Had this accommodation been achieved, it was reiterated, the outbreak of a general war in Europe in 1741 would have been prevented.[89]

On 20 September the Earl of Bath, as Pulteney was known following his elevation to the peerage, warned the Duke of Newcastle that 'Great Clamours are raised against the taking the Hanoverian Troops into our pay . . . In short there is a spirit of discontent arising & so many discontented persons at work to raise it.'[90] Although Bath was writing, appropriately, from Bath, and on the basis solely of his observations of the activities of leading opposition politicians, the grounds for heeding his warning only increased in the ensuing weeks. To be sure, before December 1742 actual attacks in the press on the award of British pay to the Hanoverians (the Hanoverians had been taken into British pay in August, following Carteret's success in persuading George II to repudiate the Hanoverian neutrality) were comparatively rare.[91] It was not yet the predominant, or even a major, issue of press concern. Nevertheless,

---

[87] *The Conduct of the Late Administration*, 11–13.
[88] *The Present State of British Influence in Holland Exemplified* (1742); *An Important Secret Come to Light*.   [89] *An Important Secret Come to Light, passim.*
[90] BL Add. MS 35407, fos. 144–5: Bath to Newcastle, 20 Sept. 1742.
[91] But see the *Champion*, 6 Nov. 1742; *A Letter to my Lord Mayor Vindicating the Late Instructions* (1742), 15.

as early as the beginning of October there were significant signs of its potential to inflame popular opinion.

By far the most important of these was the City of London's instruction to its MPs condemning the conduct of the new Whigs following Walpole's fall. The instruction referred to 'the Parade of numerous Land Armies, and the Hire of foreign troops, without the Appearance of any service in Behalf of his Majesty's *British* Dominions'.[92] This led Philip Yorke to observe two days after the instruction appeared:

I have just read the City-Instructions to their members, which is surely a chef d'œuvre of fury & Disaffection . . . I [could] wish, at the same time . . . that they had been deprived of one topic upon which, I foresee a good deal of clamour will be raised; I mean the taking of so large a Number of Foreign troops into Pay before there was an immediate use for them.[93]

Furthermore, as it has been the major purpose of the latter part, in particular, of this chapter to show, even if the Hanoverian troops had yet to become a central issue of press concern, there were other good grounds for concern regarding the likely press and popular response to the conduct of the war. The Hanoverian neutrality had already ensured that the issue of Hanover's influence on British foreign policy was going to play an important role in the press debate created by Britain's role in the war. Equally important, given the depth of popular outrage and discontent created by the political settlement that followed Walpole's fall, was the very close relationship that had been established in press debate between the issues and recriminations arising from the new Whig betrayal and the developing press campaign against the new ministry's interventionist strategy. All that was needed to bring together the various aspects of the press debate and to provide a powerful focus for the expression of popular exasperation and disillusionment with national politics was the intervention in the press of some of the Earl of Bath's 'discontented persons'. It is this area of opposition activity between 1742 and 1744 that is examined in the following chapter.

Finally, what of press interest in the war against Spain in 1742? This was almost nil. As Horace Walpole remarked in April: 'As to the Spanish war and Vernon, there is no more talk of them; one would think they had been taken by privateer.'[94]

---

[92] The possibility of British interests in the war being subordinated to Hanoverian ends was also raised by the instruction drawn up by the Westminster Society of Independent Electors.

[93] BL Add. MS 35396, fos. 79–80: Yorke to Birch, 24 Oct. 1742.

[94] Lewis, *Walpole*, xvii. 389–92: Walpole to Mann, 8 Apr. 1742.

5

CARTERET AND HANOVER, 1742–1744

GIVEN that a significant proportion of the early Hanoverian political nation was disposed to view any intervention on the Continent as proof of subserviency to Hanoverian ends, it was almost inevitable that widespread concern about the issue would be expressed once Carteret committed Britain in the second half of 1742 to providing Austria with direct military support as well as financial and diplomatic aid. What could not have been predicted, however, was the remarkable degree to which it came to dominate all levels and aspects of press and public debate during 1743–4. That this occurred was, as it is the aim of this chapter to show, the result of a combination of domestic and foreign circumstances, amongst which two of the most important were the role of the 16,000 Hanoverian troops that had been taken into British pay in the summer of 1742, and the direct intervention in the press of a number of opposition Whigs who had found themselves excluded from the political settlement that followed Walpole's fall.

Historians have hitherto tended to overlook this second factor, concentrating instead on the violent parliamentary speeches of the same group of politicians. This was not the case at the time. One contemporary, for example, observed:

Chesterfield expected to have been Secretary of State, Pitt Secretary at War, and Bedford and Sandwich to have been in the Admiralty, when disappointed, they entered the closest amity and intimacy with the leaders of the Jacobites. *In writing*, in conversation, and in their speeches, they expressed an insolent contempt and malevolence to the King and his Government beyond what had appeared under the Walpole Administration.[1]

As we have seen in another context in this work, in his pamphlet *Faction Detected by the Evidence of Facts* Lord Perceval identified the press as the Broad-Bottom opposition's most important means of achieving its goals. The same point was made even more forcefully by

[1] Quoted in J. W. Wilkes, *A Whig in Power: The Political Career of Henry Pelham* (Chicago, 1964), 22 (my italics).

another pamphleteer: 'their [the opposition Whigs] chief efforts are not in Parliament, nor in Debates: Their strength lies in the vulgar. There lie all their Hopes; there they exert all their coarse Talents, and best Ability, that of Railing and Reviling.'[2] As will be shown, the scale and success of the opposition Whig press activity is one of the most striking features of the press debate arising from the war between 1742 and 1744. It is also hoped to reveal the nature of the contribution that this made towards ensuring that the conduct of the war was debated in these years with an influence and an intensity that were unmatched throughout the rest of the war.

Before examining this, however, it is necessary first to say something about the constitutional issue that, according to the opposition, was raised by the alleged Hanoverian control of British foreign policy. What was in dispute here was the meaning and significance of the often-quoted clause in the Act of Settlement of 1701 that declared that Britain was 'not obliged to engage in any war for the defence of any dominion or territories which do not belong to the Crown of England, without the consent of Parliament'. Whatever the intentions of the framers of this clause, all elements of the patriot opposition were in no doubt that it signified that Britain should not, under any circumstances whatever, intervene in foreign disputes in support of Hanover. Even if the electorate was attacked as a consequence of British measures, as had in fact occurred in 1741, Britain was still not obliged to defend her.[3] Should the contrary have been true, Britain would, in the words of the *Old England Journal*, 'lose the very Benefit of being an Island'.[4]

If the meaning of the clause was self-evident, the implications of pursuing measures barred thereby were, at least as far as the opposition press was concerned, equally straightforward. To deploy British resources in support of Hanoverian ends was to contravene the very Act from which the Hanoverian dynasty derived its title to the British Crown. As the *Old England Journal* explained: 'As . . . it was not for the sake of one man, or one Family, but the whole people, that this transfer was made of the Crown of England, it is demonstrably our Right, it is indispensably our Duty to see that the conditions are fulfilled; and to insist that our own Act and Deed should operate to our use and Advantage.'[5] The logical conclusion of this line of reasoning was

---

[2] *A Warning to the Whigs, and to Well-Affected Tories* (1744), 13.
[3] For a rebuttal of this view, see *A Letter to a Friend, Concerning the Electorate of Hanover* (1744).
[4] *OEJ* 28 Apr. 1744.   [5] Ibid. 25 Feb. 1744.

inescapable. As Sir William Yonge expostulated during a Commons debate at the end of 1742:

Upon this occasion, things have been said, nay things have been printed and published, which, in my opinion, ought to be deemed high treason . . . for they have first represented it as a condition in the Act of Settlement, that we should never be put to any expence, or brought into any danger, on account of the Electorate of Hanover; and then they have endeavoured to shew, that all our foreign measures . . . have been calculated for the interest or aggrandisement of that electorate. If this were true, the inference would be natural, that the condition of the Act of Settlement being broke, the settlement itself is become void.[6]

On occasion, opposition polemicists suggested ways of removing the potential conflict between Hanoverian rule and the British constitution. Two options were particularly favoured: the cession of Hanover to one of George II's sons; and the enactment of stricter 'constitutional bars' to exclude Hanoverian interests from the conduct of British foreign policy.[7] Viewed in terms of such arguments, the intense and widespread concern about the role of Hanover felt between 1742 and 1744 is not only a very good illustration of the depth of popular interest in foreign policy, it is also further evidence of the central position occupied by 'Revolution Principles' and contractual notions of government in mid-century patriot argument.

Signs of both the excited state of press debate and its impact between 1743 and 1744 are easy to find. In addition to the influence of the opposition Whig propaganda, which is examined below, one rough measure of the former is provided by the remarkable number of occasional pamphlets published in this period that bore directly on the ministry's conduct of the war: 45 in 1743, rising to 50 in the following year—an increase that can be accounted for by the impact on press debate of the French invasion attempt in the spring of 1744. In 1747 the corresponding number was just 8.[8] Such was the number of occasional pamphlets that streamed from the capital's presses in late 1743 that a year later Lord Chancellor Hardwicke was provoked to remark: 'In the last Winter before this time, there were volumes of

[6] *Parl. Hist.*, xii. 941.

[7] See e.g. *OEJ* 17 Sept., 17 Nov., 3 Dec. 1743; *WJ* 19 Nov. 1743; [Chesterfield] *A Vindication of a Late Pamphlet, Intitled, the Case of the Hanover Troops* (1743), 31, 42–3.

[8] These figures are estimates based on the evidence of the book catalogues compiled by *GM* and *LM*.

virulent pamphlets published, which did infinite mischief.'[9] The 'infinite mischief' to which Hardwicke was referring was the popular outcry against Hanover's alleged control of British foreign policy of the winter of 1743–4.

The depth and intensity of popular discontent during the winter of 1743–4 impressed itself on many contemporaries. On 6 November 1743 the Reverend Dr Francis Ayscough, Clerk of the Closet to the Prince of Wales, recorded in his political journal: 'The discontents run higher than ever—the Han[overian] troops gave more universal disgust than either the Excise or convention.'[10] A few weeks previously Henry Fox had informed his elder brother, the Earl of Ilchester, that the popular uproar had grown sufficiently serious 'to disturb as sanguine a politician as I am'.[11] The same events were eliciting a rather different response from the Earl of Sandwich: 'The clamour and general discontent of all ranks of people, on account of our late Hanoverian measures is greater than I could have imagined it could have been, and if rightly pursued by a vigorous attack at the beginning of the session may be productive of very good ends.'[12] Such comments could be multiplied. It is worth noting, however, that similar concern about popular discontent is conspicuous by its absence (or virtual absence) from correspondence dating from, first, late 1742, when the Hanover issue was first seriously agitated, and, secondly, the period surrounding the opening of the 1744–5 parliamentary session, when a concerted attempt was made to rekindle popular concern about the role of Hanover.

As the remarks of Hardwicke reveal, contemporaries were in no doubt that behind the popular clamour of the winter of 1743–4 lay the influence of the press. This fact, or so it was claimed, explained the broad social and geographical dimensions of anti-Hanoverian feeling. In this context, Sandwich's emphasis on 'all ranks of people' was widely reiterated. Thus the author of the pamphlet *Popular Prejudice Concerning Partiality to the Interests of Hanover* (1743) alleged that 'the whole people, at least most of them, seem to abet those ungenerous pens that thus asperse and vilify the foreign subjects of their Prince.'[13] That the assumptions being made regarding the nation-wide extent of the outcry

---

[9] W. Coxe, *Memoirs of the Administration of the Right Honourable Henry Pelham*, 2 vols. (1827), i. 203. [10] BL Add. MS 51437 (Holland House Papers), fo. 50.
[11] Quoted in N. Rogers, *Whigs and Cities: Popular Politics in the Age of Walpole and Pitt* (Oxford, 1989), 70.
[12] Quoted in J. B. Owen, *The Rise of the Pelhams* (1957), 197.
[13] *Popular Prejudice*, 3.

were not simply an exercise in cautionary alarmism is suggested by a letter that Lord Tankerville wrote to Newcastle from Chillingham in Northumberland on 11 January 1744: 'The Hanoverians has made a great Noise here and there has not wanted proper Emissaries to throw out every invective the heart of man can invent, to make the *greatest of persons* [George II] appear as black and odious to the people as possible.'[14]

In Parliament, perhaps the most outspoken scourge of the encroachment of the press on opinion both inside and outside the Palace of Westminster was Carteret. In the course of a number of tirades against the press attacks on his conduct of the war and the Hanoverian troops, he inveighed against what he characterized as the 'extraordinary and bold attacks' that he claimed were being made 'to deceive the people'.[15] It is almost certain that, in making these comments, Carteret had in mind a wave of populist propaganda—prints, ballads, and cheap pamphlets—which were disseminated in large numbers in the capital during October and November 1743.[16] As they appeared, copies of these various forms of printed propaganda were being sent to Charles Hanbury Williams, who had been detained in Bath, by Henry Fox, at this time about to become one of the Lords of the Treasury. On 22 October Hanbury Williams wrote: 'Such a Letter and such a print as I receiv'd today from you would shake any faith less fixt than mine. Good god where will all this end. Must we fall by our own hands.'[17] A few weeks later Hanbury Williams informed Fox that he was suppressing the pieces that the latter was sending him.[18] His concern was shared by the ministry. In November two pieces, the ballad *Old England's Te Deum* and the cheap pamphlet *A True Dialogue between a Trooper and a Serjeant*, the latter of which Hanbury Williams described as being 'wrote as much *ad captum vulgi* as ever I read anything', provoked the ministry to take action to prevent their circulation.[19] The Earl of Morton declared in the Lords that the 'enormous licentiousness of writers' was a 'public evil' of such magnitude that Parliament would

---

[14] BL Add. MS 32702 (Newcastle Papers), fo. 7: Tankerville to Newcastle, 11 Jan. 1744. [15] *Parl. Hist.*, xiii. 285–93.

[16] The printer of one of the ballads, *Old England's Te Deum*, claimed that it had had an initial print-run of 15,000 (PRO, TS 11/82). See also below.

[17] BL Add. MS 51390, fos. 134–5: Hanbury Williams to Fox, 22 Oct. 1743.

[18] Ibid., fos. 149–50: Hanbury Williams to Fox, 15 Nov. 1743.

[19] PRO, TS 11/982; BL Add. MS 51390, fos. 143–4: Hanbury Williams to Fox, 6 Nov. 1743.

be entirely justified in contriving what were described as 'proper and equitable measures of restraint'.[20]

As has already been suggested, a primary dynamic behind the press attacks on Carteret's conduct of the war between 1742 and 1744 was the propagandist activities of the opposition Whigs. Certain aspects of these activities have already been discussed elsewhere in the present work. In particular, attention has been drawn to the knowledge and experience of press intervention that was gained (and the relationships within the print trade that were thereby established) during the final years of Walpolian rule by the Earl of Chesterfield, who seems to have been the tutelary influence on the press campaign, Edmund Waller, and George Dodington.[21] The operation and importance of these relationships can be further illustrated by the pamphlet *A Defence of the People*, which was published in October 1743 as a riposte to *Faction Detected by the Evidence of Facts*. This was written jointly by Chesterfield and James Ralph. Ralph, who had been one of the editors of the *Champion* between 1739 and 1741, was also, it will be recalled, one of the editors of the flagship of the opposition Whig press campaign, the weekly essay paper *Old England, or, the Constitutional Journal*, in which, as Hanbury Williams commented to Fox, *A Defence of the People* was 'advertised with pomp'.[22] It is also worth noting that Ralph came under the direct patronage of Dodington some time in the early 1740s.

Another opposition Whig who was active in the press in this period, and who had also engaged in polemical activity in the final years of the Walpolian administration, was the Earl of Marchmont. As well as contributing prominent pamphlets to both the press agitation for war against Spain in 1739 and the opposition campaign leading up to the general election of 1741, Marchmont had collaborated with William Guthrie, Ralph's fellow editor on the *Old England Journal*, on the short-lived *Englishman's Evening Post*.[23] His role between 1742 and 1744 is revealed in a letter that Chesterfield wrote to him on 5 January 1743: 'I send you a skeleton of a protest upon the Hanover Troops; it is truly

---

[20] *Parl. Hist.*, xiii. 609–18.

[21] Chesterfield's oversight of the opposition Whig press campaign was the subject of hostile comment in the pamphlet *An Apology for the Conduct of the Present Administration* (1744), esp. 1–7.

[22] BL Add. MS 51390, fos. 138–9: Hanbury Williams to Fox, 30 Oct. 1743.

[23] The major pamphlets between 1739 and 1741 of which Marchmont was the author were *A State of the Rise and Progress of the Differences with Spain and the Conduct of the Ministers Relating thereto* (1739), and *A Serious Exhortation to the Electors of Great Britain* (1740).

a skeleton yet. Therefore, I beg you give it flesh and colour which nobody can do so well.'[24] The reference here was almost certainly to the Lords protest occasioned by the rejection of a motion on 1 February against awarding British pay to the Hanoverian troops. The propaganda potential of such protests is highlighted by its publication in at least two separate pamphlets, along with the Commons division list for the vote of 10 December 1742 on the same measure. As the *Old England Journal* remarked regarding the dissemination of these lists: 'The Name of every single man who approv'd of these measures is now known, and known not to amount to one man in a hundred thousand of his majesty's British subjects.'[25]

A similar combination of a Lords protest and a Commons division list was also produced in early 1744. Again, Chesterfield seems to have been responsible for the authorship of the Lords protest, this one occasioned by the rejection of the Earl of Sandwich's motion of 31 January 1744 to pass a resolution in the Upper House declaring that the continued allocation of British pay to the Hanoverian troops was prejudicial to the interest of the King. In the account of the debate on this motion in his parliamentary journal Philip Yorke wrote with regard to Chesterfield's contribution: 'The substance of it is interwoven into the protest w[hic]h is in everybody's hand & therefore I need say less of it here.'[26] The division list gave the voting behaviour of MPs on a motion of 18 January 1744 to continue the Hanoverian troops in British pay for the coming year. Another published list pertaining to the same motion printed the names of those who had supported the retention of the troops in Hanoverian yellow, while those who had opposed their employment were reproduced in British red. The exact distribution of responsibility between Chesterfield and Waller for the major opposition pamphlets on the Hanoverian troops is an open question.[27] Similarly uncertain is the latter's contribution in 1744, along with George Dodington and James Ralph, to the weighty and 'circumstantially scurrilous' *Of the Use and Abuse of Parliaments*.[28]

The opposition Whig press initiative was launched in December 1742 with the publication of the best known of at least three pamphlets published during 1742–3 that attacked the employment of the

[24] Rose, *Marchmont Papers*, ii. 290.   [25] *OEJ* 12 Feb. 1743.
[26] *Parl. Hist.*, xiii. 244–8.
[27] See William B. Todd, 'The Number, Order, and Authorship of Hanover Pamphlets Attributed to Chesterfield', *Papers of the Bibliographical Society of America*, 44 (1950), 324–8.   [28] Lewis, *Walpole*, xviii. 463–6: Walpole to Mann, 18 June 1744.

Hanoverian troops, and for which the opposition Whigs were directly responsible. This pamphlet, *The Case of the Hanover Forces in the Pay of Great Britain*, had a particularly marked impact, with at least eight editions appearing over the next few months.[29] It was also extracted in the January issue of the *London Magazine*. At the end of 1743 Perceval claimed in *Faction Detected by the Evidence of Facts* that it was assured as wide a readership as possible by means of a concerted nation-wide distribution campaign.[30] Such assertions are a commonplace in mid-eighteenth-century press exchanges, and often seem to have had no basis in fact. In this instance, however, there is independent corroboration of Perceval's claim. In February 1743 Horatio Walpole produced a rebuttal of *The Case of the Hanover Forces*, entitled *The Interest of Great Britain Steadily Pursued*. As has been discussed elsewhere in the present work, the ministry seem actively to have discouraged Walpole's unsolicited efforts to counter the effects of the first of the opposition Whig pamphlets. This, as Walpole wrote to Robert Trevor, was in marked contrast to the fate of *The Case of the Hanover Forces*: 'The printer told me, that the *Case of the Hanover Forces* had been industriously dispersed at the expense of opponents all over the kingdom, the friends of the Government were surprised that the same care was not taken to spread the anti-dote.'[31] As Walpole's remarks reveal, considerable unease was created among supporters of the ministry by *The Case of the Hanover Forces*. More than usually sensitive to the subversive potential of domestic Jacobitism during a war against the Bourbon powers, this group (and various ministers) were understandably alarmed by a pamphlet that aimed to demonstrate the allegedly continuous sacrifice of British interests to Hanoverian ends since 1714. The possibility of its condemnation in the Commons was considered.[32] In the event, however, it was left to the Secretary at War, Sir William Yonge, and Horatio Walpole to articulate in the Lower House the concern that was felt about the pamphlet's influence.[33]

The second of the opposition Whig pamphlets, and the first to argue the necessity of dissolving the Anglo-Hanoverian union, *A Vindication of a Late Pamphlet, Intitled, the Case of the Hanover Troops*, was

---

[29] Todd, 'The Number, Order, and Authorship of Hanover Pamphlets', 225–8.

[30] [Perceval] *Faction Detected*, 124–5.

[31] HMC, Fourteenth Report, Appendix 9 (1895), 87–8: Walpole to Trevor, 25 Apr. 1743.

[32] *Richmond–Newcastle Correspondence*, 95: Newcastle to Richmond, 14 Dec. 1742.

[33] *Parl. Hist.*, xii. 941 (Yonge), 1036–7 (Walpole).

published in early January 1743. Not surprisingly, it failed to have the enormous impact of its predecessor. Nevertheless, it still went through at least four editions, its appearance creating what Horace Walpole described as 'a great noise'.[34] Moreover, it too was extracted in the *London Magazine*. The third, and least influential, of the three pamphlets, *A Farther Vindication of the Case of the Hanover Troops*, was timed to coincide with the commencement of the parliamentary session on 1 December. This pamphlet seems to have appeared in only one edition.[35] Like its immediate predecessor, it argued the necessity of separating Great Britain and Hanover. It also portrayed the coming session of Parliament as 'the last and only Hopes of this once rich, great, brave, renown'd, and independent Nation'.

Although all three of the opposition Whig pamphlets were, as indicated towards the beginning of the chapter, seconded by a plethora of anonymous pamphleteers, they were widely recognized as being the most influential contributions at that level of press debate. As well as being extracted in the *London Magazine*, various passages from them also appeared in the weekly essay papers. On 28 January 1744 one of these papers, the *Westminster Journal*, in the course of attacking the alleged subserviency of British foreign policy to the Hanoverian aim of territorial aggrandizement, remarked: 'For a full view of this we need only look into that famous pamphlet, The Case of the Hanover Troops, and the subsequent pieces that have been written to vindicate and explain it . . . the Author of these has *so well* said, and everybody almost has seen.' Very few pamphlets had such a marked impact; the vast majority were, in Thomas Birch's words, 'mushroom pamphlets which spring up and die here every week'.[36]

Two other pamphlets published in 1743 also have a claim to be considered as part of the opposition Whig press campaign. The source of the attributions is again Perceval's compendious pamphlet *Faction Detected by the Evidence of Facts*.[37] The first of the pamphlets that, in addition to those discussed above, was attributed by Perceval to the parliamentary opposition was entitled *The Question Stated with Regard to our Army in Flanders*. Published in February, this pamphlet was a summary of the major lines of argument that had been mobilized by

[34] Todd, 'The Number, Order, and Authorship of Hanover Pamphlets', 228–30; Lewis, *Walpole*, xviii. 140–4: Walpole to Mann, 13 Jan. 1743.

[35] Todd, 'The Number, Order, and Authorship of Hanover Pamphlets', 230.

[36] BL Add. MS 35396 (Hardwicke Papers), fos. 161–3: Birch to Yorke, 1 Oct. 1743.

[37] *Faction Detected*, 124–5.

the opposition during the 1742–3 parliamentary session against the deployment of British troops on the Continent. The plausibility of the attribution is strengthened by the fact that the tactic of publishing arguments at the end of the session that had failed to encroach on the ministerial majority in Parliament was regularly employed by early Hanoverian oppositions.[38] The second of the pamphlets singled out by Perceval was a riposte to Horatio Walpole's *The Interest of Great Britain Steadily Pursued*, which was predictably entitled *The Interest of Hanover Steadily Pursued* and was published in March. Apart from the similarity between the arguments rehearsed by the author of this second pamphlet and those in common use amongst Broad-Bottom politicians both in the press and Parliament, there is nothing but Perceval's insistence to link this pamphlet directly with the parliamentary opposition. The case for the inclusion of both pamphlets, moreover, is weakened by the fact that neither, unlike most of the substantial opposition Whig pamphlets published between 1743 and 1744, was 'advertised with pomp' in the weekly essay paper *Old England, or, the Constitutional Journal*.

The political forces underpinning the establishment of the *Old England Journal* in February 1743 have been discussed in depth in an earlier chapter. Two points, however, are worth reiterating here. First, and perhaps most interestingly, the paper underlines the close connections that were established in this period between the opposition Whigs and the forces of metropolitan radicalism in the form of the Westminster Society of Independent Electors. And secondly, the paper also reinforces the impression that it was Chesterfield who was co-ordinating the various aspects of opposition Whig press activity, Chesterfield being the author of the first few essays that were published in the *Old England Journal*, and appearing to have kept a close watch on it activities thereafter.[39] As was the case with the *Craftsman* in the late 1720s, the *Old England Journal* seems to have played a vital role in shaping the political role of the press in the early 1740s.[40] One indication of this is an increase in the demand for political comment that accompanied the paper's initial publication and immediate success. Not only were the bulk of the early issues of the *Old England Journal* rapidly reprinted in pamphlet form, but, under the stimulus of its success,

---

[38] See above, Ch. 1, for this.   [39] See above, Ch. 1, for this.

[40] For the *Craftsman*, see K. T. Winkler, 'The Forces of the Market and the London Newspaper in the First Half of the Eighteenth Century', *Journal of Newspaper and Periodical History*, 4 (1988), 24–5.

other papers felt compelled to give increasing attention to political comment.[41] The most salient illustration of this is the other leading opposition essay paper, the *Westminster Journal*. Taking its cue from the *Old England Journal*, the *Westminster Journal*'s leading essays became increasingly devoted, particularly from the autumn of 1743, to attacking the alleged Hanoverian control of British foreign policy. As the author of the pro-ministerial pamphlet *A Vindication of our Present Royal Family* remarked of the *Westminster Journal* in February 1744: 'the Author of the afore-said Journal, and one of his colleagues of the week [*Old England Journal*] out-do all that went before them in virulence, scandal, and violence.'[42] At its inception in late 1741, the *Westminster Journal, or, the New Weekly Miscellany*, as its full title suggests, was intended as a vehicle for moral and humorous comment as well as political analysis. On 10 December 1743 an anonymous correspondent duly complained: 'You are now grown a mere political Reasoner.'

The prominence that the author of *A Vindication of our Present Royal Family*, together with other pamphleteers such as the author of the pro-Carteret pamphlet *An Apology for the Conduct of the Present Administration* (1744), accorded to the question of the *Old England Journal*'s influence underlines the rapidity with which the opposition Whig essay paper intruded itself into the forefront of press debate. Its success can also be traced in the pages of the *Gentleman's Magazine* and the *London Magazine*. By the second half of 1743 it had largely displaced such longer-running papers as the *Craftsman* in the essay selections reprinted in the two magazines. On 19 February 1743, in the paper's third issue, the author of the leading article informed the readership that the maximum weekly print-run was 193,000 copies, which was, the author continued, 'a very small proportion to the number of those who will be sollicitous to read them'. Given that, even at its most successful, the *Craftsman* had never exceeded a print-run of 13,000 for any one issue, such boasts need not be taken very seriously. Nevertheless, the reality of a rapidly growing readership is further indicated by the very striking increase in the number of advertisers attracted to the pages of the *Old England Journal*, particularly during the winter of 1743–4. By early 1744 over half the paper was taken up with advertisements, thereby forcing significant changes in the layout

---

[41] See above, Ch. 1, for the publication in pamphlet form of early issues of the paper.
[42] *A Vindication of our Present Royal Family*, p. v.

and, in particular, a very marked contraction in the coverage of domestic and foreign news. This volume of advertising was probably unparalleled in an eighteenth-century essay paper. Needless to say, once the paper began to diminish in influence after 1745, most of these advertisers flocked to other papers.

Even a cursory glance at the early issues of the *Old England Journal* reveals that its remarkable impact during its first year was achieved by the very violence of its opposition to Carteret and the employment of the Hanoverian troops. As one pro-ministerial pamphleteer remarked: 'I should fill a volume did I attempt quoting the seditious, insolent, even treasonable paragraphs of this latter [*Old England Journal*], tho' it be scarce a year's standing.'[43] In the light of this, it is hardly surprising that its influence was the source of increasing concern amongst individuals close to the ministry. Also unsurprising are the sporadic attempts that, as was noted in an earlier chapter, were made by the ministry to disrupt the paper's publication during the first two years of its existence. Two series of letters in particular document the escalating anxiety created by the paper. The first is the correspondence between Charles Hanbury Williams and Henry Fox that has already been quoted from. On 9 October Hanbury Williams wrote: "Tis impossible to write two more inflaming & malicious papers than the two journals you send me. I wish I had material to answer them ... Indeed if such aspersions go unwhipp'd off & such reflections pass unanswer'd they must have fatal consequences.' Commenting on the attempts of the paper to realign the attitude of the political nation towards the issue of Hanoverian influence on British politics and interests, Hanbury Williams continued: 'Had Machiavel been a Jacobite now 'tis a Distinction he would have been proud to have been father of. Tis worthy a conclave, & what the assembled Jesuits of the world might glory in.'[44]

The second is the correspondence between Thomas Birch and the eldest son of the Lord Chancellor, Philip Yorke. These letters are an invaluable source of information on press activity in London, since a major part of Birch's brief was to provide Yorke with details of recent publications. During 1743 the density of references to the *Old England Journal* is yet another reflection of its remarkable impact.[45] The immediate determination of the ministry to bridle the paper is revealed by the unusually high bail that it attempted to impose on William Guthrie

[43] Ibid.   [44] BL Add. MS 51390, fo. 127: Hanbury Williams to Fox, 9 Oct. 1743.
[45] See e.g. BL Add. MS 35396, fos. 115–16: Birch to Yorke, 2 July 1743.

following his arrest for the authorship of the sixth issue.[46] In addition to this issue, three further numbers in 1743–4 provoked the ministry into issuing warrants for the arrest of the personnel of the paper, and one other issue was brought to its notice as the proper object of legal action.[47] For its part, the *Old England Journal* sought to evade the unwelcome attentions of the King's Messengers by changing the name that appeared on the colophon of the papers on three separate occasions between 1743 and 1744.

Before turning to consider the arguments mobilized by the opposition Whigs and the wider press debate of which they were a part, it is worth briefly examining the possibility that the opposition Whig intervention in the press in 1743 extended to encompass the major portion of the wave of populist propaganda that, as mentioned earlier, was published in October and November. The evidence for this is of four sorts. First, it seems that for at least two of the pieces, the cheap pamphlet *A True Dialogue between a Trooper and a Serjeant* and the print *The Confectioner General Setting Forth the H-n-v——n Desert*, the edition sizes were abnormally high, thus suggesting that the motivation behind their publication was political and not purely commercial.[48] Moreover, in the case of the print, this seems, as with *The Case of the Hanover Forces*, to have been in part a function of nation-wide distribution.[49] It is also noteworthy that at least one pro-ministerial pamphleteer singled out *A True Dialogue* as being closely linked to the tactics of the Broad-Bottom opposition during the 1743–4 parliamentary session.[50] Secondly, as has been emphasized in a different context in the present work, it is very unlikely that any other element of the opposition was also intervening in the press in this period. Thirdly, the actions of the opposition Whigs loosely grouped around Chesterfield and Lord Cobham were informed, even for eighteenth-century opposition politicians, with an uncommon degree of political cynicism. A very

---

[46] M. Harris, *London Newspapers in the Age of Walpole: A Study in the Origins of the Modern English Press* (1987), 141.

[47] PRO, SP 36/44, *passim*. The issues of the paper that provoked the ministry to issue warrants were those of 12, 19 Mar. and 14 May 1743, and 28 Jan. 1744. The one further issue that was recommended as the proper object for similar action was that of 12 Nov. 1743.

[48] Cowse claimed under examination that 11,000 copies of *A True Dialogue* had been delivered to him by an unknown porter (PRO, TS 11/982). For the large numbers of *The Confectioner General* in circulation in late 1743 (Pl. 3), see Lord Mahon, *History of England from the Peace of Utrecht to the Peace of Versailles, 1713–1783*, 7 vols. (1858), iii, Appendix, pp. vii–ix.

[49] Ibid. [50] *A Warning to the Whigs*, 24.

Pl. 3. The Confectioner General Setting Forth the H-n-v-———n Desert.

relevant disclosure of this is provided by a letter that Chesterfield wrote to Lord Gower on 2 October. Commenting on the breakdown of one of many sets of negotiations between the Pelhams and the opposition Whigs between 1742 and 1744, Chesterfield outlined the tactics that he now considered that the opposition should adopt: 'all that we have to do, in my opinion, is to prepare for battle, to procure an early and universal attendance of all our people, and to blow the Hanover Flame to height'.[51]

The fourth factor that seems to point to the opposition Whigs is the fact that the bulk of the popular anti-Hanoverian propaganda of late 1743, including both *A True Dialogue* and *The Confectioner General*, shared the same nominal publisher, one Benjamin Cowse of Paternoster Row.[52] A number of other publications with which he was involved during this period suggest that Cowse was connected with the opposition Whig campaign. The first of these was the pamphlet referred to earlier, *A Defence of the People*, for which Cowse was initially advertised as being the publisher.[53] More significantly, his was one of the four names that appeared on the colophon of the *Old England Journal* between 1743 and 1744. Another of these names was that of the leading trade publisher Mary Cooper.[54] From the testimony that he gave following his arrest for his role in *A True Dialogue*, it appears that Cowse had gone to work for Cooper in April 1743. He also claimed to transact occasional business on his own behalf.[55] As a trade publisher, Cooper provided booksellers, printers, and authors of mostly topical publications with access to an extensive and efficient distribution system. Another advantage that she provided was that of concealment. Thus, for a relatively small additional cost, any author could forgo the distributive inconvenience of a totally false imprint, and pay Cooper to stand between them and the authorities.[56] For these reasons, it seems

---

[51] Quoted in A..Foord, *His Majesty's Opposition, 1714–1830* (Oxford, 1964), 248.

[52] See e.g. *The ·Yellow Sash, or, H——r Beshit: An Excellent New Ballad* (1743): *Beef and Butt Beer, against Mum and Pumpernickle: H-n——r Scrubs, or a British Glory Revived* (1743); *Bumper to Old England, Huzza: A Drinking Song* (1743); *The Jubilade—an Ode* (1744).

[53] See *OEJ* 8 Oct. 1743. The eventual publisher was another trade publisher, Jacob Robinson.

[54] The two other names to appear on the colophon of the paper were J. Purser, the de facto printer of the paper, and Jane Morgan, who was Cooper's sister.

[55] PRO, TS 11/982.

[56] See M. Treadwell, 'London Trade Publishers, 1675–1750', The *Library*, 6th ser., 4 (1982), 91–134.

that between 1742 and 1744 Cooper was given the job of distributing the *Old England Journal*.

One further item published in 1743 for which Cowse was the nominal publisher, and which forms another possible link between Cowse and Cooper and the opposition Whigs, was the printed version of the Earl of Stair's memorial. A copy of this memorial, which justified Stair's resignation of the command of the Allied army on the Continent in September, is known to have been sent by Stair to Chesterfield.[57] Apart from Chesterfield and the Pelhams, there is no way of telling how many others received copies, but it is doubtful either that they were members of the opposition or that they numbered more than a handful.[58] Irritatingly, whether Chesterfield was himself responsible for the memorial's publication must remain an open question. Furthermore, against this possibility must be weighed Thomas Birch's claim at the time that the opposition was actually suppressing the memorial because of Stair's support for a bellicose interventionist strategy.[59] Nevertheless, what cannot be denied is that both Cooper and Cowse had links in this period with the opposition Whigs, which could have been exploited to disseminate the popular anti-Hanoverian propaganda of late 1743.

The immediate impact of the opposition Whig press campaign and, in particular, of *The Case of the Hanover Troops* can be partly explained by the effects on press and public debate of the Hanoverian neutrality, which were described in the last chapter. An important factor behind the continued success of Chesterfield and his colleagues in stimulating widespread popular support for their attacks on Carteret and the Hanoverian troops during 1743 was the changing international situation. In late 1742 (as was also shown in the last chapter) opposition and ministerial attitudes towards the war had polarized against the background of the collapse of the French military and diplomatic position in Europe and the empire. In the present context, it is worth emphasizing just how dramatic the shift in the character of the war had been during 1742, and how great had been the associated changes in domestic perceptions of the situation on the Continent.

This is very clearly illustrated by two prints, *The Queen of Hungary Stript* and *The Queen of Hungary in Splendor, or the Monsieurs Pounded*

[57] See BL Add. MS 32701, fos. 117–20: Newcastle to Orford, 16 Sept. 1743.
[58] See BL Add. MS 35396, fos. 161–3: Birch to Yorke, 1 Oct. 1743.
[59] Ibid., fos. 176–7: Birch to Yorke, 15 Oct. 1743.

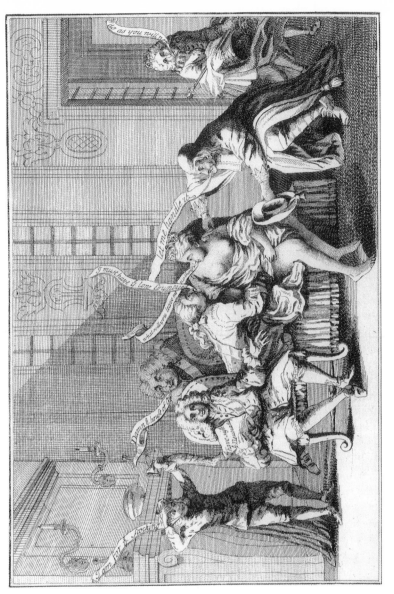

PL. 4. The Queen of Hungary Stript.

Pl. 5. The Queen of Hungary in Splendor, or the Monsieurs Pounded in Prague.

in Prague, published at the beginning and end of the year respectively.[60] In the former, Maria Theresa is being stripped by Frederick II of Prussia and Cardinal Fleury of France, while Spain steals away with Austria's Italian provinces. George II is seated in a chair, his concern for his electorate and the international situation clearly satisfied by the neutrality convention, a copy of which he holds in one hand. Behind him lurks the figure of Walpole, who is cursing the Habsburg family. In the latter the positions are reversed. Maria Theresa, supported by her Hungarian subjects, has trapped Belle-Isle and his army in Prague. The British, under the command of Stair, are coming to add their weight to her forces, dragging the reluctant Dutch along in their wake. Louis XV is kneeling in the background, surrounded by various of his now despairing allies, and lamenting the dissolution of his schemes of 'Universal Empire'.

Significantly, during 1743 not only did the position of the French continue to deteriorate, but the character of the war was altered still further by a related enlargement of British war aims associated with Carteret's ambitious diplomacy. In May 1742 British troops were deployed in Flanders with the object of disabling French schemes to dismember the Austrian empire; by mid-1743 British war aims embraced the divestment of Lorraine and parts of Alsace from France (Carteret's war of equivalents) in order to compensate Austria for the cession of Silesia to Prussia at the Peace of Breslau. As one anonymous pamphleteer exclaimed in February 1743; 'We now make war to conquer France.'[61] The predominant effect of these developments on press debate was to facilitate the efforts of opposition polemicists to dissociate the events on the Continent from recognized British strategic and commercial interests.

Both in Parliament and the press the opposition Whigs sought to exploit the changing situation in Europe by repeatedly returning to two basic propositions. The first, and one that had repercussions at almost all levels of debate, was the absence of a French threat to the balance of power in Europe and, in particular, to the Dutch Barrier in the Austrian Netherlands. The obvious reluctance of the Dutch to join Carteret's schemes substantially strengthened the opposition's counter-claims to ministerial assertions that Britain was still struggling against

[60] Pls. 4 and 5.
[61] *An Englishman's Answer to the Present Politicks of the Principal Powers of Europe*, 93.

a French ministry actively engaged in a project to enslave Europe.[62] Dutch policy, it was widely argued by opposition polemicists, was predicated on a realistic assessment of the essentially defensive aims of the French following the collapse of their original goals in 1742. As one pamphleteer remarked of the Dutch Republic:

> She justly thinks, that peace is preferable to war, but whenever her own safety, or that of her Allies, or of Europe, shall make a war necessary, she will not balance a moment: on the contrary, she will immediately engage, and will prosecute it with that vigour, resolution, and courage, which she has heretofore given so many proofs of.[63]

If the French represented no threat to the Barrier, they were also alleged to represent no threat to the balance of power in Germany.

Central to this view, the second of the opposition's basic propositions, was the assumption that the German empire was actually strengthened as a potential bulwark against the French by the elevation of a non-Habsburg, Charles VII of Bavaria, to the imperial throne in 1742.[64] In these circumstances, it was argued, Britain would be best served by working to achieve an accommodation between Austria and the German princes on the basis of the territorial status quo.[65] Whatever the weaknesses of the assumptions that underlay this position, the opposition support for a policy of what was called German union was, at least superficially, rowing with the tide of events between 1742 and 1743.[66] In particular, the closely related assumption that French military power was insufficient to overcome the supposed opposition of most of continental Europe to her domination seemed to be vindicated by the collapse of the French schemes that had driven the early stages of the war. So confident was one opposition pamphleteer of this fact that he claimed that the French plight in the present war indicated

---

[62] For the pro-ministerial portrayal of French war aims in 1743, see *The Present Measures Proved to Be the Only Means of Securing the Balance of Power* (1743), *passim*.

[63] *A Letter from a Member of the States-General in Holland to a Member of Parliament in England* (1743), 40.

[64] See esp. *German Politicks, or, the Modern System Examin'd and Refuted* (1744), *passim*.

[65] See e.g. *Britons Awake and Look Around You, or, Ruin the Inevitable Consequence of a Land-War* (1743), 29; *Free Thoughts on the Late Treaty of Alliance Concluded at Worms* (1743), 43.

[66] The notion of German union was principally flawed by its failure to appreciate the depth of Austro-Prussian rivalry and of Austrian opposition to Bavarian aggrandizement.

the prudence of Germany's princes in allegedly exploiting French ambitions in 1741 to reduce Austria's influence in the empire.[67]

The presence of such arguments in the press during 1743, along with the two propositions discussed above, reflects amongst other things the degree to which the French menace had retreated from the press discussions of Britain's role in the war since the winter of 1741–2. Moreover, their importance was increased by a series of abortive peace initiatives, notably at Prague in 1742 and Hanau in 1743, which seemed to be, at least as far as the opposition press was concerned, further proof that France, together with most of the rest of Europe, was currently disposed towards peace. Against this background, it is hardly surprising that Carteret's far-reaching schemes were widely identified as the principal obstacle to the conclusion of the war on the Continent.

This view, that it was Carteret's adventurous diplomacy that was responsible for the continuation of the war after late 1742, was held by opposition polemicists to be further revealed by the Treaty of Worms, concluded by Britain, Austria, and Sardinia in September 1743.[68] As far as the ministry and their supporters were concerned, any possible criticisms of the terms of the treaty were negated by the necessity of ensuring that Sardinia remained a member of the anti-Bourbon alliance.[69] Opposition polemicists dismissed (unfairly) ministerial claims regarding the difficulty of inducing Sardinia to continue the struggle against the Bourbons. The terms (which included the provision of a subsidy 'tant que la guerre et le Besoin durera') were, these same polemicists argued, unnecessarily favourable to Sardinia. The effects of the treaty, moreover, would simply be to exacerbate the conflict in Europe. As one opposition pamphleteer declared, the treaty was one aspect of a broader policy, the consequences of which were to 'kindle up the flames of war in Germany and Italy'.[70] Much of the argument surrounding this last assertion was focused on the tenth article of the treaty, which committed Britain to supporting Sardinian claims to the territory of Finale. Not only would Sardinian possession of this coastal area have adverse consequences for British trade and navigation, it was argued, but, by proposing the unjustified dispossession of Finale from

---

[67] *German Politicks*, 93.

[68] For the Treaty of Worms, see R. Lodge, *Studies in Eighteenth-Century Diplomacy, 1740–1748* (1930), 31–79.

[69] See *The Answer of a Milanese Gentleman . . . upon the Tenth Article of the Treaty of Worms* (1743), esp. 4.   [70] *Free Thoughts on the Late Treaty of Alliance*, 43.

Genoa, the Treaty of Worms could only inflame the conditions of war and diplomacy in Italy.[71]

Carteret's ambitious war aims, and the alleged effects of his schemes on the prospects for peace on the Continent, were not the only aspects of the conduct of the war to attract the condemnation of the opposition press. No less important, if continual reiteration is an accurate index, was the fact that they were also, as far as the opposition polemicists were concerned, both impractical and the source of a debilitating and potentially ruinous drain on Britain's resources. With regard to feasibility, the role of the Dutch again occupied a prominent position in opposition argument. That this was the case should cause little surprise. Because of the maritime and commercial basis of the British and Dutch economies, it was almost universally held that an indispensable precondition for British intervention in Europe was full Dutch co-operation. To intervene without the Dutch Republic's support would simply allow their merchants to encroach on British trade. Significantly, and this was a point principally raised in the press by the embittered Lord Hervey, Walpole had himself used the neutrality of the Dutch during the War of the Polish Succession to justify his ministry's failure to intervene on the Continent on behalf of Austria between 1733 and 1735.[72] During 1742–4 the likely opposition of many German powers and, in particular, of Prussia was also cited as a reason for doubting the practicability of a policy that aimed at re-creating Austria's ascendancy in the empire.[73] Moreover, by deploying British troops in Flanders, Carteret was actually putting vital British interests at risk by threatening to provoke France into launching a counter-attack in the Low Countries. Ironically, as will be revealed later, the strength of a large part of the opposition press critique of Carteret's conduct of the war was eroded in 1744, when the predictive accuracy of this line of argument was confirmed by the first of Saxe's campaigns in the Austrian Netherlands. With France threatening to overrun large areas of the Low Countries, it became considerably more difficult for opposition writers to deny the existence of a French threat to British interests in Europe.

[71] Ibid. 53–7. See also *The Dutch Reasoner: A Letter from the Hague on the Earl of Chesterfield's Embassy* (1745), 10.

[72] [Hervey] *Miscellaneous Thoughts on the Present Posture of our Foreign and Domestick Affairs* (1742), 52.

[73] See e.g. [Chesterfield] *The Case of the Hanover Forces in the Pay of Great Britain* (1742), 32, 51–2.

The vast bulk of the opposition press argument about the domestic strains imposed by Carteret's bellicose schemes was simply a restatement of the traditional isolationist critique of British participation in so-called land wars, and does not need reformulating here. One feature of this area of debate that is deserving of further comment, however, is the comparisons that many opposition polemicists made between domestic conditions at the outbreak of the War of the Spanish Succession and the outbreak of the present war. Not surprisingly, it was Walpole who was (unfairly) held responsible by the opposition polemicists for the allegedly weakened state, when compared with the situation in 1702, of the British nation in 1742. In particular, his failure to reduce appreciably the size of the national debt and to relieve the British people and commerce from relatively high levels of taxation imposed, it was argued, strict limitations on Britain's room for manœuvre in foreign affairs.[74] In this context, the lessons of the War of the Spanish Succession were obvious. As well as providing an incontrovertible illustration of the domestic strains that would accompany even a successful land war, the earlier war also demonstrated the defensibility of the French position once they were attacked on their own territory. Moreover, it was further argued, Britain no longer possessed military leaders of the calibre of Marlborough.[75]

If Carteret's conduct of the war inevitably carried with it the prospect of ruin, the alternative of a blue-water strategy avoided, it was predictably asserted, all the disadvantages associated with intervention on the Continent. Two features of the opposition press advocacy of a blue-water strategy between 1742 and 1744 stand out. The first is the widespread recommendation of combined operations against the French coast. As is well known, a succession of coastal raids against the French were the Elder Pitt's most original (and unsuccessful) contribution to Britain's role in the Seven Years War.[76] Between 1742 and 1744 all the arguments associated with the expeditions of the late 1750s, along with the vast ignorance regarding the technical difficulties of mounting such

[74] See e.g. *An Important Secret Come to Light, or, the States General's Reasons for Refusing to Guaranty the E——e of H——r* (1743), 51–3; *Britons Awake and Look Around You*, 49–54; *The Case of the Hanover Troops*, 53.

[75] *Britons Awake and Look Around You*, 54.

[76] For the most recent examination of Pitt's contribution to the Seven Years War, see R. Middleton, *The Bells of Victory: The Pitt–Newcastle Ministry and the Conduct of the Seven Years War, 1757–1762* (Cambridge, 1985).

operations, were enthusiastically rehearsed in the opposition press.[77] Thus, coastal raids were widely portrayed as a relatively inexpensive and easy means of diverting large numbers of French troops from other theatres of war.[78]

The second feature is the emergence, albeit as yet submerged under the weight of consideration accorded to the war and diplomacy in Germany, of what was to become the dominant issue of the later stages of the war: namely, Anglo-French commercial rivalry. Perhaps the most interesting example of this was the publication in 1743 of George Burrington's pamphlet *Seasonable Considerations on the Expediency of a War with France*. Like most other opposition polemicists, Burrington opposed the wastage of Britain's resources in a land war. Unlike his fellow opposition writers, however, Burrington was a forceful advocate of war against the French. Behind this position was a deep-seated concern about the French commercial advance over the previous thirty years. In order to arrest and, ultimately, remove the threat posed by this advance, Burrington argued, Britain should undertake military action against the springs of French commercial development. Thus, the French West Indies trade, the French Levant trade, the French fisheries in North America, the French commercial involvement in the Spanish empire, all should be destroyed or disrupted by British naval power. It is worth noting that Burrington, like many of the later proponents of military action against French trade and colonies, had close connections with Britain's North American colonies. He had also made sporadic attempts at the beginning of the decade to draw popular attention to the commercial possibilities represented by the colonies by writing a number of essays on the subject, which were published in the *Champion* between 1741 and 1742.[79] Between 1742 and 1744 the essay paper that displayed the greatest signs of having heeded Burrington's arguments was the *Westminster Journal*. As the paper demanded on 1 September 1744:

Could it be imagined that *England* should call herself emphatically a *maritime power* and affect to despise the naval force of *France*, and yet that after the

[77] For a recent discussion of the many problems associated with combined operations, see R. Harding, 'Sailors and Gentlemen of Parade: Some Professional and Technical Problems concerning the Conduct of Combined Operations in the Eighteenth Century', *Historical Journal*, 32 (1989), 35–55.

[78] *Britons Awake and Look Around You*, 36–41; *Craftsman*, 19 May 1744.

[79] Burrington had served two periods of office as Colonial Governor of North Carolina, 1724–5 and 1731–4. *Champion*, 24 Oct., 3 Nov. 1741; 30 Jan., 4, 11 Feb. 1742.

Danger had been so carefully and early pointed out, we should have been so negligent as not to make any attempt on *New France* [Canada], which is such a check to our *North American* colonies?

In the same issue the paper also drew the attention of its readers to French aggression in North America, exploiting the French attacks on the settlement of Canso in Nova Scotia to underline the immediacy of this threat to Britain's empire.

A major stimulus to the arguments about the prudence of Carteret's so-called 'Don Quixote' diplomacy was the victory over the French at Dettingen in June 1743. The predominant effect of the battle on the British political nation was undoubtedly the creation of a brief wave of enthusiasm for the war in Europe. As Archbishop Herring of York remarked: 'The action was indeed a glorious one and has done more to help the king and his friends to the affection of the public than the most just and prudent administration of twenty years. It has stopped the mouth of malignancy and falls in exactly with our natural pride and vain glory.'[80] The magnitude of the shift in the popular mood and of the expectations raised by Dettingen are indicated by the *Westminster Journal*. Unlike the *Old England Journal*, which attempted to belittle the significance of the battle, the *Westminster Journal* portrayed Dettingen as having created a historic opportunity to impose a conclusive peace on France. As the paper argued on 6 August:

All *Europe* has long felt the power, and seen the views of the *French* court, and I make no scruple to say that her *money* alone hath so long enable them to take Effect. But she has of late too much extended her *liberality*, and too open exposed her *machinations*: The Funds begin to fail and the *conspiracy* against human liberty to unfold itself. The *Refinements* of *Fleury* in all probability will overset the colossus projected by *Richelieu*, and raised under his successors.

Given such popular and press euphoria, even amongst opposition opinion, the doubts that quickly emerged concerning the circumstances both before and after the battle were easily brushed aside. 'Victory', as Joseph Yorke observed at the time, 'has always a right, like charity, to cover a multitude of faults.'[81] Yet if Dettingen represented a great opportunity for, on the one hand, Britain and her allies in the struggle to bridle French ambition and, on the other, the ministry in its relations with the wider political nation, it also created a new set of risks. Failure

---

[80] *The Life and Correspondence of Philip Yorke, Earl of Hardwicke*, ed. Philip Yorke, 3 vols. (Cambridge, 1913), i. 317.
[81] BL Add. MS 35396, fos. 125–6: Yorke to Birch, 24 July 1743.

to realize the popular expectations of quick results from the war would almost inevitably produce an unusually fierce backlash against the ministry. As the Duke of Newcastle remarked to Carteret soon after news of victory had reached London: 'This victory seems to make us masters of every thing, and it is our own fault, if we do not make good use of it.'[82]

What, then, was the significance of these various arguments, and the developments to which they were a response, for the opposition Whig-led press onslaught against Carteret and the Hanoverian troops during 1743? In the first place, they serve to illuminate the development and power of the central feature of the opposition Whig critique of the alleged Hanoverian control of British foreign policy between 1742 and 1744: the identification of Hanoverian aims as the principal cause of the continuation of the war after 1742. Carteret's support for the Hanoverian goals of territorial aggrandizement and enrichment, it was argued, was preventing the pacification of central Europe. Why all these strands of debate should have become so closely intertwined is explained by the same body of propaganda's exploitation of the policies pursued during the initial stages of the war by George II as Elector, and of the doubts raised about the possible military contribution of the Hanoverian troops almost as soon as they were taken into British pay in August 1742.

Together with the Hanoverian neutrality, the other major plank in the opposition press attack on Hanover's role in the early stages of the war was a scheme to dismember the Prussian dominions, which was briefly envisaged by George II in the winter of 1740–1.[83] The scheme seems to have been inadvertently disclosed in early 1742 through the inadequate censorship of diplomatic papers placed before Parliament on the eve of Walpole's fall.[84] Armed with this information, the near effacement of Austrian power in 1741, and even the expansion of the original dispute between Austria and Prussia into a general European war, could be attributed by opposition polemicists to British support for Hanover's incendiary aims. The anti-Prussian scheme, it was argued, was behind the mobilization of the Hanoverian army and the deploy-

---

[82] BL Add. MS 32700 (Newcastle Papers), fo. 245: Newcastle to Carteret, 24 June 1743.
[83] For this, see U. Dann, *Hanover and Great Britain, 1740–1760: Diplomacy and Survival* (Leicester, 1991), 27–31.
[84] This was the explanation of the disclosure of the scheme put forward by various opposition writers. See e.g. *The Detector Detected* (1743), 49.

ment of the British-paid Danes and Hessians in the electorate in 1741. Had Britain ignored Hanover's aims and supported a policy of accommodation with regard to the differences between Austria and Prussia following Frederick II's invasion of Silesia in late 1740, it was further alleged (as it had been between 1741 and 1742), France would never have had the opportunity to enter the war. Moreover, that such a policy had been practicable in 1741 was revealed by the proposals that Frederick II had put forward at the time for very limited cessions of Austrian territory to satisfy Prussia's larger dynastic claims.[85] In this context, it was once again the Dutch, who had advocated supporting an accommodation between Austria and Prussia in 1741, who provided the contrast to the imprudent and self-interested conduct of George II and Hanover.[86]

These arguments, and the closely related claim that Hanover's desire for territorial gain continued to direct Britain's role in the war, were supported by frequent references to the diplomacy of George I and, in particular, to the debates occasioned by the Hanoverian acquisition of the duchies of Bremen and Verden, Hanover's spoil from the collapse of the Swedish empire in the Great Northern War (1700–21). The need to retain Bremen and Verden, and Hanover's further aim of controlling the duchy of Mecklenburg, was held to be the spring of the allegedly anti-Austrian direction of foreign policy during the years of Walpolian rule, and the underlying cause of the problems confronting Europe in the 1740s.[87] The importance that contemporaries attached to the issue of the purchase of Bremen and Verden is suggested by a number of attempts made by pro-ministerial pamphleteers to refute the opposition allegations that George I had used British diplomatic and naval resources to acquire the duchies.[88] Rehearsing the debates of the late 1710s had the additional advantage for the opposition of not only recalling the Whig split of 1717–20, thereby countering to some extent ministerial accusations that disloyalty was the motivating force behind the present anti-Hanoverian outburst, but also of casting further doubt on Hanoverian (and therefore Carteret's) commitment to the declared aim of supporting Austria.

---

[85] See esp. *The Question Stated with Regard to our Army in Flanders* (1743), 56–7; *A Defence of the People* (1743), 137–8.

[86] See esp. *A Letter from a Member of the States-General in Holland, to a Member of Parliament in England* (1743), *passim*.

[87] *The Case of the Hanover Troops*, 1–15; *A Vindication of a Late Pamphlet, 1–15; A Farther Vindication of a Late Pamphlet, passim*.

[88] [Horatio Walpole] *The Interest of Great Britain Steadily Pursued* (1743); *A Vindication of our Present Royal Family*.

The concrete proof that Carteret was allowing the aims of Hanover to dictate his conduct of Britain's role in the war was, of course, the award of British pay to the 16,000 Hanoverian troops in 1742. The employment of the Hanoverians, or so the opposition Whig polemicists argued, provided the single most important explanation of Britain's intervention on the Continent. Thus, the deployment of British troops in Flanders and the mobilization of the Pragmatic army were, it was alleged, simply a means to justify this measure.[89] Again, as with so many other strands of the opposition Whig press campaign during 1743, the plausibility of this claim was increased by the dramatic collapse of the French threat to European stability during the second half of 1742.[90] Moreover, as a means of arousing popular concern about the influence of Hanoverian interests, the value of the Hanoverian troops was greatly enhanced by the terms and circumstances under which they were initially taken into British pay. In the first place, although payment to the electorate had commenced in August, the 16,000 Hanoverians did not set out from Hanover until mid-September, and then, on reaching Flanders, almost immediately took up winter quarters. Equally suggestive was the fact that the terms of service agreed between the ministry and George II compared very unfavourably, from a British point of view, with those that had been stipulated in a similar subsidy treaty in 1702. Perhaps the most glaring difference between the treaties of 1702 and 1742, as the opposition press was quick to point out, was the latter's provision for the payment of levy money, a payment that also seemed to ignore the fact that the Hanoverians had been fully mobilized in 1741.[91]

The military utility of the Hanoverians was also questioned in terms of the threat of an imperial ban that, it was confidently predicted, would be enforced against the electorate in the event of its troops undertaking military action against the head of the empire in Germany. Hanover's recognition of imperial authority was alleged to have been manifested by George II's vote as Elector for Charles VII of Bavaria's election to the imperial throne in 1742, and by his participation in a vote of a imperial tax to the new Emperor.[92] The fear of incurring an

---

[89] For this, see esp. *A Vindication of a Late Pamphlet*, 40–54.

[90] For the argument that the mobilization of the Pragmatic army served no military purpose, see esp. *The Question Stated with Regard to our Army in Flanders*, *passim*.

[91] See e.g. *A Vindication of a Late Pamphlet*, 48–9; *A Defence of the People*, 132–3; *OEJ* 5 Nov. 1743; *WJ* 12 Nov. 1743.

[92] The most detailed discussion of the contemporary relevance and operation of the imperial ban was provided by the author of *German Politicks*. See also *The Question Stated with Regard to our Army in Flanders*, 39–46.

imperial ban, it was further argued, had prevented the Hanoverians from pursuing the retreating Maillebois across Germany during the summer of 1742, and thereby preventing his junction with the besieged Belle-Isle at Prague. The importance of these opposition allegations is indicated by the anxiety of Newcastle and some of his ministerial colleagues when Carteret and George II decided to leave the Pragmatic army in Flanders in late 1742 rather than marching it into Germany to take up winter quarters. To have taken the latter course, as Newcastle pointed out in a memorandum in late 1743, would have effectively undermined the opposition's assertion that the Hanoverians 'can't, won't, nor ought to act'.[93]

It has recently been argued that the campaign against Hanover in this period was primarily concerned with domestic politics.[94] It is not necessary to accept this view to recognize the very great contribution that certain domestic factors (and one domestic factor in particular) made to the intensity of the press campaign against Carteret and Hanover. As might be expected, the particular domestic circumstance that exerted a powerful influence on both the content and reception of the propaganda of the opposition Whigs and others was the reaction of the bulk of the political nation to the narrow political settlement that followed Walpole's fall. The importance of popular and press responses to what was seen as a great betrayal by Pulteney and his fellow new Whigs has already been sufficiently emphasized in a number of places in the present work. Moreover, as we saw in the last chapter, the influence of the popular indignation created by the events that followed Walpole's departure from office was already very clearly manifest in the latter part of 1742 at most levels of the developing press debate about the new ministry's conduct of the war.

In the longer term, it was another of the effects of the political settlement of 1742—the growing disillusionment and indifference towards national politics—which can be seen to have most influenced the continuing debate about the war. In fact, as early as the first issue of the *Old England Journal* Chesterfield was forced to remark of the widespread cynicism about the possibilities of opposition arising from Pulteney's betrayal:

---

[93] *The Case of the Hanover Forces*, 42, 60, 68; *An Impartial Review of the Present Troubles of Germany* (1743), 10; *A Great Man's Speech in Downing Street against the Enquiry* (1743); Yorke, *Hardwicke*, i. 318–19.

[94] Dann, *Hanover and Great Britain*, 48.

I know that the conduct of those who sneak'd and abandon'd their principles upon the late change of ministry, is sometimes made use of as an Argument why all opposition must be *fruitless*, since all mankind, they say, employ it only as the *means of their preferment*. This Argument is in point of *Fact* absolutely False, and in point of *Reasoning* extremely inconclusive.[95]

By late 1744 the opposition Whigs were themselves attacking the pervasiveness of popular indifference towards national politics as part of their efforts to revive hostility towards Carteret's conduct of the war on the eve of a new parliamentary session.[96] In the short term, however, Pulteney's apostacy in 1742 created a large residuum of popular hostility towards the new Whigs that could be exploited in a campaign to drive Carteret from power. That this animus towards the new Whigs was vital to the success of the opposition Whig press campaign in 1743 is disclosed not only by opposition Whig propaganda itself, but also by the arguments articulated in other papers and pamphlets in this period.

Perhaps the most important illustration of the undisguised appeal that the opposition Whigs made to the popular hatred of the new Whigs is the one aspect of the attacks against the employment of the Hanoverian troops that has not yet been discussed: the emphasis on the role of Carteret. It was not simply that it was argued that this measure had been contrived to establish Carteret's influence over George II; similar allegations had been levelled against Walpole for most of his period in office. Rather, what was significant about the opposition Whig allegations was that it was argued that taking the Hanoverians into British pay had been necessitated by the particular circumstances of the admission of the new Whigs into the ministry. To overcome the resentment of George II on being forced to part with his chief minister, and to circumvent the distrust of the old corps Whigs left in the administration, Carteret, or so opposition Whig propaganda claimed, had made the advantage of Hanover his only goal in the conduct of the war. Given that, following the French intervention in the war, the territorial aggrandizement of Hanover was no longer practicable, the chosen vehicle for this scheme was the subsidization of the Hanoverian troops.[97] One aspect of this measure that was alleged to underline Carteret's motivation was his failure to submit it to prior discussion in Parliament. Carteret's actions in this respect, and his supposed view of Parliament as simply an institution to ratify and provide financial

---

[95] *OEJ* 5 Feb. 1743.   [96] Ibid. 29 Sept. 1743.
[97] See e.g. *A Vindication of a Late Pamphlet*, 41–3; *OEJ* 5 Nov. 1743.

support for the measures of the executive, led the opposition Whigs to dub the ministry 'a prerogative administration'. Furthermore, by employing the Hanoverians, Carteret was, it was alleged, outdoing anything essayed by his predecessor. As Chesterfield wrote in the *Old England Journal*: 'the safety and profit of H——n Dominions had never been made the immediate, open, and avow'd cause of sacrificing the nearest and dearest of this nation.'[98] In the same issue the paper also declared that it had been established to oppose 'those who have found the secret of acquiring more infamy in ten months than their predecessors with all the pains they took could acquire in twenty years'.

As was referred to above, the contemporary importance of such declarations is further revealed by the evidence of other papers and pamphlets published in 1743. Of the papers, the most vigorous scourge of Carteret and the new Whigs was the *Craftsman*. Throughout 1743–4 the *Craftsman* returned again and again to the issue of the position of the monarch's favourite in English history, comparing Carteret with other past favourites who had aroused the hatred of the English people, such as Buckingham and Strafford. The lesson provided by these historical parallels was inescapable: by allowing Carteret to remain in power, George II was endangering the security of the Hanoverian and Protestant succession.[99] In February 1743 the same paper argued a rather different case for opposition to the new Whigs. On 12 February this was summarized in the blunt declaration: 'If it was a breach of Trust and Abuse of Confidence that they opposed in ******* [Walpole], it is the same with double and treble Aggravations, that we oppose in them, and will oppose, till they meet with the Punishment which they remitted to him, for fear of a precedent which might prove fatal to themselves.'[100]

Among the many pamphlets published during 1743, the one that stands out, and one that revived all the animosities and recriminations created by the apostacy of the new Whigs in 1742, was Perceval's *Faction Detected by the Evidence of Facts*. As was shown in an earlier chapter, this muscular vindication of the new Whigs, published in September, had an impact that was unparalleled in the press of the 1740s. Despite its enormous length of over 170 pages and its relatively high cost of 2*s.*, it had sold out in at least six editions by the end of the year. Over the next few months it provoked at least seven substantial

---

[98] *OEJ* 5 Feb. 1743.
[99] See e.g. *Craftsman*, 14, 21, 28 May, 4 June, 8 Oct. 1743; 25 Feb., 3, 17 Mar., 22 Sept. 1744.   [100] See also ibid. 5 Feb. 1743.

pamphlets that directly addressed themselves to rebutting the major lines of argument employed by Perceval.[101] It also immediately provoked the publication of *A Congratulatory Letter to a Certain Right Honourable Person upon his Late Disappointment* (1743), a scathing satire on the Earl of Bath's failure to be appointed First Lord of the Treasury following Lord Wilmington's death during the summer. Like *Faction Detected*, this pamphlet quickly sold out in a number of early editions. What is very striking about these pamphlets is that they were creating a stir just when popular concern about the role of Hanover and the Hanoverian troops was reaching its climax. In this respect, it is also worth noting that *Faction Detected*, as Horace Walpole observed at the time, provided, amongst other things, the most comprehensive contemporary rebuttal of the anti-Hanoverian arguments of the opposition Whigs.[102]

The immediate cause of the public uproar in the winter of 1743–4 was the mutual influence of the press and the events of the summer's military campaign. Even before the campaign had commenced, Horatio Walpole remarked to Robert Trevor that the failure to avoid 'disgrace on the other side or inaction' would 'cause a most troublesome and boisterous scene next sessions'.[103] Unfortunately for supporters of the ministry, despite the initial success at Dettingen, the military campaign of 1743 fully confirmed this prediction. No attempt was made to exploit the military opportunities that had been created by the victory of Dettingen, and for the major part of the remainder of the campaigning season the Pragmatic army, on arriving at Hanau, was completely inactive. When the army did finally move towards the Rhine in conjunction with the Austrian forces under Prince Charles of Lorraine, no significant actions resulted. Although the Rhine was eventually crossed, the campaign ended without any further military engagements with the French.

Nor did the bad news stop there. Even more alarming, at least as far as the ministry was concerned, were the disagreements and antagonism between the British and Hanoverian contingents in the army during the campaign. The discontent among the British troops and officers was brought to a head by George II's unguarded demonstrations of his preference for the Hanoverian rank and file after he joined the army at Aschaffenburg on the river Main just before Dettingen. Any possibility

---

[101] See above, Ch. 2, for these pamphlets.
[102] Lewis, *Walpole*, xviii. 315–21: Walpole to Mann, 3 Oct. 1743.
[103] HMC, Fourteenth Report, Appendix 9, 87: Walpole to Trevor, 25 Apr. 1743.

that the ministry would be able to minimize the impact of these events was completely removed in September, when the Earl of Stair resigned his command in protest at his lack of influence and the conduct of the campaign after Dettingen. As has already been referred to, Stair presented George II with a memorial in justification of this action. In this memorial Stair was not only openly critical of the dependence on what he described as 'inferior channels', by which he meant the Hanoverians, following George II's arrival in the army, but he also alleged that the Hanoverians had been allowed to exercise complete control over all aspects of the campaign, including even 'the minutest detail of Bread and Forage'. The memorial also described various schemes that Stair had unsuccessfully proposed during the summer, designed, first, to harry the French retreat from Germany and, second, to invade French territory. It concluded by reaffirming Stair's long-standing support for an aggressive anti-French foreign policy, citing as evidence, amongst other things, the memorial of 1734 that had been submitted to Queen Caroline arguing the necessity of intervening in support of the Austrians in the War of the Polish Succession.

The impact of Stair's action was significantly increased by the fact that his loyalty to the Hanoverian dynasty was unassailable. He was, moreover, also a veteran of Marlborough's glorious campaigns of the 1700s. As the *Old England Journal* exclaimed, he was a '*British General*, bred up in camps, where *British* views, supported by *British* valour, had been crown'd with deserv'd success'.[104] His resignation and memorial, published in London in October, thus gave credibility to the numerous reports, rumours, and allegations regarding the role of George II and the Hanoverian troops during the summer's campaign that were being disseminated in the capital in late 1743. The most inflammatory reports came from the army abroad, and concerned the discontent caused by George II's conduct and the alleged precedence accorded to the Hanoverians in the allocation of quarters and supplies. As Thomas Birch wrote on 29 October:

[The] general conversation of the people here turns upon nothing else than the tragical stories brought from our army of the contempt & ill treatment, which they pretend to have receiv'd on all occasions. I am well convinc'd that all these Accounts are monstrously aggravated, but the Effect of them is real & extremely unseasonable at the Beginning of a session of Parliament.[105]

[104] *OEJ* 5 Nov. 1743. See also *A Letter to the E—— of S——r* (1743), 9; *A Letter from an Officer in the Army of the Allies* (1743), esp. 5–6.
[105] BL Add. MS 35396, fos. 184–5: Birch to Yorke, 29 Oct. 1743.

At the beginning of October the role of George II and the Hanoverian troops during the summer had provoked Birch to exclaim: 'I need make no Reflections upon the consequences of such conduct; But you will readily see, what a new fund of materials it will afford next winter to sollicit the passions, & feed the ill humour of the Nation.'[106] Birch, as mentioned earlier, was a seasoned observer of the press community, yet it is unlikely that he foresaw the scale and fury of the press onslaught against the sacrifice of British interests to Hanoverian ends during the winter of 1743–4.

This press outcry can be broadly divided into two parts: first, the press attacks against the conduct and character of the summer's military campaign; and secondly, the press criticism and abuse provoked by the respective roles of George II and the Hanoverian troops at the head of, and as part of, the Pragmatic army. The task of vilifying the conduct of the 1743 military campaign was greatly facilitated by the facts that emerged during the months after Dettingen concerning the inept strategy of the Allied Generals, which had enabled the French, under Marshal Noailles, to outmanœuvre the Pragmatic army before the battle. Having marched to Aschaffenburg, the Pragmatic army had found that the French were threatening their supply lines along the river Main, and, as a consequence, they were forced to attempt a difficult retreat to Hanau.[107] As the Duke of Richmond had written on 7 July, 'we were then certainly in a cul de sac'.[108] Moreover, the fact that, in a position of huge strategic inferiority, the allies had avoided a crushing defeat at Dettingen owed less to their own military capabilities than to a rash charge at the start of the battle by the Duke de Grammont at the head of the French cavalry.[109] Not surprisingly, Stair was vigorously (and undeservedly) absolved by the opposition press from any responsibility for the decisions that had created this potential disaster.[110] Dettingen itself, meanwhile, dwindled to a 'chance-medley Escape' and 'the Escape of the Army', its significance being further questioned in the light of, first, the failure (contrary to Stair's advice) to pursue the French forces in the immediate aftermath of the battle

---

[106] Ibid., fos. 161–3: Birch to Yorke, 1 Oct. 1743.

[107] For details of the battle, see R. Butler, *Choiseul: Father and Son, 1719–1754* (Oxford, 1980), pp. 409–18.

[108] HMC, Fourteenth Report, Appendix 9, 89: Richmond to Trevor, 9 July 1743.

[109] *WJ* 22 Oct. 1743; *The Triumphant Campaign* (1743), 9.

[110] *OEJ* 24 Sept. 1743; *WJ* 22 Oct. 1743; *The Triumphant Campaign*, esp. 44; *The Mysterious Congress* (1743), 15.

and, second, the decision to leave the field of battle, along with the English dead and wounded, to the defeated French.[111]

It is a measure of how far the exploitation of such facts in the opposition press had transformed popular attitudes towards Dettingen by late 1743 that the City of London's address to the Crown on George II's return from the Continent in November deliberately omitted to make any mention of the battle.[112] This omission provoked vigorous condemnation from at least one pro-ministerial pamphleteer, and was also in pointed contrast to the other addresses to the Crown on the same occasion.[113] Another consequence of the disclosure of the various facts about Dettingen discussed above, together with the inactivity that characterized the rest of the campaign, was that a number of opposition polemicists strongly questioned whether George II and Carteret had had any real intention of attacking the French. Rather, just as the deployment of the Pragmatic army in Flanders in 1742 had been portrayed as having been designed solely to justify the employment of the Hanoverian troops, the march into Germany, it was alleged, was motivated by the need to defuse the popular opposition created by this measure. As one pamphleteer exclaimed, the 1743 campaign had been a 'parading pacifick scheme'.[114]

These arguments were made all the more plausible by the ambiguities that surrounded the role of the Hanoverians at Dettingen. In this context, much was made of the positioning of the Hanoverian troops at the rear of the army during the retreat from Aschaffenburg. Ministerial claims that the French had been expected to launch their attack from the rear were derided, and the deployment of the Hanoverians was unequivocally asserted to have been motivated by the overriding aim of keeping them isolated from any actual fighting. The operation of this motive, it was claimed, was placed beyond all reasonable doubt by the refusal of the Hanoverian General who had been placed in command of the Hanoverian and British troops that made up the rearguard to bring his troops to the front of the army at the end of the battle to facilitate the pursuit of the fleeing French forces. Unsurprisingly, this General, dubbed the Confectioner General by the opposition press, was the object of a volley of press outrage and abuse

---

[111] *OEJ* 31 Dec. 1743; 7 Jan. 1744.   [112] *London Gazette*, 19 Nov. 1743.

[113] *A Vindication of our Present Royal Family*, p. ix. The other addresses were published in successive issues of the *Gazette* between Nov. 1743 and Feb. 1744.

[114] *An Impartial Review of the Present Troubles of Germany*, 22. See also *The Triumphant Campaign, passim.*

that included a number of extremely crude and scatalogical ballads.[115] One claim that was frequently reiterated was that cowardice was an important feature of the Hanoverian national character. In support of this assertion, opposition polemicists disinterred William III's alleged remarks during the Nine Years War that the Hanoverians were only good for running away.[116] Predictably, as well as emphasizing the supposed pusillanimity of the Hanoverian soldiery, the same opposition polemicists also spared no efforts to praise the bravery of the 'free-born' Englishmen, which, it was asserted, had been displayed to full advantage at Dettingen. In this respect, it was once again Stair's role, this time at the head of the victorious Allied army, which provided the exemplar against which the military shortcomings of the Hanoverians were measured.[117]

As these and similar polemical strategies reveal, an important element of the popular discontent of the winter of 1743–4 was the extreme xenophobia of the majority of the English people. The depth of the popular commitment to hatred of foreigners throughout the eighteenth century has been noted again and again; and between 1742 and 1744 opposition polemicists vied with each other to heap more and more abuse on to both Hanover and the Hanoverian troops. In this context, none doubted the extreme poverty and insignificance of the electorate. According to the *Westminster Journal*, Hanover was 'a spot of German Furze and Heath'; while the *Old England Journal* declared that it was a 'province scarce known to the world, scarce to be found on the map'.[118] Somewhat inconsistently, opposition polemicists also argued that Hanover's present wealth and international influence were solely derived from its connection with Britain. By way of contrast, Britain was portrayed as a country of potentially limitless wealth and an imperial destiny. As one pamphleteer exalted, Britain was 'the most splendid throne in Europe'.[119] The immense gulf between the two countries was portrayed in a different way in the ballad *The Wife and the Nurse*, in which Hanover was depicted as an upstart 'tatter'd Nurse of Aspect Glum', and her charge, Britain, as 'an Island-Nymph most fair'. Union with Hanover, opposition polemicists further argued, was

[115] See e.g. *OEJ* 26 Nov., 10, 31 Dec. 1743; *WJ* 31 Jan. 1744; *The Yellow Sash, or, H——r Beshit; Beef and Butt Beer.*

[116] See esp. *The English Nation Vindicated from the Calumnies of Foreigners* (1744), 8–12.

[117] See esp. *A Letter from an Officer in the Army of the Allies*, 2–3; *The Triumphant Campaign*, 45.   [118] *WJ* 13 Oct. 1743; *OEJ* 29 Oct. 1743.

[119] *English Loyalty Opposed to Hanoverian Ingratitude* (1744), 12.

depriving Britain of the advantages of her island position, and entangling her in continental rivalries. Such claims played remorselessly on the great upsurge of bellicose mercantilism that swept through the English nation at the end of the 1730s.[120] It is also worth noting here that a prominent theme in the opposition Whig propaganda was Carteret's abandonment of the so-called 'national war' against Spain, which, it was continually recalled, he had advocated between 1738 and 1741, when he had been a leading member of the opposition.

One other factor that ensured that the full force of popular xenophobia was directed against Hanover and the Hanoverians was the popular perception, at least before early 1744, that the French had temporarily ceased to represent a major threat to British interests and security. As the aptly entitled pamphlet *Popular Prejudice Concerning Partiality to the Interests of Hanover* (1743), the author of which purported to be a Hanoverian officer, observed: 'All our Advices agree that their [the English] jealousy to Foreigners, so natural to that selfish Nation, is of late confined to us H——ns; Their Rancour to the French holds at present, but the second place.'[121]

The exploitation of popular xenophobia was also a prominent element in the opposition press attacks provoked by George II's role at the head of the Pragmatic army, and the resulting discontent of the British soldiery (the second major element of the anti-Hanoverian press outcry of late 1743). Not only was George II and Carteret's connivance at the Hanoverian control of the summer's military campaign portrayed as a reversal of the normal relationship between paymaster and mercenary, it was also alleged to have inflicted a huge blow to English national honour. As the *Old England Journal* declared on 24 December: '*Injuries* were aggravated by *Insults*; nor was *victory* over our *Interests* thought sufficient without a Triumph over our *Honour*.' Of the 'injuries' to the British soldiery that were singled out for particular press attention, the gravest was held to be the supposed favour shown to the Hanoverians regarding the provision of supplies and the allocation of quarters during the campaign. In this context, the image of the starving but courageous British soldier was exploited most intensively in the more populist polemic. The trooper in the cheap pamphlet *A True Dialogue between a Trooper and a Serjeant* (1743) was made to declare: 'I am sure they [Hanoverian troops] were not us'd as they deserv'd now; for they were

---

[120] See esp. K. Wilson, 'Empire, Trade and Popular Politics in Mid-Hanoverian Britain: The Case of Admiral Vernon', *Past and Present*, 121 (1988), *passim*.
[121] *Popular Prejudice*, 3.

well-us'd. They had their Bellies full, while we were starv'd; and the *English* could have nothing till the H-n——ns were first serv'd.'[122] Similarly, one of the verses of the cheap ballad entitled *Beef and Butt Beer, against Mum and Pumpernickle* (1743), read:

> Our Men almost starv'd, yet in Heart were full stout,
> They repuls'd, they attack'd, and the French were put to rout.
> The H-n——ns tho' cram'd to the Eyes with good food,
> Fac'd about to the Right and sneak'd into the wood.

A number of opposition polemicists made little attempt to disguise the fact that they held George II primarily responsible for the conduct of the Hanoverians during the campaign, a conviction that was reinforced by his decision to sport the yellow sash of Hanover rather than the red of England during the battle of Dettingen. However, few were as blunt as the author of *A True Dialogue*, who asserted that Stair's exclusion from a position of influence over the affairs of the Pragmatic army had only occurred 'after *Somebody* [i.e. George II] came to the Army'.[123] As with the role of the Hanoverians at Dettingen, the grievances arising from George II's role at the head of the army were magnified in the opposition press by constant references to, on the one hand, past scenes of British military glory such as Agincourt and Blenheim and, on the other, the Hanoverians' alleged national cowardice.[124]

This alleged contrast between Hanoverian 'slaves' and 'free-born' Englishmen was also at the heart of the allegations made by a number of opposition polemicists that George II's conduct during the summer was a direct threat to the English constitution and English liberties. On this issue, as with so many other areas of press debate between 1742 and 1744, the most outspoken elements of the press were the two leading opposition weeklies, the *Old England Journal* and the *Westminster Journal*. In fact, as early as the first issue, the *Old England Journal* had signalled its willingness both to exploit the possible constitutional implications of Hanover's alleged control of British foreign policy and to employ radical Whig language to arouse popular concern. Thus Chesterfield had declared that the Crown had been settled on the Hanoverian dynasty in the belief that its rulers would never act to the disadvantage of British interests. In the same issue Chesterfield had also included the minatory observation that the people had never alienated their right to

---

[122] *A True dialogue*, 3.   [123] Ibid., esp. 7–8.
[124] See esp. *OEJ* 8, 29 Oct. 1743.

cashier their rulers should the latter again infringe English liberties. The libertarian theme was reiterated in the second issue of the paper, with the claim that Carteret's conduct of the war had reduced politics to the simple alternatives of either 'National Independence' and 'constitutional Allegiance' or 'immediate poverty' and 'Eventual slavery'.[125] Before the winter of 1743–4 the vehemence of the *Old England Journal*'s concern for the integrity of the English constitution was unmatched amongst the other opposition papers. However, between December and January of the following year both the *Old England Journal* and the *Westminster Journal*, under the stimulus of George II's role at the head of the Pragmatic army, carried alarmist warnings to the effect that the Anglo-Hanoverian union represented a very immediate threat to English liberty.

Not surprisingly, the *Old England Journal* was the first to publish such a warning. On 3 December the paper argued that the dangers implicit in the Anglo-Hanoverian Union were twofold. First, Hanover represented a continual drain on British power and wealth. Secondly, George II, as an arbitrary ruler in Hanover, would necessarily confer his favour on those ministers who would support an attempt to establish arbitrary rule in England. In the same issue it was also argued that George II's conduct during the 1743 military campaign threatened to 'annihilate fundamental Rights and to extinguish 'British liberty and Independency for ever and ever'. Recommending the seventeenth-century Whig exclusionists as a model for emulation, the paper concluded by calling for the immediate legislative dissolution of the Anglo-Hanoverian union. Early in 1744 the *Old England Journal* further reminded its readers of the libertarian origins of the Hanoverian regime:

Whatever might be the Fact, we all know the pretence of the Revolution was to redress the Grievances of the Deliver'd, and not to gratify the Ambition of the Deliverer: And when the Act of Settlement took place, the only compliment thereby made to the House of Hanover was the national belief that under those princes, only our liberties would be safe.[126]

The *Westminster Journal*, meanwhile, avoided the dangers of commenting directly on the role of the monarch in politics, and concentrated instead on exposing the threat to British liberty alleged to be

---

[125] *OEJ* 12 Feb. 1744.   [126] Ibid., 25 Feb. 1744.

represented by the Hanoverian troops. As the paper declared on 14 January 1744:

> *Envy* would at all times prompt them to assist in a *levelling* scheme amongst the subjects of the same Prince, and the very motive that makes the *Devil* tempt souls to *Damnation*, because he is himself already a *damnable state*, would be at any Time sufficient to induce *Hanoverians* or even *mercenary Danes* and *Saxons* to endeavour to effect in *England*, a Throne of Tyranny after the *German* or *Danish* model.

That the threat posed by the Hanoverian troops was more than unsubstantiated alarmism was revealed, the paper further argued, by the absence of any other explanation or purpose for their employment. Moreover, the *Westminster Journal* added: 'Did they not in the Field insult the very men, who tho' in the same Rank of *Service*, and only distinguished by their idea of *Liberty* might be properly said to be *their masters*'. In the same month this line of argument was reiterated in the pamphlet *The English Nation Vindicated from the Calumnies of Foreigners*, which also alleged that the duchy of Bremen was a potential port of embarkation for a Hanoverian-led assault on British liberty.[127]

The impact of these and similar allegations during the winter of 1743–4 is suggested by the efforts of at least two pro-ministerial pamphleteers to rebut the charges that George II and the Hanoverian troops represented a possible threat to the constitution. In late 1743 the author of *Popular Prejudice Concerning Partiality to the Interests of Hanover* asserted that the claims being made in the opposition press regarding the possible use of the Hanoverian troops to enslave Britain were no more than 'whim and chimera'. Moreover, such fears were, the same pamphleteer continued, hardly consistent with the charges made by the same opposition polemicists regarding the deep-seated cowardice of the Hanoverians: 'Surely so eminently brave a Nation as the E——h, are above dreading to be enslaved by a people whom they themselves represent as the most cowardly Nation *in Europe*.'[128]

In April 1744, following the scare created by the French invasion attempt of late February/early March, the author of *An Address to the People of Great Britain* attempted to debunk another of the assumptions that underpinned much of the opposition argument about the threat to English liberty supposedly represented by the Anglo-Hanoverian union; namely, the assumption that German government was tyrannical.

---

[127] *The English Nation Vindicated*, 25. [128] *Popular Prejudice*, 55–6.

The powers of German Princes, this pamphlet asserted, were closely circumscribed by the 'protectorium or conservatorium powers' that resided in the office of the German Emperor. This authority, it was alleged, ensured that the rule of individual Princes in the empire was 'kept within reasonable Bounds'.[129] In this context, the author of *An Address* could also have pointed out that the tendency towards absolute power in Hanover had been arrested in 1714 by the assumption of the British Crown by the electorate's ruling dynasty.[130] Interestingly, the claim that the Hanoverian dynasty aspired to arbitrary rule in England was raised again by a patriot opposition in 1756, when Hanoverian troops were actually deployed in England as part of the ministry's defensive preparations against a possible French invasion. The catalyst on this later occasion was the Attorney-General's decision to issue a warrant releasing a Hanoverian soldier from Maidstone gaol, where he had been placed by local authorities for allegedly stealing some pocket handkerchiefs.[131] The opposition polemicist who was primarily responsible for fanning the flames of popular disquiet created by this incident was the Tory-patriot John Shebbeare. Shebbeare's famous *Letters to the English People* recall amost exactly the arguments that had been exploited to such effect in 1743 by many elements of the opposition press and, in particular, by the *Old England Journal*.

In one major respect, despite the heat generated 'without doors' by the anti-Hanoverian press outcry in the winter of 1743–4, the opposition Whig press campaign failed to achieve its real objective. Largely as a result of the efforts of the veteran Earl of Orford, the ministry's majority in the Commons held relatively firm during the crucial divisions of the 1743–4 parliamentary session.[132] This failure, however, did not cause any abrupt cessation of the opposition Whig intervention in the press. Nor did it provoke any very marked reduction in the intensity of their press campaign against Carteret's conduct of the war and the alleged subserviency of British interests to Hanoverian ends. One measure of their determination in this respect is the relative neglect by the *Old England Journal* of the naval miscarriage that took place at Toulon in March 1744, when the Mediterranean squadron under Admiral Matthews failed, in controversial circumstances, to

---

[129] *An Address to the People of Great Britain by a Country Clergyman* (1744), 8–9.

[130] F. L. Carsten, 'The Empire after the Thirty Years War', in F. L. Carsten (ed.), *Essay in German History* (1985), 115–16.

[131] See M. Peters, *Pitt and Popularity* (Oxford, 1980), 50, 64.

[132] See Owen, *Rise of the Pelhams*, 210–11.

destroy the bulk of the combined Bourbon fleets.[133] Although the paper
printed a letter on 12 May calling for the *Old England Journal* to provide information about the miscarriage, and subsequently itself called
for an inquiry into its causes, it was not until early 1745 that either
Toulon or the broader issue of the shortcomings of the condition and
deployment of the navy became objects of major concern in the paper.

During the spring and summer of 1744 the *Old England Journal*
chose instead to concentrate on events on the Continent and, in
particular, on Hanover's alleged control of Britain's role in the war.
Moreover, this assessment of priorities was shared by its fellow
opposition essay paper, the *Westminster Journal*.[134] Yet, despite the
persistence with which these two essay papers and other elements of the
opposition press continued to exploit popular sensitivity regarding
Hanover's role in British politics, the influence of the opposition press
seems to have considerably diminished in 1744. In part, as noted
earlier, this can be explained by the increasing impact of the disillusionment with national politics that had been produced by Pulteney's
apostacy in 1742. It also owed a great deal to a steady alteration in the
international situation, which commenced in the spring with the French
invasion attempt.

The news in early February that the French planned to invade
Britain was initially received with widespread scepticism. On 7 February the *London Evening Post* declared:

The sudden Disappearance of a certain Young Gentleman in the South [the
Young Pretender], the Pretences that are given for his Absence, and the
mysterious motions of the Brest Fleet, are at present subjects of various
speculations—but the known prudence of the French which seldom suffers
them to make any rash Attempt should be, perhaps, sufficient to satisfy us, that
all is Amusement only, in order to cover their real Designs.

In the next issue the paper hinted strongly that the invasion scare was
being manufactured by the ministry to deflect opposition criticism
of the conduct of the war, an allegation that was widely reiterated
throughout the opposition press.[135] Philip Yorke argued at the time that
the 'perfect deadness and incredulity' of the people was removed by the

---

[133] For Toulon, see H. Richmond, *The Navy in the War of 1739–1748*, 3 vols.
(Cambridge, 1920), ii. 1–54.

[134] The only opposition paper to provide sustained coverage in 1744 of the issues
arising from the miscarriage at Toulon was the *Craftsman*. See e.g. *Craftsman*, 30 June,
21, 28 July, 13 Oct., 3 Nov. 1744.

[135] See e.g. ibid. 18 Feb. 1744; *OEJ* 25 Feb. 1744.

public notification of the French schemes that both Houses of Parliament received from the King on 15 February.[136] The King's message to Parliament, which also alleged that the French plans had been drawn up in conjunction with a number of disaffected persons in Britain, was reinforced on 24 February, when a number of papers were submitted to Parliament's inspection that, the ministry claimed, provided proof of both the reality of the French design and the preparations that had been undertaken to expedite it. On the earlier occasion leading opposition Whigs had unsuccessfully attempted to tack on to the respective addresses of thanks in both Houses motions calling for an immediate inquiry into the state of the navy and the causes of the present danger.[137] These attempts were obliquely defended by the *Old England Journal* on 25 February, when the paper argued that if the threat of a French invasion was in fact real, the situation now facing Britain was proof, if any were needed, of both the imprudence of Carteret's policies and the negligence of the ministry.[138] The invasion scare, it was further argued, also revealed the empty nature of the ministerial claims that had been made throughout the previous year regarding France's vulnerability to attacks against her own territory.[139] On 25 February the *Westminster Journal* asserted that susceptibility to fear was the index of a 'weak and little' mind, and repeated the earlier warnings of the opposition press of the ministry's alleged interest in inducing alarm amongst the people.

Perhaps the most remarkable attack that the opposition press levelled against the ministry's response to the French invasion threat was published in the *Old England Journal* on 3 March. Prefacing its remarks with the admission that the present situation was 'an alarming one', the paper proceeded to question in detail the nature of the information that had been provided by the ministry to substantiate the facts asserted in the King's message to Parliament of 15 Feburary. After describing various alleged shortcomings of this information, the paper concluded: 'The sum total amounts to this that his majesty has heard the Pretender's son is in France: That it is said he is at Calais: Add to that it is the Talk of this place, that Kent or Scotland is to be invaded by 15,000 men in two Dozen transports from Dunkirk.' Furthermore, the paper observed, the information that had been submitted to Parliament had been notably

[136] *Parl. Hist.*, xiii. 641–9.   [137] Owen, *Rise of the Pelhams*, 212–13.
[138] This allegation was also made in the *Craftsman* on 25 Feb. 1744.
[139] *OEJ* 10 Mar. 1744.

silent on the subject of domestic disaffection.[140] On 10 March the paper continued its remorseless hounding of the ministry by attacking the call for 6,000 Dutch troops to help defend Britain against a possible invasion, and alleging that the invasion threat was merely a feint by the French to deflect attention from the opening of an offensive in the Austrian Netherlands.[141]

Despite the fact that as late as 12 March Edward Weston, the Under-Secretary of the southern department, was writing to Newcastle about the publication in pamphlet form of the papers already submitted to Parliament, in order, as Weston remarked, 'to convince Everybody of the Truth of Embarkation', it seems unlikely that either the *Old England Journal* or the *Westminster Journal* made much headway against the wave of defensive loyalism that overtook popular opinion towards the end of February.[142] On 1 March so numerous were the manifestations of this loyalism that Horace Walpole exclaimed: 'The spirit of the Nation has appeared extraordinarily in our favour.'[143] Almost a month later Nicholas Paxton, the former Treasury Solicitor and a key figure in the policing of the press during the previous decade, was advising Newcastle that the favourable movement of opinion as a result of the French invasion attempt had created an opportunity for a full-scale legal attack against the *Old England Journal*: 'Old England was very sawcy last Saturday. With submission to your Grace, if there be anybody to be try'd for libels, I think, according to the present Disposition of the People, they may be convicted in London, or anywhere else.'[144] Perhaps still more significantly, even those opposition papers which maintained their position of hostility towards the conduct of the ministry during the invasion scare, including the *Old England Journal* and the *Westminster Journal*, acknowledged the unanimity of the popular response to the invasion threat. Thus, on 10 March the *Westminster Journal* exploited the upsurge of defensive loyalism to restate the opposition axiom that the 'people', as opposed to either foreign mercenaries or a standing army, were the '*invincible strength and real security*' of the English nation. The *Old England Journal*, meanwhile, argued that the loyalty being demonstrated by the bulk of the nation proved that ministerial claims that the opposition supported

---

[140] See above, Ch. 2, for the opposition press and the question of domestic disaffection.
[141] *OEJ* 10 Mar. 1744.
[142] BL Add. MS 32700, fos. 193–4: Weston to Newcastle, 12 Mar. 1744.
[143] Lewis, *Walpole*, xviii. 497–510: Walpole to Mann, 1 Mar. 1744.
[144] BL Add. MS 32700, fo. 268: Paxton to Newcastle, 29 Mar. 1744.

the Stuart cause had no foundation. It also proved, the paper further argued, that the encouragement that had been provided in recent times to the enemies of the Hanoverian regime proceeded from the measures of the ministry, and not from the conduct of the opposition.[145]

As was to be the case during the Jacobite Rebellion of 1745–6, a principal element of the effusion of loyalist feeling during early 1744 was the widespread revival of popular animosity towards the French. As the author of the pamphlet *A Warning to the Whigs, and to Well-Affected Tories* (1744) remarked:

> The present Tender of her Good will to us, hath made one Discovery notably to her disadvantage and mortification, but equally to our Benefit and Glory, that however Englishmen may differ and dislike and even calumniate, one another, they are unanimous against France, against French Falsehood, French invasion, and a King of French creation.[146]

Pro-ministerial polemicists sought to exploit this reawakening of anti-French feeling by arguing that the invasion attempt had once more revealed the reality of the French threat to European stability and British independency. Thus, the French support for the Jacobites was portrayed as a function of France's historic goal of universal monarchy, and the aim of the invasion attempt as the extinction of Britain's opposition to her schemes. Should the attempt succeed, it was argued, Britain would inevitably be reduced to the status of a mere viceroyalty of France.[147] In support of these claims, much of the history of alleged French ambition and duplicity in the seventeenth century was restated, and great emphasis was placed on Britain's traditional hostility to France.[148] One pamphleteer even alleged that Anglo-French rivalry could be traced back to the Norman Conquest. This rivalry, the pamphleteer claimed, would only cease if France were to change 'all the maxims of her Government'; motives of religion, commerce, and differing principles of government all conduced towards enmity between the two nations.[149] In such circumstances, Britain's interests and security, it was claimed by a number of writers, could only be safeguarded by a policy that aimed permanently to disable France from

---

[145] *OEJ* 17 Mar. 1744.　　[146] *A Warning to the Whigs*, 42.

[147] See e.g. *An Address to the People of Great Britain on the Present Posture of Affairs* (1744); *An Address to the People of Great Britain, on the Present Enterprises of France* (1744).

[148] See esp. *An Apology for the Conduct of France* (1744), 30–40.

[149] *Considerations on the Politics of France* (1744), 2–16.

essaying her ambitious schemes. As the author of *Considerations on the Politics of France* (1744) explained: 'We can never be safe while France is powerful, never be secure in the Possession of our liberties and our properties, if we are not in a condition to prevent any projects she can form for the subversion of both.'[150]

Another effect of the French invasion attempt was to encourage ministerial supporters to commence the reclamation of much of the vocabulary of patriotism.[151] Thus one pamphleteer declared that the 'very zeal' that had been shown in the opposition to the measures of the ministry was 'now the strongest reason for joining with it'. For what was at stake in the present crisis was the 'cause of British Liberty'.[152] Much of the press discussion of the implications of the imposition of a Catholic Stuart monarch supported by France was to be amplified during the Jacobite Rebellion, and is examined in detail in the following chapter. What requires emphasizing here is the fact that the allegations in the opposition press that the Hanoverian control of British foreign policy and the employment of the Hanoverian troops represented a threat to British liberty were rapidly overtaken in the spring of 1744 by strident declarations of the Franco-Jacobite threat to these same liberties.

If, therefore, the French invasion attempt revived the issue of the French threat to British interests and security, the *Old England Journal* and the *Westminster Journal* showed, as their reaction to the invasion scare itself has already demonstrated, few signs of acknowledging this fact. Their determination not to be deflected from attacking Hanover's role in the war, despite the suspension of the Habeas Corpus Act for three months from late February, was further disclosed, almost as soon as the invasion scare had ended, by their respective responses to the French declaration of war against Britain on 15 March. This declaration understandably placed great emphasis on the Hanoverian neutrality convention of 1741, which, the French insisted, had included Britain as well as Hanover within its terms. Rather than follow the court-led rejection of the allegations made in the French declaration, both opposition papers chose to exploit them in order to revive the controversy that had been created by the neutrality and by Haddock's failure to prevent the Spanish expedition to Italy in late 1741. The *Old England Journal* called for an inquiry into the truth of the French allegations,

---

[150] Ibid. 1.
[151] See above, Ch. 2, for the intensification of this process after the '45.
[152] *An Address to the People of Great Britain, on the Present Enterprises of France*, 21.

arguing that the facts cited in the French declaration in defence of their interpretation of the neutrality convention had hitherto gone uncontradicted.[153] The following issue of the paper rehearsed in their entirety the claims that had been made in opposition Whig propaganda during the previous year about George II's anti-Prussian schemes of 1741, in order both to reaffirm the opposition Whig's contention that the war was a 'German war' unrelated to British interests, and to underline Hanoverian responsibility for the situation in which Britain now found itself.[154] On 31 March the *Westminster Journal* remarked: 'War is at length *declared* by the *French* King, against the King of *England*, Elector of *Hanover*; and declared in *such Terms* as fully confirm what has been repeated in this Journal, that the management of *somebody* at Home has fix'd in our Enemies an opinion of our *Disunion* and *Disaffection*.'

In the same issue and in the two following issues the *Westminster Journal*, rather like the *Old England Journal*, proceeded to restate many of the allegations that had been made in the opposition press during the previous eighteen months about Hanover's supposed control of Britain's role in the war between 1741 and 1744. Moreover, on 14 April the paper reiterated its view of the gravity of these allegations: 'The very idea of the sacrifice of *British* Interest to any *foreign consideration*, had *Mr Locke* thought of it in the *Light* it has since been depicted, would certainly have been placed *first* in his list of the *causes* of the *Dissolution of Government*.'

Despite the continued prominence accorded to the alleged subserviency of British interests to Hanoverian ends by the *Old England Journal* and the *Westminster Journal* throughout 1744, both these papers and the other elements of the opposition press could not ignore the second major development in the war (after the French invasion attempt) in the first half of the year: the French invasion of the Austrian Netherlands. The principal effect on press debate of this development, and of the defensive measures undertaken by Britain and her allies to repulse the French armies in the Low Countries, was the raising of a number of new issues that were to assume increasing prominence as the war progressed. The first of these was Britain's interest in the defence of the Dutch Barrier. As has long been established, the widespread contemporary recognition that vital British strategic and commercial interests would be endangered by French control of the

---

[153] *OEJ* 21 Apr. 1744.   [154] Ibid. 28 Apr. 1744.

Low Countries tended to undermine the otherwise clear-cut distinction between blue-water and interventionist positions. The problems that Marshal Saxe's assault on the Barrier fortresses posed to some elements of the opposition were highlighted on 28 April 1744 by the *Old England Journal*.[155] In the first half of the essay reprinted in the paper the author simply reiterated the allegations that had been made throughout the opposition Whig propaganda of 1743 regarding Hanover's responsibility for both the outbreak of a general European war in 1741 and for Britain's role in the war up to the present day. In the second half, however, the author laid down various conditions that, if adhered to, would enable every 'true Briton' to support the ministry's intervention in Europe. Significantly, the second of these was that the war should be carried on 'for the necessary Defence of that part of the continent, *only*, in which *England* has any concern: I mean the *Barrier*'. To facilitate this end, the *Old England Journal* further argued, it was essential that Britain enter into an unambiguous agreement with the Dutch that the defence of the Barrier should be the sole object of the war.

As the remarks of the *Old England Journal* indicate, the second major issue to emerge under the stimulus of events in the Low Countries in 1744 was the ability and political will of Britain and her allies, particularly the Dutch, to resist the French attack on the Barrier. Before 1744 the fundamental infirmity of the Dutch as a military power had been effectively obscured by the concentration of military activity in Germany. During the military campaign of 1744, however, the Dutch Republic's unwillingness and inability to oppose the French was fully exposed. The same was true of Austria's lack of commitment to the defence of the Austrian Netherlands. In the first instance, both were revealed, or so it was claimed by opposition polemicists, by the shortfalls in the numbers of Austrian and Dutch troops designated to the Allied army in the Low Countries in early 1744. As the *Craftsman* remarked on 19 May: 'By what I can at present learn the Troops of Great Britain in Flanders, including all in our Pay, bear a proportion enormously superior to our Allies who seem immediately concerned. And what is yet stranger these Britons seem to be more in earnest than any others.'

Even more alarming was the comparative ease with which, in the early stages of the campaign, the French were able to capture the

---

[155] For divisions amongst the opposition on this question, see Owen, *Rise of the Pelhams*, 204–5.

Barrier fortresses of Menin and Ypres. In this context, the opposition press placed considerable emphasis on the failure of the Dutch to provide anywhere near full-strength garrisons to defend the Barrier fortresses. Ypres, one pamphleteer noted in June, had had a garrison of 2,500, which was only just over a quarter of the minimum strength allegedly required to defend it adequately. Moreover, the same pamphleteer argued, the Dutch conduct was unlikely to change. Burdened with considerable indebtedness, and aware of Britain's inability to sustain her present levels of military expenditure, the Dutch were prudently continuing to pursue a policy that aimed at peace in central Europe.[156] Another reason for the Dutch stance, it was alleged, was the States General's desire to preserve the Republic's commercial links with France.[157]

Despite the jeremiads of a number of opposition polemicists, there is little doubt that widespread hopes of seeing some military advantage emerge from the campaign in the Low Countries in 1744 were briefly raised in June, when a major part of the French army was withdrawn from the Austrian Netherlands to counter the invasion of Alsace by an Austrian army under Prince Charles of Lorraine.[158] As Lord Chancellor Hardwicke wrote to his son Joseph Yorke, who was then serving in Flanders: 'We are in daily expectation of further news from your side, either of a battle or of some town having fallen into your hands, or at least of your having penetrated further.'[159] As in 1743, however, expectations of military success were to be frustrated by disputes and friction between the various powers that comprised the Allied army. Little agreement could be reached between the Allied officers regarding the goals of the campaign, and once again an opportunity to exploit temporary French vulnerability was thrown away. As had also occurred in the previous year, the campaign ended with the Allied army marching on to French territory only to disperse almost immediately amid arguments between the various contingents in the army about responsibility for the lack of real military achievement.

Amongst the opposition press, the events of the latter part of the military campaign in particular were exploited most vigorously and most exhaustively in the pamphlet *The Operations of the British and*

---

[156] *A Letter from Flanders* (1744), 16–17.   [157] Ibid. 23–4.

[158] For the military campaign in Flanders in 1744, see A. W. Massie, 'Great Britain and the Defence of the Low Countries, 1744–48', D.Phil. thesis (Oxford, 1987), 11–59.

[159] *Henry Fox, First Lord Holland: His Family and Relations*, ed. Earl of Ilchester (1920), i. 351–2: Hardwicke to J. Yorke, 6 Aug. 1744.

Allied Arms, during the Campaigns of 1743 and 1744, which was published in December and was the second of two substantial pamphlets attacking Carteret's conduct of the war for which the opposition Whigs were responsible in 1744.[160] Purporting to have been written by an eyewitness, the pamphlet provided a detailed narrative of all the controversial events of the military campaigns of the previous two summers. As regards the most recent campaign, the author reiterated and clarified many of the criticisms that had been levelled during the previous six months, not least in the *Old England Journal,* against Carteret and the role of Austria and the Dutch. Thus, public attention was directed again both to the shortfalls in Allied troop numbers and, in particular, to the lack of Dutch will to resist the collapse of the Barrier. Allied inferiority in the Low Countries, it was emphasised, had only been reversed by the adventitious irruption into France of the Austrians under Prince Charles of Lorraine midway through the campaign. The failure to exploit the position of superiority created by the Austrian invasion of Alsace was unequivocally attributed to fundamental differences between the war aims of Britain and her allies, and to the absence of strategic foresight and care, which, it was claimed, had characterized the campaign from beginning to end. One particular example of inadequate planning that was understandably highlighted was the failure to supply the Allied army with any heavy artillery, an omission that effectively prevented it from laying siege to the French fortress of Lisle. In early 1745, as will be shown in the next chapter, the events of what one opposition pamphleteer was to call the 'last shameful and never to be forgotten campaign', and, in particular, the conduct of the Dutch were to be raised again by opposition polemicists in order to question the practicability of the continued deployment of British troops in Flanders.[161]

The importance of the failure to extract any substantial military advantage from the summer's campaigning in the Low Countries was, as far as politics at home were concerned, considerably increased by the event that dominated press discussion of the war during the second half of 1744: namely, Frederick II of Prussia's invasion of Bohemia in July. As Richard Lodge has described elsewhere, not only did Frederick II publish a manifesto defending his actions in terms of the alleged ill-treatment of the Emperor, Charles VII of Bavaria, he also forwarded to

---

[160] For the other opposition Whig pamphlet, see below.
[161] *The Present Ruinous LAND-WAR Proved to Be a H——r War* (1745), 12.

his envoy in London a dispatch that was intended as a special manifesto for the British nation.[162] Both documents, which were widely reprinted in the London press in August, refocused the attention of the British political nation on the question of Britain's role in the abortive peace negotiations that had taken place at Hanau during the summer of 1743. In addition to alerting the British people to their ministry's refusal to engage Britain in support of the terms stipulated by the so-called Treaty of Hanau, a treaty that, it was alleged, would have secured the pacification of central Europe, the Prussian manifesto and rescript (Frederick II's dispatch to Andrié, the Prussian diplomatic representative in London) also referred to a possible Hanoverian motive for the British ministry's opposition to the peace project. Thus, the Prussian manifesto asserted that Maria Theresa had, in her determination to recover Austria's former position in the empire, engaged to indemnify certain powers for what the manifesto termed 'the extraordinary Helps they have afforded her'. These indemnifications, it was further alleged, were to comprise the alienation of various fiefs of the empire, and the secularization of a number of bishoprics. These allegations, moreover, were amplified in a further Prussian document, *Remarques d'un Bon Patriote Allemand sur l'Ecrit Intitulé: Expose des Motifs, &c.*, published in translation in London in September. This last document, a reprint of the manifesto, with its main contention restated and confirmed, claimed that Hanover and Britain had engaged to support Austria in her aim of regaining the imperial throne and adding Bavaria to the Habsburg dominions (as compensation for the loss of Silesia), in return for the secularization of Osnabrück and the cession of Ostend respectively.[163]

The impact on press debate of Prussia's second intervention in the war was, broadly speaking, twofold. First, the Prussian invasion of Bohemia, and its seemingly disastrous consequences for the military position of Britain and her allies, was widely held by the opposition press to have finally discredited Carteret's conduct of the war. As the *Old England Journal* remarked on 15 September: 'Their [the Hanoverians] E——h Agent [Carteret] has, like the evil Angel of B——n, rode in the whirlwind, and directed the storms of *Europe*, which he can now no longer control, and which beat up so high, and rage so fierce against that very interest he pretended to espouse.' The same point was made more concisely by the author of the pamphlet

---

[162] R. Lodge, 'The Hanau Controversy in 1744 and the Fall of Carteret', *English Historical Review*, 38 (1923), 509–31.

[163] *The Remarks of a True German Patriot* (1744), 5–6.

Serious Considerations on the Present State of Affairs, who asked: 'What less can be expected than that the Queen of *Hungary* will be *stript of all?*' Wherever one chose to look, the same pamphleteer asserted, whether it was to Germany, the Italian peninsula, or the Low Countries, the military balance held out only the prospect of further Bourbon success.[164] What made the situation worse, or so opposition polemicists alleged, was that it had been clearly foreseeable and foreseen.

In support of this view, great emphasis was placed on the arguments that had been articulated across the gamut of the opposition press since late 1742, regarding the failure of Carteret's policies to accommodate either the reality of Austro-Prussian rivalry in the empire or the antipathy of the Dutch to what was alleged to be an unnecessary war. In this context, it is worth noting that as recently as May 1744 the *Old England Journal* had directly addressed itself to the issue of Prussia's role in the war. On this occasion, the paper had not only reiterated the opposition Whig contention that Frederick II would never tolerate the despoliation of Bavaria in order to reinstate Austria as the dominant power in the empire, but it had also argued that Prussia held the key to the balance of power in Germany.[165] As regards the role of the Dutch, all the reasons that had been advanced earlier in the year to explain the Republic's reluctance to commit itself fully to the defence of the Barrier were now restated and confirmed.[166] One additional factor allegedly guiding Dutch conduct that was put forward in late 1744 was the supposed absence of any French threat to the Republic. As the *Old England Journal* observed on September 1: 'The French are now perfectly convinced that they have nothing to dread from *Holland*; and therefore will take care that she shall have nothing to dread from them.' In these circumstances, it was argued, the Dutch would never commit themselves to war against the French, thereby relinquishing all the advantages that their present conduct secured.

On 22 September Thomas Birch remarked that Frederick II had been the hero of 'our political malcontents ever since the manifesto appear'd'.[167] As Birch's comments indicate, the second major consequence for press debate of Prussia's actions was the fillip that they provided to the opposition Whig-led press campaign against Carteret and his alleged sacrifice of British interests to Hanoverian ends. Almost

[164] *Serious Considerations* (1744), 8.   [165] *OEJ* 12 May 1744.
[166] See e.g. *WJ* 1, 24 Sept. 1744; *OEJ* 6, 20 Oct. 1744; *Craftsman*, 13 Oct. 1744.
[167] BL Add. MS 35396, fos. 257–8: Birch to Yorke, 22 Sept. 1743.

as soon as the Prussian manifesto and rescript had appeared, the opposition Whigs had sought to exploit the suspicions that these documents had aroused regarding the role of Carteret and Hanoverian territorial ambitions at Hanau by the publication in the same month (August) of the pamphlet *Natural Reflexions on the Present Conduct of his Prussian Majesty*. Commonly attributed to Chesterfield, this pamphlet revived many of the basic lines of argument that had been so successfully deployed in the previous year. Carteret's conduct and policies were once again unfavourably compared with the Walpolian regime, and his alleged undisguised pursuit of Hanoverian ends in the war was portrayed as a necessary consequence of the circumstances surrounding the new Whigs' admission to office in 1742. Similarly, Frederick II's claims that his renewed participation in the war had been motivated by his concern for the interests of both the Emperor and the empire were exploited to reaffirm the opposition Whig assertion that the war was solely concerned with the distribution of power in Germany, and that a foreign policy that aimed at German union was Britain's proper role on the Continent. The Treaty of Hanau was portrayed, as it had been in the Prussian documents that had stimulated the opposition Whig pamphlet, as having created a major opportunity to put an end to the war. But, as the author of *Natural Reflexions on the Present Conduct of his Prussian Majesty* exclaimed:

Peace, tho' extremely useful to a mortgag'd, over-burden'd bleeding *Kingdom*, may not turn to the Account of a cherish'd *Dukedom*, that feels not the weight of *Taxes*, or interruptions of *Trade* and industry; and *profit* by a war. An Equitable peace would not so soon produce the Alienation of *Imperial Fiefs*, and the secularisation of German *Bishopricks*, as a successful war.

In early 1745 another opposition pamphleteer amplified this view of the abortive Hanau peace project by comparing Carteret's alleged opposition to the peace with the notorious refusal of the Whig ministry during the War of the Spanish Succession to accept the terms that had been proposed by the French at Gertruydenburg in 1709. As had occurred at the Peace of Utrecht, Carteret's actions at Hanau, the pamphleteer argued, would inevitably lead to a less favourable conclusion to the war.[168] The stimulus to opposition press activity provided by the Prussian manifesto and rescript is also disclosed by the *Old England Journal* and the *Westminster Journal*. As the *Westminster Journal* observed of the

[168] *The Visible Pursuit of a Foreign Interest* (1745), *passim*.

content of the Prussian documents: 'These particulars are the more worthy of consideration, as many of them are agreeable to the sentiments of the *wisest men* at home, and have been inculcated in the writings for the constitution and natural independency of England.'[169] Between August and mid-November both essay papers reiterated many of the arguments that had been set out in detail in the pamphlet *Natural Reflexions on the Present Conduct of his Prussian Majesty*. In this respect, both papers emphasized the contention that the war was principally a 'German war'. As the *Old England Journal* declared on 25 August: 'The Balance of Europe proves a phantom and vanishes; the Balance of Germany rises in its place; an English minister espouses it in the Face of the Sun, and resolves to support it at all Hazards, and an Effrontery beyond Example.' On 15 September the same paper added a new dimension to press debate, when it argued explicitly that Carteret's policies and pursuit of Hanoverian interests were actually endangering Britain's capacity to defend itself against the French. The paper also revived an allegation that had been made by a number of opposition polemicists in the previous year: namely, that the Dutch stance in the war was guided by the recognition that, under Carteret, British interests were being subordinated to Hanoverian ends.[170]

The supposed Hanoverian control of Britain's conduct in the war was also held, by both the *Old England Journal* and the *Westminster Journal*, to be responsible for Prussia's actions since 1741. In this context, George II's anti-Prussian schemes of 1741 were again made to bear an importance that they did not in reality justify.[171] On 29 September the *Old England Journal* made a call for grand juries to exercise their constitutional right to petition the throne to urge George II to remove Carteret from office. This tactic was justified, the paper asserted, as 'ALL IS AT STAKE'. In the next issue the *Old England Journal* repeated its call for the people to declare their support for Carteret's dismissal, arguing that 'The pretences are now removed why the people ought not to apply, by way of Instruction to their constituents; they have long, thro' Decency forborn, let them now, for safety, resume that privilege.'[172] In the event, instructions or addresses to the Crown were neither necessary nor forthcoming. In late November the developing

---

[169] *WJ* 18 Aug. 1744.

[170] See e.g. *OEJ* 15 Dec. 1744. For the development of this allegation in 1743, see esp. *An Important Secret Come to Light, passim; A Letter from a Member of the States-General in Holland to a Member of Parliament in England, passim.*

[171] *OEJ* 25 Aug. 1744; *WJ* 8 Sept. 1744.   [172] *OEJ* 6 Oct. 1744.

press onslaught against the role of Carteret and Hanover at Hanau was abruptly arrested when Carteret was finally forced from office by the Pelhams, and the bulk of the opposition leadership, including Chesterfield and most of his fellow opposition Whigs, were admitted to the newly formed Broad-Bottom ministry.

As part of his introductory remarks to the 1744–5 parliamentary session in his parliamentary journal, Philip Yorke wrote of Carteret's position in late 1744:

by the Nation in general he was held in abhorrence, not only from the character he had acquired of insincerity and falseness, but from an opinion taken up, that he was desirous of prolonging a war to the conduct of which he had shewn himself unequal, and that instead of checking and discountenancing the King's unhappy partiality to his electoral interests, he had from private views raised and fomented it to such a degree, as greatly to lessen the affections of the people. The public ill-humour was increased by the inactivity of the campaign in Flanders and the unlucky alteration in Germany from the King of Prussia's infamous breach of faith. It brought back to their minds in how unaccountable a manner the success at Dettingen had been thrown away, and the emperor's overtures neglected last Summer, when this noble lord was in the fulness of his power.[173]

It would be wrong to exaggerate the role of popular detestation of Carteret and his measures in bringing about his downfall. Eighteenth-century ministers were very rarely, if ever, brought down simply by the force of popular opinion. Nevertheless, the contribution that the intense and widespread anti-Carteret feeling 'without doors' in late 1744 made to the resolve shown by the Pelhams and the leaders of the Broad-Bottom opposition to dislodge Carteret from office and to establish a 'national' administration cannot be discounted. As has been argued elsewhere in the present work, if the actions of mid-century politicians were not usually governed by the press and popular opinion, neither were they isolated from either of these pressures.

Following Carteret's fall from power, the press debate of the issues arising from the war was never to regain the momentum and influence that had been imparted to it by the opposition Whig campaign to force the 'Hanover Troop master' from power.[174] As this chapter has attempted to show, the opposition Whig intervention in the press between 1742 and 1744 was also primarily responsible for ensuring that

[173] *Parl. Hist.*, xiii. 975–83.   [174] The phrase was Pitt's (ibid. xii. 1033–6).

Hanover's role in the war had remained at, or near to, the forefront of popular and press concern for most of this period. In achieving this, the opposition Whigs had demonstrated the remarkable extent to which, in their pursuit of political power, they were prepared to exploit the alienation of the majority of the political nation from the personnel and politics of the Hanoverian regime. Not surprisingly, both at the time and later, ministerial supporters berated the opposition Whigs for providing succour to the Jacobite cause; and when the Jacobite manifestos and declarations issued during the '45 reiterated much of the anti-Hanoverian argument that had been articulated in the opposition press between 1742 and 1744, the myth rapidly emerged that the opposition press was one of the factors primarily responsible for the Jacobite invasion.[175]

Finally, it is worth noting that this myth, and the opposition Whigs' conduct between 1742 and 1744, was recalled in 1756, when Pitt and Leicester House, aided by William Beckford, were attempting to revive popular concern about the alleged Hanoverian control of British foreign policy by attacking the ministry's conclusion of subsidy treaties with Hesse-Kassel and Russia, which, Pitt and his allies claimed, were designed solely to protect Hanover. James, second Earl Waldegrave, was to write of the success of this later anti-Hanoverian campaign:

But what inflamed the multitude and shook the very Foundation of Government, were the treasonable Falsehoods pointed even at the very Throne itself. His Majesty's very Natural Affection for his German Electorate was brought as an undoubted proof of his settled Aversion to his British subjects. All these calumnies which had been formerly very successfully employ'd by some of the same persons, when Lord Granville was minister and had rais'd that National Discontent which had been the forerunner of the last Rebellion. Not that Rebellion was the Point they aimed at nor did they it on the present occasion. They only desired to create as much confusion as might be necessary to bring themselves into Power; which being once obtained they were ready to talk a different language . . .[176]

Ironically, a leading supporter of the ministry in 1756, who was to warn the Lords of the dangers of the anti-Hanoverian platform of Pitt and the opposition, was Pitt's former ally of the early 1740s, and the principal architect of the anti-Hanoverian press campaign of 1742–4, the Earl of Chesterfield.[177]

---

[175] See above, Ch. 2.
[176] *The Memoirs and Speeches of James, 2nd Earl Waldegrave, 1742–1763*, ed. J. C. D. Clark (Cambridge, 1988), 175–6.
[177] See Walpole, *Memoirs of King George II*, ii. 94.

6

THE BROAD-BOTTOM MINISTRY AND THE JACOBITE REBELLION, 1745-1746

THE fall of Granville, together with the dismissal from British pay of the 16,000 Hanoverian troops at the end of 1744, was a turning-point. Between 1742 and 1744, as we saw in the previous chapter, Carteret and the Hanoverian troops had provided the focus for an often violent and influential opposition press campaign. For the remainder of the war nothing attracted the same degree of press abuse. The effects of this were only amplified by the admission into the new ministry, the so-called Broad-Bottom ministry, of most of the opposition politicians who had intervened so vigorously in the press between 1742 and 1744. Consequently, late 1744 marked the beginning of a further noticeable slowing of the tempo and violence of press and popular debate about the war. Yet the extent of this should not be exaggerated. As the first part of this chapter attempts to show, the drift of events both at home and abroad, especially in the Low Countries, in the first half of 1745 ensured that intense press and popular hostility towards the conduct of the war persisted for most of that year. Events also continued to provide a fund of material for attacks on Hanoverian influence. On occasion, moreover, these attacks were as violent as anything that had been published during the previous two years.

There were, therefore, few grounds for confidence at court about the prospective domestic reaction when the Young Pretender arrived off the west coast of Scotland in late July 1745. Yet the bulk of popular opinion was to line up firmly behind the Hanoverian regime as the threat to it from the Jacobite invasion became clear. The contribution of the press to this apparently dramatic about-turn of popular sentiments, the subject of the second part of this chapter, has never been systematically studied.[1] This is perhaps not so surprising an omission.

---

[1] But see R. C. Jarvis (ed.), *Collected Papers on the Jacobite Risings* (Manchester, 1972), ii, 3–36; W. A. Speck, *The Butcher: The Duke of Cumberland and the Suppression of the '45* (Oxford, 1981), 53–77, 183–203. There is also useful information on the press during the '45 in Henry Fielding, *The 'True Patriot' and Related Writings*, ed. W. B. Coley (Oxford, 1987).

Given the prevailing view that political stability was the foremost achievement of the early Hanoverian period (a belief that obtained at least until the 1970s), the defensive loyalism of 1745–6, together with the role of the press in its stimulation, seemed to require neither detailed examination nor explanation. More recent work, however, has challenged a number of key elements of the view that political stability took firm root under the first two Georges. In particular, a number of historians have argued that Jacobitism continued to represent a potent threat to the Hanoverians at least until it was crushed militarily at Culloden, and perhaps until 1759.[2] Against this background, the response of the press to the '45 acquires additional interest.

As in 1743, it is impossible to dissociate press discussion of Britain's role in the war during the first half of 1745 from the frustration of the widespread expectations of political change created by the recent admission of leading opposition politicians into the administration. The revival of the hopes for a new dawn of patriot government that followed Granville's fall, and the subsequent disillusionment and indignation expressed by all elements of patriot opinion at a second betrayal of patriotism, were examined in an earlier chapter. In the immediate context, what is significant is the expectations that the change in ministry signalled a major change in the direction of Britain's war effort. These expectations were articulated most forcefully, but not exclusively, in the *Old England Journal* and the *Westminster Journal*. As the *Westminster Journal* remarked on 16 March:

Let us recollect what were the principal charges against the late Adm——n. I will reduce them only to three; the Engaging in a *Land War*, and pursuing it in a manner not calculated for the service of Gr——t Br——n; the paying of a large body of *foreign mercenaries*, who were not only useless to, but an actual impediment to the common cause: the neglecting of our *Naval Affairs* to such a Degree, as to leave Trade unprotected, and bring disgrace upon our numerous Fleets.

It was 'upon the pretence of remedying' these shortcomings in Britain's role in the war, the paper continued, that the 'voice of the people' had supported the removal of Granville from office.

If patriot opinion was to be disappointed in early 1745 by the absence of any concerted attempt to instigate a programme of domestic reform, it confronted a similar lack of significant change in official foreign policy. In fact, as a number of opposition polemicists were

---

[2] See esp. E. Cruickshanks, *Political Untouchables: The Tories and the '45* (1979); P. Monod, *Jacobitism and the English People, 1688–1788* (Cambridge, 1989).

quick to point out, far from seeing a diminution in Britain's participation in the land war, the commitment of both men and money to the continental theatre actually intensified in 1745.[3] The contribution that this made to popular discontent in the first half of 1745 is suggested in the first place by the publication in May of the influential pamphlet *An Expostulatory Epistle to the Welch Knight*, which attacked the leading Tory Sir Watkin Williams Wynn. (As was noted in a previous chapter, in early January Wynn had given his vote and had spoken in support of a motion in a Committee of Supply to increase the number of British troops to be deployed in Flanders for the ensuing year.) It is also suggested by the desperate efforts that Thomas Carte, the probable author of *The Case Fairly Stated in a Letter from a Member of Parliament in the Country Interest to One of his Constituents* (1745) (the major pamphlet defence of the role of the Tory leadership in the Broad-Bottom ministry), made to shield Wynn and his colleagues from accusations that they had reneged on the patriot commitment to a bluewater strategy.[4] The Tory leaders, Carte remonstrated, had correctly seized the last available opportunity for 'propping up a falling nation', and had supported a prudent policy aimed solely at securing a general European peace and extricating Britain from the disastrous situation created by Granville's wild schemes. In response to the widespread criticisms of Tory support for increased military commitment to the Continent, Carte, referring to the wider aim outlined above, declared:

Upon these considerations, when our Army in *Flanders* came to be voted, we were induced to add that weight which unanimity gives to Parliamentary Resolutions, and surely this Behaviour cannot be thought inconsistent with the Principles we have always professed, for you will consider Sir, that though we have constantly opposed, though we still detest those measures that have brought this land-war upon us: yet it now becomes our Duty to get out of it as well as we can.[5]

Unfortunately for the Tory leadership, the credibility of Carte's arguments was strained by the Tories' own opposition to a vote of credit towards the end of the session, which seemed to run counter to the declared intention of expediting a rapid conclusion to the war in

[3] *WJ* 2 Feb., 16 Mar. 1745; *An Address of Thanks to the Broad-Bottoms* (1745), 37–46; *An Expostulatory Epistle to the Welch Knight*, 10; *Dutch Faith, Being an Enquiry Founded on Facts, into the Probability of the Success of the British Arms, on the Continent Next Campaign* (1745), 8–10, 38–40.

[4] For a detailed discussion of the contemporary importance of both *An Expostulatory Epistle* and *The Case Fairly Stated*, see above, Ch. 2.

[5] *The Case Fairly Stated*, 17–20.

Europe. As one scornful pamphleteer correctly observed, the key to this inconsistent behaviour was the state of progress of the 'darling' of the Tory leaders, the remodelling of the commissions of the peace in various counties.[6]

It is unlikely that Tory-patriot opinion would have been mollified by Carte's apologetics under any circumstances. Two further factors effectively removed the remote possibility of this occurrence. The first was the efforts of a number of pamphleteers to vindicate Granville. Two of their pamphlets, *The Plain Reasoner, wherein the Present State of Affairs Are Set in a New, but Very Obvious Light* and *A Continuation of the Plain Reasoner*, published in December 1744 and March 1745 respectively, seem to have attracted particular attention.[7] Both contained closely argued defences of Granville's interventionist diplomacy, and the allegation that the Pelhams had deliberately contrived to undermine Granville by conniving with the opposition to raise the cry of Hanover. In their task of directing popular anger against the Broad-Bottom ministry, Granville's apologists were substantially aided by the new ministry's efforts to reassure Britain's major allies that Granville's dismissal did not portend any significant alteration in Britain's role in the war. As a result, it was an easy enough matter to portray the Broad-Bottom ministry as the product of the Pelhams' desire for a monopoly of political power, and to identify those who had played leading roles in the opposition of 1742–4, and who were now part of that ministry, with a vigorously interventionist foreign policy.[8] The allegation that the Pelhams had actively sought the support of the opposition to force Granville from office, and the further claim that the Broad-Bottom ministry was ineffectively pursuing, or had ineffectively pursued, a foreign policy modelled on Granville's diplomacy were to be restated in a number of places both before and immediately after the end of the war.[9]

[6] *A Letter to the Author of the Case Fairly Stated, from an Old Whig* (1745), 67. For the Tories' opposition to the vote of credit, and the importance of Tory demands for admission to commissions of the peace, see J. B. Owen, *The Rise of the Pelhams* (1957), 259–60.

[7] Other pro-Granville pamphlets published in early 1745 include *The Modern Patriot, or, Broad B-tt-m Principles Examin'd* and *A Letter to a Certain Foreign Minister*. One hostile pamphleteer claimed that *The Plain Reasoner* 'has found its way into most Hands in Town' (*A Plain Answer to the Plain Reasoner*, 6).

[8] *The Modern Patriot*, 63; *A Letter to the Author of the Case Fairly Stated*, 9.

[9] *The State of the Nation Consider'd in a Letter to a Member of Parliament* (1747); *The State of the Nation for the year 1747, and Respecting 1748* (1747); [Egmont] *An Examination of the Principles, and an Enquiry into the Conduct of the Two B———rs* (1749); *OEJ* 4, 25 Oct., 20 Dec. 1746.

In 1745, meanwhile, *The Plain Reasoner* provoked at least one direct pamphlet rebuttal, entitled *A Plain Answer to the Plain Reasoner*. This did little more than restate the allegation that Granville's adventurous policies were directed by Hanoverian interests, and assert the view of rigid isolationists that Britain could, irrespective of the prevailing diplomatic and international conditions, defend itself against the French without the aid of foreign alliances. In retrospect, of greater interest here is a series of essays, also provoked by *The Plain Reasoner*, which appeared in the *Daily Post* and which attacked many of the basic assumptions underlying the pro-Granville arguments.[10] Opposition polemicists argued throughout the war that the diplomatic concepts favoured by Granville and his supporters—'universal monarchy' and the 'common cause', for example—were merely shadows raised to induce support for misguided policies of intervention in Europe or for even more sinister ends. The essays in the *Daily Post*, however, went a stage further, explicitly asserting that the current distribution of power on the Continent rendered such concepts anachronistic.[11] Another factor that draws attention to the same essays is the high degree of pessimism that informs their analysis of the military prospects. This culminated on 5 January with a warning about France's commitment to the idea of invading Britain:

This Design, if we may judge by present Appearances, France has not yet laid aside . . . To defeat their projects, there is no way left but bringing home our troops; for, as France has no manner of Business now for an Army in Alsace, it follows that the Allies will be greatly over-match'd either in Flanders or Westphalia; and, therefore, it is high time to look to ourselves.

Such pessimism about the military situation was shared by a number of other opposition writers in early 1745. It also provoked one pro-ministerial pamphleteer to attack the opposition for its allegedly defeatist attitudes.[12]

The second factor feeding the alienation of patriot opinion from the Broad-Bottom ministry in the early months of 1745, and accurately

---

[10] *Daily Post*, 2, 3, 4, 5, 18, 24 Jan., 8, 11, 12, 28, 30 Mar., 3, 6 Apr., 3, 4 May, 23 July, 8, 31 Aug. 1745.

[11] See esp. ibid. 8 Mar., 3 Apr., 3 May, 16 Aug. 1745.

[12] For other pessimistic accounts of the military prospects in early 1745, see esp. *The Free and Impartial Examiner, Being a Candid Enquiry into the Causes of our Present Melancholy Situation with Regard both to Domestick and Foreign Affairs* (1745), *passim*; *The Present Ruinous LAND-WAR, Proved to Be a H——r War* (1745), *passim*. Such accounts were attacked in *The Criterion of the Reason and Necessity of the Present War* (1745), 45.

foreseen by the essayist in the *Daily Post*, was the desperate military situation that unfolded during the first half of the year. As far as politics at home was concerned, the central features of this were Marshal Saxe's devastating military campaign in the Low Countries, and the obvious lack of Dutch military and political will to resist the collapse of the Barrier. Even before the start of the military campaign, the likelihood of the Dutch co-operating fully and vigorously in military action against the French had been questioned by a number of writers, the most detailed discussion of the issue being undertaken by the author of the pamphlet *Dutch Faith, Being an Enquiry Founded on Facts, into the Probability of the Success of the British Arms on the Continent Next Campaign* (1745). This pamphlet, purporting to have been written by an English officer in Flanders, revived the criticisms of Dutch conduct raised during the 1744 campaign, notably the alleged treachery involved in the capitulation to the French of the fortresses of Menin, Ypres, and Furnes, and the Dutch refusal to act offensively against the weakened French forces in the Low Countries following the invasion of Alsace by Prince Charles of Lorraine. In the light of this record, the author reasonably asked what grounds there were for believing that the Dutch would alter their stance in 1745. The improbability of any shift in their role in the war, it was further argued, was also suggested by their fail- ure to declare war against France, and their supposed rejection of the bellicose Earl of Stair as Commander of the Allied army for the coming year.[13] Without the full co-operation of the Dutch, the opposition press asserted, as it had done since 1742, British intervention in Flanders was doomed to failure. As the author of *The Present Ruinous LAND-WAR, Proved to Be a H——r War* (1745) argued, despite the obvious French threat to the strategically sensitive Low Countries:

All we would infer from hence is, if the Dutch will not come into the Alliance heartily and *totis viribus*; if, by temporizing, they can provide for the security of their Barrier, and of the Netherlands; it will be absolutely necessary for us, to desist from our military operations by Land, and convert our intended Assistance of the Queen of Hungary into a pecuniary Aid.[14]

In the event, the military campaign of 1745 seemed to confirm all the apprehensions of the opposition press. Renewed frictions between the British and Dutch over quotas of men and money for the military effort; the capitulation of further Barrier fortresses; and the relative

---

[13] *Dutch Faith*, 41–5.   [14] *The Present Ruinous LAND-WAR*, 15.

military failure of the Dutch troops at the Battle of Fontenoy on 11 May—all were unsurprisingly portrayed as clearly foreseeable and foreseen, and the culpability of the ministry as correspondingly greater. As the *Old England Journal* remarked on 6 July: 'Thus the great point, which the Nation has gain'd by the Broad-Bottom Revolution, has been the Exchange of insolent mercenaries [the Hanoverian troops] for treacherous Auxiliaries, of those whom Experience has told us, would fight, for those whom Reason might of convinced us, would not.'[15]

Various explanations of the Dutch stance were put forward by the opposition press. Many of them recalled the arguments about the Republic's conduct that had begun to be developed in the second half of the previous year. Thus, great emphasis was again placed on Anglo-Dutch commercial rivalry and on the allegedly overriding ambition of the Dutch to maintain their trade with France and protect their commercial links with other neutral powers.[16] Similarly, the view that Dutch reluctance to support Britain's military schemes was a consequence of the States General's recognition that Britain's conduct in the war was being controlled by Hanoverian ends was also restated.[17] Another factor, which had only been raised infrequently in the previous year, but which received much attention in early 1745, was the importance of the divisions in Dutch politics, and the fear of the Republicans that to declare war against France would lead to a repeat of the events of 1672 and the elevation of the Prince of Orange to the stadtholderate.[18] A number of opposition polemicists also alleged that the Dutch had made secret agreements with the French to safeguard the Republic, a possibility lent weight by, amongst other things, the continuing negotiations between the French and the States General in 1745.[19]

The strength of the popular animus towards the Dutch created by the combined effect of the press and the events in Flanders is indicated by the depth of concern over anti-Dutch feeling expressed by a number of leading ministerial figures during the summer months. One member of the ministry who, more than most, was disturbed by the mood of the

---

[15] See also *Considerations on the Conduct of the Dutch* (1745), *passim*; *A Modest Enquiry into the Present State of Foreign Affairs* (1945), *passim*.

[16] *OEJ*, 17 Aug., 21 Sept. 1745; *WJ*, 24 Aug. 1745; *Christmas Chat, or, Observations on the Late Change at Court* (1745), 54–5; *Hanoverian Politicks, in a Letter from a Gentleman at the Court of Hanover* (1745), 4; *The Free and Impartial Examiner*, 46.

[17] *The Free and Impartial Examiner*, 35–40.

[18] See esp. *Considerations on the Conduct of the Dutch*, 38–9.

[19] See esp. *Dutch Faith*, 35–7.

people was the Earl of Chesterfield. As well as being a principal architect of the Broad-Bottom ministry, Chesterfield had travelled to The Hague at the beginning of 1745 as the official representative of the British ministry, with the task of attempting to cajole the Dutch into closer union with British schemes. On 9 July, now back in London, he wrote to Robert Trevor: 'I never in my life saw the public in a worse humour than at present, and I am very sorry to tell you, that the Dutch and your humble servant are the principal objects of it.'[20] As was the case with the anti-Hanoverian outcry in late 1743, letters from the British contingent in the Allied forces in Flanders giving details of the Dutch role in the military campaign were also fanning the flames of popular anti-Dutch sentiment.[21]

While the Dutch undoubtedly bore the brunt of popular dissatisfaction with the Broad-Bottom ministry's conduct of the war during the first seven months or so of 1745, the continued commitment to the Continent also kept alive the allegations that Hanoverian interests were controlling Britain's foreign policy. And although there was no equivalent to the employment of 16,000 Hanoverian troops to draw press attention, the continued prominence accorded to the issue in the opposition press, again particularly in the *Westminster Journal* and the *Old England Journal*, suggests that it would be unwise to underestimate the continuing strength of popular anti-Hanoverian sentiments during the months immediately preceding the Jacobite Rebellion. In the second half of 1744, as was described in the last chapter, popular and press attention had been refocused on the question of Hanoverian control of British foreign policy by Frederick the Great's attempts to vindicate his re-entry into the war on the side of the Bourbon powers. The formation of the Broad-Bottom ministry temporarily arrested the developing press onslaught against Granville and Hanover stirred up by Frederick the Great. Yet, as the comments of the *Westminster Journal* quoted at the beginning of this chapter demonstrated, the removal of the 'Germaniz'd' Granville also created expectations, first, that the Hanoverian troops would be dismissed from British pay and, secondly, that the alleged influence of Hanover would be seen to be removed from the conduct of Britain's foreign policy. Significantly, in this context, the necessity of dislodging Granville from office was presented by a number of opposition polemicists as the major reason, or the only justification, for the co-operation of the former leaders of the opposition with the old corps Whigs. Commenting on the possibility that the Broad-Bottom ministry might prove to constitute a repeat of the betrayal of 1742, the *Westminster Journal* warned: 'But should this prove true, what has been done by this great siege [the Broad-Bottom opposition of 1742–4]? Han——r thou shalt flourish! B——n thou shalt tremble and languish.'[22]

Against this background, it was almost inevitable that the ministry's continued intervention in Europe would be attributed to Hanoverian interests, and that attacks on Granville's role in the peace negotiations at Hanau in 1743 would be revived. Furthermore, any hopes that the dismissal of the Hanoverians would temper press sensitivities were undermined by the provision of an additional subsidy to the Queen of Hungary that was widely, and correctly, recognized as designed to enable her to take 8,000 of the dismissed Hanoverians on to the Austrian payroll. Nor did the concessions to George II's Hanoverian interests stop there. Instead of the usual six weeks', the Hanoverian troops were paid eight weeks' march money.[23] As the *Old England Journal* concluded:

During the last M——y a H——n spirit might have been easily enough smelt throughout our C——ls: But then it was simple, it was undistinguish'd, and the Anti-dote to it was ready and easy. But the H——sm of this M——y is double distill'd, it is refin'd from all savour of B——sh spirit, even the vessels which export it are foreign.[24]

A further impetus behind opposition press criticism of the role of Hanover and Hanoverian interests in early 1745 was the Battle of Fontenoy. The large number of British losses in the battle was exploited by both the *Old England Journal* and the *Westminster Journal* to launch vitriolic assaults against the impact of Hanover on British interests and, more specifically, on George II's departure for his electorate in early May. The most remarkable of these was printed in the *Old England Journal* on 18 May, and immediately provoked the ministry to issue a warrant for the arrest of the printer, publisher, and author of the paper.[25] In this issue the *Old England Journal* argued that

[22] *WJ* 16 Feb. 1745.
[23] See U. Dann, *Hanover and Great Britain, 1740–60: Diplomacy and Survival* (Leicester, 1991), 61–2.
[24] *OEJ* 20 Apr. 1745.   [25] PRO, SP 44/82, fos. 207–8.

James II had been removed from office for having, in current constitutional language, 'done wrong' in abdicating the throne at a time of 'public calamity'. Ostensibly referring to both James and his elder brother Charles II, the paper continued:

Supposing one of them had managed Parties ill at home, and matters abroad, so that he had been forc'd to put his *civil* Affairs into the Hands of a *motley ministry* [the Broad-Bottom ministry]... and supposing that a public calamity [Fontenoy] had overtaken the Nation, and in that melancholy state of Things, the K——g and his W[hore] [George II's mistress, Amelie Sophie von Walmoden] had march'd off; and that he had been so wholly engross'd in his Passion for *foreign Business*, that he had disregarded the Remonstrances of all his M——y, which AGREED in nothing but in their Entreaties to keep him at home. Supposing that, like a Dog who had broke from his Halter, he had been afraid of even looking back upon the place of his prison, as he thought this *island* to be. I say, supposing all this, can we suppose such a *king to have done no wrong*.

The implication was clear; by going to Hanover in the midst of the disasters of the military campaign, George II was forfeiting his right to the British throne. The pursuit of Hanoverian interests, the same issue of the paper further intimated, had involved Britain in a 'cruel, bloody, expensive, and unnecessary war'. Moreover, in a bitter glance at the opposition Whigs admitted to the ministry in late 1744, the paper concluded that opposition to Hanoverian interests was merely 'the method by which *men get places* and compliance with it, the means by which *they keep them*'.

The *Westminster Journal* commenced its onslaught on the role of Hanover even before the Battle of Fontenoy, and maintained it until just three weeks before the Jacobite victory at Prestonpans in the last week of September.[26] Some index of the importance that the paper attached to the issue in this period is provided by the fact that, of the twenty-one issues of the *Westminster Journal* published between 13 April and 7 September, all but five bore directly on it. On 13 April the paper remarked:

The office of *limited monarch*, a monarch whose will is not the *sole law* of his Government, should not, methinks, be very desirable to a man of *violent Passions*. Such a man may indeed *tyrannize* over a Nation of slaves, may satiate, with high Gust, his unjust and brutal *Appetites*; but must meet with many

---

[26] The last attack on the role of Hanover before Prestonpans was published on 31 Aug. 1745.

Restraints, many *Mortifications* from a *free people.* . . . A little *German Count,* who rules over a District no bigger than an *English* Hundred, may, with this Temper, think himself much happier than if he was king of *England.*

On 20 April, in the next issue, the paper advocated the desirability of a legislative dissolution of the Anglo-Hanoverian union.[27] As with the *Old England Journal,* the attack on the role of Hanover came to a climax after news of the Battle of Fontenoy had reached London. On 11 May the *Westminster Journal* exclaimed: 'See there, Sir, what are the Effects of our connexion with Han——r! Behold those Fields *crimson'd* o'er with the Blood of our *Countrymen,* who fell a sacrifice to the scheme of enlarging a *pitiful Duchy,* and the vengeance of that Duchy against *France* for obstructing her views!' On 18 June the paper was arguing that the union with Hanover was distorting Britain's relations with the major northern Protestant powers—Prussia, Sweden, Hesse-Kassel, and Denmark—all countries against which Hanover, the paper further alleged, had territorial ambitions. Britain's historic role at the head of the 'Protestant Interest' was thus being undermined by its connection with Hanover. Finally, on 6 July the pseudonymous correspondent 'A Citizen of the World' offered the embittered suggestion that the seat of the 'British Empire' should be transferred from London to the electorate.

That these press attacks fell on a receptive readership, at least in London, and did have an impact is suggested by two factors. The first —and evidence that anti-Hanoverianism was maintaining its hold over at least one centre of metropolitan opposition in early 1745—is the toasts that were proposed at the anniversary dinner of the Westminster Society of Independent Electors, which took place at Vintners' Hall on 15 February. These included 'Great Britain unGermaniz'd', and 'That German measures may never get the better of English liberty'.[28] The second is the desperate efforts of the Tory pamphlet referred to earlier, *The Case Fairly Stated,* to defend the Tory element in the Broad-Bottom ministry against the charge that they had failed to remove Hanoverian influence from the conduct of the war. To this end, the pamphlet attempted to portray the dismissal of the Hanoverian troops as a historic patriot triumph. All the major criticisms that had been levelled against the measure between 1742 and 1744 were carefully restated to support such a view of the scale and nature of the achieve-

---

[27] For the continued advocacy of the same measure in *WJ* after the '45, see below, Ch. 7.   [28] *GM* 15 (1745), 107.

ment. 'And if we remember all this,' Carte pleaded, 'can we think the Dismission of these troops a light matter, and that it was not attended with difficulties from a certain Quarter much easier to be guessed at than described?' Moreover, Carte continued,

the great consideration of all was that this vote was giving the Discharge in full to the *Hanoverians*, and dismissing them for ever from the Pay of *Great Britain*. This Estimate was to appear on our journals, as the declared sense of the legislature, that these Troops ought on no Pretence whatsoever, to be taken into *British* Pay for the future.[29]

The more sober reality that lay behind these claims was laid bare by the author of the principal rebuttal of Carte's pamphlet, *A Letter to the Author of the Case Fairly Stated, from an Old Whig.* The author repeated the allegations of a number of other opposition polemicists that the former members of the opposition who had been admitted to the Broad-Bottom ministry had engaged to support the provision of money to the Hanoverians provided that it did not appear on the Estimates, and further alleged, correctly, that this cynical exercise in political camouflage had, by causing the withdrawal of half of the Hanoverian contingent in the Allied army, severely weakened the Allied military position in Flanders. One of the consequences of this was the crushing military defeat by the French at Fontenoy.[30]

On 13 May George Grenville wrote to his younger brother Thomas Grenville: 'God send us some good news somewhere or other, or else send us a peace.'[31] Just over two months later came the news that a body of New England troops, under their American Commander William Pepperell, had, with the assistance of a naval squadron under Admiral Warren, forced the surrender of the fortress of Louisbourg, thereby gaining control of the Island of Cape Breton in the Gulf of the St Lawrence. There can be little doubt that this capture outside Europe had a huge and almost immediate impact on popular opinion. On 24 October Chesterfield wrote to Lord Cobham:

As to the point of Cape Breton, you may remember I was aware at first of the difficultys it would create, and when I heard people bawling and huzzaing for its being taken I wish'd it in their throats. But I think you have no option left,

---

[29] *The Case Fairly Stated*, 23–5.
[30] *A Letter to the Author of the Case Fairly Stated*, 34–5. For modern confirmation of this view of the repercussions of the dismissal of the Hanoverians, see A. W. Massie, 'Great Britain and the Defence of the Low Countries, 1744–48', D.Phil. thesis (Oxford, 1987), esp. 76.   [31] *The Grenville Papers*, ed. W. J. Smith, 4 vols. (1852), i. 35–9.

and you might much easier give up Gibraltar and Minorca; and I don't think you could find a plenipotentiary who would venture to sign it away.[32]

Earlier, on 13 August, Chesterfield had remarked to Robert Trevor that the island had become 'the darling object of the whole Nation', and that people had begun 'laying on their claims and protesting already against the restitution of it upon any account'.[33] The last part of Chesterfield's remarks is corroborated by Thomas Birch. On 27 July he wrote of Cape Breton: 'Our merchants universally consider it as more than an equivalent for the loss of Flanders, & talk of procuring an Act of Parliament next session to annex it for ever to the Crown of Great Britain.'[34] And even Henry Pelham, usually indifferent to the swirls and eddies of popular opinion, was forced to concede that the people were 'mad' about the island.[35] Following the news of the success, most of the opposition papers, and the carefully neutral *St James's Evening Post*, printed essays listing the 'prodigious Advantages' held to be secured by control of the island.[36] The *Gentleman's Magazine* joined in this wave of press enthusiasm by reprinting Robert Auchmuty's influential memorial, *The Importance of Cape Breton to the British Nation*.[37]

That the expositions in the press of the alleged benefits that would flow from Cape Breton's capture were being widely assimilated by the political nation is revealed by the loyal addresses provoked by the Jacobite Rebellion that poured in from September onwards. Out of a total of 307 printed in the *London Gazette* between September 1745 and April 1746, 112 referred directly to the capture of the island. Of these, many proclaimed one or more of the supposed advantages of possession of the island expounded in the press during August and September 1745. The corporation of Bideford, for example, observed that, as a result of the capture, 'France is deprived of that grand nursery of sailors, and the maritime power of that Kingdom is undermined, and her Colonies in North America are render'd useless to her.'[38] The corporation of Poole, meanwhile, remarked on the security that Britain's own North American colonies would derive from British

---

[32] *Private Correspondence of Chesterfield and Newcastle*, 74.
[33] HMC, Fourteenth Report, Appendix 9 (1895), 127–8.
[34] BL, Add. MS 35396 (Hardwicke Papers), fos. 298–9: Birch to Yorke, 27 July 1745.
[35] HMC, Fourteenth Report, Appendix 9, 131–2: Pelham to Trevor, 10 Sept. 1745.
[36] *WJ* 3 Aug. 1745; *St James's Evening Post*, 25–7 July 1745; *OEJ* 29 Sept. 1745; *LEP* 20–3 July 1745.
[37] *GM* 15 (1745), 356–7. For Auchmuty, see below, Ch. 7.
[38] *London Gazette*, 15–19 Oct. 1745.

control of Cape Breton.[39] Furthermore, eight of the loyal addresses explicitly called for the island's retention in all eventualities. One of these was submitted by the corporation of London, which declared that Cape Breton was

a place of the greatest consequence to this Nation, as it secures your Majesty's subjects free and uninterrupted Trade in America, and protects them from the Insults of a dangerous and inveterate Enemy. And we intirely rely on your Royal patronage and Protection, to secure to these Kingdoms, the perpetual Enjoyment of this invaluable Acquisition.[40]

It is not difficult to explain why the capture of Cape Breton had such a remarkable impact on the British political nation. Apart from the island's perceived commercial and strategic importance, its capture provided at least one instance of military success upon which a harassed people, otherwise consumed with the spectacle of a seemingly unstoppable French advance in the Low Countries, could congratulate itself. It seems unlikely, however, that it engendered any significant shift in popular opinion in favour of the ministry. Rather, at least as far as the opposition press was concerned, it simply provided still further evidence of the imprudence of the ministry's interventionist strategy, as well as of the possibilities of a well-conducted blue-water policy. As the *Westminster Journal* observed: 'But if all our Expeditions had been undertaken with the *same views*, views to the increase and security of our commerce and conducted with the same *secrecy* and *Regularity*, does not this success afford a very good specimen of what *might* have been done.'[41] Moreover, the paper argued in the same issue, there was little evidence to support the view that the ministry were primarily responsible for the capture of Cape Breton; rather, all the evidence pointed to the primary role played by the uncorrupted New Englanders.[42] In fact, in the opinion of most opposition polemicists, the Broad-Bottom ministry had provided few signs of utilizing Britain's naval power to any greater effect than their predecessors. Calls for a wide-ranging parliamentary inquiry into the state of the navy were met with the less satisfactory reality of a far narrower inquiry into the naval disaster at Toulon, and criticisms of the condition and deployment of the navy continued unabated during the first six months of 1745.

[39] Ibid. 17–21 Sept. 1745.
[40] Ibid. 7–10 Sept. 1745. The other addresses calling for Cape Breton to be retained came from Exeter, Liverpool, Lincoln, Maidstone, Southampton (town and county), Bridport, and the borough of Fowey.
[41] *WJ* 3 Aug. 1745.   [42] Ibid.; *OEJ* 27 July 1745; *Craftsman*, 3 Aug. 1745.

On 11 May the *Old England Journal* called for an investigation into the nomination of allegedly inadequate officers to important naval commands, and provided a short list of experienced officers, including Sir John Norris and Admiral Vernon (both of whom were to play an important role in the defence of Britain's coasts during the '45), who were currently unemployed. Another, and rather anomalous, inclusion on the *Old England Journal*'s list was Admiral Lestock, who was popularly believed to have been responsible for the débâcle at Toulon. As with Britain's role on the Continent, the dominant tone of much press comment on the conduct of Britain's navy in this period was one of extreme disillusionment. Thus, on 13 July the *Westminster Journal* printed a letter from a correspondent that suggested that Britain's navy could be more usefully employed by catching mackerel, at least until the end of the fishing season. And in September the opposition City MP George Heathcote was echoing a widely held view, when he described the navy as 'a neglected, dishonoured, and ruined fleet'.[43]

Viewed from almost all angles, therefore, the press and popular reactions to the war in the first half of 1745 provided very few grounds for optimism regarding the likelihood of a rapid rallying of support for the Hanoverian regime at the outset of the Jacobite Rebellion. Furthermore, even after the defeat at Fontenoy, there was still more news of military set-backs to reinforce popular discontent with the war. A strategically inept retreat from the Allied army's defensive position at Lessines left much of Flanders open to further French advance and exposed further instances of supposed Dutch treachery.[44] As Horace Walpole wrote on 1 July to his close friend Henry Conway (Conway was serving in the British forces in Flanders at the time): 'We hear nothing but of your retiring, and of Dutch treachery; in short, 'tis an ugly scene.'[45] In August further disaster occurred, when the strategically important port of Ostend fell to the French. The loss of Ostend threatened to cut off the Allied army in Flanders from direct communication with Britain, and was one factor behind press speculation that Britain would be forced to evacuate its troops from the Continent and submit to a peace settlement imposed by the victorious French.[46] This view was strengthened by the Prussian military success against Austrian forces in Germany during the summer.[47]

[43] Rose, *Marchmont Papers*, ii. 341–2: Heathcote to Marchmont, 6 Sept. 1745.
[44] See Massie, 'Great Britain and the Defence of the Low Countries', 112–15.
[45] Lewis, Walpole, xxxvii. 200–3.
[46] See *Hanoverian Politicks*, *passim*; *LEP*, 16–18 May 1745; *WJ* 17, 24 Aug. 1745.
[47] See e.g. *Hanoverian Politicks*, esp. 23–6.

That the impact on popular opinion of Britain's desperate military position was causing concern amongst the ministry and their supporters during the very early stages of the Jacobite Rebellion is clear from a letter that Archbishop Herring of York wrote to Lord Chancellor Hardwicke on 7 September: 'The common topics of conversation', even between 'friends of the Government', were, Herring reported, 'the disaster at Fontenoy, the perfidy or the weakness of the D[utch], the frightful consequences of our engagements on the Continent.'[48] Just over a week later the Duke of Richmond was writing to Newcastle that the behaviour of the Dutch was threatening to 'raise the whole Nation into a flame about it'.[49] Yet, despite the deteriorating position of Britain and her allies during the first seven months of 1745, and despite the widespread dissatisfaction with the Broad-Bottom ministry's conduct of the war, most elements of the political nation were to demonstrate their loyalty to the Hanoverian regime at some stage during the Jacobite Rebellion. Furthermore, all those papers which had been prominent in the attacks on the Broad-Bottom ministry were to join with almost all the other elements of the London press in supporting the wave of defensive loyalism that overtook popular opinion towards the end of September.

Two basic features of this loyalist effort stand out. The first is the depth of support among London's various essay papers, newspapers, and periodicals for the Hanoverian regime. All of London's papers, not least those which under normal circumstances avoided all political controversy and contained no political comment, contributed to the deluge of anti-popery and anti-Jacobite polemic that streamed from London's presses during the height of the rebellion. Thus, the *General Advertiser*, the *St James's Evening Post*, the *Daily Gazetteer*, the *General London Evening Mercury*, the *Daily Advertiser*, the *General Evening Post*, and the *Penny London Post, or, Morning Advertiser* all opened their pages to pro-Hanoverian material. Two of these papers, the *General Advertiser* and the *Penny London Post*, distinguished themselves from other elements of the newspaper press by printing the slogans 'No Popery', 'No Pretender', 'No Arbitrary Power', 'No Slavery', and 'No Wooden Shoes' in the margins of their front pages between October 1745 and February 1746. The *General Advertiser* also joined a number of other papers in printing series of anti-Jacobite essays under such

---

[48] R. Garnett, 'The Correspondence of Archbishop Herring and Lord Hardwicke during the Rebellion of 1745', *English Historical Review*, 19 (1904), 532–3.
[49] *Richmond–Newcastle Correspondence*, 179–80: Richmond to Newcastle, 16 Sept. 1745.

titles as 'The Subject' (the *General Advertiser*) and 'The Briton' (the *General Evening Post*, the *Daily Gazetteer*). The *Universal Spectator* abandoned its strict 'Neutrality in Politicks' to defend the 'present Constitution' in early November.[50] Among the periodicals, the September issue of the *Gentleman's Magazine* discontinued its self-proclaimed function as a 'fund of profit and entertainment to the learned, ingenious, and public spirited' in order to devote its pages to rousing '*English* Virtue in each *English heart*'.[51] The opposition papers, meanwhile, uniformly enjoined a cessation of the 'rage against corruption', and advocated positive action in defence of the established regime. As the *Old England Journal* observed: 'The dispute now is not who shall set the sail or handle the rudder, but whether rudder, sails, and all shall sink or swim: it is not about modes of government but about the existence of our constitution.'[52] By the end of the year the existing papers had been joined by two newcomers: namely, the *London Courant, or, New Advertiser* and Henry Fielding's the *True Patriot*.

The second notable feature of the response of London's newspapers to the '45 is the timing of their support for the Hanoverian regime. The two leading opposition weeklies, the *Old England Journal* and the *Westminster Journal*, followed identical courses. As late as 21 September both papers were still publishing leading essays attacking the Broad-Bottom ministry's conduct of the war. A week later, however, following the Jacobite victory at Prestonpans (21 September), they were vigorously averring their loyalty to the Hanoverian regime, and counselling their readers to show resolution and unanimity in opposing the Jacobite threat. As is well known, the defeat of the Hanoverian forces under Sir John Cope at Prestonpans sent shock waves of alarm throughout the nation, firmly dispelling the view that the Jacobite army was an ill-equipped and ill-disciplined force that represented little threat to the regular soldiery of the British state.[53] The widespread hardening of anti-Jacobite feeling following the battle was reflected across the gamut of the London press, which almost immediately responded to the Jacobite victory by a very significant increase in the volume of anti-Jacobite polemic printed in most papers. As with the *Old England Journal* and the *Westminster Journal*, it was only after Prestonpans that the *Penny London Post* began to carry anti-Jacobite comment.[54] Similarly, it was on 28 September that the front page of the *General Advertiser* first carried the margin slogans referred to earlier.

---

[50] *Universal Spectator*, 2 Nov. 1745.   [51] See *GM* 16 (1746), preface.
[52] *OEJ* 12 Oct. 1745.   [53] Speck, *The Butcher*, 53–5.
[54] *Penny London Post*, 25–7 Sept. 1745.

A number of papers had already embarked upon an anti-Jacobite press campaign during the weeks before Prestonpans. In this respect, the activities of the two influential opposition papers, the *London Evening Post* and its sister publication the *Daily Post*, are of particular interest. Both these papers fell within the ambit of the printing interests of Richard Nutt. Unlike the situation for the vast majority of individuals who make up the personnel of the London press in this period, a limited amount of external evidence survives to illuminate Nutt's politics.[55] In 1736 Nutt had been elected to the Common Council for the opposition stronghold of Farringdon Without. Moreover, in the list of the corporation of London prepared for the Jacobites in 1743 Nutt was described as a Jacobite patriot.[56] Unfortunately, no evidence exists to shed light on either Nutt's precise contribution to either paper or the nature of his relationship with John Meres, who took over the printing of the *London Evening Post* in 1737. It is worth noting, however, that Meres's assumption of this responsibility coincided with a number of innovations in the paper's content that signalled a more determined phase in its opposition to Walpole.[57]

What is remarkable about the role of both the *London Evening Post* and the *Daily Post* in 1745 is that, issue for issue, they matched the loyalism of any of London's other papers. As early as 5 September the *London Evening Post* printed an item warning of the danger of party spirit in the present circumstances. On 7 September the *Daily Post* included a similar item on the need for unanimity in the face of the Jacobite Rebellion. The event that is most likely to have precipitated this response was the King's official communication to the Lord Mayor, Henry Marshall, that the Young Pretender had raised his standard in Scotland, an event that occurred on the same day that the *London Evening Post* began its anti-Jacobite campaign. On 14 September the *Daily Post* remarked:

I likewise heartily rejoice at the Laudable spirit that begins to appear in some of our publick papers against popery, and as I was the *first*, I think, that put a

[55] See M. Harris, 'London Printers and Newspaper Production during the First Half of the Eighteenth Century', *Journal of Printing Historical Society*, 12 (1977/8), 33–51.

[56] The list, apparently given to a Jacobite agent during talks with a number of leading City politicians in 1743, is reprinted in Cruickshanks, *Political Untouchables*, appendix 2: 139–47. There is no record of Nutt's personal participation in any of the various loyal schemes in London during the '45. For this, see N. Rogers, 'London Politics from Walpole to Pitt: Patriotism and Independency in an Era of Commercial Imperialism, 1738–63', Ph.D. thesis (Toronto, 1975), appendix 21: 658–64.

[57] G. A. Cranfield, 'The London Evening Post, 1727–1744', *Historical Journal*, 6 (1963), 20–37.

Hand for this plough, in warning and advising how to avert the storm, so now that it is come, I shall endeavour not to be behind-hand, with any serving the Nation.

The *Daily Post* was not grossly exaggerating its own role and originality. Only one of its rivals had been 'before-hand' in alerting its readership to the seriousness of the threat posed by the Jacobites: this was the *Daily Gazetteer*, formerly the vehicle for the pro-Walpole writers, which printed its first loyal item on 2 September. In addition, only one other paper, the *General Evening Post*, matched the efforts of the *Daily Post* and the *London Evening Post*.[58] A week later the loyal activities of these four papers were being emulated by a further two, the *St James's Evening Post* and the *General Advertiser*.[59]

As well as being measured against other London newspapers, the support that the *London Evening Post* and the *Daily Post* displayed for the Hanoverian regime also needs to be seen in terms of the dominant view of the Jacobite invasion circulating in the capital during the weeks before Prestonpans. On 9 November a letter in the *Old England Journal* attempted to explain the widespread indifference to the early stages of the '45. This, the correspondent asserted, had been primarily a function of popular expectations that the rebellion would be quickly extinguished by the British army. Cope's march to intercept the rebels had been popularly regarded as merely 'a parade of Triumph', and the people had 'in idea' seen 'Gibbets loaded with Highlanders'. 'But chiefly', the correspondent explained, 'we were animated by the Accounts publish'd by Authority, a few Days before the fatal Action at Gladsmuir [Prestonpans], that the Rebels were not above 3,000 naked, needy, miserable wretches, and that their Numbers were rather diminishing than increasing.' Even a brief glance at the reports of rebel activity printed throughout London's newspapers before Prestonpans would show that there was a close correlation between this explanation and the facts. For example, as the *Old England Journal*'s correspondent alleged, there was little in the *London Gazette* during the week before Cope's defeat to suggest that the rebel forces represented a grave threat to the security of the Hanoverian regime. The first official notice of the Young Pretender's landing in Scotland was published in the *London Gazette* on 17 August. The next information concerning the subsequent military movements of the rebels appeared in the issue dated 14

---

[58] *General Evening Post*, 5–7 Sept. 1745.
[59] *St James's Evening Post*, 12–14 Sept. 1745; *General Advertiser*, 13 Sept. 1745.

September—that is, barely a week before the defeat. In this respect, it is noteworthy that, before Prestonpans, even leading members of the old corps Whigs privately accepted the view that the rebellion would, in Henry Pelham's words, 'end in smoke' as soon as the rebels confronted 'a regiment or two with good officers at their head'.[60] Viewed from at least two perspectives, therefore, the *Daily Post* and the *London Evening Post* provide instances of two leading opposition papers not merely supporting, but actually leading, the loyal reaction against the Jacobites.

What, then, was the precise nature of the contribution made by these and other papers to the outpouring of defensive loyalism during the winter of 1745–6? For the purposes of elucidation, it makes sense to divide this contribution into three parts. While all three may overlap at many points, their separation helps to illustrate the various means by which London's papers and periodicals bolstered loyalist sentiments.

First, and at the most basic level, all of London's papers and both the major periodicals, the *Gentleman's Magazine* and the *London Magazine*, acted as vehicles for the dissemination of the various forms of anti-Jacobite polemic. As was briefly mentioned earlier, a number of papers printed series of essays designed to rouse popular opinion against the invading Jacobites. Of all the essays directly provoked by the rebellion, the virulent anti-popery pieces written under the pseudonym 'Montanus', first published in the *General Evening Post*, seem to have had a greater impact than most. A number of them were reprinted in both magazines, and all were collected together for separate publication in pamphlet form.[61] One political writer from the past to be disinterred was Addison. On 11 September the *Daily Gazetteer* remarked:

At the Desire of several of our Readers, who are firmly attached to the present Establishment, we present the publick with Mr Addison's Freeholder No. 9 which being the *Declaration* of the Freeholders of Great Britain, in answer to that of the Pretender, will, we think, be seasonable at this Juncture, and agreeable to all true lovers of Liberty.

The *Daily Gazetteer*'s lead was followed by a number of the other papers, which printed various essays from both the *Freeholder* and other works by Addison.[62]

[60] HMC, *Fourteenth Report*, Appendix 9, 131–2: Pelham to Trevor, 10 Sept. 1745.

[61] In its Nov. issue the *GM* noted that 'There are many other pieces by this author, which are collecting in a separate pamphlet' (*GM* 15 (1745), 80). Various essays by Montanus were also included in the pamphlet *Miscellaneous Pieces Relating to the Present Rebellion* (1745).

[62] *Daily Gazetteer*, 11, 14, 27 Sept. 1745; *GM* 15 (1745), 532–4; *St James's Evening Post*, 5–7 Nov. 1745; *General Advertiser*, 9 Oct. 1745.

Another major source of loyalist polemic was the multitude of cheap anti-popery pamphlets published between September and the following January. A typical example is the threepenny tract *The Pope's Dreadful Curse*. This tract, one of many emphasizing the allegedly cruel and bloodthirsty nature of the Catholic Church, was reprinted in the *General Evening Post* on 1 October, the *Daily Advertiser* on 2 October, and twice in the *General Advertiser*, initially on 21 September and then, allegedly owing to popular demand, on 25 September. It was also reprinted in the *Gentleman's Magazine*.[63] As well as reproducing items originally published in the newspapers, the two monthly magazines also extracted most of the more important pamphlet defences of the Hanoverian regime to appear during the rebellion.[64]

The final major source of anti-Jacobite polemic reprinted throughout the capital's papers was the English episcopacy's letters to the clergy of their respective dioceses. These letters, particularly of Gibson of London, Hoadly of Winchester, Secker of Oxford, and Herring of York, appeared across the gamut of London's newspapers.[65] As is revealed again by correspondence between Herring and Hardwicke, the importance of these letters as propaganda was clearly appreciated, with both men discussing the propriety of Herring's insistence in his letter on the certainty of a French invasion attempt in support of the rebellion.[66] However, it was Gibson's letter to the clergy of the diocese of London that seems to have elicited the most favourable response. On 21 September Thomas Birch wrote to his regular correspondent Philip Yorke: 'The Bishop of London's circular letter to the clergy is admir'd by the laity as the best performance of the kind, that has yet appear'd.'[67] As well as Herring's letter to the clergy of York, another of the Archbishop's loyal statements to be widely reprinted in London's papers, including the *London Gazette*, was his speech of 24 September to the loyal association in Yorkshire, in which he played a leading role.[68]

Perhaps as important as, and closely related to, this function of the

---

[63] *GM* 15 (1745), 490.   [64] See e.g. ibid. 531–2; 657–60.

[65] See e.g. *St James's Evening Post*, 12–14, 17–19 Sept. 1745; *General Advertiser*, 13, 18, 21 Sept. 1745; *General Evening Post*, 19–21, 21–4 Sept. 1745; *LEP* 12–14 Sept. 1745; *Universal Spectator*, 14 Sept. 1745. A number of the episcopal letters were also printed in pamphlet form and extracted in *GM* and *LM*.

[66] Garnett, 'The Correspondence of Herring and Hardwicke', 534–5, 538–9, 541–3.

[67] BL Add. MS 35396, fos. 325–7.

[68] See e.g. *General Evening Post*, 26–8 Sept. 1745; *London Gazette*, 21–4 Sept. 1745; *General Advertiser*, 28 Sept. 1745; *GM* 15 (1745), 471–2. Herring's speech was also printed in pamphlet form both in York and London.

press, was the coverage in London's papers and periodicals of the multifarious demonstrations of support for the Hanoverian regime that occurred country-wide during the rebellion. Particularly after Cope's defeat at Prestonpans, all of the capital's papers teemed with paragraphs and private letters giving the details of loyal associations, the size of individual and collective subscriptions to loyalist funds, and notable instances of loyal activity, such as popular demonstrations of pro-Hanoverian support. Just a few examples will suffice to give some indication of the range and nature of the press reportage of these activities.

On 22 October the *London Evening Post* noted that the keelmen of Newcastle had entered into a loyal association. The keelmen, the report continued, had been armed at the expense of a certain Crawley (the first name was omitted by the paper) and 'other persons of distinction'. As a coda, the *London Evening Post* declared: 'Which piece of news we mention with so much more Pleasure, as it was lately given out by the Faction that now disturbs our Repose that those Keelmen would join their Party whenever the Enemy should draw near.' Another form of support for the Hanoverian regime that was widely reported was the enthusiastic reception that greeted Cumberland's army on its march northwards. A vast array of paragraphs and private letters described instances of two outstanding features of the popular reaction to the army's presence: the billeting of soldiers in private houses at the express request of the inhabitants of a particular town; and the provision of horses to speed up the progress of Cumberland's forces. On 26 December, for example, the *St James's Evening Post* printed a paragraph that reported that the Tory MP Sir Lister Holt had sent 250 horses from his estate at Acton Hall near Birmingham to Coventry to expedite the movement of Cumberland's army to Chester. Holt, it is worth noting, was to play a prominent part in the crypto-Jacobite demonstrations at the Lichfield races two years later.[69] A final example comes from the *Westminster Journal* of 19 October, which reported that a Mr Scott of Fulham and a Mr Barat of Brentford, both brickmakers, had raised a company of their own employees to serve within fifty miles of the capital. These examples could be multiplied many times over, and the London press remains a much neglected source for loyalist activity during the '45.

In a number of cases the newspaper printers may have been paid

[69] See Cruickshanks, *Political Untouchables*, 107.

to insert particular paragraphs describing loyal demonstrations and actions.[70] In one or two others they may have been subjected to another kind of pressure. Certainly this is what happened to the printer of the *St James's Evening Post*, Thomas Read. Among the State Papers Domestic for 1745 survives a letter to Read from a certain Abraham Corbitt of Dublin, informing him that if he did not either publish the list of papist militia in Dublin that Corbitt had sent him on an earlier date or advise the government of it, he, Corbitt, would inform the ministry of Read's disaffection. Why Read should have been singled out by Corbitt is unclear. In the spring of 1745 Read had been arrested by the ministry for publishing a book of pornographic prints, *A Compleat Set of Charts of the Coasts of Merryland*. On that occasion he had assured Thomas Waite, one of the Clerks of the Signet, that henceforward he would abandon such dubious ventures, and, furthermore, he had offered to act as a press spy.[71] However they came to be published, the coverage in the London press of the various manifestations of loyalism ensured that they realized their maximum propaganda potential, which, as leading members of the ministry appreciated at the time, was their primary value. As Hardwicke remarked to the Duke of Newcastle on 25 September: 'I don't find any mention in the Gazette of the number of Lords, Gentlemen etc., who have desir'd to raise regiments. Surely some authentic publication should be made of that, in order to give spirit to the people, and to do justice to the persons who have desir'd it.'[72]

Given the scale and degree of attention shown by the press to the nation's demonstrations of support for the Hanoverian regime, it is hard to avoid the conclusion that it played an important role in creating a climate of opinion, both in the capital and elsewhere, which placed enormous pressure on individuals to demonstrate their loyalty in their respective communities.[73] In this respect, it is also significant that the opposition papers gave, at most, equivocal support to those sections of the opposition which argued that they should only join court-sponsored

---

[70] For this, see M. Harris, *London Newspapers in the Age of Walpole* (1987), 59.

[71] PRO, SP 36/68, fo. 110; SP 36/55, *passim*.

[72] *The Life and Correspondence of Philp Yorke, Earl of Hardwicke*, ed. Philip Yorke, 3 vols. (Cambridge, 1913), i. 458–9.

[73] For Tory MP Humphrey Sydenham's complaint that Tories were being threatened with being branded as disloyal if they did not take both subscriptions and associations, see *Parl. Hist.*, xiii. 1351–2. In Yorkshire a record was kept of those who did not chose to support the loyal subscription (N. J. Arch, ' "To Stop this Dangerous Mischief": Yorkshire and the Jacobite Rebellion of 1745', *York Historian*, 3 (1980), 27–31).

loyal schemes following a commitment from the ministry that it would support the people's loyalty with the passage of the various patriot measures designed to remedy the alleged corruption of Parliament and the electoral process.[74] Although the *Westminster Journal* and the *Craftsman* did print essays in response to an attempt by a number of opposition MPs to secure an amendment to the Commons address of thanks of 17 October proposing the passage of a number of 'popular' bills (the 'country' trinity of place and pension bills and the repeal of the Septennial Act) to buttress popular loyalty to the Hanoverian regime, these were far outweighed by press support, even in these same opposition papers, for unconditional identification with loyal schemes.[75] Neutrality in such circumstances, when 'All was at Stake', it was trumpeted from almost every other page of London's papers, was an unforgivable dereliction of patriotic duty.[76] Moreover, almost nothing was heard in the press during the final months of 1745 of the questions that were raised by a number of individuals regarding the constitutional propriety of the loyal subscriptions.[77] The only criticism of the loyal associations expressed in the papers concerned the prudence of committing resources to locally based measures, possibly to the detriment of the centrally organized defence effort. Thus, the *Old England Journal* argued that the associations were desirable if, and only if, they served as 'so many Reservoirs for supplying the great channels of Government'.[78]

Before leaving the subject of the press's support for, and publicization of, the vast array of contemporary loyal schemes and initiatives, it is worth briefly considering the response of a number of the capital's papers to the tightening of public credit and the run on the Bank of England that occurred during the last week of September.[79] The factors that lay behind this temporary collapse in financial confidence are sufficiently well known not to need rehearsing here. Suffice it to say that, in order to restore confidence, a large number of London's merchants agreed to issue a signed declaration stating that

[74] N. Rogers, *Whigs and Cities: Popular Politics in the Age of Walpole and Pitt* (Oxford, 1989), 70–86. [75] *Craftsman*, 5, 12 Oct. 1745; *WJ* 9 Nov. 1745.

[76] See e.g. *Daily Post*, 24 Oct., 15 Nov. 1745; *Craftsman*, 2 Nov. 1745; *WJ* 12 Oct. 1745; *St James's Evening Post*, 24–6 Dec. 1745; *General Advertiser*, 1 Oct. 1745; *General Evening Post*, 19–22 Oct. 1745.

[77] Speck, *The Butcher*, 57. But for rebuttals of these objections, see *General Advertiser*, 18 Jan. 1745; *True Patriot*, 24 Dec. 1745, 21 Jan. 1746.

[78] *OEJ* 26 Oct. 1745. See also *General Evening Post*, 12–15 Oct., 12–14, 17–19 Nov. 1745; *The Folly and Danger of the Present Associations Demonstrated* (1745).

[79] Speck, *The Butcher*, 66–7.

they would not refuse to accept Banknotes as payment for any sum of money owing to them. On 28 September the *London Gazette* published the first part of a list of those merchants who had subscribed to the declaration, which, as W. A. Speck has noted elsewhere, covered six columns of the paper. The second part of the list was published in the next issue, on 1 October. The complete list was also published, likewise over two issues, in both the *London Evening Post* and the *Daily Advertiser*.[80] On 26 September, the day the merchants' scheme commenced, the *General Evening Post* printed an essay that defended the desirability of the measure and the practicability of supporting public credit in such a situation. The same essay also appeared three days later in the *Daily Gazetteer*. On 1 October the *General Evening Post* returned to the issue of public credit, when it printed a monitory essay alerting its readers to the dangers represented by the dissemination of falsehood and rumour by the agents of the Pretender. On 2 October, to the same end, the *Daily Post* reported: 'We hear for certain that in a late Run on the Bank, (set on foot no doubt by evil-disposed persons) many were hinder'd from receiving their money by a crowd of people, several of whom had no Business there.' A number of other papers reported that another 'base Artifice employed to hurt publick credit' had been the activities of 'a certain noted Gentleman', who had repeatedly drawn out the sum of £5,000, taken the money immediately to a banker, changed it back to Banknotes, and then recommenced the operation of drawing out his money.[81] Meanwhile, the *Gentleman's Magazine* was reporting that twenty-four hours after the initiation of the merchants' scheme to support public credit, the declaration had been signed by a total of 1,140 individuals. Furthermore, the report continued, the run on the Bank was widely agreed to have been caused by papists and Jacobites.[82] The message thus being conveyed to the readers of London's papers was that the operations of the Bank of England were underwritten by the vast majority of the capital's mercantile élite, and that, rather than reflecting any deep-seated crisis in the stability of the Hanoverian regime, the run on the Bank had largely been caused by the machinations of a few disaffected individuals.

The importance of the contribution of the London press to defensive loyalism in 1745–6 is further suggested by the third and last aspect of

---

[80] *LEP* 26–8 Sept., 28 Sept.–1 Oct. 1745; *Daily Advertiser*, 28 Sept., 1 Oct. 1745.
[81] *Penny London Post*, 30 Sept.–2 Oct. 1745; *General Advertiser*, 28 Sept. 1745.
[82] *GM* 15 (1745), 500.

the press's role during the '45 to require comment here. In the course of writing about the role of a number of mainly, but not exclusively, northern provincial papers, R. C. Jarvis noted that the private letters published in the newspapers provided a great deal of information, albeit not always accurate, concerning local conditions during the Jacobite Rebellion.[83] The details of loyalist endeavour to be found in some of the private letters printed in London's papers, many of which seem to have been reprinted from the pages of the provincial press, has already been alluded to. Amongst the vast number of such letters published throughout the press at this time, a significant proportion were primarily designed by their authors to allay suspicions that particular localities or towns had shown anything but exemplary loyalty to the Hanoverian regime during the rebellion. In particular, letters from Edinburgh, Carlisle, and Manchester, all towns whose allegiance was under question following either their capitulation to, or their allegedly favourable reception of, the Young Pretender on his march southwards to Derby, were printed in many of the capital's papers vigorously defending the loyalty of their inhabitants.

Especially striking, in the light of the recruitment of a regiment by the Jacobites from there in November, are the various letters from Manchester. A typical example is the letter signed 'A. B.' that was printed in the *London Evening Post* on 28 December. This letter asserted, in response to the allegations that the town's inhabitants had aided the rebels, that out of a total population shared between Manchester and Salford of near 30,000, only 50–60 individuals had actually joined the Jacobites. And as regards those actions which occurred at Manchester at the time of the rebels' first arrival in the town, such as the illumination of windows in honour of Charles Edward's presence in the town, the author of the letter further retorted that these had all been undertaken under duress. Moreover, if any additional confirmation was needed of the town's essential loyalty, it was provided by the fact that as the rebels passed through the town on their retreat to Scotland, they had been pelted with stones by the town's inhabitants. The presence of large numbers of similar letters in London's papers at this time reflects not only the strength of anti-Jacobite feeling provoked by the '45, but also the importance that contemporaries attached to the press as a vehicle for the expression of that feeling.

[83] Jarvis, *Collected Papers*, ii. 3–36.

Yet another factor that points to the importance of the role played by the press during the '45 is the evidence of an increase in the demand for London's papers and periodicals. Not only did the rebellion immediately prompt the establishment of the *London Courant* and the *True Patriot*, it also improved the circulation of existing papers. One paper that seems to have attracted a very marked increase in readership was the *London Gazette*.[84] The major reason for this was undoubtedly the paper's role as the source of official information about the progress of the Jacobite army and the defensive measures taken by the ministry. Confirmation of this is provided by the compendious extracts from its news columns that were printed in the *Gentleman's Magazine* for the duration of the rebellion. In its December issue the magazine announced that it was temporarily ceasing its reports of parliamentary debates, hitherto one of its most popular features, in order to concentrate on the accounts of the activities of the rebel forces and the King's forces published in the *London Gazette*.[85] The success of this venture, together with the magazine's other loyal efforts, is indicated by the boast of the preface to the 1746 volume that its monthly circulation had increased by 3,000 as a consequence of the rebellion.

In the case of the *General Advertiser*, it is possible to provide figures for the increase in the circulation of the paper during and after the rebellion. Between December 1745 and December 1746 the number of copies printed per issue rose from 1,350 to 2,300.[86] In the light of these figures, it is worth noting that the *General Advertiser* continued its assiduous promotion of loyal sentiment for a considerable length of time after most of the other papers had reverted to their usual content. In addition, towards the end of 1746 the paper printed a number of very forceful pro-Cumberland items in response to the allegations of undue cruelty on the part of the British army at Culloden and during the Highland clearances that were being disseminated by, amongst others, the crypto-Jacobite paper the *National Journal, or, the Country Gazette*, first published on 22 March 1746.[87]

That the alarm produced by the Jacobite army was, in one sense, good news for the London press is also confirmed by the small wave of new papers and periodicals that emerged alongside the *National Journal*

---

[84] On 25 Jan. 1746 the *LEP* referred to the 'present Extraordinary demand' for the *London Gazette*.   [85] *GM* 15 (1745), 619.
[86] Harris, *London Newspapers*, 57.   [87] See esp. *General Advertiser*, 7 Oct. 1746.

in 1746.[88] A number of these newcomers also provide further evidence
that the primary dynamic behind this upsurge of press activity was
increased demand for news, and not comment. Thus, the *Whitehall
Evening Post, or, London Intelligence*, first published in March 1746,
advertised its establishment with the declaration that an unparalleled
news coverage would be provided, 'without the interruption of ingenious councils or profound speculations'. However, it would be wrong to
make too much of this growth in the demand for news. As has been
shown elsewhere, many of the news reports published in London's
papers during the rebellion emphasized the cruel actions and depreda-
tions allegedly carried out by the Jacobite army during its progress
and retreat, thus further kindling anti-Jacobite feeling.[89] Furthermore,
as has been illustrated above, all of London's papers contained a
vast quantity of anti-Jacobite comment and news of the many loyal
associations and schemes undertaken throughout the country during the
period of greatest threat to the Hanoverian regime. In this respect, the
London Gazette was no different from other papers. Between October
and December at least two-thirds of the *London Gazette* was filled with
loyal addresses from all parts of Great Britain and all sections of British
society.

In July 1746 Ralph Griffiths, at this stage just embarking on what
was to become a highly successful career in the London press, was
taken up by the King's Messengers for the publication of a pamphlet
entitled *Copies of Letters and Papers Delivered in their Execution by
the Nine Rebels who Suffered Death on 30 July*. Under examination,
Griffiths pleaded: 'During the late Rebellion I wrote and published at
my own Expence, several Tracts against the Pretender & his wicked
attempt, but by most of these Pieces, I was a considerable loser, as were
many others who contributed to glut the publick with such writings. At
the same Time all other Literary work were suspended.'[90] Griffiths's
remarks on the efforts of his fellow printers seem to have been basically
accurate. Moreover, some of them seem to have had considerably
greater success than the hapless Griffiths. Many advertised pamphlets
at discount rates for those gentlemen who intended to distribute them
in their respective neighbourhoods and among their social inferiors.

---

[88] The papers established in 1746 included the *Extraordinary Gazetteer* (28 July 1746–
50) and the *Anatomist, or, News Regulator* (Oct. 1746–50). The first issue of the new
periodical, the *Museum*, published by Robert Dodsley, appeared in Mar. 1746.
[89] For this, see Jarvis, *Collected Papers*, ii. 3–36.   [90] PRO, SP 36/86, fo. 350.

Thus, on 14 September 1745 the *London Evening Post* advertised a pamphlet entitled *An Address to the Honest Part of the Nation on the Subject of Popery and the Pretender* as follows:

This small tract is wrote with a view to undeceive the common people of this Kingdom, as to the groundless suggestion that they would enjoy their Religion and Liberties under a Popish Prince and to engage all Degrees of People in a just defence of their Country against any such Popish Pretender, and in order that so useful and well-tim'd a work should have the good and earnest desired Effects, by our Noble patrons disposing them so that they come to the Hands of all sorts of persons they are now sold . . . at a Guinea and a half per 100 and 6d a single book.

It is only possible to guess at how widespread this practice was, but it seems that it may have occurred on quite a large scale. On 21 September the *Daily Post* included a paragraph praising a particular 'very worthy Patriot' for distributing 500 copies of *The Pope's Curse* to his neighbours and tenants. In October the *Gentleman's Magazine* printed an abridged version of another cheap anti-popery pamphlet, *The Question, whether England Can Be Otherwise than Miserable under a Popish King*. The pamphlet, the magazine alleged, had been 'read in country churches, reprinted in different parts of the Kingdom, and many thousands given away by noblemen, gentlemen, and others'.[91] Similarly, Josiah Tucker, the Whig pampleteer and future Dean of Gloucester, claimed of his pamphlet *A Calm Address to All Parties in Religion Concerning Disaffection to the Present Government*: 'In the year 1745, the year of the Rebellion, I wrote a little tract which, with the approbation and by order of the Recorder of Bristol . . . was printed and given away in large numbers.'[92] Of the more conventionally priced and sized pamphlets, Henry Fielding's *A Serious Address to the People of Great Britain*, published at the beginning of October, was probably one of the more successful. The initial print-run of 3,000 was far in excess of the majority of comparable pamphlets. A second edition of 2,000 copies quickly followed, and in the course of the next month two pirate editions were also placed before the capital's inhabitants.[93]

In the 1770s Tucker was to claim that both his *Calm Address* and Archbishop Herring's speech to the loyal association in Yorkshire on

[91] *GM* 15 (1745), 522–6.
[92] Quoted in G. Shelton, *Dean Tucker: Eighteenth-Century Economic and Political Thought* (1981), 37.
[93] *The 'True Patriot' and Related Writings*, ed. Coley, pp. xxxvi–xxxvii.

24 September were reprinted and circulated throughout the nation by the government.[94] In the first place, however, this claim is hard to reconcile with the absence of a reference to any such action in the correspondence maintained between Hardwicke and Herring during the '45. Letters between the two men were otherwise meticulous in detailing ministerial actions to publicize Herring's loyal activities at York. On 28 September Hardwicke wrote to Herring regarding the speech to the loyal association:

His Majesty read it from beginning to end, and gave it the just praise it so highly deserves, and said it must be printed. I said I believed it was printed at York, but it was determined to print it in the Gazette. If in this my commission be exceeded, I plead my masters command, but I hope your Grace will not disapprove it, since my sincere opinion is that it deserves to be published, and that the topics and animated spirit of your composition are calculated to do much good.[95]

The same letter also told Herring that a paragraph that he had written describing the unanimity that informed the proceedings at York to establish the county's loyal association had also been placed in the London newspapers.

In the second place, it seems highly unlikely that Fielding received any direct ministerial support for either his weekly paper, the *True Patriot*, or any of his anti-Jacobite pamphlets.[96] The general absence of substantial ministerial intervention in the press at this stage is also suggested by remarks that Fielding himself made in the *True Patriot* on 10 December. Referring to the forceful anti-Jacobite pamphlet *An Occasional Writer in Answer to the Manifesto of the Pretender's Eldest Son*, Fielding somewhat bitterly observed that it was 'A pamphlet which some Administrations would have thought worth propagating by Authority'. In an earlier issue Fielding had also reflected on Henry Pelham's general indifference to the press.[97]

Finally, and perhaps most conclusively, we also have the testimony of Philip Carteret Webb, author of the pamphlet *Remarks on the Pretender's Eldest Son's Second Declaration* (1745). Webb's pamphlet had been prompted by a declaration issued by the Young Pretender from Holyrood House in Edinburgh on 10 October. In this declaration

[94] Shelton, *Dean Tucker*, 37. Tucker made his claim in *A Series of Answers to Certain Popular Objections* (1776).

[95] Garnett, 'The Correspondence of Herring and Hardwicke', 545–7: Hardwicke to Herring, 28 Sept. 1745.

[96] For this, see above, Ch. 1.   [97] *True Patriot*, 4 Feb. 1745.

loyal propagandists, the clergy, and the weekly papers had all come under attack for endeavouring to 'cloud the truth'.[98] In response, Webb exclaimed: 'Instead of the Government's having employed the pens of ill-designing men, to cast a cloud on the Truth, it is notorious that the Administration think the Pretender, and his cause, so little worthy of being answered, that they have not employed a single pen to write against him.'[99] The value of Webb's testimony is increased by the fact that he had come under the patronage of Hardwicke. In 1745 Hardwicke appointed Webb to be Secretary of Bankrupts in the Court of Chancery.[100]

Two other notable features of the output of London's presses during the '45 were the reprinting of classic anti-popery polemic, and the remarkable number of sermons published.[101] With regard to the latter, the *General London Evening Mercury* was to claim on 3 July 1746 that 'While the late Rebellion made any Figure, the sale of sermons was, perhaps higher, than in all preceding years of this century.' In many cases these sermons seem to have been printed with the encouragement of the same local élites that formed the bedrock of the defensive loyalism expressed during the rebellion. They were also one aspect of what seems to have been a colossal effort by the clergy of almost all denominations to imbue their respective flocks with 'loyal principles' and a due hatred of popery. In 1749 Lord Orrery, recalling the circumstances that had surrounded his return to Ireland from England in 1745, remarked: 'When my affairs called me into this Kingdom, the Clergy were roaring at the Devil, the Pope, and the Pretender. Europe was in arms, the Goddess of Discord was triumphant.'[102] A rough indication of the number of sermons that were published in London during the '45 is provided by the *Gentleman's Magazine*'s catalogue of books and pamphlets, which lists as many as forty-eight sermons directly bearing on the Jacobite Rebellion.[103]

[98] *A Collection of Declarations, Proclamations, and Other Valuable Papers Published by Authority at Edinburgh, in the Years 1745 and 1746* (1948), 15–19.

[99] [Carteret Webb] *Remarks on the Pretender's Eldest Son's Second Declaration*, 39.

[100] L. B. Namier and J. Brooke (eds.), *History of Parliament: The House of Commons, 1754–1790*, 3 vols. (1964), iii. 615–17.

[101] For the reprinting of classic anti-popery pamphlets, and the most recent discussion of the role of anti-Catholic feeling during the '45, see C. M. Haydon, 'Anti-Catholicism in Eighteenth-Century England, *c*.1714–*c*.1780', D.Phil. thesis (Oxford, 1985).

[102] *The Orrery Papers*, ed. E. C. Boyle, Countess of Cork and Orrery, 2 vols. (1903), i. 50–1: Orrery to Dr Mead, 13 Jan 1749.

[103] This figure underestimates the number of sermons published, as it does not include, for example, those preached on 5 Nov.

The principal aim of most of these sermons, together with the major part of all the anti-Jacobite polemic published during the '45, was to arouse the intense anti-Catholic prejudices that pervaded all levels of mid-eighteenth-century society.[104] The volume of anti-popery material printed in the capital's papers during the rebellion provoked the *Westminster Journal* to allege in early December that so numerous had been the 'Railings against popery' that they were now being widely ignored.[105] Whatever the truth of this, it is certain that a number of key themes in this strand of polemic surfaced again and again. Foremost amongst these was the contention that neither the Protestant religion nor the Church of England could ever be safe with a Catholic on the throne. This was a question not of personal disposition, but of the duty of any Catholic Prince to further the cause of the Church of Rome and to extirpate heresy. If proof were needed of the inevitable insecurity of the Anglican Church under Catholic rule, as well as of the inherent untrustworthiness of the promises of any Catholic monarch to protect that Church, this was provided by the reigns of Mary Tudor and James II. As Benjamin Hoadly advised the clergy of the diocese of Winchester:

If such promises are now made, you can inform your people, they come from one, who, supposing him disposed to keep them (which we have no reason to suppose) yet, is devoted to a religion, which not only sets him free from all the ties of faith, but, as soon as the proper time shall come, and the blow may be given with the safety guided by power, makes it his absolute duty, without which he shall neither enjoy earth nor heaven, to break thro' them all, and lay waste the religious and civil rights of that wretched people, who can be unmindful of what has happened in two former popish reigns, (remarkable for the strongest promises of security, and the most scandalous violations of these promises:) and be again deceived, by smooth words, into the same miserable condition.[106]

Behind a popish king, therefore, there stalked the Inquisition, the Jesuits, and the full apparatus of Catholic persecution. Nor did the ramifications of the imposition of a Catholic monarch stop there. Britain would also be subjected to the rule of Rome, and the Church lands that had been sold off during the Tudor period would be seized.[107]

---

[104] For the evolution of anti-Catholicism during the eighteenth century, see Haydon, 'Anti-Catholicism in Eighteenth-Century England'.

[105] *WJ* 7 Dec. 1745.   [106] *GM* 15 (1745), 483.

[107] For seizure of Church lands, see e.g. *True Patriot*, 12, 19 Nov. 1745; *Remarks on the Pretender's Declaration and Commission* (1745), 19.

The closeness of the relationship between the Pope and the Jacobite cause was underlined by a number of polemicists by drawing attention to the support and protection that the papacy had given to the exiled Stuart court in Rome. As the author of the cheap tract *The Question, whether England Can Be Otherwise than Miserable under a Popish King* asked of the Young Pretender: 'Has he not been bred up under the eye of the Pope? Is he not obliged to him, and other popish princes, for the subsistence of himself and his family? Do you imagine a Pope would protect him unless he had the strongest assurances of their zeal in his cause?'[108] Much of the anti-popery polemic was extremely crude, relying on direct emotional appeal for any impact that it may have had. Typical in this respect was a print entitled *The Pope's Butcher, or, the Massacre of Paris*, which depicted the streets of Paris swollen with the blood of the Huguenots slaughtered on St Bartholomew's Day, 1572.

If, then, the promises of the Young Pretender that the Church of England would be safe under Stuart rule lacked credibility, this was also true, or so it was argued, of his promises that Britain's constitution and the liberties of the English would remain untouched following a Stuart restoration. The claims that the Young Pretender would not only respect the cause of liberty, but advance it by purging away corruption and removing the influence of Hanover over British government, were met with a vast array of counter-claims. In the first place, and perhaps most importantly, the only title by which the Stuarts had a claim to the Crown, namely indefeasible hereditary right, was not only a 'ridiculous and exploded notion', it was also irreconcilable with the constitutional settlement that the Young Pretender was alleging that he had come to protect.[109] Such a title represented, in fact, a complete negation of freedom. As Philip Carteret Webb declared in his pamphlet *Remarks on the Pretender's Eldest Son's Second Declaration*:

The safety of the people is the *supreme* law, and is to be preferred to all *hereditary Titles*: And, therefore, in all *free* Countries, whenever the Prince, by a series of illegal proceedings, becomes a *Tyrant*, and endeavours to destroy his subjects whom he is bound to protect, he thereby forfeits the Crown . . . whoever can doubt of this, must be of the opinion *Princes* were not made *for* their people, but that the people were made for their king.[110]

---

[108] *GM* 15 (1745), 522–6.
[109] See e.g. *GM* 15 (1745), 471–2; *The Layman's Sermon* (1745), 7–9; *General Advertiser*, 6 Jan. 1746; [Fielding] *A Serious Address to the People of Great Britain* (1745), 4.
[110] *Remarks on the Pretender's Eldest Son's Second Declaration*, 31.

Furthermore, the implications for the governance of Britain of overthrowing the Hanoverian regime were obvious. The only means by which the Stuarts could hope to retain power was by destroying the fabric of government established by the Revolution.[111] In this context, the Young Pretender's education was also relevant again. If Charles Edward had been educated in the bosom of the Catholic Church, he had also been educated in the 'maxims of tyranny', amongst the Princes of Italy, Spain, and France.[112] By way of contrast, the Hanoverians, unlike the previous Stuart Kings of England, had shown only unimpeachable respect for Britain's constitution in both Church and State. As Archbishop Herring declared in his speech to the Yorkshire association: 'We are now bless'd under the Administration of a just and protestant King, who is of so strict an adherence to the laws of our Country, that not an instance can be pointed out, during his whole reign, wherein he made the least attempt upon the liberty, property, or religion, of a single person.'[113]

The threat posed by Jacobite success could also be discerned from the major sources of support for the rebellion. In this respect, the most significant aspect of the '45 was the involvement of the French. On 12 September Hardwicke remarked to Herring: 'One thing I have always observed is:—that representing the Pretender as coming (as the truth is) under a dependence upon French support; I say, stating this point with popery, in a strong light, has always the most effect.'[114] Hardwicke need not have worried. The loyal essays, pamphlets, prints, sermons, and addresses provoked by the rebellion bristled with declarations of detestation for France's support for the Young Pretender, and its consequences for the liberty and independence of Britain should the rebellion succeed. A number of polemicists and addresses even argued that the '45 was, in design and execution, a French scheme finally to extinguish Britain's opposition to France's historic aim of universal monarchy. Thus, the corporation of Bristol remarked:

It gives us no manner of surprize that the common enemy, in Resentment of your Majesty's zeal and magnanimity in Defence of the liberties of Europe, should endeavour to place a Dependant of his own on the Throne of Great

---

[111] *The Layman's Sermon, passim.*
[112] See e.g. *The Spirit and Principles of the Whigs and Jacobites Compared* (1746), 40.
[113] *GM* 15 (1745), 471–2.
[114] Garnett, 'The Correspondence of Herring and Hardwicke', 53–5.

Britain: For the system of Universal Monarchy can never take place, while Great Britain remains a Free and Independent Nation.[115]

In the event of the Jacobites dislodging the Hanoverians, Britain would inevitably become a province of France. Even if the Young Pretender genuinely desired to maintain Britain's independence, motives of gratitude and necessity would impel a Stuart monarchy to recompense France and her ally, Spain, for their support both in regaining and retaining the Crown. As a result, not only would Britain's liberties be further threatened, but the bases of her commercial power would be imperilled. As the author of the pamphlet *Remarks on the Pretender's Declaration and Commission* asked: 'Should they [France] insist on the most extravagant Terms, should Spain demand *Gibraltar* and *Jamaica*; and France besides *Cape Breton*, insist on *Plymouth* and *Portsmouth*, nay *Chatham* itself, should be delivered into their Hands, with what Face can the Pretender refuse it.'[116]

The importance of the connection that the bulk of loyal polemic established between France and the Jacobite invasion is hard to exaggerate. Not only did French support enable anti-Jacobite polemicists to allege that the success of the rebellion would inevitably result in the elevation of France to a new pinnacle of international power, it also underscored the threat that the rebellion posed to English liberties. As has been noted many times elsewhere, for the majority of the English nation aggressive hostility towards the French and all aspects of French culture and politics defined what it meant to be a 'free-born Englishman'. As Lord Orrery observed in 1731: 'It is the duty of every Englishman to hate the King of France: we look upon it as an eleventh commandment to which we pay more strict obedience than to all the other ten.'[117] French methods of arbitrary government, and an impoverished and oppressed French peasantry provided the antithesis, or so most Englishmen thought, to the rule of law and prosperity and contentment secured by Britain's constitutional government. Thus, just under two months before the outbreak of the rebellion, the *Old England Journal* had remarked:

Thanks be to that secret Reverence, which her worst of M——rs have had, in the worst of Times, for the Liberty of the Press: The Common People of *England* have at this time *English* principles . . . That Aversion to *France* which

[115] *London Gazette*, 17 Sept. 1745.
[116] *Remarks on the Pretender's Declaration and Commission*, 24.
[117] Quoted in Cruickshanks, *Political Untouchables*, 13.

ought to be Nearest to a *British* Heart, has . . . broke out with a spirit, which had it been carefully conducted would have been irresistable [*sic*]. Our naval Glory is still the pride of the community of *England*: the hatred of arbitrary power is their darling passion, and standing armies are by them considered as necessary Evils.[118]

During the rebellion one pamphleteer attempted to add to the anti-French feeling by drawing on the national myths constructed around Britain's supposedly glorious role in the coalitions led by William III and Marlborough against Louis XIV's France. How could France's present schemes, this pamphleteer argued, not fail to raise the indignation of every 'Briton', the same 'Britons' whose names had formerly caused the French to tremble at the mere sound.[119] France's support for the Jacobites was demonstrated, above all else, by the French invasion threat of early 1746. The defensive measures taken to repulse a possible invasion not only further exposed Britain's military vulnerability, they also stimulated more demonstrations of popular support for the Hanoverian regime in those coastal areas which formed the bridgehead of Britain's defences against the French. The foundation of the Laudable Society of Anti-Gallicans in 1745 was another appropriate expression of the intensity of popular anti-French feeling created by the rebellion.[120]

A resurgence of this feeling also seems to have produced a ground swell of popular support for Britain's participation in the war on the Continent in early 1746. Thus, the justices, grand jury, gentlemen, and freeholders of the county of Huntingdon, addressing the Crown after the defeat of the Jacobite army at Culloden, remarked that Cumberland's victory had created 'great Hopes to see that proud prince [Louis XV] yet humbled Abroad, whose Perfidious Attempts on your Majesty's throne and the inseparable Happiness of your people, has been so remarkably defeated in this Country'.[121] Similar statements were made in many of the other addresses that flowed in following Culloden, and the popular desire for revenge against the French was an important factor behind the very muted discussion in the opposition press of the propriety of recommitting British troops to the war in Flanders in the spring of 1746. A further factor tending to push popular

---

[118] *OEJ* 22 June 1745.

[119] *Remarks on the Pretender's Declaration and Commission*, 28–9.

[120] For the anti-Gallicans, see L. Colley, 'Radical Patriotism in Eighteenth-Century England', in Raphael Samuel (ed.), *Patriotism: The Making and Unmaking of British National Identity* (1989), i. 168–88.   [121] *London Gazette*, 2 Aug. 1746.

attitudes towards the war in the same direction was the widespread belief, also expressed in many of the loyal addresses occasioned by the rebellion, that the election of Francis, Grand Duke of Tuscany, as Holy Roman Emperor in September 1745 presaged a substantial accretion of military strength to the anti-Bourbon alliance.[122]

The last group whose support for the rebellion was used to arouse popular anti-Jacobite feeling was the Highlanders, who formed the bulk of the Young Pretender's army. This last fact operated against the Young Pretender at a number of levels. At one level, as W. A. Speck has pointed out elsewhere, it reinforced the view of the rebellion, already established by the support from Rome, Paris, and Madrid, as an alien intrusion.[123] At a deeper level, it could also be used to underline the basic illegitimacy of the Jacobite cause. Not only was the Young Pretender faced with the overwhelming hostility of the English nation, a number of loyal polemicists argued, he had only found support amongst a section of Scottish society that was outside the confines of civilization, and whose members were motivated solely by a desire for material gain. As the author of *A Proposal for Arming, and Disciplining the People of Great Britain* remarked:

How great an Indignation must it raise in the Breast of every *Englishman*, to see a crew of beggarly Highlanders, headed by attainted Rebels, march from their own barren mountains, into the very Heart of *England*, not only without obstruction, but with what they chiefly aimed at, the plunder of every country, through which they passed?[124]

The tenacity with which popular opinion held to the view that the Highlanders were an inherently bloodthirsty race also provided a further opportunity to portray the 'bloody' consequences that would inevitably follow should the rebellion be successful. On 26 October the *General Evening Post* described the rebel army as 'a bloody Host of Robbers from the woods and Bogs of *Ireland*, Droves of Savages from the Rocks and caverns of the *Highlands*, void of letters, and, even of Humanity, armed with Ignorance, Brutality, and barbarous zeal, must be turned into a Army to secure a violent Establishment by Acts of Violence.'

We have already seen how press reports for the duration of the rebellion contained stories and allegations of acts of violence and plunder committed by the Highlanders. And, as was the case with the

---

[122] For this, see below, Ch. 7.   [123] Speck, *The Butcher*, 187.
[124] *A Proposal for Arming, and Disciplining the People of Great Britain* (1746), 3.

French support for the rebellion, the propaganda potential of these reports did not go unrecognized by the ministry and its supporters.[125] Moreover, that they were having the desired impact is suggested by the comments made in a number of the loyal addresses to the Crown that were reprinted in the *London Gazette*. The address from the county of Pembroke, for example, referred to the 'uncommon cruelty' with which the rebels had 'ravag'd and plundered the Northern Parts of our dear Country'.[126]

On 12 July 1746 the *Westminster Journal*, looking back to the height of the Jacobite Rebellion, remarked:

It was at this Time, if ever, that the Liberty of the Press was the great Palladium of our other Liberties. All who made use of it, except those who had engag'd to be the Engines of its Destruction, turn'd it to awaken a too secure and drowsy People. They accomplished their Design, as soon appear'd in the spirit of zeal and loyalty that was every where diffused.

The mid-eighteenth-century press was apt to attribute almost every event of which it approved to the much-vaunted 'Liberty of the Press'. Yet, as it has been a major purpose of this chapter to demonstrate, here the *Westminster Journal* had at least reasonable grounds for making such claims. It is true, as the *Westminster Journal* indicated, that there do seem to have been a number of fly-by-night printers who were prepared to use their presses to produce Jacobite manifestos and declarations during the '45. However, their very exceptional and marginal position, when viewed against the response of London's printing trade as a whole, only confirms the impression of a staunch and vigorously loyal press.[127] It is also true that although all of London's papers displayed those features of press support for the Hanoverian regime described in the above account, they did so to varying degrees. Thus, not only was the *Old England Journal* one of the last to join the anti-Jacobite press campaign, it was also one of the first to break ranks and to publish essays that, if not disloyal, were openly critical of the ministry. On 4 January the paper's editor declared:

As I believe no Reader is *weak enough* to imagine, that a public writer at this Time is *mad enough* to blame; and, as I have never yet dealt so much in *Praising*

---

[125] See Garnett, 'The Correspondence of Herring and Hardwicke', 545: Herring to Hardwicke, 27 Sept. 1745.
[126] *London Gazette*, 11 Feb. 1746.   [127] PRO, SP 44/83, fos. 471–80.

as to acquire the Fluency of Panegyrick; I shall therefore use the Freedom with the Publick for one week more to make a borrow'd Extract from a pamphlet entitled *The Occasional Writer*. In the mean Time, I promise to break off my political Taciturnity the following week and be the Event what it will communicate to the Public my sentiments, and Praise where I can, and where I cannot, be *dutifully* silent.

On 18 January the *Old England Journal* duly printed an essay attacking the response of the ministry to the rebellion, and blaming their ineffectual measures for the initial success of '6–7,000 shabby, cowardly Highlanders headed by a beardless wanderer'. Similarly, as early as 21 December the *Westminster Journal* had printed a series of queries bearing on the same issue. Both these papers, however, had only reverted to attacking the ministry more than two weeks after the Jacobite retreat from Derby (6 December). If, as W. A. Speck has written elsewhere, the intelligence coming into the government during the '45 was one of mass support for the Hanoverian regime, the basic message being conveyed to the readers of the capital's papers, pamphlets, and other forms of printed propaganda was that the vast majority of the nation was united, in an almost unprecedented manner, by its repugnance for the Jacobite cause.[128]

It might be argued that the response of opposition newspaper printers and publishers to the '45 could hardly have been any different: in displaying loyalty, they were merely being prudent in seeking to avoid legal or physical harassment. Given the general paucity of information about the personnel of the mid-century press, it is impossible to prove anything conclusively about the motivations of the individuals concerned. Yet a number of the features of the press response to the crisis that have been described in this chapter suggest that such an explanation of opposition press behaviour in the winter of 1745–6 has only very limited applicability. First, in the case of one of the individuals about whom some information does exist, Richard Nutt, and who also moved in political circles frequented by Jacobites, the two papers with which he was associated, the *London Evening Post* and the *Daily Post*, were in the vanguard of defensive loyalism in late 1745. As we have seen, the loyalist efforts of these two papers pre-dated those of other opposition papers and of most non-political papers by between one and three weeks. Secondly, other opposition papers were not merely keeping their heads below the parapets in the crucial weeks

[128] Speck, *The Butcher*, 63.

between Prestonpans and the second half of December; rather, when the threat to the Hanoverian regime was most acute, they sought to play a full part in bolstering loyalist sentiment. In this context, a comparison can also usefully be made with their behaviour during the French invasion scare in the spring of the previous year. Then, despite the suspension of habeas corpus and a brief surge of loyalist feeling, the ferocity of their attacks against the ministry and Hanoverian influence continued undimmed for the duration of the scare.[129] Thirdly, the response of the *opposition* press to the '45 must be seen against that of the press as a whole and, in particular, against the wave of loyalist fervour that swept through all levels and aspects of the press after Prestonpans. In this, as at other moments, the press, including those opposition papers which had until that moment remained aloof from loyalist activity, appears to have been doing what success (or survival) necessitated: namely, responding to an abrupt shift in the popular mood.

One further and final conclusion is suggested by the response of London's presses to the '45. However much they may have disliked the personnel and politics of Hanoverian Britain, most English people seem to have viewed the imposition of a Catholic monarch supported by Catholic foreign powers as a worse evil. Amongst other things, this, as has been argued elsewhere and as is disclosed by the anti-Jacobite press campaign of the '45, reflected the existence of a broad-based consensus in favour of the constitution as established by the Revolution and the Act of Settlement. As the *Craftsman* declared on 12 October:

The Revolution under K. *William* the *Third* was undertaken, carry'd on, compleated on principles of civil and religious liberty, and to that revolution the Prince on the *British* throne owes his crown . . . A *Pretender* and a *Popish Pretender*, who attempts to break into this settlement . . . is actuated by principles destructive of these liberties on which the late Revolution is founded, and on which the Act of Settlement is made.

[129] For this, see above, Ch. 5.

7

WAR OR PEACE, 1746–1748

THE last chapter discussed the response of the London press to the Jacobite Rebellion of 1745–6. During the height of the rebellion press discussion of Britain's role in the war ceased as the capital's presses disgorged an unceasing stream of anti-popery and loyalist polemic. When the debate resumed in early 1746, the issues arising from the ministry's conduct of the war never engendered the same degree of concern or intensity as those which had overshadowed the press argument of the earlier 1740s. One measure of this is provided by the press reaction to the award of British pay to 18,000 Hanoverian troops in the spring of 1746, a measure very similar to that which had created such popular uproar in 1743. Although two pamphleteers argued the merits and demerits respectively of the ministry's renewed commitment of men and money to the Continent in 1746,[1] a subject also tentatively discussed in the leading opposition weeklies, no opposition polemicist commented on the measure itself.[2] Three weeks after the employment of the Hanoverians had been ratified by Parliament, twenty opposition peers issued a protest against carrying on the war in Flanders in which they expressed alarm at the absence of that 'Patriot zeal' which had characterized reactions to similar measures in previous years.[3] Two years later the situation was unchanged. During the debate over the Peace of Aix-la-Chapelle one opposition pamphleteer remarked: 'But for our parts we seem to be so entirely regardless whether Things are well or ill managed, that one would think the people of England did not so much as dream of their most essential Rights and Priviledges being settled by this Treaty. To what this general Despondency is owing . . . I am at a loss to ascertain.'[4] Yet if the press debate of the final years of

---

[1] *The Important Question Discussed, or, a Serious and Impartial Enquiry into the True Interest of England with Respect to the Continent* (1746); *A Detection of the Views of those who Would, in the Present Crisis, Engage an Incumber'd Trading Nation, as Principals, in a Ruinous Expensive Land-War* (1746).

[2] But for attacks on Pitt's defence of the measure, see above, Ch. 2.

[3] *Parl. Hist.*, xiii. 1411–13.

[4] *The Advantages of the Definitive Treaty to the People of Great Britain Demonstrated* (1749), 10.

the war was generally less vigorous, and certainly less influential, than that of the early 1740s, many of the issues that were raised, most notably those of trade and empire, were arguably of wider significance.

Many of the political factors that lay behind the depressed state of opposition writing and the wider lack of concern with issues of national politics have been examined in an earlier part of this work. It is as well, however, briefly to recapitulate the more salient domestic causes. First, the admission of Chesterfield and the Cobhamites into the ministry in late 1744 denuded the parliamentary opposition not only of its principal debating strength, but also of those politicians who had intervened so actively in the press between 1742 and 1744. As Horace Walpole acidly observed in his first *Letter to the Whigs* in 1747: 'We see no lists now in different colours of who voted for or against *Hanover* Troops; no journals to assure mankind, that whoever has a place, must be a villain; no *Grubstreet* Ballads on Yellow sashes, Brunswick mum and pumpernickle; no satirical odes on new ministries.'[5] Secondly, there was the increasing impact on the press and politics 'without doors' of the widespread cynicism about national politics that had been created, most notably, by Pulteney's great betrayal of 1742, but also by the failure of the Broad-Bottom ministry to pursue a programme of patriot reforms and measures in early 1745. Thirdly, opposition 'without doors' was still further weakened by the divisive effects on the opposition of the '45 and by the upsurge of loyalism provoked by the rebellion.

One last factor that also had the effect of constraining the opposition press was the suspension of the Habeas Corpus Act until February 1747. It will be recalled that in the spring of 1744 this same measure had remarkably little impact on the ferocity of the attacks that the leading opposition essay papers in particular levelled against the ministry and the conduct of the war. In 1746–7, however, its influence seems to have been considerably greater. This is suggested by, amongst other things, the fact that on more than one occasion during the winter of 1746–7 the *Old England Journal* felt compelled to remind its readers of the limitations placed upon it by the suspension of habeas corpus. In one particularly noteworthy issue it was claimed that it was this measure that had been principally responsible for the paper's dullness and caution during the previous six months.[6]

Against this background, and in view of the demoralized state of much of the parliamentary opposition and, in particular, of the Tories

---

[5] [Walpole] *Three Letters to the Whigs, Occasion'd by the Letter to the Tories* (1748), 14–15. [6] *OEJ* 4 Oct. 1746. See also ibid., 17 Jan., 7 Feb. 1747.

in the later 1740s, it is perhaps unremarkable that almost all the substantial pamphlets published between 1746 and 1748 regarding Britain's role in the war were either, on the one hand, written or inspired by the fallen Earl of Granville or, on the other, occasioned by the resignation of the Earl of Chesterfield in February 1748 from his position as Secretary of State for the northern department. The re-emergence of Leicester House as a centre of opposition only influenced press debate at the very end of the war (the first issue of the Leicester House essay paper, the *Remembrancer*, appeared on 12 December 1747), and it was only after the Peace of Aix-la-Chapelle that the Prince's followers provoked a significant response with detailed polemical attacks on the Pelhams' conduct of the war, and a revival of the controversy surrounding the abortive Treaty of Hanau of 1743. The central figure in this belated polemical assault was the Earl of Egmont, whose pamphlet *An Examination of the Principles, and an Enquiry into the Conduct of the Two B——rs* rapidly went through six editions in 1749.[7] Ministerial intervention in the press seems to have been correspondingly slight. For the final stages of the war Henry Fielding was almost alone in defending the ministry's conduct in his heavyweight election pamphlet of 1747, *A Dialogue between a Gentleman of London and an Honest Alderman of the Country Party*, and in his weekly essay paper, the *Jacobite's Journal* (5 December 1747–5 November 1748), a role that made him the object of a colossal outpouring of highly personal abuse.[8] In addition to just two issues of Fielding's *Jacobite's Journal*, only one pamphlet emerged in late 1748 to defend the ministry's negotiation and conclusion of the Peace of Aix-la-Chapelle.

The general torpor in politics and the press after 1746 was also, in part, a function of the circumstances of the war. The importance of external factors was remarked on at the time by Charles Yorke, who, in seeking to account for what he chose to describe as 'the right and happy temper' of the nation, suggested that 'Dread of France' was one of a number of 'deeper and more weighty causes'.[9] An important aspect of the loyalist fervour expressed during and after the '45 was an enhanced

---

[7] Egmont was also the likely author of *An Occasional Letter from A Gentleman in the Country to his Friend in Town, Concerning the Treaty Negociated at Hanau in the Year 1743* (1749).

[8] That the attacks of the *OEJ* and the *LEP* in particular were reaching their target is evident in Fielding's shrill remarks on the press and personal libel in his *A Charge to the Grand Jury* (1749).

[9] *The Life and Correspondence of Philip Yorke, Earl of Hardwicke*, ed. Philip Yorke, 3 vols. (Cambridge, 1913), ii. 79: C. Yorke to J. Yorke, 6 Aug. 1747.

perception of the French threat to British interests and liberties. Throughout the winter of 1745–6 the spectre of a French-backed Stuart tyranny formed a central plank of loyalist polemic, which also echoed with defiant celebrations of Britain's historic role as a principal obstacle to French hegemonic ambition. The significance of this for the debate over the war is demonstrated by recalling that, before the '45, an important strand of the opposition platform was either the denial or minimalization of the French threat to British interests in Europe and the Hanoverian and Protestant succession. The opposition Whigs and the *Old England Journal*, as has been emphasized in an earlier chapter, had even attempted to deny, despite impressive evidence to the contrary, the reality of the French invasion attempt of the spring of 1744.[10] Obviously, this line of argument was no longer a possibility after the rebellion, and both opposition and ministry were united in accepting the gravity of the French threat. And if anyone needed additional help in reaching this conclusion, it was provided by continued French military success in, first, the Austrian Netherlands and then, towards the end of the war, in the United Provinces. As will be illustrated later, the problem of the defence of the Low Countries was to assume an increasingly prominent position in the press debate as the war drew to its close.

The most striking feature of the discussion of Britain's role in the war after 1746 is the emphasis that was placed in the opposition press on the issue of Anglo-French commercial rivalry. Typical in this respect was William Horsley, author of the 'Fool' essays in the *Daily Gazetteer*. On 2 January 1747 Horsley declared: 'Two great points to be considered in this war, are the preservation of our Trade, and Ruin of that of the Enemy.' It would be wrong to exaggerate the novelty of this development. Advocates of a blue-water strategy, such as the *Westminster Journal*, had been preaching the gospel of commercial and colonial aggrandizement at the expense of the French throughout the 1740s.[11] Furthermore, important commercial interest groups had been publicizing the danger represented by the expansion of French commerce, notably in the sugar trade, since the late 1720s.[12] Nevertheless,

---

[10] See above, Ch. 2.

[11] See esp. Ch. 5. See also *The Present Ruinous LAND-WAR Proved to be a H——r War* (1745) esp. 20–30; *A Key to the Present Politicks of Europe* (1743) esp. 6; *Considerations on the Politics of France* (1744), *passim*.

[12] See C. M. Andrewes, 'Anglo-French Commercial Rivalry, 1700–1750', *American Historical Review*, 20 (1914–15), 539–56, 761–80.

there was a very perceptible change in both the nature and the emphasis of the debate about the commercial possibilities of the war after 1746. The scale of this shift is perhaps best brought out by a brief consideration of opposition attitudes to the central issue of the final years of the war: namely, to what extent, and under what conditions, peace with France was an immediate imperative.

This question, first raised in the press as a result of the dispatch of the Earl of Sandwich to the peace conferences convened at Breda in August 1746, not only cut across the Whig–Tory political axis, but also divided the ministry. As Horace Walpole wrote in late 1747: 'Except Mr Pelham, the Ministry in general are for the war; and what is comical the Prince and the opposition are so too!'[13] The enthusiasm for the war expressed by the opposition both in Parliament and the press during 1747–8 provoked justifiable accusations of inconsistency from ministerial supporters.[14] The extent and timing of the shift in their attitude is revealed by the Lords protest of May 1746 referred to earlier. The signatories not only attacked the ministry's conduct of the war, but also asserted the primacy of 'domestic welfare' as opposed to the demands of a foreign policy tending towards 'national calamity, bankruptcy, and military government'. Domestic welfare, it was further declared, would only be secured by 'the re-establishment of Peace, and of order, by wise economy, and temperate reformation, by regaining the confidence and authority to government, and reviving, in the nation a truly British and moral spirit'.[15] In short, the policy that, broadly speaking, had been advocated by the opposition since the second half of 1742. The principal cause of the sea-change in opposition attitudes was the growing conviction that Britain's naval forces would allow her to engross French commerce and colonies. As a consequence, James Ralph, writing in the *Remembrancer* in early 1748, was able to argue that 'the war ought to be condemned and yet *now* ought to be prosecuted'.[16]

A vital factor behind the growing recognition of the commercial possibilities being opened up by the war was Cape Breton, Britain's 'new American idol'.[17] As Paul Langford has noted elsewhere, the capture of Cape Breton added a new dimension to the debate over imperial opportunity, establishing the North American Continent,

---

[13] Lewis, *Walpole*, xix. 447–50: Walpole to Mann, 24 Nov. 1747.
[14] *The Resignation Discussed* (1748), 24–5; *Jacobite's Journal*, 22 Oct. 1748.
[15] *Parl. Hist.*, xiii. 1411–13.   [16] *Remembrancer*, 9 Jan. 1748 (my italics).
[17] HMC, Fourteenth Report, Appendix 9, xiv, 9, 151: Horace Walpole to Robert Trevor, 26 July 1746.

alongside the West Indies and the Spanish empire, as a key area in the struggle with France for 'power and plenty'.[18] The extent of the continuing popular enthusiasm for Cape Breton, particularly in 1746, is hard to exaggerate. On 23 December 1746 Newcastle wrote: 'The nation is now universally for war. All parties in Parliament seem to agree to it, and that which has thus united everybody, I am convinced, is their hopes, and expectations of keeping Cape Breton, and distressing and making impression upon the French in North America.'[19] As in the second half of 1745 (after the news of the capture of Cape Breton had first arrived in England), similar comments are easy to find, and the impact that the popular attachment to the island had on, most importantly, Newcastle led prominent members of the pacific wing of the ministry to bemoan what one of them called the 'servitude to popularity at home'.[20] As was suggested in the last chapter, a large element of the explanation for the value attached by the wider political nation to Cape Breton must lie in its symbolic significance. Against a background of grinding failure and successive military defeats on the Continent, Cape Breton shone forth as the proper object for a trading nation to pursue in war, tapping deep-seated popular beliefs regarding Britain's natural affinity with the sea, and maritime war as a vehicle for getting rich quick. It can also be more specifically related to a wave of pamphlets, essays in newspapers, and extracts in the monthly magazines published between 1746 and 1747.

This wave of printed material actually represented an amplification of the range of comment on Cape Breton that had begun to appear in the London press almost as soon as news had arrived in August 1745 of the capture of the island. A particularly influential and widely reprinted contribution to that first barrage of pamphlets and essays had been Robert Auchmuty's memorial, *The Importance of Cape Breton to the British Nation*.[21] In 1746, after the Jacobite Rebellion was over, it was again Auchmuty, a Vice-Admiralty Judge at Boston and a close friend of the architect of the expedition against Cape Breton, Governor William Shirley of Massachusetts, who was one of the most important contributors to the renewed press debate about the value of the island.[22]

---

[18] P. Langford, *The Eighteenth Century, 1688–1815* (1976), 124–5.

[19] Quoted in H. Richmond, *The Navy in the War of 1739–1748*, 3 vols. (Cambridge, 1920), iii. 49.

[20] See HMC, Fourteenth Report, Appendix 9, xiv, 9, 145: Trevor to Chesterfield, 17 May 1746.   [21] See above, Ch. 6.

[22] [Auchmuty] *The Importance of Cape Breton Consider'd, in a Letter from an Inhabitant of New England* (1746).

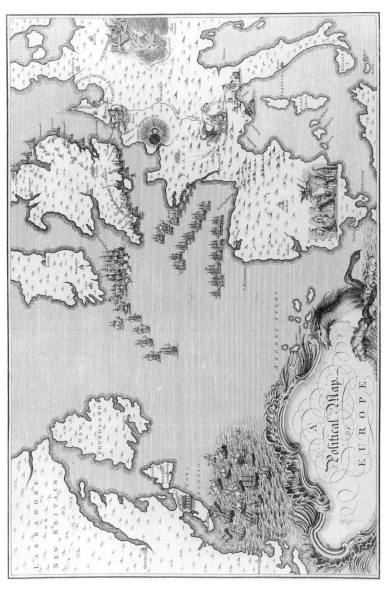

PL. 6. A Political Map of Europe. The capture of Cape Breton in July 1745 galvanized popular interest in North America, here reflected in its inclusion as one of the major theatres of the war.

A close colleague of Auchmuty's who supported his polemical efforts in 1746 was William Bollan. Bollan had been sent to London to attempt to recover from the ministry the costs of the expedition incurred by Massachusetts.[23] Perhaps somewhat ironically, one of the most commonly cited sources of information on the commercial value of the island was the recently published *Histoire et description générale de la Nouvelle France* (Paris, 1744) by the French Jesuit Pierre Xavier de Charlevoix.[24] Charlevoix's work included memorials written between 1706 and 1713 by Jacques Raudot, the Intendant of French Canada, to the metropolitan administration pointing out the potential value of the development of Cape Breton to both Canada and French trade in general. It was from Charlevoix and Raudot that the English press plundered the details of the enormous expenditure of the French on the fortress of Louisbourg, and French attempts to develop the commercial potential of their share in the Newfoundland fishery following the cession of Newfoundland and Nova Scotia to Britain at the Peace of Utrecht in 1713.

The benefits that the press claimed would accrue to Britain from possession of Cape Breton were broadly threefold. First, possession of the island would enable Britain to establish an exclusive monopoly on the Newfoundland cod fishery. The potential value of the fishery, with assured markets in the Catholic countries in Europe, particularly Spain and Portugal, was represented as almost limitless. One pamphleteer eagerly concluded

That the Fishery of Newfoundland Island and Banks, (under which general name I include *Cape Breton*, and all the rest in those seas) and the opposite coasts along the continent, might, if carried to the highest, and made the most of by any one Nation, be render'd of more value than the mines of *Peru* and *Mexico*, or than any other Possession of Property that can be had in any part of the World.[25]

Not only did the fishery promise wealth beyond a nation's wildest dreams, it also provided an ideal 'nursery of seamen'. Estimates of the numbers involved ranged from 20,000 to 50,000, thus representing a

---

[23] [Bollan] *The Importance and Advantage of Cape Breton, Truly Stated and Impartially Considered* (1746). Bollan was also related by marriage to Governor Shirley. One other pamphlet about Cape Breton that received much attention, but for which the authorship is unknown, was *The Great Importance of Cape Breton, Demonstrated and Exemplified* (1746).

[24] Extracts from Charlevoix were also reprinted in both the *LM* and *GM*.

[25] *The Great Importance of Cape Breton Demonstrated*, 69.

potentially huge accretion of maritime strength.[26] The fishery, it was further argued, would also create a 'vast consumption of British commodities, of most kinds', providing a particular fillip to the country's largest export industry, woollen textiles.[27]

Secondly, British possession of Cape Breton would stem the tide of the French commercial advance that had taken place in the thirty years after the Peace of Utrecht. Great emphasis was placed by a number of writers on the role of the French First Minister, Cardinal Fleury (1726–43), as an assiduous steward of French commerce and manufactures (one pamphleteer portrayed Fleury as the successful guardian of the legacy of France's great seventeenth-century Finance Minister, Colbert), and the Newfoundland fisheries were represented as the spring of French commercial expansion.[28] Louisbourg, it was noted, had acted as a safe harbour for French East and West Indian merchant shipping, and Cape Breton as a source of supply of fish and lumber to the French sugar islands in the West Indies. As one pamphleteer remarked: 'By these and other advantages join'd to their policy and prudent management, 'tis notorious, they had before the war well nigh beaten the English quite out of the foreign sugar trade.'[29] Furthermore, Louisbourg was the key to Canada. English control of the Gulf of St Lawrence, secured by the possession of Cape Breton, could either provide a starting-point for an expedition against Canada or enable the isolation of the French settlement and its slow dissolution. Eventually, therefore, in addition to the fishery, Britain would acquire the fur trade, 'which is', one pamphleteer alleged, 'perhaps next to the fishery the most valuable in that part of the world'.[30] In short, it was argued, hold on to Cape Breton, and you would be cutting off the source of the expansive potential of France's commerce and thus, it was assumed, French military might.

The third and last advantage that, according to the press, was to be gained from the possession of the island was the security not only of Britain's trade with the North American Continent, but also of her North American colonies. Without Cape Breton, one pamphleteer declared, 'the *British* Empire in *America* can be no otherwise compleated, nor our Trade to *New England, New York*, the *Jersies*,

---

[26] Auchmuty estimated the number of French fishermen employed in the fishery at 25,000–30,000, and the value of the fishery at £2 million per annum. The author of *The Great Importance of Cape Breton Demonstrated* put the number of fishermen at 30,000–50,000.   [27] *The Great Importance of Cape Breton Demonstrated*, 69.
[28] See esp. *The Importance of Cape Breton Consider'd*, 15.
[29] Ibid. 2.   [30] *The Great Importance of Cape Breton Demonstrated*, 72.

Maryland, Virginia, Carolina, and *Georgia* be secured'.[31] The threat that a French presence at Cape Breton posed to the British in North America was, therefore, twofold. First, it provided a base for the French privateers who preyed on English merchant shipping on route to and from the English colonies. Secondly, and more ominously, it also provided a base from which to launch expeditions, first, against Nova Scotia and then, from there, against New England and the other major English North American colonies. Interestingly, the gathering menace of French attempts to link up their settlements in Canada with those at the mouth of the Mississippi, the precipitant of the Seven Years War, was raised in a number of places. Thus, on 30 April 1748 the *Westminster Journal* remarked that the 'French were artfully working for universal Empire in America'.

The weight of these warnings was increased by the French attacks on Canso, one of two English settlements in Nova Scotia, at the beginning of the war. The vulnerability of Nova Scotia, with its large French Catholic population and its biddable Indian population, was a continually reiterated theme in press discussion concerning Cape Breton, and it was an increased awareness of the potential threat of expanding French power in North America that lay behind the widespread enthusiasm with which the post-war scheme, sponsored by the Duke of Bedford as Secretary of State for the southern department (1748–51) and the Earl of Halifax at the Board of Trade, to colonize Nova Scotia with demobilized troops and seamen was received in 1749.

Perhaps surprisingly, given the repreated expressions of ministerial concern over the possible domestic consequences of the restoration of Cape Breton to the French, the restitution of the island at the Peace of Aix-la-Chapelle failed to provoke a popular outcry. What is not clear is how far this was simply a result of a diminution of popular concern over the island during the last two years of the war. In early 1747 a number of opposition writers continued the call, first raised in late 1745 by London's merchants, for the annexation of the island by Act of Parliament.[32] As late as August 1747 the Earl of Sandwich was writing to his patron, the Duke of Bedford: 'Whatever we may flatter ourselves to the contrary, the clamour that will be raised in consequence of any arrangements that may be taken about that acquisition [Cape Breton] will, I am certain, have very great weight in the nation.'[33] Continued

---

[31] Ibid. [32] See esp. *WJ* 31 Jan., 28 Feb. 1747.

[33] Russell, Lord John (ed.), *The Correspondence of John, Fourth Duke of Bedford*, 3 vols. (1842–6), i. 241–5: Sandwich to Bedford, 29 Aug. 1747.

ministerial sensitivity to the popular dimension to Cape Breton's future was also articulated in Fielding's *Jacobite's Journal* in the period between the signing of the peace preliminaries in April 1748 and the conclusion of the definitive peace in October. On 24 September the leading article in the paper anxiously attacked the *London Evening Post* for its objections to the restoration of the island to the French, and urged readers to view that one provision of the peace settlement in terms of the whole: 'Who doth not see that the Question is not whether *Cape Breton* be, or be not of Importance; but whether it be of greater Importance to us than the terms upon which we are to surrender it?' Furthermore, the theme of Anglo-French commercial rivalry was kept firmly in the forefront of debate by the efforts of the British navy. On 3 July 1747 Horace Walpole wrote that 'we shine at sea',[34] and the victories of Anson off Cape Finistère in May, and Hawke off Belle-Isle in October signalled to the political nation Britain's increasing command of the sea.

The impact of these naval victories on press debate was intensified by their sharp contrast with the apparent shortcomings of the condition and deployment of the navy before the end of 1746. Up until then, press discussion of the naval aspect of the war was still being overshadowed by the inconclusive engagement that had occurred south of Toulon in February 1744. As was shown in an earlier chapter, the immediate impact of this débâcle was lessened by the degree to which the opposition press was preoccupied with the war on the continent and, in particular, with the role of Hanover. By early 1745, however, stimulated by the formation of the Broad-Bottom ministry and by a number of further instances of naval misfortune (or mismanagement) in 1744, the press clamour for the punishment of those responsible was gaining momentum.[35]

We have already noted how early 1745 also saw widespread calls from the press for a comprehensive inquiry into the condition and management of the navy, a demand that was met with the far more limited Commons inquiry into the miscarriage at Toulon.[36] After sifting through a mountain of evidence, this inquiry ended with the Commons

---

[34] Lewis, *Walpole*, xix. 423–5: Walpole to Mann, 3 July 1747.

[35] Apart from the usual criticisms of inadequate naval protection of commercial shipping, one particular incident that provided a focus for the expression of discontent in the press regarding the management of the navy was the loss of the 110-gun ship, the *Victory*, in a storm in the autumn of 1744. See e.g. *WJ* 12 Jan. 1745; *LEP* 20 Oct., 8 Dec. 1744.

[36] See above, Ch. 6.

addressing the King to hold courts martial on Matthews, his second in command, Admiral Richard Lestock, and a number of other officers who appeared to be culpable.[37] When Matthews and Lestock were eventually tried by court martial in early 1746, the opposition press felt that justice was evaded. In particular, Lestock's acquittal at the hands of his fellow officers, and his subsequent joint command of a combined operation against Brittany in late 1746 (Lestock was known to have connections with leading figures among the old corps Whigs), was portrayed as a further instance of the debilitating encroachment of corruption.[38] It also led to calls for an alternative to trial by courts martial.[39] Lestock's fate was widely contrasted with that of the patriot hero Edward Vernon, who had been struck from the list of Admirals after disagreements with the Admiralty Board concerning his role in the defence of the Channel during the '45.[40] In 1746 Vernon attempted to vindicate his position by publishing his correspondence with the Board, in which he had criticized many areas of current naval practice and administration, in pamphlet form.[41]

The extent of the impact of the naval victories can also be related to the expectations of effective naval action raised (and frustrated) during the previous year. As part of an attempt to extend the appeal of the ministry, the King's speech of 14 January 1746 included a paean to Britain's naval force, and a declaration of intent 'to be particularly attentive to this important service; and to have such a fleet at sea early in the Spring; as may be sufficient to defend ourselves and annoy our Enemies'.[42] William Horsley was again typical in heralding the possibilities of effective naval action from August 1746 onwards.[43] Words, however, were not matched by deeds. Not only did a planned expedition against Canada fail to depart during the summer, but the navy failed to intercept a French squadron under the Duke d'Enville that had been dispatched to recapture Louisbourg. As various sections of the opposition press were quick to point out, the reasons for the failure of D'Enville's expedition had nothing to do with effective

---

[37] J. B. Owen, *The Rise of the Pelhams* (1957), 264–6. I am also grateful to Dr P. A. Luff for allowing me to read a copy of his unpublished paper, 'Matthews versus Lestock: Parliament, Politics, and the Navy in Mid-Eighteenth Century England'.

[38] *WJ* 14 Feb., 15 Aug. 1747; *Daily Gazetteer*, 4 Feb. 1747.

[39] *WJ* 27 Sept., 8, 14, 29 Nov. 1746.

[40] Richmond, *The Navy in the War*, ii. 184.

[41] [Vernon] *A Specimen of Naked Truth (in Letters) from a British Sailor* (1746); *Original Letters to an Honest Sailor* (1746).

[42] *Parl. Hist.*, xiii. 1395.   [43] See *Daily Gazetteer*, 14 Aug., 26 Sept. 1746.

preparations for the defence of Britain's celebrated acquisition.[44] Furthermore, when the abortive expedition to Canada was redirected to raid the coast of Brittany, it ended in a foolish retreat. On 23 October Alexander Hume Campbell wrote to his brother the Earl of Marchmont: 'The silly, not secret, expedition to France is exclaim'd against as ill-conducted, worse contrived and not possible to have any but a bad effect.'[45]

British naval commanders in the West Indies added to the dismal picture by demonstrating a seemingly unerring capacity to allow French convoys to sail undisturbed to and from Martinique. Particularly damaging to the ministry in this respect were the efforts of Commodore Mitchell, who surpassed himself by failing to engage a weaker contingent of French men-of-war stewarding a French convoy sailing out from the West Indies that had already evaded Mitchell's colleague, Commodore Lee.[46] Thus, on 28 October Hume Campbell was again writing to his brother of naval shortcomings: 'The news stirring here is a misbehaviour in one Commodore Mitchell who it seems with five ships ran away from three French in the West Indies.'[47] In India, too, the news was bad, with La Bourdonnais, the Governor of the French islands in the Indian ocean (the Seychelles and île de France (Mauritius)) capturing Madras in September. This loss, however, excited nowhere near the same degree of attention in the press as, in particular, D'Enville's unhindered passage to the coasts of North America.

The effect on popular opinion of the following year's naval success and of the steady tightening of the British navy's grip on France's major trading routes was, as already mentioned, exploited most vigorously by pro-Granville polemicists. Between the beginning of 1747 and the end of 1748 Granville either directly sponsored or inspired four substantial pamphlets, two urging the continuation of the war, and two, published after the signing of the peace preliminaries, condemning the ministry's sacrifice of Britain's supposed prospects of gain for an unsatisfactory peace. The first of these pamphlets, *The State of the Nation Consider'd in a Letter to a Member of Parliament*, went through four editions and was extracted in the *London Magazine*.[48] The impact of the pamphlet is

[44] *WJ* 14 Feb., 18 Apr., 15 Nov. 1747; *The State of the Nation Consider'd* (1747), 17–18.   [45] HMC, Polwarth Papers, v. (1961), 183.
[46] See Richmond, *The Navy in the War*, iii. 53–8.
[47] HMC, Polwarth Papers, v. 183.   [48] LM 16 (1747), 65–7.

also detectable in Fielding's *A Dialogue between a Gentleman of London and an Honest Alderman of the Country Party*. In an easily decipherable allusion to Granville's conduct of the war between 1742 and 1744, Fielding warned that an opposition victory in the elections of 1747 would either lead to the desertion of Britain's allies and interests in Europe or 'a shameful and no less ruinous Forwardness to continue the war upon objects or Passions in which the Interest and Honour of *England* hath no real or weighty concern, which the past conduct of others who bear a principal part in the same opposition gives too much cause to apprehend'.[49] In early 1748 the second of the pro-Granville pamphlets, *The State of the Nation for the Year 1747, and Respecting 1748*, had a similar impact to its predecessor, going through three editions and being extracted in both the *London Magazine* and the *Westminster Journal*.[50] It also earned the distinction of being one of only two pamphlets published between 1747 and 1748 to elicit a direct rebuttal from pro-ministerial writers.[51]

The principal war aims advanced by the pro-Granville polemicists were the destruction of French trade in its entirety, and the capture of all spheres of French colonial influence: North America, the French sugar colonies in the West Indies, the French settlements in India—all were to be swept up in a whirlwind of British naval success. Destroy French commerce and naval power, it was argued, and Britain would be able to command a peace on her own terms:

> It is no paradox to say, that commerce is the Basis of Dominion, nor is it difficult to conceive that what the *French* lose, is our Gain. All agree, that *French* commerce, before the war, was more extensive than our own, nor will any one dispute that it brought them more wealth. It naturally follows that such Addition must increase our Power, and proportion lessen that of *France* who, by having no commerce, must drop all her destructive projects for want of pecuniary support; and consequently the destroying *French* commerce produce such a Peace as we want.[52]

The use of growing fiscal strain as a possible objection to the prolongation of the war was dismissed in a stream of accusations of fiscal mismanagement and proposals for spreading the tax burden more

[49] [Fielding] *A Dialogue between a Gentleman of London and an Honest Alderman* (1747), 44.   [50] *LM* 17 (1748), 13–18; *WJ* 20 Feb. 1748.

[51] *The Case Restated, or, an Examine of a Late Pamphlet, Intitled, the State of the Nation for the Year 1747* (1748). The other pamphlet to provoke direct rebuttal was Chesterfield's *An Apology for a Late Resignation* (1748). See below.

[52] *The State of the Nation for the Year 1747*, 30–1.

evenly.[53] Rather inconsistently, however, it was also argued that the mounting size of the national debt was a factor behind the need to secure the bulk of French trade and the majority of her colonies. Only by the increase in revenues that this would provide could Britain free itself from the current scale of national indebtedness.[54] The consequences of failing to pursue these war aims and of acceding to a 'shameful peace' were represented as being as dramatic as the possibilities created by continuing the war. Britain, emasculated by the burden of a colossal national debt, would be unable to counter a France emancipated from the control of the British navy and allowed to recover her commercial and naval position. Following a bad peace, it was argued, 'One Summer's campaign by Land and Sea may ruin the work of Ages, and render the power of *France* wholly irresistible.'[55] Even if military defeat were avoided, the tax burden on Britain's trade, a consequence of the need to service the expanded national debt, would inevitably depress Britain's commercial standing, primarily to the advantage of the French.

Of course, there were many obvious weaknesses in these arguments, and a number of them were attacked at the time. Two central assumptions that were justifiably contested were, first, the closeness of the link between French military power and the extent of her colonial trade and, secondly, the ease with which French colonies would fall into Britain's eagerly outstretched hands.[56] Nevertheless, the evidence of other elements of the press suggests that both these assumptions and the war aims promulgated by the pro-Granville pamphleteers were widely accepted, at least amongst the opposition. The *Westminster Journal*, the *Old England Journal*, and the influential *London Evening Post* all advocated the continuation of the war and echoed the Granvillite declarations regarding the huge accretion of commercial strength awaiting capture. Even the ministry, in the form of the King's speech at the close of the 1746–7 parliamentary session, acknowledged the extent to which naval success was transforming the circumstances of the war: 'The signal success which by the blessing of God, has already attended my Fleet has happily disappointed some very pernicious

---

[53] *The State of the Nation Consider'd*, 29–31; *The State of the Nation for the Year 1747*, pp. vii, 7–8. Both pamphlets included unfavourable comparisons between levels of expenditure during the War of the Spanish Succession and the present conflict to support the general allegation of financial mismanagement.

[54] *The State of the Nation for the Year 1747*, p. xiv.

[55] *The State of the Nation for the Year 1747, and Respecting 1748* (1748), 15.

[56] *The Case Restated*, 42–5.

projects of our enemies, and given a considerable blow to their naval strength, as well as to their commerce: which will be the most probable means of reducing them to reason.'[57] The only dissentient voice in the press seems to have been the *Craftsman*, by this stage already far advanced into obscurity, which was still printing essays calling for the extrication of Britain from the war, and the instigation of a policy of domestic reform. Nevertheless, the paper acknowledged the domestic impact of the naval success, remarking that it had 'rendered the people almost forgetful awhile of their Grievances'.[58]

By contrast to the maritime aspect of the war, the military prospects on the Continent between 1746 and 1748 gave far fewer grounds for optimism. As was mentioned earlier, a prominent feature of the press debate in this period was the increasing intrusion of the problem presented by the continued French military advance in the Low Countries. As far as the opposition press was concerned, however, this issue decreased in importance for the major part of 1746 as a result of the success of the combined Austro-Sardinian armies in Italy, which opened up the prospect of an invasion of France through Provence early in the following year. On 16 April 1746 Horace Walpole wrote to Sir Horace Mann: 'Your triumphs in Italy are in high fashion: till very lately Italy was scarce ever mentioned as part of the scene of war.'[59] It seems that the favourable prospect created by events in Italy engendered a temporary revival of confidence amongst a broad section of the political nation regarding the conflict in Europe. In Parliament the leading City MP Sir John Barnard proposed an unsuccessful motion to alter the Commons address of thanks in reply to the King's speech to assert that the victories in Italy 'over-balanced' the failures in the Low Countries.[60] Throughout the second half of the year William Horsley showered plaudits on the Earl of Granville, the author of the Treaty of Worms, and proclaimed him to be the architect of the improved situation in Italy.[61] Horsley also remarked on the significance of the Peace of Dresden (1745), which had brought to an end the second Silesian War, and which, together with the elevation of Francis, Grand Duke of Tuscany, to the imperial throne in September 1745, had effectively settled those issues which had led to war in Germany in the early 1740s. Horsley's optimism was shared by the author of the *Westminster*

[57] *Parl. Hist.*, xiv. 63–6.
[58] *Three Letters to the Members of the Present Parliament* (1747), 21.
[59] Lewis, *Walpole*, xix. 239–44.   [60] *Parl. Hist.*, xiii. 1428–32.
[61] *Daily Gazetteer*, 22 Aug., 6, 26 Sept., 30 Oct., 28 Nov. 1746.

Journal. On 1 February 1746 the paper asserted the possibility of constructing a bellicose anti-Bourbon alliance encompassing Saxony-Poland and Prussia and the empire, and largely financed by Britain. This alliance, it was argued, would effect the dismemberment of 'Alsace, Lorrain, French Luxemburgh, French Hainault, Artois, Flanders' from the French. The central assumption underlying this scheme—namely, that Prussia and the empire would naturally intervene in the war on behalf of the anti-Bourbon powers—was unrealistic. Nevertheless, it was an assumption shared by many writers in the final stages of the war, and is yet another instance of the failure of most British writers to comprehend the depth of Austro-Prussian rivalry after 1740. The hopes of an Austro-Sardinian invasion through Provence came to an early end in February 1747, when the Allied army ground to a halt, immobilized by differences between the two powers and by the insurrection of Genoa, which cut their supply lines.[62]

In order to appreciate the gravity of the problem introduced into the debate by the near total collapse of the Dutch Barrier between 1746 and 1747 and by the French military irruption into the United Provinces in the spring of 1747, it is necessary to recognize the strength of the consensus throughout the political nation regarding the vital strategic and economic importance of the Low Countries to Britain. On 16 January the *Remembrancer*, although at the same time advocating a blue-water strategy, declared that 'The people of *England*, I am persuaded, will submit chearfully to the pressures of a war, which hitherto they have had abundant Reason to complain of, for the sake of preserving a State [Holland], which is so immediately the Barrier of their own. Such an *object* they would call a British *object*.' Throughout 1747–8 other elements of the opposition press and pro-ministerial pamphlets rang with similar comments. The pro-Granville pamphlet *The State of the Nation for the Year 1747, and Respecting 1748* warned: 'When *Holland* is gone, we not only lose a Country, but at the same time erect a naval power, equal to our own, facing us at a small Distance, and then have but a faint chance to preserve our commerce, if we shall be able to defend ourselves at Home, our domestic Rights and Liberties.'[63] While supporting the ministry, Fielding included a lengthy exposition of the gravity of the situation in the Low Countries in his pamphlet *A Dialogue between a Gentleman of London and an Honest*

---

[62] R. Lodge, *Studies in Eighteenth-Century Diplomacy, 1740–1748* (1930), 201–3.
[63] *The State of the Nation for the Year 1747*, 30.

Alderman of the Country Party.[64] Furthermore, looking forward to the debate over the Peace of Aix-la-Chapelle, argument concerning the continued defensibility of Holland, and the possible role of the Russian auxiliaries who were marching across Germany to join the Allied forces in Holland in early 1748, assumed an important position in the controversy over the necessity of the peace. The existence of this broadly based consensus should cause little or no surprise. Of greater interest, however, is the evidence that suggests that, together, the widespread concern over events in the Low Countries between 1747 and 1748, and the visions of commercial aggrandizement created by Britain's recent achievement of naval mastery, tended to undermine the usually exaggerated distinctions between the blue-water and interventionist positions.

That this was in fact occurring is suggested initially by the infrequency with which isolationism was advocated in the opposition press. After 1746, only one pamphlet was published before the end of the war that expounded a rigid isolationist position.[65] Similarly, support for withdrawal from Flanders was only sporadically articulated in the opposition papers. In this respect, the Leicester House paper, the *Remembrancer*, was unusual in its forthright support for confining Britain's role in the war to the maritime sphere. Criticism of the allies, usually a major feature of isolationist argument, was very subdued, and this was despite recurring shortfalls in the quotas of Austrian and Dutch troops in the Allied armies. Moreover, neither of the military defeats in Flanders during these years, at Roucoux in 1746 and Laffeldt in 1747, provoked a similar outburst to that created by the defeat at Fontenoy. In what is another peculiar twist to the debate over the war, it was actually Pelham's 'Whig' ministry, particularly during 1748, which placed the greatest emphasis on the shortcomings of the allies' contribution to the war effort.[66] Obviously, a major part of the explanation for the enfeebled condition of isolationism lies in the state of the parliamentary opposition, discussed at the beginning of this chapter, and the prominence of the contribution made to press debate by Granville and his supporters, who, although advocating a predominantly naval strategy at this stage in the war, had no hesitation in

---

[64] *A Dialogue between a Gentleman of London and an Honest Alderman*, 36–7. See also *OEJ* 14 Nov. 1747.

[65] *Considerations on Both Sides, or, Remarks on the Conduct of Great Britain and Holland, at the Present Critical Conjuncture* (1747). But see also *A Letter from a Travelling Tutor to a Young Noble Lord* (1747). [66] See e.g. *Parl. Hist.*, xiv. 331–8, 371–6.

defending the deployment of British troops and money in Europe for the defence of the Low Countries.[67] Careful examination of the *Westminster Journal*, however, suggests that this is only a partial explanation.

It will be recalled that the *Westminster Journal* seems to have received no direct political support. Hitherto it had advocated a basically blue-water strategy, only departing significantly from this position in the summer of 1743, following the victory over the French at Dettingen in June. For a number of issues during June and July 1743 the paper had responded to the wave of enthusiasm for the continental war created by both the victory and the prospects of a military invasion of French territory by outlining far-reaching schemes for despoiling France of her remote provinces. Between 1746 and 1748 the paper reaffirmed its commitment to a naval-based war by reiterating the Granvillite claims of the huge gains to be achieved by aggressive naval action, and also by defending, despite the unfavourable example of the Brittany expedition of 1746, the merits of naval descents on the coast of France.

Significantly, however, the paper's attitude towards Britain's role on the Continent changed over the same period. In early 1746, as has already been noted, the paper supported, against the background of a seemingly favourable situation in Europe, an aggressive policy of subsidization. By March 1747 the paper seems to have accepted that if Britain was to force an acceptable peace from France, including the unconditional restitution of the Austrian Netherlands and the cession of Cape Breton to England, the continued deployment of British forces in the Low Countries was inevitable. On 21 March the paper declared:

France is not unconquerable: we found so in the last war, tho' we made no Advantage of the Discovery: And we have seen in this, that her projects may be defeated . . . we know that perseverance has in former times done wonders and that if any thing be done in this war, towards reducing the exorbitant power of the *House of Bourbon*, the sole object of it to us as a land war in *Europe*, it must be done with perseverance.

In the same issue the 'shameful' Peace of Utrecht was held up as a warning of the probable result that awaited Britain if the ministry failed to exploit the 'good allies and fair prospects' of the present situation.

One factor that, in the face of the continued failure in the Low Countries, underlay both the determined stance of the *Westminster*

---

[67] See *The State of the Nation for the Year 1747, and Respecting 1748, passim.*

Journal and the optimism of a number of other writers in 1747 was the recent change of regime in Holland. The elevation of the Prince of Orange to the stadtholderate during March and April engendered a swell of ill-founded confidence amongst both the opposition and some pro-ministerial supporters that Britain's fellow maritime power would finally assume a vigorous and effective role in the struggle against France.[68] During the summer this optimism was reinforced by a number of measures taken by the Orangeist regime that were explicitly directed against the French.[69] The first substantial sign that the capabilities of the Dutch were being overestimated occurred in September, when, after a prolonged siege, Cohorn's giant fortress of Bergen-op-Zoom fell to the French.[70] The shift in mood caused by the capitulation of the fortress was almost immediately reflected in a newly despondent tone in the *Westminster Journal*. On 26 September the paper remarked:

It would be better for us that the whole *Seven Provinces* should be next year in the Hands of *France*, and that we should have that year to recruit our spirits, and mind only our sea war, than that, with our utmost help, the Dutch should faintly resist for three years longer, and at last irretrievably fall leaving us twenty millions of money poorer, and a hundred thousand men weaker, which would be so much taken from the Defence of ourselves which would then be absolutely necessary.

However, by early 1748 the paper had resumed the determined optimism of the second third of 1747, influenced partly by the ministry's schemes to raise an unprecedentedly large Allied army in the Low Countries for the coming military campaign, and partly by the news from France of the famine affecting large areas of that country. On 20 February 1748 the paper asked: 'Have we not Hopes of acting offensively by Land as well as by Sea?' In the event, both the ministry's schemes and the expectations of successful military action were undermined by the Dutch inability to contribute effectively, either financially or militarily, to the defence of their country.

---

[68] *The Conduct of the Government with Regard to War and Peace Stated* (1748), 17; *Ministerial Artifice Detected* (1749), 20; *A Dialogue between a Gentleman of London and an Honest Alderman*, 30.

[69] The Dutch anti-French measures of the summer of 1747 were largely directed against French trade and shipping, and were enthusiastically reported in the London press. See e.g. *WJ* 19 Sept. 1747.

[70] For the intense public interest in the fate of Bergen-op-Zoom, see Lewis, *Walpole*, xix. 434–5; *The Orrery Papers*, ed. E. C. Boyle, Countess of Cork and Orrery, 2 vols. (1903), ii. 5–6; *The Correspondence of Philip Doddridge, 1702–1751*, ed. G. F. Nuttall (Northants Record Society, 29; 1979), 256.

Despite claims to the contrary by both ministerial and opposition speakers in Parliament, there can be little doubt that the Peace of Aix-la-Chapelle, finally signed in its definitive form on 18 October 1748, stirred up no more than acquiescence from the vast majority of the political nation.[71] On 24 October, following the arrival of news of the definitive treaty in London, Horace Walpole noted: 'The peace is signed . . . but does not give the least joy; the stocks do not rise, and the merchants are unsatisfied. . . . In short, there is not the least sign of public rejoicing. . . .'[72] The absence of popular enthusiasm is easily explicable. Following nine years of war, during which the ministry had expended unprecedented sums of money and considerable human resources, Britain had been forced to accept a peace, having rejected similar terms in 1747, which provided very few tangible gains. In addition, many of the articles of the peace clearly reflected France's military superiority during the negotiations—most notably, the stipulation that Britain should send two noblemen to France as hostages against the restitution of Cape Breton. Perhaps even more fundamentally, the peace settlement resolved very few of the principal areas of dispute between Britain and France, and promised only a brief period of recuperation before the renewal of war between the two powers.[73] In these circumstances, even the ministry itself seems to have announced the peace with a minimum of celebration. In Parliament the peace preliminaries were never submitted for scrutiny and discussion, an omission that was vigourously attacked in the opposition press.[74] While in the press, as mentioned earlier, Fielding only devoted two issues of the *Jacobite's Journal* to defending the terms and timing of the peace.[75] Furthermore, it seems probable that the only pamphlet published in 1748 to defend the ministry's conclusion of the peace was written without ministerial guidance or support.[76]

As far as the opposition press was concerned, the gravest charge

---

[71] For opposition and ministerial claims about the popular reaction to the peace, see *Parl. Hist.*, xiv. 353–83.

[72] Lewis, *Walpole*, xix. 510–11: Walpole to Mann, 24 Oct. 1748.

[73] For Pelham's acknowledgement that the peace settlement was inherently unstable, see *Parl. Hist.*, xiv. 346–57.

[74] *Remembrancer*, 25 June, 3 Dec. 1748; *WJ* 3 Dec. 1748; *Some Thoughts on the Constitution, Particularly with Respect to the Power of Making Peace and War* (1748).

[75] *Jacobite's Journal*, 22, 29 Oct. 1748.

[76] Although it was widely alleged in the opposition press that the pamphlet, entitled *Considerations on the Definitive Treaty, Signed at Aix-la-Chapelle* (1748), was directly inspired by the ministry, the dissimilarity of the arguments employed by the ministry in Parliament and those developed in the pamphlet suggests that it was written and published without ministerial encouragement.

against the peace was the ministry's supposed sacrifice of the possibilities and leverage created by Britain's establishment of naval
supremacy after 1747. This is most clearly disclosed by the arguments
levelled against the timing of the ministry's accession to the peace
preliminaries in April. The ministerial claims that fiscal necessity and
imminent military disaster had compelled Britain to seek an immediate
end to the war in early 1748 were vigorously rejected by most opposition polemicists. In contrast to the ministry's emphasis on the extreme
vulnerability of the allies' position in the Low Countries in early 1748,
the military prospect was portrayed in almost wholly favourable terms.
A large part of the opposition argument in this respect was simply a
reiteration of the positions that had been widely articulated between
1746 and early 1748. Thus, France's trade and colonies were alleged to
be on the point of, on the one hand, extinction and, on the other,
capture, thereby leaving Britain, once these ends were achieved, able to
command an advantageous and durable peace.[77] The capture of Port
Louis on St Domingo, and the dispatch of a naval squadron under
Boscawen to the East Indies in 1748 only served to reinforce the
convictions of the opposition press regarding the practicability of such
war aims.[78] As to the situation in the Low Countries, very few opposition polemicists accepted that the position was irretrievable. Most
argued that the French advance against Holland could have been
arrested until the arrival of the Russians had altered the military
balance in favour of Britain and her allies.[79] Some went even further,
and suggested that it would have needed only one substantial military victory to dislodge the French from all the provinces that they
had captured in the Low Countries since 1745.[80] Other polemicists
argued that too great a degree of French military success in Holland
would simply cause the creation of a powerful anti-French continental
alliance.[81]

Interestingly, in the light of the press debate concerning Britain's
role in Europe before the peace preliminaries were signed, only one
pamphleteer suggested that even if Britain had been forced to abandon the Continent, her naval position alone was sufficient to justify

[77] *Remembrancer*, 21 May 1748; *WJ* 6 Aug., 10 Sept. 1748; *The State of the Nation with
a General Balance of Publick Accounts* (1748), 38; *A Supplement to the State of the Nation*
(1748), 25.

[78] *WJ* 4 Nov., 29 Oct. 1748; *LEP* 20–2 Dec. 1748; *OEJ* 21 May 1748.

[79] *A Supplement to the State of the Nation*, 28; *The Advantages of the Definitive Treaty
to the People of Great Britain Demonstrated* (1748), 16; *OEJ* 7, 21 May 1748.

[80] *Ministerial Artifice Detected*, 20; *A Supplement to the State of the Nation*, 30.

[81] *Ministerial Artifice Detected*, 20.

prolonging the war.[82] As Henry Pelham remarked during a parliamentary speech defending the peace, much of this opposition argument, most notably with respect to the situation on the Continent, had entered the realms of fantasy: 'With regard to what might have happened afterwards, if the war had been continued, gentlemen may, if they please, build castles, and imagine great things, but I am afraid, the event would have shewn, that they imagined vain things.'[83] Nevertheless, it is not hard to see why such arguments were so readily advanced. In addition to the indisputable fact of Britain's naval superiority, by the winter of 1747–8 France was displaying very visible signs of the strains that the war was imposing on her economy and population. As one pamphleteer remarked: 'the Armies the Crown of *France* has maintained, have in Effect ruin'd their manufactures, and drawn off their labouring people in such a manner, as to leave the land uncultivated, and, in consequence thereof, produced a Famine, however, that Affair had been glossed over by some people.'[84]

The famine in France had initially attracted the attention of a broad section of the press at the beginning of 1748. Following the Christmas recess, an attempt was made by a number of opposition MPs to induce Parliament to pass a bill banning the export of corn to France.[85] During January and February the desirability of such a measure was thoroughly debated across the gamut of the London press. Supporters of the bill, ignoring the lessons of 1709, argued that a prohibition on the export of corn to France would rapidly weaken the French military position.[86]

The straitened condition of the French economy also ensured that great prominence was accorded to the comparative dimension of the arguments put forward in the opposition press in support of the view that Britain's own economy was capable of bearing the extra strain that would have been imposed by prolonging the war. As in so many areas of press debate between 1747 and 1748, it was the pro-Granville pamphleteers who went the furthest in exploiting France's economic distress.[87] In contrast to the situation in France, they argued, Britain's

---

[82] *The Advantages of the Definitive Treaty*, 17–18.   [83] *Parl. Hist.*, xiv. 346.

[84] *A Supplement to the State of the Nation*, 25.

[85] W. Coxe, *Memoirs of the Administration of the Right Honourable Henry Pelham*, 2 vols. (1827), i. 383–6.

[86] See esp. *GM* 18 (1748), 20–1, 30–1; *Impartial Remarks on the Present Posture of Publick Affairs* (1748).

[87] *The State of the Nation with a General Balance of Publick Accounts*; *A Supplement to the State of the Nation*.

economy had navigated the war with relative ease. The supply of specie was alleged to be at about the same level as it had been before the outbreak of war, and the supplies of corn and other essential provisions were described as 'moderate but cheap'.[88] Moreover, Britain's trade had allegedly benefited from the war and the concomitant destruction of the bulk of French trade. With the aid of the navy, Britain's merchants were portrayed as having managed to regain much of the ground lost to the French in the years of Walpolian peace. This apparent recovery of trade, it was further argued, would have ensured Britain's continued capacity to underwrite the costs of war.[89]

The importance of such arguments was undoubtedly increased by the depth of unease widely expressed, not least by other elements of the opposition press, concerning the escalating costs of the war, and the domestic strains created by the current levels of taxation.[90] Thus the author of *The Advantages of the Definitive Treaty to the People of Great Britain* (1749) argued: 'But if it had been true that we were in that weak condition as we have been industriously represented, was it not true that the French were reduced to the last Extremity.'[91]

By far the most glaring obstacle that opposition polemicists had to overcome in order to support the contention that Britain had been capable of continuing on a wartime footing was the rapid tightening of credit after January 1748 and the near failure of the loan of 1748, which were only arrested and prevented respectively by the signing of the peace preliminaries. The financial background and details of the loan (ironically, given the support expressed in the opposition press for Sir John Barnard's schemes to widen the base of anticipatory finance in 1746, the loan was raised by open subscription), and the very serious difficulties that it ran into following the unfavourable war news of the start of the 1748 military campaign, have all been closely examined elsewhere.[92] What is of interest here is the crude political explanation of the financial crisis provided by the opposition press. The ministry, it was widely alleged, had deliberately contrived to undermine the loan in order to induce a crisis in public credit and thereby to force Britain into accepting peace on any terms. Various suggestions were advanced as to the means by which this piece of financial skulduggery had been effected. The author of *The Advantages of the Definitive Treaty* asserted

---

[88] *A Supplement to the State of the Nation*, 30.
[89] *The State of the Nation with a General Balance of Publick Accounts*, 50.
[90] See below. [91] *The Advantages of the Definitive Treaty*, 17.
[92] P. G. M. Dickson, *The Financial Revolution in England: A Study in the Development of Public Credit, 1688–1756* (1967), 226–8.

that the loan's failure had been secured by preventing the monied men from taking subscriptions for the loan; rather, it was alleged, the subscriptions had been given to 'people who were known not to be worth a Groat'.[93] The *Remembrancer*, meanwhile, argued that Pelham's own opposition to the continuation of the war, openly expressed in Parliament in early 1748, had caused him not to intervene in support of public credit by using his supposed influence over the Bank of England.[94] Most of the explanations of the ministry's successful depression of public credit, however, failed to reach even this limited degree of sophistication, and it is difficult to avoid the conclusion that they were reliant as much upon financial ignorance as on political inclination for any impact that they may have had.

On 14 May 1748 Fielding, writing in the *Jacobite's Journal*, complained: 'If we make a peace, then it is base, dishonourable, injurious; our successes in the war magnified, in Defiance of manifest Truth and Experience, and to make the terms we have accepted disadvantagious we are in a moment elevated to the situation of giving laws to *all Europe*.' Fielding's analysis of opposition argument is basically sound, if only because no opposition writer was prepared to acknowledge (or, more likely, understand) the limited leverage that Britain's naval mastery gave it over events on the Continent. Unable to accept that power followed trade, but only at a respectable distance, opposition polemicists were uninhibited in arguing that both the peace and the peace terms, which were viewed as almost wholly favourable to France and her allies, represented a senseless capitulation to the French. Thus, on 5 November the *Westminster Journal* described the suspension of Britain's 'prodigious naval successes' and the return of Cape Breton as 'entirely *free gifts* to the House of *Bourbon*'. Moreover, these 'gifts', the paper acidly added, had not prevented the French from extracting an establishment for Don Philip in Italy: 'by the free sacrifices we prevailed upon the Enemy, then in distressed and doubtful circumstances, not to *give back* his conquests in the *Low Countries*, but to accept of an Equivalent for these conquests, by way of cession, in the Establishment made for Don *Philip* in *Lombardy*.' Similarly, the French domination of the actual peace negotiations between April and October 1748, in large part a consequence of Anglo-Austrian differences (a factor that the opposition press seems to have either conveniently overlooked or again, more likely, failed to perceive), was also portrayed

---

[93] *The Advantages of the Definitive Treaty*, 17.   [94] *Remembrancer*, 2 Apr. 1748.

as exclusively the result of ministerial pusillanimity. In support of this view, the convention of 2 August, by which the British agreed to the retirement of the Russians, and France undertook to withdraw 35,000 men from The Netherlands, was singled out for particular criticism.[95] Yet even if Britain's naval position had been significantly less favourable in 1748, it is unlikely that the terms of the peace would have elicited a less hostile response from the opposition press.

After having allegedly prevented the establishment of a global British commercial supremacy, perhaps the next most unacceptable feature of the peace, as far as the opposition press was concerned, was the fact that Britain was being forced to make sacrifices, over and above the enormous financial support that she had provided for the duration of the war, to shore up the weaknesses of her continental allies. A number of opposition polemicists were even prepared to suggest, with no concessions to diplomatic realism, that Britain's interests should have been considered independently of the settlement on the Continent. Thus, on 26 April, just before news of the preliminary articles of peace had arrived in London by means of the Dutch French language press, the *London Evening Post* had remarked: 'And as to the Disputes on the Continent of Europe, the *Cessions, Partitions, Secularizations*, and other *Dispositions*, that it may be thought necessary to make, they should all answer to one another *within themselves*; no *EQUIVALENT*, of any kind, being requir'd from Great Britain, on account of *any such Disposition*.' That Britain's sacrifices at the peace involved essential British interests—namely, her commerce and international reputation—only increased the ministry's culpability. Predictably, the restoration of Cape Breton to the French caused the opposition press to resurrect all the old claims concerning the island's commercial potential.[96] In addition to Cape Breton's value, opposition polemicists also emphasized the contrast between the supposed impregnability of the fortress of Louisbourg and the vulnerability of France's principal restitution, the Austrian Netherlands, which was being restored denuded of many of its major fortifications.[97] The stipulation that Britain should provide hostages against Cape Breton's return, meanwhile, provoked a stream of jeremiads lamenting the alleged extinction of Britain's

---

[95] See esp. ibid. 13 Aug. 1748. See also *OEJ* 13 Aug. 1748.

[96] See esp. *LEP* 8–10, 22–4 Sept., 29 Sept.–1 Oct., 25–7 Oct., 3–5 Nov. 1748; *WJ* 12 Nov. 1748; *OEJ* 30 Apr., 7 May 1748.

[97] *A Letter from a Gentleman in London to his Friend in the Country, Concerning the Treaty of Aix-la-Chapelle* (1748), 15; *A Letter to a Noble Negociator Abroad* (1748), 34.

national honour, and the ramifications of this for her international position. As the author of the pro-Granville pamphlet *The State of the Nation, with a General Balance of the Publick Accounts* remarked: 'It will operate on our Foreign Affairs like a malignant star, that sheds a baleful influence wherever it appears.'[98]

The conviction of the opposition press that Britain's interests had been entirely subordinated to those of other powers at the peace was strengthened by a number of the other provisions of the peace settlement. First, and most seriously, by referring outstanding commercial differences between Britain and Spain to future negotiations, the peace had failed to provide a favourable—or, indeed, any—resolution to those disputes which had provoked war between the two countries in 1739. The only provision specifically related to Anglo-Spanish commercial relations, the renewal of the *Asiento* for a further four years, was dismissed as nugatory.[99] On 19 November, writing of the failure to secure any settlement of the more important issues of freedom of navigation in American waters and Britain's right to cut logwood on the coast of Honduras, the *Westminster Journal* bitterly observed:

If these discussions [over Anglo-Spanish commercial differences] must still be *future*, we are in the same state as we were ten years ago, only thirty millions more in debt: which, with the Lives of many thousand subjects, as well as the former labours of Don Benjamino [Benjamin Keene, Minister Plenipotentiary at Madrid during the negotiation of the Convention of Pardo (1739)], are all thrown away to no effect.

Unfortunately for the ministry, they were laid open to further attack over the question of Anglo-Spanish commercial relations by the diplomatic ineptitude of their own negotiators at Aix-la-Chapelle, who succeeded in omitting Dodington's commercial treaty with Spain in 1715 from the terms of the treaty's guarantees.[100] Many opposition polemicists also compared the failure to secure the payment from Spain of the £95,000 that the Convention of Pardo had awarded in settlement of agreed damages to British merchants with the ninth article of the peace. This article affirmed Hanover's right to the payment of an old debt dating from the War of the Spanish Succession, and the claims of the Elector Palatine to the Abbey of St Hubert. On 10 November the *London Evening Post* asked: 'Whether the petty Interests of H——r, the

---

[98] *The State of the Nation with a General Balance of Publick Accounts*, 36.

[99] See esp. *OEJ* 5 Nov. 1748.

[100] *A Letter from a Gentleman in London*, 23–6; *Remembrancer*, 11 Feb. 1749.

Abbey of *St. Hubert*, and of the *Palatine House*, as well as of the *actual Allies* of the House of Bourbon, have not *more Regard* shewn to them, in that T——y, than the *real* and *particular Interests* of G——B——?' Although the *Westminster Journal* revived the suggestion that the problems created for Britain's foreign policy by the Anglo-Hanoverian union should be solved by ceding the electorate of Hanover to the Duke of Cumberland,[101] in general the issue of Hanover and its impact on Britain's interests aroused only minimal comment during the press debate over the peace.[102]

Another provision of the peace that was singled out by the opposition press as encapsulating the ministry's basic indifference to national interests was the article concerning the condition of Dunkirk. The treaty, principally by allowing the French to fortify Dunkirk from the land, partially relieved France of the obligations to render the port useless that had been imposed by the Treaty of Utrecht. On 5 November the *Westminster Journal*, comparing the new stipulation regarding Dunkirk with the recovery of the Low Countries from the French, remarked that the 'ports of Flanders, not the inland Towns, are the proper *English* Barrier, and in respect to those we are manifest losers'. The issue of Dunkirk also stimulated the opposition press to embarrass the ministry with their recent past. As the *Remembrancer* pointedly observed on 31 December:

By the Treaty of *Utrecht* (which to this very Day has been so outrageously decried by all the *Court Whigs* in the Kingdom), it was provided That Dunkirk should be *totally demolished*: And such a value did even those *Whigs* themselves set on that provision, That they clamoured louder, if possible, for the effectual Performance of it against the conduct of Those who had the Honour to make it.

Not surprisingly, given the propensity of the ministry to taunt the opposition with recitals of past Tory conduct, the comparison between the Treaties of Utrecht and Aix-la-Chapelle was a common theme in the opposition press. Another feature of the peace settlement that encouraged this comparison was the fact that the ministry had concluded the peace preliminaries in April independently of two of Britain's three principal allies, thus recalling the supposed betrayal of the Dutch and the Austrians by Harley's ministry in 1711.[103]

In addition to the timing and terms of the peace, the other major

---

[101] *WJ* 6 May 1746.   [102] But see *Remembrancer*, 7 Jan. 1749.
[103] Ibid. 25 June 1748; *LEP* 4–6 Oct. 1748; *OEJ* 29 Oct. 1748.

aspect of the peace settlement to attract the condemnation of the opposition press was its obvious failure to provide any prospect of long-term peace. A number of opposition writers made what were designed to be damning comparisons with the earlier Peace of Ryswick (1697), which was portrayed as having sacrificed British naval mastery and, more ominously, as having laid the basis of the advance of Bourbon power into Flanders, Spain, Italy, and the Indies.[104] The current moderation of the French, it was argued, masked a design to rebuild their military strength in preparation for a new, more opportune, onslaught against Europe. In support of this argument, the opposition press was able to appropriate the view of France's international role mobilized by the ministry for much of the 1740s. Thus, the author of the pro-Granville pamphlet *A Supplement to the State of the Nation, Being Free-Thoughts on the Present Critical Conjuncture* (1748) urged: 'It is evident to Demonstration, if Facts and Evidence are capable of convincing, that the *French* Court never did, nor by parity of Reasoning never will conclude a Peace, but to recover strength, and to revive the war again as the best opportunities present.'[105] Furthermore, it was also alleged that the French would enter a new war significantly stronger than Britain and her allies.

This position was urged most forcefully, but not exclusively, by the pro-Granville pamphleteers, who in large part were again simply reiterating many of the arguments initially advanced in the earlier pamphlets. In the first place, it was claimed that France, having learnt the lessons of the last years of the war, would indubitably establish her naval power 'on a firm and lasting basis'.[106] Measures taken during 1748 to rebuild France's much depleted naval forces, including the purchase of ships from Sweden, were widely cited in the opposition press as proof of both this and of the wider aggressive aims of the French state.[107] Secondly, French commerce would allegedly continue its alarming expansion of the 1720s and 1730s, a concern that was reinforced in early 1749 by French encroachments on the so-called neutral islands in the West Indies.[108] In contrast to this picture of a rapidly recovering France, Britain's trade and recovery were portrayed as being closely constrained by the huge national debt accumulated

---

[104] See e.g. *WJ* 23 July 1748.
[105] *A Supplement to the State of the Nation*, 50.   [106] Ibid. 35.
[107] *LEP* 14–16 June, 30 Aug.–1 Sept. 1748. See also *OEJ* 20 Aug. 1748.
[108] *A Supplement to the State of the Nation*, 36.

during the conflict. Most opposition polemicists envisaged little prospect of either reducing the principal of the debt or, more immediately,
of freeing Britain's commerce and manufactures from a sufficiently high
proportion of the current tax burden to prevent French products
underselling British exports in vital markets. Of course, in retrospect
it is possible to see that, particularly in relation to the predictions of
comparative commercial growth, the opposition press was being unduly
pessimistic. In fact, as we now know, the war had been holding back
what Ralph Davis has called 'a great expansive potentiality' in Britain's
export trade.[109] And in the area of public finance, opposition writers
had understandably failed to foresee Henry Pelham's successful
reduction in 1749 of the rate of interest payable on the national debt,
a measure that went a long way, along with his broader policy of
domestic retrenchment, towards bringing Britain's fiscal position firmly
back under control.[110]

The third and final area in which the French were alleged to have
emerged from the war in a much stronger position was in relation to
their allies and the balance of power in Europe. The balance of power
in both Italy and Germany, opposition polemicists argued, had shifted
significantly in favour of the Bourbon powers. It was widely noted that
Austria, traditionally the bulwark of Britain's position on the Continent,
had been divested of important territories in both areas. In short, as the
Remembrancer remarked on 7 January 1749, Europe was now dependent
on the 'quiet Disposition' of France. The ministry were hardly helped
in this area of press debate by the efforts of one of their supporters,
who wrote a very weak defence of the peace entitled *Considerations on
the Definitive Treaty, Signed at Aix-la-Chapelle* (1748). This pamphlet,
largely eschewing the reasonable plea of necessity, attempted to argue
that the peace provided the basis for a 'solid and lasting peace'. In
defence of the indefensible, the pamphlet's author asserted that by
means of the peace the Pragmatic sanction had been 'set upon a firmer
foundation than ever', and that the only territorial cessions to the
House of Bourbon—Parma and Piacenza—were, in effect, temporary.[111]
The author also advanced the view that the period following the peace
would witness a rapid revitalization of the 'old system' (the Grand

---

[109] R. Davis, 'English Foreign Trade, 1700–1774', in W. E. Minchinton (ed.), *The
Growth of English Overseas Trade in the Seventeenth and Eighteenth Centuries* (1969), 113.

[110] See Dickson, *The Financial Revolution*, 229–43.

[111] In the event of Don Philip's succession to Naples, or his death without male heirs,
both duchies were to revert to their present holders.

Alliance of the maritime powers and Austria). Not surprisingly, this pamphlet was eagerly attacked by the opposition press, which was also able to draw attention to the effective destruction of the Dutch Barrier, and the extreme vulnerability of the Low Countries to renewed French military attack, in order to deride the pro-ministerial pamphleteer's optimism regarding the probable re-emergence of the Grand Alliance as an effective instrument of international politics.[112]

However obvious the weaknesses of the arguments advanced by the author of *Considerations on the Definitive Treaty*, the opposition press was itself being unrealistic. In part, this was a result of naïve assumptions concerning the possibilities of contriving favourable diplomatic and military outcomes.[113] But even more fundamentally, the view of both the opposition press and the pro-ministerial pamphleteer were predicated upon a conception of European diplomacy and power politics that was increasingly at odds with international realities. Of those polemicists writing in 1748, not one displayed any sign of having recognized the increasing redundancy of the categories of foreign policy debate that had emerged in the conditions of the wars against Louis XIV's France. As has been noted elsewhere, the Peace of Aix-la-Chapelle signalled the break-up not only of the Grand Alliance, but also of the traditional Franco-Spanish alliance.[114] Unfortunately for the ministry, however, the international situation was far in advance of the views of the vast majority of the British political nation. As we have seen, the significance of the rise of Prussia after 1740 seems not to have been adequately grasped by most writers. Likewise, the growing distance between the aims of France and Spain went either largely unnoticed or was actually denied.[115] The failure of opposition polemicists to either acknowledge or perceive the essential fluidity of the international system after the end of the war led them to exaggerate the weakness of Britain's international position following the peace.

An additional factor that encouraged the opposition press attack on the nature of the peace settlement, and that also added a further dimension to the wider press debate over the peace, was the publication in early 1748 of a pamphlet defending the Earl of Chesterfield's resignation from his position as Secretary of State for the northern depart-

---

[112] See esp. *Remembrancer*, 17 Dec. 1748, 7 Jan. 1749.
[113] For this, see above, Ch. 3.
[114] Langford, *The Eighteenth Century*, 129.
[115] See esp. *The State of the Nation with a General Balance of Publick Accounts*, 50.

ment.[116] This pamphlet, *An Apology for a Late Resignation*, had a number of implications for press debate, of which the most important was its publicizing of the ministerial divisions over the war and, in particular, over the question of how Britain should have responded to the French overtures of peace that had been conveyed to Sir John Ligonier by Marshal Saxe after the Battle of Laffeldt in July 1747.[117] Previous to the pamphlet's appearance, the only public confirmation of these overtures had been a brief statement in the King's speech to Parliament of 17 June 1747 to the effect that terms had been proposed by the French, but had been rejected as inadequate.[118]

An Apology for a Late Resignation immediately provoked two rebuttals, both of which seem to have been written by supporters of the ministry.[119] Unfortunately for the public defence of the ministry's future conduct, the principal reasons offered by the pro-ministerial polemicists for the ministry's rejection of the Saxe–Ligonier overture could, with equal facility, be deployed against the Peace of Aix-la-Chapelle. Thus, the two pro-ministerial pamphlets raised both the question of the desirability of concluding a separate peace with France and the dangers of being duped by French diplomatic restraint. As regards the former, the author of one of the pamphlets declaimed:

Should we again *desert* our *Allies*, and should a ministry formed upon a *coalition* make such another *separate peace* as that [Utrecht]; it might be justly considered as a *national* and *indelible* stain; and when we had once, by such a *stroke* as this, *separated* ourselves from all the *rest* of the *world*, France would find it no difficult matter to make an *End* of us.[120]

Ironically, in the light of the later debate over the Peace of Aix-la-Chapelle, the author of the other pamphlet raised the spectre of the Peace of Ryswick as a warning against capitulation in the face of

[116] Chesterfield actually denied that he was the author of the pamphlet. For this and the wider question of the authorship of *An Apology for a Late Resignation*, see Sidney L. Gulick, jun., 'A Chesterfield Bibliography to 1800', *Papers of the Bibliographical Society of America*, 39 (1985), 228–34. A correspondent of Lord Orrery's reported Lord Harrington as observing that 'whoever has wrote it . . . cannot be of the common class of men as he asserts from his own knowledge of what has pass'd in the most private councils' (*Orrery Papers*, ii. 27–8: Dr Barry to Lord Orrery, 11 Apr. 1748).

[117] For details of the Saxe–Ligonier peace overture and the divided response of the ministry, see Lodge, *Studies in Eighteenth-Century Diplomacy*, 266–77.

[118] *Parl. Hist.*, xiv. 63–6.

[119] *The Resignation Discussed* (1748); *An Impartial Review of Two Pamphlets Late published, One Intituled, an Apology for a Late Resignation, the other, the Resignation Discussed* (1748). [120] *The Resignation Discussed*, 33–4.

moderate French peace demands.[121] Furthermore, both pamphlets also argued that a durable peace settlement was a feasible goal in the war, even after the failure of the 1747 military campaign in the Low Countries.[122] At a more basic level, from the vantage-point of 1748, the ministerial rejection of the French peace proposals in 1747 seemed to have secured no advantages for Britain; rather, as William Horsley pointed out towards the end of 1748 in one of his 'Fool' essays, 'Notwithstanding so many more Lives have been lost and so many millions have been spent, I am such a Fool, as not to be able to discern the least advantageous Difference or Alteration for the Nation, between the terms now accepted, and those that were then rejected.'[123]

If, given both the circumstances surrounding the peace settlement and the hostility of the opposition press reaction to the ministry's conduct of the settlement, it is unsurprising that the peace induced little enthusiasm among the wider political nation, it is perhaps more surprising that it failed to provoke a popular outcry. Obviously, a major part of the explanation for this, as was mentioned at the beginning of this chapter, is to be found in the conditions of domestic politics. Nevertheless, it is also necessary to point out that even the opposition press was betraying signs in 1748—as, indeed, it had done during the previous year—of the impact of other factors on popular opinion, most notably the fiscal strain being caused by the current scale of Britain's military commitments. On 29 January 1748 the *Remembrancer*, its remarks coloured by the absence of popular support for the newly launched Leicester House opposition,[124] commented: 'Now, as there is no Evil that we *Englishmen*, as individuals, regard with so much Horror as poverty, it is most amazing that as a people, we can see the same Evil, approaching full speed, and in the most threatening manner without any of that Horror.' In the same issue the paper quoted the country-Tory Charles Davenant's view that once Britain had encumbered itself with an annual supply of about £6 million, the country was on the brink of national bankruptcy. In 1747, the paper duly noted, the supply raised had been over two times this sum, at £13,041,671. Britain, the paper continued, was 'on the point of sinking under the manifold load of impositions, which have from time to time, been heaped upon her'.

In such circumstances, the salient question was how best to extricate

[121] *An Impartial Review of Two Pamphlets*, 40–1.
[122] *The Resignation Discussed*, 55–6; *An Impartial Review of Two Pamphlets*, 50.
[123] *LEP* 29 Sept.–1 Oct. 1748.   [124] See above, Ch. 2.

Britain from the difficulties created by the fiscal situation. In the judgement of the *Remembrancer*, the only solution was the Granvillite policy of continuing the war, in the confidence that Britain could, through the capture of French trade and colonies, acquire the means to discharge the principal of the huge national debt with which the conflict had saddled the country. In an earlier issue the paper had also argued that it was only by abandoning the war on the Continent, and confining Britain's role to maritime activity, that the ministry could possibly keep the country in the war.[125] A similar degree of anxiety over the fiscal dimension of the war was disclosed in the *Westminster Journal*, which, like the *Remembrancer*, reiterated the Granvillite argument that the financial situation was a factor behind the desirability of prolonging the war. On 27 February 1748 the paper described public distress as 'universal and visible', and argued that it was imperative that the ministry give immediate consideration to schemes to relieve the poor, manufactures, and commerce from the present burden of taxation. One such scheme that drew support from both the *Westminster Journal* and a number of other writers was a reassesssment of the land-tax to bring all areas of the country into a position of broad equality as regards its payment.[126] The debate concerning the incidence of taxation and its deleterious effect on Britain's trade was given increased urgency in 1748 by the imposition of an additional 5 per cent on the overall customs rate. The remarks of the *Remembrancer*, the *Westminster Journal*, and other polemicists on the issue of fiscal strain provide some support for Henry Pelham's remarks to Newcastle in late July that 'the country is resolved, no land war, no more subsidies'.[127]

Finally, what were the longer-term consequences of the War of the Austrian Succession for press and popular views of Britain's international role? Two of these stand out. First, it seems reasonable to suggest that, particularly after 1746, the war was the forcing-house for the development towards a new maturity of the ideology of aggressive commercial expansion that reached the summit of its influence at the end of the following decade, under the sanction of the military successes of the Seven Years War. Of course, many of the strands of this ideology were already firmly in place long before the outbreak of war in 1739. As John Brewer has recently remarked, the belligerence

---

[125] *Remembrancer*, 16 Jan. 1748.
[126] *LEP* 29 Nov.–1 Dec. 1748; *An Essay on the Inequality of our Present Taxes* (1746).
[127] Quoted in Lodge, *Studies in Eighteenth-Century Diplomacy*, 369.

of popular and mercantile opinion in the late 1730s was a product less of commercial optimism than of concern over the increasingly visible success of Britain's principal competitors.[128] Nevertheless, starting with the capture of Cape Breton in 1745, and further encouraged by the naval successes of 1747, the issue of Anglo-French rivalry for trade and empire came to occupy a qualitatively and quantitatively new position at the vanguard of press debate. Paradoxically, as has been demonstrated above, a crucial agency in this development was the efforts of the pro-Granville faction, who, more than any other group in the politics of the 1740s, represented the legacy of Stanhopian interventionist diplomacy. The importance of Anglo-French commercial rivalry as an issue of press concern in the post-war period was revealed in early 1749 by the high degree of anxiety expressed in the opposition press over French attempts to gain control of the West Indian islands of St Lucia and Tobago.[129] And, as Jeremy Black has remarked elsewhere, much of the opposition propaganda concerning Anglo-French commercial disputes between 1748 and 1755 was characterized by its extreme distrust of the French, and a belief in the efficacy of violence.[130] By 1755 French encroachments on the British position in North America and in the West Indies had created a wave of popular indignation and support for bellicose measures to secure Britain's empire and trade against the French.[131]

The second principal consequence seems to have been to reinforce the convictions of the isolationists that Britain would be best served by detachment from the disputes of continental Europe. As has been emphasized elsewhere in the present work, and as was recognized at the time by ministers, only success in foreign policy could induce popular commendation. The apparent failure of the continental strategy pursued during the war seemed, therefore, to provide a vindication of the isolationist stance. On 8 October the *Westminster Journal* printed a letter, written under the pseudonym of Civicus, which advanced the most forceful contemporary statement of this view. In the course of a detailed exposition of the isolationist position, which even took in the

[128] J. Brewer, *The Sinews of Power: War, Money and the English State, 1688–1783* (1989), 173.

[129] See e.g. *OEJ* 13 May 1749.

[130] J. Black, *Natural and Necessary Enemies: Anglo-French Relations in the Eighteenth Century* (1986), 57–8.

[131] For Josiah Tucker's remarks on the popular clamour for war in 1753–4, see G. Shelton, *Dean Tucker: Eighteenth-Century Economic and Political Thought* (1981), 168.

beginnings of Haugwitz's reform of Austrian administration, Civicus remarked:

My concern is not only that she [Britain] is greatly in debt, but that she has been duped into a great part of this Debt; since those engaged with her, who were more interested than she in the consequences of the war, came out of it, in a manner, free and vigorous, but she with such incumbrances about her, that scarcely will she be able, on future occasions that may probably more nearly concern herself in a manner suitable to her natural strength.

The lesson was obvious: Britain could only flourish by 'attending chiefly to her own distinct and separate interest as an island, and a commercial nation'. In 1755 Pitt was to remark during his famous Rhône and Saône speech against the 1755 subsidy treaty with Russia: 'These incoherent un-British measures are what are adopted instead of our proper force—it was our navy that procured us the restoration of the Barrier and Flanders in the last war, by making us masters of Cape Breton. After that war, and even with that indemnification in our hands, we were forced to accept a bad peace.'[132]

Interestingly, Pitt's great ally and link with City opinion, William Beckford, was one of the new group of MPs in the 1747 Parliament. In the course of the debates during the last stages of the war, he was one of only a handful of opposition MPs who argued that Britain should continue the naval struggle against the French, leaving a supposedly self-regarding anti-Bourbon balance of power on the Continent to take care of the French threat to Holland.[133] In 1755 Beckford's paper, the *Monitor*, was to argue that Britain could best prevent France from expediting her bellicose schemes in Europe by the destruction of French trade and the capture of the French colonies. It seems most unlikely that both Beckford and the *Monitor*'s position was not shaped considerably by the events and arguments of the last years of the War of the Austrian Succession.

---

[132] Walpole, *Memoirs of King George II*, ii. 71.   [133] *Parl. Hist.*, xiv. 188–202.

8

CONCLUSION

ONE of the principal themes of this book has been the various ways in which the existence of a relatively unfettered press shaped the political culture of mid-eighteenth-century Britain. In recent years there has been growing scepticism about the political influence of the press in this period: the press was never the engine of faction that some contemporaries feared; its commentary on politics was superficial and episodic; religious difference, and not the press, was the forcing-house of extra-parliamentary politics; at best, the press merely confirmed existing prejudices; its ability to sway the unconvinced was negligible. All these views can be found in recent works on the eighteenth-century press.

Yet the role of the press in the politics of the 1740's was, as I have tried to show, both vigorous and important. This reflected, amongst other things, its ability to link the world of the court and Parliament to the world of the tavern and the tradesman's club. The press was a crucial intermediary between various levels and aspects of mid-century politics. Commercial viability dictated that most elements of the press voice the views of a substantial cross-section of the wider political nation. Motivated partly by the same commercial imperative, important elements of the press also displayed great ingenuity in circumventing the obstacles placed in their way by the law and parliamentary privilege, and succeeded in providing, for much of the time, a vigorous commentary on parliamentary affairs and rivalries. Nor was the press without influence in Parliament and at court. The political opportunities that it opened up were, unsurprisingly, seized on by successive opposition factions. The potential for disturbance that this created is very clearly illustrated by the press activity of the opposition Whigs during 1742–4. Had the political influence of the press really been as limited as some have recently suggested, then the scale of this activity, and the level of concern that it created, would be impossible to explain satisfactorily.

To emphasize the importance of the press as a medium of political communication under the first two Georges is hardly novel. More novel, however, is the reiteration of this view in relation to the 1740s. Historians of both early Hanoverian politics and the eighteenth-century press have tended to overlook the press of the 1740s, choosing rather to concentrate on the 1720s and 1730s, and the second half of the 1750s. Amongst other things, this has led to a tendency to underestimate the political influence and vigour of the press of the 1740s.[1] As we have seen, any validity that such a view does possess is confined to the latter part of the decade. Before 1746 the combination of war and political instability provided a great stimulus to press activity. Moreover, that the press ended the decade with a reduced political influence was a reflection of neither limited popular interest in politics nor, *pace* Michael Harris, a longer-term trend amongst London's papers and periodicals towards respectability and political quiescence.[2] Rather, it was the consequence of a very specific set of circumstances: namely, the failure of, first, the fall of Walpole and, then, the formation of the Broad-Bottom ministry to bring about a patriot reform of government, and the impact on the opposition 'without doors' of the '45.[3]

When we look at the question of the light that the press can shed on the politics of the 1740s, perhaps the most significant thing to emerge is its reflection of the importance and influence of patriot or 'country' ideology. In recent years a number of historians have been remarkably reluctant to recognize this as one of the central features of politics before the later 1750s. As both Nicholas Rogers and Harry Dickinson have suggested elsewhere, this can in part be explained by an unwilling-ness to look beyond the parliamentary arena and the assumption made by a number of historians that politics 'without doors' was a simple reflection of rivalries at Westminster.[4] To assert the importance of patriotism is not to pronounce the non-existence of the Tory party or of Whig–Tory divisions. Yet what the evidence of the press does

---

[1] For this, see esp. J. Black, *The English Press in the Eighteenth Century* (1987), 137; M. Harris, *London Newspapers in the Age of Walpole* (1987), esp. 113–33.

[2] Harris, *London Newspapers, passim.*

[3] See also Nicholas Rogers's comment on the much weakened state of opposition politics in London in the later 1740s in his *Whigs and Cities: Popular Politics in the Age of Walpole and Pitt* (Oxford, 1989), esp. ch. 3.

[4] See ibid. 3–4; J. Cannon, *The Whig Ascendancy: Colloquies on Hanoverian England* (1981), 178.

suggest is that their relevance to the public debate of national politics was extremely limited. For many of the participants in this debate, it was patriotism that gave meaning to their political viewpoint. Furthermore, it is only by recognizing this, that the progress of press debate during the 1740s becomes at all intelligible.

The evidence of the press also suggests that we should be wary of exaggerating the influence of Jacobitism on the evolution of patriotism. A Jacobite *presence* in patriot politics is not the same thing as control or even significance. That the strength of patriotism was in fact largely dependent on factors other than Jacobitism is suggested not just by the negligible contribution that the Jacobites seem to have made to press debate, but also (and more importantly) by the participation of patriot papers and writers in the influential loyalist activities of the London press during the '45. Patriotism, their staunch loyalism would seem to indicate, did not, in most cases, signify disaffection.

As we saw in Chapters 5 and 6, the support that patriot papers and writers gave to the Hanoverian succession during its darkest moments is all the more impressive when viewed against the remarkable degree of alienation from the personnel and politics of the Hanoverian regime expressed in the patriot press, particularly between 1742 and 1744. Although intense anti-Hanoverianism was without doubt the dominant feature of the public and press debate created by the war, at least until early 1745, in retrospect it was in another area of this debate that the most significant developments took place between 1740 and 1748. When the nation emerged from war in 1748, most opposition writers felt that the foremost challenge facing Britain in her relations with foreign powers was French rivalry for trade and empire and, in particular, for control of North America. Concern about French commercial and colonial ambitions was nothing new; the prominence that it was accorded, and the identification of North America as a vital area of Anglo–French rivalry, however, were. Of the factors that account for this transformation, one stands out: Cape Breton. The capture of the island provided great impetus to the articulation of concern about the French commercial advance since the Peace of Utrecht. It was also the cause of an explosion of interest and excitement regarding the commercial possibilities of North America.

In this, as in so many other areas, the press activity and debate of the 1740s looks forward to the rise of the Elder Pitt and the Seven Years War. As has been suggested at various points in this work, what it reveals in this context is that if the future lay with Pitt, patriotism, and empire, then this owed a significant amount to longer-term trends in early Hanoverian politics. It was Pitt's achievement to harness these trends, first, to help force himself into high office and, then, once in office, to induce widespread support for the Newcastle–Pitt administration.

APPENDIX: THE TORY-PATRIOT PAMPHLETS OF THE 1740s

While the intermingling of ideologies—true Whig, Tory, and Jacobite—that was such a prominent feature of the opposition argument of the early Hanoverian period has been frequently remarked upon, curiously few attempts have been made to identify polemic produced under the first two Georges that was of Tory provenance. For the 1740s, only two historians have addressed this problem: Archibald Foord and, most recently, Linda Colley.[1]

Of the two attempts, Colley's is the most seriously flawed. As P. D. G. Thomas has recently noted elsewhere, one of the principal weaknesses of her portrayal of early Hanoverian Toryism is her insistence that 'the country party' and 'country independents' were synonyms for 'the tories and not for parliamentary independents'.[2] As far as the party origins of printed polemic are concerned, this (false) assumption causes her to make a series of serious misjudgements. Two examples will suffice to illustrate the scale of the problem. The first is her description of the *Westminster Journal, or, the New Weekly Miscellany* as a Tory journal.[3] As should be evident from Chapter 2 of the present work, this is to ignore the frequent protestations of the paper's editor concerning his independence of party and faction. Equally importantly, it is also to ignore the content of the paper and, in particular, the editor's willingness to attack the conduct of both Whig and Tory ministries during the wars against Louis XIV's France. The second is the pamphlet *National Unanimity Recommended*, which was published in 1742. This pamphlet, Colley asserts, 'linked a prospective Tory administration with the repeal of the Riot, Black, and Smuggling Acts, and of a "thousand coercive clauses in Acts relating to the Excise"'.[4] Here one can only speculate that Colley failed to read the pamphlet with any care. In fact, it was only an opposition 'as general and unanimous as is consistent with the Nature of the Constitution'—that is, one constructed independently of party identities—that could secure the above objectives.[5] And as the author actually professes at one stage: 'I have been a whig from my cradle.'[6]

Colley's concern to identify a substantial quantity of patriot polemic as Tory-inspired can be related to her conviction that it was the initiative of the

[1] A. Foord, *His Majesty's Opposition, 1714–1830* (Oxford, 1964); L. Colley, *In Defiance of Oligarchy: The Tory Party, 1714–60* (Cambridge, 1982).

[2] P. D. G. Thomas, 'Party Politics in Eighteenth-Century Britain: Some Myths and a Touch of Reality', *British Journal for Eighteenth Century Studies*, 10 (1987), 204.

[3] Colley, *In Defiance of Oligarchy*, 170.   [4] Ibid. 242.

[5] *National Unanimity Recommended*, 54.   [6] Ibid. 30.

parliamentary Tory party that was the principal dynamic behind developments in politics 'without doors' under the first two Georges. As the present work has attempted to show, the historical reality was considerably more complex. Another claim that she makes, and one that is hard to reconcile with the appropriation of country principles for Toryism, is that Toryism retained its partisan bias by perpetuating the traditional Tory emphasis on Crown and Church. Colley's evidence for the Tories' 'superior consideration of the Crown' consists largely of a small number of anonymous pamphlets that undoubtedly emphasize traditional Tory attitudes towards the Crown.[7] As has been noted elsewhere, a major difficulty here is that there are good grounds for supposing that these pamphlets were actually written by Whigs. In the case of one, *Advice to the Tories who Have Taken the Oaths* (1715), this was certainly the case.[8]

Much more problematic is another of Colley's 'traditional Tory' pamphlets, *The Sentiments of a Tory*, published in 1741. This purported to be a straightforward defence of the failure of a group of Tories to support the opposition Whig-inspired motion to address George II to remove Walpole from his councils, the famous *motion* of 13 February 1741. A number of prominent features of this pamphlet are worth noting. The first is its scathing attack on Bolingbroke's *Dissertation upon Parties*.[9] As far as Colley is concerned, this is evidence of the importance of the Tory detestation (or suspicion) of Bolingbroke and his ideas on politics.[10] It is also cited by Colley as evidence of the Tory resolution not to submerge themselves in a 'country amalgam'. The second feature, not remarked upon by Colley, is the author's remarks about the imminent general election. Here the author made efforts to warn his readers of the dangers represented by 'influence' at the elections, under which denomination pains were taken to include printed lists of MPs' voting behaviour and inflammatory polemic.[11] In short, both the tactics and one of the basic aims of the 'country party'—namely, the eradication of party differences—were to be rejected. Colley cannot have it both ways. If this was a Tory pamphlet, then it is evidence against the Tory appropriation of country principles and the promotion of populist tactics. Clearly, here was one Tory, if it was a Tory, who did not, by any stretch of the imagination, conceive of Toryism as a vigorous anti-oligarchical force.

However, there are two other possibilities that are worth considering. First, even if *The Sentiments of a Tory* was written by a Tory, there is every reason to suppose that it was articulating the views of a very specific group of Tory MPs —those Tories led by Lord Cornbury who had actually voted with the ministry

---

[7] See Colley, *In Defiance of Oligarchy*, 102–3.

[8] See E. Cruickshanks, 'The Political Management of Sir Robert Walpole', in J. Black (ed.), *Britain in the Age of Walpole* (1984), 23–43. For an example of a pro-ministerial pamphlet published in 1747 that argued that the traditional Tory attitude towards the Crown should be placed in support of the Hanoverians and thus, it was argued, the ministry, see *A Letter to the Tories*.   [9] *The Sentiments of a Tory*, 4–8.

[10] Colley, *In Defiance of Oligarchy*, 97.   [11] *The Sentiments of a Tory*, 38, 45–63.

on 13 February 1741.[12] The hostility that it expressed towards the eradication of party as espoused by Bolingbroke may also reflect the effects on these same Tories of the death of the Tory leader, Sir William Wyndham, in 1740. As Colley notes, Wyndham's death was a serious set-back for the leaders of the parliamentary opposition. It was Wyndham who had been largely responsible for securing the degree of co-operation that had been achieved during the 1730s between the various elements of the opposition. With him dead, long-standing suspicions that Pulteney and Carteret were using the opposition only to force themselves into the ministry took on a much greater significance.[13] Thus, the Tories whom the pamphlet was ostensibly defending, later dubbed by Samuel Johnson 'the high-heeled party', may have represented a strand of Tory opinion that, without Wyndham's steadying influence, was unhappy about the country tactics and coloration of various other elements of mid-century Toryism.[14] But a more likely possibility is that *The Sentiments of a Tory* was a pro-ministerial pamphlet that aimed to exploit the opposition disarray following the débâcle of the *motion*. What makes this seem all the more plausible is the evidence, presented in Chapter 2, that most of the Tory-patriot pamphlets that can be more confidently identified in this period had as their basic task the reassertion of both an alleged historic Tory commitment to patriot government and the contemporary Tory commitment to the eradication of party in the politics of Hanoverian Britain.[15]

Archibald Foord's attempt to identify the Tory-inspired polemic of the 1740s is altogether more convincing than Colley's. He correctly notes that one of the best (and, in many cases, the only) means of identifying the Tory authorship of a pamphlet in this period is remarks made by the author regarding past Tory conduct.[16] It is arguable, however, that Foord's exclusive focus on the arena of parliamentary politics has led him to misinterpret the scale and significance of the Tory contribution to patriot argument. His principal concern was to emphasize, using polemical evidence, alleged divisions between the Tories and 'Broad-Bottoms' who made up the parliamentary opposition of 1742–4. Concentration on these two categories of parliamentary politician caused Foord to ignore the role of patriot polemic produced independently of factions at Westminster. The result is a tendency to identify (incorrectly) polemic as Tory merely on the grounds that it employs similar arguments to those expressed by more easily identifiable Tory-patriot pamphleteers. He does this even in cases where the author makes no, or only minimal, reference to party identities. A

[12] For this, see Foord, *His Majesty's Opposition*, 140 n. 5.

[13] Colley, *In Defiance of Oligarchy*, 227. For the role that suspicions of the motives of Pulteney and his colleagues had in shaping the Tory response to the *motion*, see Foord, *His Majesty's Opposition*, 139.

[14] *GM* 13 (1743), 181.

[15] The Tory commitment to the extirpation of party is also expressed in many of the constituency instructions of 1742. For this see above, Ch. 2.

[16] Foord, *His Majesty's Opposition*, 235.

good example is *The Case of the Opposition Impartially Stated* (1742). As was noted in Chapter 2, this pamphlet actually located the origins of the opposition in the period immediately following the South Sea crisis, thereby implicitly underlining the opposition's allegedly non-partisan nature. It is also worth noting that in the case of another pamphlet identified by Foord as Tory, *The Conduct of the Late and Present M——ry Compared* (1742), his attribution is undermined not least by the fact that the probable author of this pamphlet was an opposition Whig, George Dodington.[17]

How, then, are we safely to identify Tory polemic published in the 1740s? As might be expected, and given that (as we saw in Chapter 2) Tory polemicists generally avoided using the label of Tory, there is no easy or universally applicable rule. In a number of cases, as Foord noted, it is possible because of the partisan attitude of the author towards past Tory conduct and, in particular, towards Harley's ministry of 1710–14. In others we are entirely reliant on external evidence. The rest of this appendix consists of a list of all those pamphlets published in London between 1740 and 1748 which it seems reasonable to attribute to Tory authors. Accompanying each is a brief summary of the grounds on which the identification is based. It cannot be emphasized too strongly, however, that, as was shown in Chapter 2, the vast bulk of Tory argument articulated in these pamphlets is notable for its continuity with patriot argument that came from other sources.

1. *Opposition More Necessary than Ever* (1742). Published in September 1742, this was a direct riposte to the polemical defence during the second half of 1742 of Pulteney and his fellow new Whigs and of the political settlement that followed Walpole's fall. Its Tory authorship is disclosed by its attempts to show, by means of an extremely selective survey of events since the reign of William III, that, unlike Whigs such as Pulteney, the Tories had never deviated from a path of patriot purity.

2. *Seventeen Hundred and Forty Two, Being a Review of the Conduct of the New Ministry, the Last Year, with Regard to Foreign Affairs: in Answer to the Most Celebrated Vindications Published of Late in their Favour* (1743). Published in February 1743, as the title indicates, this was another response to the new Whig polemic of the second half of 1742. It was devoted almost exclusively to issues of foreign policy, and was basically a reiteration of the critique of Carteret's conduct of the war that had been expounded most influentially in Chesterfield's *The Case of the Hanover Forces* (1742). Its Tory authorship is suggested by the dedicatee, the Tory peer Lord Quaranden, and by its view that the accession of the Hanoverians, with its 'importation of foreign piety and foreign policy', and the onset of corruption in Britain were contemporaneous events. Quaranden was undoubtedly selected as the dedicatee because of his speech in the

---

[17] Lewis, *Walpole*, xviii. 7–9: Walpole to Mann, 29 July 1742.

Commons on 10 December 1742 attacking the employment of the Hanoverian troops. In this speech he retrospectively defended Tory foreign policy during the wars against Louis XIV's France, a defence that was reiterated in the pamphlet.

3. *Public Discontent Accounted for, from the Conduct of our Ministers in the Cabinet, and of our Generals in the Field* (1743). Published in November 1743, this was one of the earliest of the many patriot rebuttals of Perceval's *Faction Detected by the Evidence of Facts* (1743). Its Tory provenance is disclosed by its articulation of a defence of 'Tory' patriotism that is virtually identical to that advanced in *Opposition More Necessary than Ever* (1). The Tory commitment to patriot principles was thus illustrated by a partisan portrayal of events from the Glorious Revolution to the present day, which was then contrasted with the new Whig betrayal of 1742.

4. *The Opposition Rescued from the Insolent Attacks of Faction Detected* (1744). Published in the spring of 1744, this was another rebuttal of *Faction Detected by the Evidence of Facts*. The only grounds for supposing that it was of Tory origin are the remarks that the author made in defence of Tory conduct between 1710 and 1714. In this context, the author described Harley and Bolingbroke as 'Two of the wisest men that were ever produced in this or any other country'. They were also portrayed as having succesfully pursued a necessary pacific policy at the end of the War of the Spanish Succession. It is worth noting that the pamphlet began with an unequivocal recommendation of Chesterfield and Ralph's *The Defence of the People* (1743). It is perhaps also worth noting that this was despite the fact that the opposition Whigs Chesterfield and Ralph were notably less keen to be seen to be defending Tory conduct between 1710 and 1714. Thus, Chesterfield and Ralph had argued that it was only the 'leaders of the Tories' who were responsible for any misconduct that had taken place while Harley was First Minister; the present 'tories', they added, had no possible connection with alleged Tory misdeeds between 1710 and 1714.

5. *The English Nation Vindicated from the Calumnies of Foreigners* (1744). Published in January 1744, this was a direct reply to a pamphlet defending the role of the Hanoverian troops and the alleged benefits that accrued to Britain as a consequence of the Anglo-Hanoverian union, *Popular Prejudice Concerning Partiality to the Interests of Hanover to the Subjects of that Electorate, and Particularly to the Hanoverian Troops in British Pay* (1743). The vast bulk of *The English Nation Vindicated* consisted of a point by point refutation of the arguments developed in *Popular Prejudice*, and made no reference to party identities. At one stage, however, it contrasted the principles of what the author called the 'Modern Tories' with the self-interest that, as had allegedly been shown in 1742, characterized Whig conduct. 'Modern Tories', it was observed, 'retain nothing of the Principles of their Fathers but the Name.' They also, the pamphleteer continued, 'speak and act upon true *whiggish* principles'. Apart

from the comparison made between Whig and Tory patriotism, which, as should be clear from the above, was common to a number of Tory-patriot pamphlets of the early 1740s, what makes the Tory authorship of *The English Nation Vindicated* seem all the more probable is the fact that the label of Modern Tory was revived in the mid-1750s by the leading Tory-patriot journal, the *Monitor*. The circumstances surrounding its emergence in the early 1740s indicate that it was employed as a political label because of its utility in dissociating Tory patriotism from the great new Whig betrayal of 1742.

6. *A Plain Answer to the Plain Reasoner* (1745). Published in the spring of 1745, this was a riposte to a pamphlet defence of Carteret's conduct of the war between 1742 and 1744 called *The Plain Reasoner* (1745). The pro-Carteret pamphleteer attempted to buttress his defence of Carteret's foreign policy by arguing that it represented a timely revival of the great Whig tradition associated with Marlborough and William III. The author also poured scorn on the Tory conduct of foreign policy during the Nine Years War and the War of the Spanish Succession. The Tory authorship of *A Plain Answer* is suggested by the pamphlet's uncompromising defence of the Tories' involvement in foreign affairs between 1689 and 1714.

7. *An Address of Thanks to the Broad-Bottoms* (1745). Published in early 1745, this was a withering attack on the participation of the leadership of the Broad-Bottom opposition of 1742–4 in the Broad-Bottom ministry. This, it was argued, represented a second and successive betrayal of patriotism within three years. Of the various factors indicating Tory authorship, the most significant is the pamphlet's reprinting of eight of the nine so-called 'Broad-Bottom promises' that Lord Noel Somerset, the rising star of the Tory party in 1745, and Sir Watkin Williams Wynn submitted to Lord Gower, one of the architects of the Broad-Bottom ministry, in early 1745.

8. *An Expostulatory Epistle to the Welch Knight* (1745). Published in February 1745, this was principally an attack on Sir Watkin Williams Wynn for supporting the Broad-Bottom ministry in the early stages of its existence. Apart from its target, its reiteration of many of the arguments advanced in *An Address of Thanks* (7) suggests that its author was a Tory. This is also suggested by the apparent discomfort that the pamphlet caused to Wynn.[18]

9. *The Case Fairly Stated in a Letter from a Member of Parliament in the Country Interest to one of his Constituents* (1745). Published in May 1745, this was a detailed defence of the Tory leaders' support for the Broad-Bottom ministry. A central feature of the pamphlet was the reproduction of all nine of the 'Broad-Bottom promises' referred to above.

[18] For this, see above, Ch. 2.

BIBLIOGRAPHY

MANUSCRIPTS

Bodleian Library

Carte MS 175.
Dashwood MS DD (Bucks) 11–33.
Rawlinson MS D 367.

British Library

Hardwicke Papers, Add. MSS 35354, 35360–3, 35385, 35396–7, 35407–8, 35423–4, 35587–8.
Newcastle Papers, Add. MSS 32699–704.
Egmont Papers, Add. MSS 47012B, 47013B, 47093, 47159.
Holland House Papers, Add. MSS 51390–1, 51417, 51437.

Public Record Office

State Papers Domestic, George II, SP 36; Regencies, SP 43; Entry Books Criminal, SP 44.
Treasury Solicitors Papers, TS 11.
King's Bench Papers, Precedents, KB 33; Rules of Court, KB 21.

Westminster Public Library

Vestry Minutes, St Paul's, Covent Garden (1737–51).

PRINTED SOURCES

Newspapers and Periodicals

All Alive and Merry, or, the London Daily Post.
Annals of Europe.
Champion, or, British Mercury.
Common Sense, or, the Englishman's Journal.
Craftsman.
Daily Advertiser.

Daily Gazetteer.
Daily Post.
General Advertiser.
General Evening Post.
General London Evening Mercury.
Gentleman's Magazine.
Jacobite's Journal.
London Courant, or, New Advertiser.
London Evening Post.
London Gazette.
London Magazine.
National Journal, or, the Country Gazette.
Old England, or, the Constitutional Journal (in 1746 the title changed to *Old England, or, the Broad-Bottom Journal*).
Penny London Post.
Publick Register.
Rayner's London Morning Advertiser.
Remembrancer.
St James's Evening Post.
True Patriot.
Universal Magazine.
Universal Spectator.
Westminster Journal, or, the New Weekly Miscellany.
Whitehall Evening Post.

Pamphlets and Ballads

At least one library location is given for each item. The following abbreviations have been used: BL, British Library; BodL., Bodleian Library; C, Codrington Library, All Souls, Oxford.

Pamphlets Published before 1741

An Address to the Electors and Other Free Subjects of Great Britain, Occasioned by the Late Secession (1739), BodL.
Considerations on the Management of the Late Secret Negociations and the Conduct of the Court of France (1740), BodL.
The Convention (1740), BodL.
Copies of Some Letters from Mr Hutcheson to the Later Earl of Sunderland (1722), BodL.
[Earberry, M.] *An Historical Account of the Advantages that Have Accru'd to England by the Succession in the Illustrious House of Hanover* (1722), BodL.
[———] *The Second Part of the Advantages that Have Accrued to England by the Succession in the Illustrious House of Hanover* (1722), BodL.
[———] *The whole System of English Liberty Formed from the Ancient Laws and*

Constitutions of our Forefathers, Compar'd with the Modern Practices in Courts of Justice and Other Places (1738), BodL.

An Epistle from a Noble L——d to Mr P——y (1740), BodL.

[Gordon, Thomas] *An Appeal to the Unprejudiced, Concerning the Present Discontents Occasioned by the Late Convention with Spain* (1739), BodL.

An Historical View of the Principles, Characters, Persons &c. of the Political Writers of Great Britain (1740), BodL.

An Impartial Enquiry into the Properties of Places and Pensions as they Affect the Constitution (1740), BL.

The Livery-Man, or, Plain Thoughts on Publick Affairs (1740), BodL.

[Lyttleton?] *A Letter to a Member of Parliament Concerning the Present State of Affairs at Home and Abroad* (1740), BodL.

[Marchmont, Earl of] *A Serious Exhortation to the Electors of Great Britain, wherein the Importance of the Approaching Elections Is Particularly Proved from our Present Situation at Home and Abroad* (1740), BodL.

The Original Series of Wisdom and Policy, Manifested in a Review of our Foreign Negociations and Transactions for Several Years Past (1739), BL.

The Place Bill—A Ballad (1740), BodL.

The Present State of the Revenues and Forces of France and Spain, Compar'd with those of Great Britain (1739), BodL.

[Pulteney] *A Short View of the State of Affairs with Relation to Great Britain for Four Years Past* (1730), BodL.

[——] *An Humble Address to the Knights, Citizens, and Burgesses, Elected to Represent the Commons of Great Britain in the Ensuing Parliament, by a Freeholder* (1734), BodL.

[——] *Politicks on Both Sides with Regard to Foreign Affairs* (1734), BodL.

A Review of the Late Excise Scheme, in Answer to a Pamphlet Intitled the Rise and Fall of the Late Projected Excise, Impartially Considered (1733), BodL.

The Rise and Fall of the Late Projected Excise, Impartially Considered, by a Friend of the English Constitution (1733), BodL.

A Series of Wisdom and Policy, Being a Full Justification of our Measures ever since the Year 1721, Including and Especially of our Late Convention (1739), BodL.

A Serious Address to the Electors of Great Britain (1740), BodL.

[Walpole, Horatio] *The Convention Vindicated from the Misrepresentations of the Enemies of our Peace* (1739), C.

What or That! Occasion'd by a Pamphlet, Intitled Are these Things So!, and its Answer, Yes, they Are (1740), BodL.

Pamphlets Published during 1741

The Conduct of Admiral Vernon Examin'd and Vindicated, BodL.

A Dialogue between G——s E——e and B-b D——n, BodL.

The False Accusers Accused, or, the Undeceived Englishman, Being an Important

Enquiry into the General Conduct of the Administration, and Compared with that of their Enemies, whereby it Will Appear who Merit Impeachment, &c., BodL.

A Farther Account of the Property which the Royal and Electoral House of Prussia and Brandenburg Claims in the Silesian Dutchies of Jagendorff, Bries, Wohlau, and the Lordships thereto Appertaining, as Is Founded on the Laws of Nature and of the Empire, BodL.

The Grand Retreat, or, the Downfall of the S-d——an Party, BodL.

Great Britain's Memorial, Containing a Collection of the Instructions, Representations, &c. of the Freeholders and Other Electors of Great Britain to their Representatives in Parliament after these Two Years Past, BL.

The Groans of Germany, or, the Enquiry of a Protestant German into the Original Cause of the Present Distractions of the Empire, BodL.

The Plain Truth, a Dialogue between Sir Courtly Jobber, Candidate for the Borough of Guzzledown, and Tom TellTruth, Schoolmaster and Freeman in the Said Borough, BodL.

The Present Influence and Conduct of Great Britain Impartially Considered, BodL.

Reasons Founded on Facts for a Late Motion, BodL.

A Review of the Late Motion for an Address to his Majesty against a Certain Great Minister, and the Reasons for it, with Some Remarks upon the Minister's Speech, in Defence of himself, to which Is Added a Short Address to the Electors of Great Britain at this Critical Conjucture, BodL.

A Second Letter to a Member of Parliament Concerning the Present State of Affairs, BodL.

The Sentiments of a Tory, in Respect to a Late Important Transaction, and in Regard to the Present Situation of Affairs, BodL.

The True Principles of the Revolution, Revived and Asserted, Being a Defence of the Present Administration, in a Letter to a Friend, BodL.

Truth and Moderatio | odL.

Pamphlets Published during 1742

Address to the Electors of Great Britain, Occasion'd by the Report of a Late Secret Committee, BodL.

The Affecting Case of the Queen of Hungary, in Relation both to Friends and Foes, Being a Fair Specimen of Modern History, BodL.

Behind the Screen—A Vision, BodL.

Britannia in Mourning, or a Review of the Politicks and Conduct of Great Britain with Regard to France, the Balance of Power, and the True Interest of these Nations, from the Present Times, and Particularly since the Accession of the Ilustrious House of H——r, BodL.

[Campbell, J.] *The Case of the Opposition Impartially Stated,* BL.

[Chesterfield] *The Case of the Hanover Forces in the Pay of Great Britain,* BodL.

The Conduct of the Late Administration with Regard to Foreign Affairs from 1722 to 1742, wherein that of the Right Honourable the Earl of Orford (Late Sir Robert Walpole) Is Particularly Vindicated, in a Letter to a Certain Right Honourable Gentleman, Member of the Present Parliament, BodL.

Considerations on the War, wherein the Transactions Antecedent thereto, and Consequent thereon, Are Fairly Stated and Impartially Examined, BodL.

The Country Girl: An Ode, BodL.

The Court Secret: A Melancholy Truth, BodL.

The Dangerous Consequences of Parliamentary Divisions, Occasion'd by Refusal of the Place Bill, the Act of Indemnity, &c., BodL.

[Dodington?] *The Conduct of the Late and Present M——ry Compar'd, with an Impartial Review of the Public Transactions since the Resignation of the Right Honourable the Earl of Orford, and the Causes that Immediately Effected the Same, to which Is Added Remarks on a Farther Report of a Certain Committee, in a Letter to a Friend*, BodL.

A Draught of a Bill of Complaint in the High Court of Chancery by Mrs Magna Britannia, Complaint against Robert de Houghton, and Others, Defendants, BodL.

An Enquiry into the Present State of our Domestick Affairs, Shewing the Danger of a New Opposition, BodL.

An Epistle to William Pulteney Esq., upon his Late Conduct in Publick Affairs, BodL.

The False Patriot, a Satirical Epistle to W—— P——y Esq., on his Being Created E——l of B-th &c. BodL.

A Full Answer to the Letter from a By-Stander, BodL.

[Hervey, John Lord] *Miscellaneous Thoughts on the Present Posture of our Foreign and Domestick Affairs, Humbly Offer'd to the Consideration of the Parliament and the People*, BodL.

An Impartial Review of the Opposition and Conduct of the Late Minister since his Accession, BodL.

The Independent Briton, or, Free Thoughts on the Expediency of Gratifying the People's Expectations, BL.

An Inquiry into the Revenue, Credit, and Commerce of France, in a Letter to a Member of this Present Parliament, BodL.

A Key to the Business of the Present Session, BodL.

The Late Minister Unmask'd, or, an Answer to a Late Pamphlet, Entitled Conduct of the Late Administration, with Respect to Foreign Affairs, from 1722 to 1742, wherein that of the Right Honourable the Earl of Orford, Late Sir Robert Walpole, is Particularly Vindicated, BodL.

A Letter from a Member of the Last Parliament to a New Member of the Present, Concerning the Conduct of the War with Spain, with Some Observations on the Hanover Neutrality, as far as it May Relate to or Affect Great Britain, BodL.

A Letter of Condoleance, and Invitation from Cardinal Fleury, to the Right Honourable the E—— of Or——d, BodL.

A Letter to a Member of this New Parliament, from a True Lover of the Liberties of the People, BL.

A Letter to a Right Honourable Member of Parliament, Demonstrating the Absolute Necessity of Great Britain's Assisting the House of Austria, BL.

A Letter to my Lord Mayor, Vindicating the Late Instructions from the City of London for Postponing the Subsidies to Redress of Grievances, BodL.

A Letter to the Author of the Enquiry into the Revenue, Credit, and Commerce of France, wherein the Former and Present State of the Power and Commerce of that Kingdom Are Fully Consider'd, and Deduced from Authentic Accounts, BodL.

A Letter to the Secret Committee, Concerning Certain Extraordinary Practices of the Late M———r, Intended to Have Been Laid before them in a Private Manner, and Now Submitted to their Publick Consideration, BodL.

A Modest Enquiry into the Present State of Foreign Affairs, by a Lover of his Country, BL.

[Morris, Corbyn] *A Letter from a By-Stander to a Member of Parliament*, BodL.

National Unanimity Recommended, or, the Necessity of a Constitutional Resistance to the Sinister Designs of False Brethren, BodL.

The New Ministry, Containing a Collection of All the Satirical Poems, Songs, &c. since the Beginning of 1742, BodL.

Observations on the Conduct of Great Britain in Respect of Foreign Affairs, in which All the Objections that Have Been Thrown out in Some Late Pamphlets and Discourses Are Fairly Answered, BL.

The Old Coachman: A New Ballad, to which Is Added, Labour in Vain, BodL.

[Oldmixon, John] *Memoirs of the Press, Historical and Political, for Thirty Years Past, from 1710–40*, BodL.

Opposition More Necessary than Ever, or, a Review of the Principles, Designs, and Conduct of the Two Parties, Joined in the Opposition to the Late Minister, and after his Resignation, Shewing who Have Been, and Are Most Likely to Continue the Friends, and who Are the Enemies of the Public, BodL.

Plain Matter of Fact, or, Whiggism the Bulwark of these Kingdoms, BL.

The Present State of British Influence in Holland Exemplified, BodL.

A Proper Answer to the By-Stander, BodL.

Sapho to Phaon, an Epistle from a Lady of Quality to a Noble Lord, Occasioned by the Late Publication of his Miscellaneous Thoughts, BodL.

Seasonable Expostulations with the Worthy Citizens of London, upon their Late Instructions to their Representatives, by a Country Gentleman, BodL.

The Thoughts of a Private Gentleman on the Late Indemnifying Bill, BodL.

A Vindication of the Conduct of a Certain Eminent Patriot, BodL.

Pamphlets Published during 1743

Beef and Butt Beer, against Mum and Pumpernickle, H-n———r Scrubs, or, British Glory Revived, BodL.

Britons Awake and Look Around You, or, Ruin the Inevitable Consequence of a Land-War whether Successful or not, BodL.

Bumper to Old England, Huzza, BodL.

[Burrington, George] *Seasonable Considerations on the Expediency of a War with France*, BodL.

A Caveat against Concluding this Session with an Act of Indemnity, BodL.

[Chesterfield] *A Vindication of a Late Pamphlet, Intitled, the Case of the Hanover Troops*, BodL.

[——] *A Farther Vindication of the Case of the Hanover Troops*, BodL.

[—— and Ralph] *A Defence of the People, or, a Full Confutation of the Pretended Facts Advanced in a Late Huge Angry Pamphlet, Called Faction Detected*, BodL.

A Compleat View of the Present Politicks of Great Britain in a Letter from a German Nobleman, to his Friend at Vienna, BodL.

A Congratulatory Letter to a Certain Right Honourable Person upon his Late Disapointment, BodL.

[De Coetlogan] *Serious and Impartial Reflections on the Conduct of the Several Princes and States of Europe*, BodL.

The Desertion Discussed, or, the Last and Present Oppositions Placed in their True Light, wherein the Characters Aspersed in a Late Tedious and Prolix Libel, Entitled Faction Detected by the Evidence of Facts, Are Fully Vindicated, the Design of that Treatise Rendered Manifest, and the Deserters of their Country's Cause Properly Exposed, BodL.

The Detector Detected, or, the Danger to which our Constitution Now Lies Exposed, Set in a True and Manifest Light, BodL.

A Dialogue between the Proud Horse, the Tame Lion, and Crab the Master's Cudgel, as they Lay together One Night in a Stable near Mentz in Germany, with Some Historical Particulars, BodL.

The Emperor's Plan for a Peace, with Remarks upon it, BodL.

The Englishman's Answer to a German Nobleman, Containing Some Observations upon the Political System of the Present Administration, as it Is Exposed in the German's Letter, BodL.

An Enquiry into the Independency of a Dependent Lord, BodL.

An Essay on Maritime Power and Commerce, Particularly those of France, BodL.

Four Letters Published in the Old England Journal, BodL.

A Free and Impartial Enquiry into the Extraordinary and Advantageous Bargain for Remitting Money for the Pay of the Forces Abroad, for the Year 1743, BodL.

Free Thoughts on the Inevitable Consequences of a Land War, BL.

A Full and Clear Vindication of the Full Answer to a Letter from a By-Stander to a Member of Parliament, BodL.

A Great Man's Speech in Downing Street, against the Enquiry, C.

The Groans of Britons at the Gloomy Prospect of the Present Precarious State of their Liberties and Properties, Compared with what it Has been, BodL.

The H—— T—— Come again, BL.

An Impartial Review of the Present Troubles of Germany, BodL.

An Important Secret Come to Light, or, the States General's Reasons for Refusing to Guaranty the E——e of H——r, and to Act Offensively against France in the Netherlands, as Lately Proposed by the Ministers of Great Britain, BodL.

The Interest of Hanover Steadily Pursued, BodL.

J——L's Wife: A New Ballad, in Answer to One, Intitled S——s and J——L, BodL.

A Key to the Present Politicks of the Principal Powers of Europe, BodL.

A Letter from a Member of the States-General in Holland, to a Member of Parliament in England, BodL.

A Letter from an Officer Abroad, Giving an Account of the Earl of Stair's Resignation, BL.

A Letter from an Old Discarded Minister to One Lately Disgraced in China, BodL.

A Letter to a Friend in the Country, upon Occasion of the Many Scurrilous Libels which Have Been Lately Publish'd, BodL.

A Letter to a Great Man in France, in which Are Briefly Considered, the Following Popular Points, BodL.

A Letter to the E—— of S——, in which Are Examined the Conduct of the Several Ministries with Respect to the Ballance of Power in Europe and the Necessity of Supporting the House of Austria, and Prescribing Bounds to the Power of France, BodL.

A Letter to the Rev Mr T. Carte, Author of the Full Answer to the By-Stander, BodL.

A Letter to the Rev Dr Zachary Pearce, Occasion'd by his Advertisement in the Daily Advertiser of Oct. 28, 1743, in which the Secret History and Real Tendency of a Late Pamphlet Intitled Faction Detected by the Evidence of Facts Are Clear'd up, together with Some Observations as to the Danger of the Press, and the Necessity of Preserving its Freedom, BL.

Letters and Negociations of M. Van Hoey, BodL.

The Memorial of the E——l of S——r, BodL.

Miscellaneous Reflections on Miscellaneous Thoughts, in a Letter to the Honourable Author, BodL.

The Mysterious Congress, a Letter from Aix-la-Chapelle Detecting the Late Secret Negociations there, Accounting for the Extraordinary Slowness of the Operations of the Campaign since the Action at Dettingen, and Particularly for the Resignation of the E——l of S——r, BodL.

A New Song on the Sharp and Bloody Battle of Dettingen, BL.

Observations on the Conduct of Great Britain in Respect to Foreign Affairs, BL.

Old England, or, the Constitutional Journal Extraordinary, BL.

Old England's Te Deum, BL.

Opposition not Faction, or, the Rectitude of the Present Parliamentary Opposition to the Present Expensive Measures, Justified by Reason and Facts, in Answer to Faction Detected, BodL.

The Patriot and the Minister Review'd by Way of Dialogue, BodL.

[Perceval] *Faction Detected by the Evidence of Facts*, BodL.

Plain Thoughts in Plain Language: A New Ballad, BodL.

Popular Prejudice Concerning Partiality to the Interests of Hanover, BodL.

The Present Measures Proved to Be the Only Means of Securing the Balance of Power in Europe, as well as the Liberty and Independency of Great Britain, BL.

A Proper Reply to a Late and Scurrilous Libel, Intitled a Congratulatory Letter to a Certain Right Honourable Person upon his Late Disappointment, BodL.

Public Discontent Accounted for, from the Conduct of our Ministers in the Cabinet, and of our Generals in the Field, wherein Proper Observations Are Made on the Late Ministerial Apology, Intitled Faction Detected, BodL.

The Question Stated with Regard to our Army in Flanders, and the Arguments for and against this Measure Compar'd, BodL.

[Ralph, J.] *A Critical History of the Late Administration of Sir Robert Walpole, Now Earl of Orford*, BodL.

A Review of the Whole Political Conduct of a Late Eminent Patriot and his Friends, BL.

S——s and J——l: A New Ballad, BodL.

Serious Consideration on the Several High Duties which the Nation in General, as well as its Trade in Particular Labour under, BodL.

Seventeen Hundred and Forty Two, Being a Review of the Conduct of the New Ministry the Last Year, with Regard to Foreign Affairs, BodL.

A State of the Expence of the Late War, BodL.

The Steady Pursuit of the Interest of Great Britain Dispassionately Examin'd, BL.

Three Private Letters from Persons in the Army of Hanau, BodL.

The Triumphant campaign, a Critical, Panegyrical, Poetical History of the Late Active Glorious German Campaign, BodL.

A True Dialogue between Thomas Jones, a Trooper, Lately Return'd from Germany, and John Smith, a Serjeant in the First Regiment of Foot Guards, BodL.

Two Letters Publish'd in Old England, or, the Constitutional Journal, BodL.

[Walpole, Horatio] *The Interest of Great Britain Steadily Pursued*, BodL.

The Wife and the Nurse: A New Ballad, BodL.

The Yellow Sash, or, H——r Beshit: An Excellent New Ballad, BodL.

Pamphlets Published during 1744

An Address to the People of Great Britain by a Country Clergyman, BodL.

An Address to the People of Great Britain, on the Present Enterprises of France, BodL.

An Address to the People of Great Britain on the Present Posture of Affairs, BodL.

The Answer of a Milanese Gentleman to a Member of the British Parliament, BodL.

An Apology for the Conduct of the Present Administration as to Foreign Affairs Generally, but Particularly with Regard to France, BodL.

Considerations on the Politics of France, BodL.

The Emperor's Commissorial Decree for Raising the Whole Force of the Empire against the Queen of Hungary, and the Motives of the King of Prussia for Acting Totis Viribus in Support of the Emperor, BodL.

English Loyalty Opposed to Hanoverian Ingratitude, Being a Vindication of the Present and All Former Ministries since the Accession, in Answer to a Late Libel on the English Nation in General, Called a Letter from Hanover, Shewing the True Cause of the Present Broils of Germany, and Confusions of Europe &c., BodL.

The English Nation Vindicated from the Calumnies of Foreigners, BL.

[Fielding?] *An Attempt towards a Natural History of the Hanover Rat*, BL.

Free Thoughts on the Late Treaty of Alliance Concluded at Worms, BodL.

French Perfidy Illustrated in General, but Particularly in the Present Pretended Invasion, and the State of Dunkirk, BodL.

French Snakes in British Clover, or, a Discourse Shewing that the Swarms of Frenchmen in the Service of the Families of Great Britain Are Inconsistent with the Love of our Religion and Country, and Destructive of the Interests, and that they Are in a Dangerous Situation to Act a Bloody Part in Concert with their Countrymen in Case of Invasion, BodL.

German Politicks, or, the Modern System Examin'd and Refuted, wherein the Natural Strength of Germany and France Are Compar'd, and the Nature of the Ballance of Power Explained, BodL.

The H——r Heroes, or, a Song of Triumph in Laud of the Immortal Conduct, and Marvellous Exploits of those Spirits, during the Last Campaign, and Action of Dettingen, BL.

The Instructions Sent by the Regency of Hanover to the Privy Counsellor to Busch, Electoral Minister of the King of Great Britain at the Court of Dresden, together with a Letter from a Hanoverian Minister to a Member of Parliament, Containing a Justification of the Hanoverians and his Sentiments on the Present Critical Conjuncture of Affairs, BL.

A Letter from a Genoese Gentleman to a Member of Parliament of Great Britain, Relating to the Treaty of Worms which Regards the Town and Marquisate of Finale, BodL.

A Letter from Flanders, Giving an Account of the Present State of the War in the Netherlands, the Weakness of the Allies, and the Strength of the French, BodL.

A Letter from Hanover, Shewing the True Cause of the Present Broils of Germany, and Confusions of Europe, BodL.

A Letter to a Friend, Concerning the Electorate of Hanover, wherein her Connexion with these Kingdoms Is Endeavour'd to Be Impartially Considered, BodL.

A Letter to his Prussian Majesty, upon his Most Extraordinary Breach of Publick and Solemn Faith, BodL.

The Lords Protest, to which Is Added a List of the Members of Parliament who Voted for and against Continuing the Hanover Troops in British Pay, Jan. 18 1743, Likewise the State of the National Debt down to Christmas 1743, BodL.

The Manifesto of a Certain Power, BodL.

The New Opposition Compared with the Old in Point of Principles and Practice, in which All the Malevolent Aspersions Scattered through a Late Bulky Performance, Entitled Faction Detected by the Evidence of Facts, Are Fully Refuted and the Friends of Liberty and Independency Clearly Vindicated, BL.

The Operations of the British and the Allied Arms, during the Campaigns of 1743 and 1744, Historically Deducted, by an Eye Witness, BodL.

The Opposition Rescued from the Insolent Attacks of Faction Detected, wherein Is Considered the Rectitude of our Present Measures with Regard to Foreign Affairs, BodL.

The Political Cabinet, or, an Impartial Review of the Most Remarkable Occurrences of the World, Particularly of Europe, BodL.

The Political Views of the Court of France Delineated, Shewing the Perfidious Conduct of the French with Regard to the Treaties of the Pyrenees, Aix-la-Chapelle and Nimegen, from the Spanish of Don Pedro Ronquillo Ambassador of Spain to King Charles II, BodL.

The Remarks of a True German Patriot upon a Writing, Intitled, Exposition of the Motives which Obliged the King of Prussia to Supply the Emperor with Auxiliaries, BodL.

A Rescript of his Majesty the King of Prussia to M. D'Andrié his Minister at the British Court, BodL.

The State of the Nation, as it Stood Dec. 31 1742, BL.

A Vindication of our Present Royal Family Principally with Regard to Hanover, BodL.

A Warning to the Whigs, and to Well-Affected Tories, BodL.

Pamphlets Published during 1745

An Address of Thanks to the Broad-Bottoms, BodL.

An Address to the Electors of the Empire, Concerning the Approaching Dyet of Election, BodL.

The Advantages of the Hanover Succession and English Ingratitude Freely and Imparitally Considered and Examined, BL.

An Apology for the Welch Knight, and View of the Principles and Present Dissensions between the Chiefs of the Broad-Bottoms, BodL.

A Brief and True Representation of the Posture of our Affairs, Containing a

Particular Account of the Dangers to Be Apprehended from the Present Invasion, BodL.

[Carteret Webb] *Remarks on the Pretender's Eldest Son's Second Declaration, Dated the 10th of October 1745*, BodL.

The Case Fairly Stated in a Letter from a Member of Parliament in the Country Interest to One of his Constituents, BodL.

Christmas Chat, or, Observations on the Late Change at Court, on the Different Characters of the INS and OUTS, and on the Present State of Affairs, BodL.

A Compliment of Congratulation to a Nobleman, on his Return from Boetia, BodL.

Considerations Addressed to the Publick, BL.

Considerations on the Conduct of the Dutch, Containing a Candid Examination whether there Was Any Just Reasons to Expect they Should Concur with us in Declaring War against France, BodL.

The Criterion of the Reason and Necessity of the Present War, and of Pursuing it with Steadiness and Vigour, BodL.

Dutch Faith, Being an Enquiry Founded on Facts, into the Probability of the Success of the British Arms, on the Continent, Next Campaign, BodL.

The Dutch Reasoner, a Letter from the Hague on the Earl of Chesterfield's Embassy and Success, and the Emperor's Death, BodL.

An Enquiry into the Causes of our Late and Present National Calamities, BodL.

An Expostulatory Epistle to the Welch Knight, on the Late Revolution in Politicks, and the Extraordinary Conduct of himself and his Associates, BodL.

[Fielding] *A Dialogue between the Devil, the Pope, and the Pretender*, BodL.

[———] *The History of the Present Rebellion in Scotland*, BodL.

[———] *A Serious Address to the People of Great Britain, in which the Certain Consequences of the Present Rebellion Are Fully Demonstrated*, BodL.

The Folly and Danger of the Present Associations Demonstrated, BodL.

The Free and Impartial Examiner, Being a Candid Enquiry into the Causes of our Present Melancholy Situation, BodL.

[Gibson] *The Bishop of London's Pastoral Letter to the People of his Diocese . . . Occasion'd by our Present Dangers*, BodL.

Hanoverian Politicks, in a Letter from a Gentleman at the Court of Hanover, to his Friend in England, Concerning the Present Posture of Affairs on the Continent, BodL.

[Herring] *The Speech Made by his Grace, the Lord Archbishop of York, at Presenting an Association, Entered into at the Castle of York*, BodL.

The Heroes: A New Ballad, BodL.

The Layman's Sermon, Occasioned by the Present Rebellion, BodL.

A Letter to a Certain Foreign Minister, in which the Grounds of the Present War Are Truly Stated, BodL.

A Letter to a Member of Parliament on the Importance of Liberty, BL.

A Letter to a Young Member of the House of C-m———ns, BL.

A Letter to the Author of the Case Fairly Stated, from an Old Whig, BL.

The Measures of the Late Administration Examin'd, with an Enquiry into the Grounds for the Present Revolution, BodL.

Miscellaneous Thoughts, Moral and Political, upon the Vices and Follies of the Present Age, the Septennial, Triennial, Pension and Place Bills, the Act of Settlement, the Qualifying Act, and the Coalition of Parties, or what Is Now Called, the Broad Bottom, BodL.

The Modern Patriot or, Broad B-tt-m Principles Examin'd, BodL.

A Modest Enquiry into the Present State of Foreign Affairs, BL.

Observations on a Late Letter to a Certain Foreign Minister, BodL.

Peace to Britain, or, No Popish Pretender, an Address to the Protestants, Shewing why we Should Oppose the Pretender, and how we May Do it Effectively, BL.

A Plain Answer to the Plain Reasoner, wherein the Present State of Affairs Is Set, not in a New but a True Light, BodL.

The Plain Reasoner, wherein the Present State of Affairs Are Set in a New, but Very Obvious Light, BodL.

The Present Ruinous LAND-WAR, *Proved to Be a H——r War, by Facts as well as Arguments, or, the Opposition Fully Vindicated*, BodL.

The Question, whether England Can be Otherwise than Miserable under a Popish King, BL.

Remarks Occasion'd by the Plain Reasoner, BodL.

Remarks on the Pretender's Declaration and Commission, BodL.

The Reply of the British Member of Parliament to the Answer of a Milanese Gentleman, BodL.

A Survey of the National Debts, the Sinking Fund, the Civil List, and the Annual Supplies, BodL.

[Tucker] *A Calm Address to All Parties in Religion, Concerning Disaffection to the Present Government*, BL.

The Visible Pursuit of a Foreign Interest, in Opposition to the Interest of Great Britain, BodL.

[Yorke, C.] *Some Considerations on the Law of Forfeiture, for High Treason, Occasion'd by a Clause in the Late Act for Making it Treason to Correspond with the Pretender's Sons, or Any of their Agents*, BodL.

Pamphlets Published during 1746

An Apology for the Conduct of a Late Celebrated Second-Rate Minister, BodL.

[Auchmuty, Robert] *The Importance of Cape Breton Consider'd, in a Letter to a Member of Parliament from an Inhabitant of New England*, BodL.

[Bollan, William] *The Importance and Advantage of Cape Breton, Truly Stated and Impartially Considered*, BodL.

[Burgh, James] *Britain's Remembrancer, or, the Danger not Over*, BodL.

A Defence of Several Proposals for Raising Three Millions for the Service of the Year 1746, BodL.

A Detection of the Views of those who Would, in the Present Crisis, Engage an Incumber'd Trading Nation, as Principals, in a Ruinous Expensive Land-War, BodL.

An Examination of the Expediency of Bringing over Immediately the Body of Hanoverian Troops Taken into our Pay, BodL.

The Great Importance of Cape Breton, Demonstrated and Exemplified, by Extracts from the Best Writers, French and English, who Have treated of that Colony, BodL.

An Impartial Enquiry into the True Cause of our Present National Troubles, BodL.

The Important Question Discussed, or, a Serious and Impartial Enquiry into the True Interest of England with Respect to the Continent, BodL.

A Letter to Sir John Barnard upon his Proposals for Raising Three Millions of Money for the Service of the Year 1746, BodL.

A Letter to the Author of the National Journal, BL.

A Letter to the People of Great Britain and Ireland of Every Denomination, on Matters of the Utmost Importance to them All, in this Critical and Dangerous Crisis, BL.

A Letter to William Pitt, BL.

The Lords Protest on the Motion to Address his Majesty for Keeping our Forces at Home, till the Dutch Has Declared against France, BodL.

The New System, or Proposals for a General Peace upon a Solid Foundation, BL.

The Present Condition of Great Britain, BL.

A Proposal for Arming, and Disciplining the People of Great Britain, with Some Occasional Reflections on the Late Conduct of France, BodL.

Remarks on a Letter to Sir John Barnard, in which the Proposals of that Worthy Patriot Are Vindicated, BodL.

The Sp——ch of Major S-w-n, the First Day of the Session, Being the 18th of November, BL.

The Spirit and Principles of the Whigs and Jacobites Compared, BodL.

[Squire, Samuel] *A Letter to a Tory Friend, upon the Present Critical Situation of Affairs*, BodL.

[Vernon] *Original Letters to an Honest Sailor*, BodL.

[——] *A Specimen of Naked Truth (in Letters), from a British Sailor*, BodL.

Pamphlets Published during 1747

Considerations on Both Sides, or, Remarks on the Conduct of Great Britain and Holland, at the Present Critical Conjuncture, BL.

A Critical, Expostulatory, and Interesting Address to a Certain Right Honourable Apostate, on his Present Unaccountable Conduct at this Critical Juncture, and on Several Other Important and National Affairs, BodL.

[Dashwood] *An Address to the Gentlemen, Clergy, and Freeholders of All the Counties of Great Britain*, BodL.

An Essay on Liberty and Independency, Being an Attempt to Prove, that the People under a Popular Form of Government, May Be as much Slaves, as those Subject to the Arbitrary Will of One Man, BodL.

An Expostulatory Letter to a Certain Right Honourable Gentleman upon his Late Promotion, BodL.

[Fielding] *A Dialogue between a Gentleman of London and an Honest Alderman of the Country Party,* BodL.

A General View of the Present Politics and Interests of the Principal Powers of Europe, BL.

[Granville?] *The State of the Nation Consider'd in a Letter to a Member of Parliament,* BL.

[——?] *The State of the Nation for the Year 1747, and Respecting 1748, Inscribed to a Member of Parliament.* BodL.

History of the Rise, Progress, and Tendency of Patriotism, Drawn from a Close Observation of the Conduct of Many of our Late Illustrious Patriots, BodL.

King Harry the Ninth's Speech to Both Houses of Parliament, BodL.

A Letter on the Dangers Arising from Popery and Disaffection, BodL.

A Letter to the Author of the Whitehall Evening Post, BodL.

A Letter to the Tories, BodL.

Liberty and Right, or an Essay, Historical and Political, on the Constitution and Administration of Great Britain, BodL.

National Union Recommended, BL.

The Ordinary of Newgate's Account of the Behaviour, Dying Words, and Confession, Birth, Parentage and Education of the Several Malefactors that Were Executed at Westminster on Friday Last, for the Horrid Crimes of B——y and C——n, BL.

Three Letters to the Members of the Present Parliament on Kings and Ministers of State, to which Is Added a Letter to Sir John Phillips Bart, Occasioned by his Recess from Parliament, BodL.

[Walpole, Horace] *A Letter to the Whigs,* BodL.

Pamphlets Published during 1748

An Apology for a Late Resignation in a Letter from an English Gentleman to his Friend at the Hague, BodL.

The Case Restated, or, an Examine of a Late Pamphlet, Intitled, the State of the Nation for the Year 1747, BL.

A Collection of Political and Humorous Letters, Poems, and Articles of News, Published in an Evening Paper, Intitled, the National Journal, or, Country Gazette, BodL.

The Conduct of the Government with Regard to War and Peace Stated, BL.

Considerations on the Definitive Treaty, Signed at Aix-la-Chapelle, BodL.

An Essay upon Publick Credit in a Letter to a Friend, Occasioned by the Fall of Stocks, BodL.

[Fielding] *A Proper Answer to a Late Scurrilous Libel, Entitled an Apology for the Conduct of a Late Celebrated Second-Rate Minister*, BodL.

The Finesse of Rantum Scantum, a New Diverting Dialogue betwixt Tom and Harry, Fratres Fraterrini, BodL.

The Fool, Being a Collection of Essays, Epistles, Moral, Political, Humourous and Entertaining, Published in the Daily Gazetteer, BodL.

A Free Comment on the late Mr W——g——ns Apology for his Conduct, BL.

Impartial Remarks on the Present Posture of Publick Affairs, Addressed to his Grace the Duke of Bedford, One of his Majesty's Principal Secretaries of State, Proving that it Is the Interest of Great Britain not to Conclude a Peace at Present with France, BL.

An Impartial Review of Two Pamphlets Late Published, One Intituled, an Apology for a Late Resignation, the other, the Resignation Discussed, BodL.

The Interests of the Empress Queen, the Kings of France and Spain, and their Principal Allies, BodL.

A Letter from a Gentleman in London to his Friend in the Country, Concerning the Treaty of Aix-la-Chapelle, BL.

A Letter to a Noble Negociator Abroad, on the Present Prospect of a Speedy Peace, BL.

The Patriot Analized, or, a Compendious View of the Publick Criticism of a Late Pamphlet Called, an Apology for the Conduct of a Late Second-Rate Minister, BL.

The Remembrancer, by George Cadwallader Gent, (first 12 issues), BodL.

The Resignation Discussed, in which Many False Facts Are Detected and Sophistical Reasonings Refuted, in a Pamphlet Intitled, an Apology for a Late Resignation, BodL.

A Review of the Late Mr W——s Conduct and Principles, BL.

Some Thoughts on the Constitution, Particularly with Respect to the Power of Making Peace and War, BodL.

[Squire] *An Historical Essay upon the Balance of Civil Power in England, from its First Conquest by the Anglo-Saxons, to the Time of the Revolution, in which Is Introduced a New Dissertation upon Parties*, BL.

A Supplement to the State of the Nation, being Free Thoughts on the Present Critical Conjuncture, BL.

The State of the Nation with a General Balance of Publick Accounts, BodL.

[Swift] *Good Queen Anne Vindicated, and the Ingratitude, Insolence, &c. of her Whig Ministry and the Allies Detected and Exposed, in the Beginning and Conducting of the War* (this was actually a reprint of *The Conduct of the Allies*), BodL.

[Walpole, Horace] *Three Letters to the Whigs, Occasioned by the Letter to the Tories*, BodL.

Ways and Means, or an Easy Method to Raise the Supplies in a Letter to the High Constable, BodL.

Pamphlets Published after 1748

The Advantages of the Definitive Treaty to the People of Great Britain Demonstrated (1749), BL.

Alive, Alive, Alive, Ho! To Be Seen at Paris, the Pacquet Boat, just Setting out from Dover, the Rarest Raree Shew that ever Was Shewn in France, Ho! The Two Most Famous Ostriches (1749), BodL.

The Conduct of the Two B——rs Vindicated, the Examiner's Numerous Contradictions and Inconsistencies Exemplified, his False Facts Delineated and his Romantic Conjectures Exploded (1749), BodL.

[Davenant, Charles] *An Essay upon Universal Monarchy, Written in the Year 1702, Soon after Lewis the Fourteenth Had Settled his Grandson upon the Throne of Spain, by Charles Davenant, to which Is Prefixed, an Abstract of Eassay upon the Ballance of Power, Published at the same Time* (1756), BodL.

A Dialogue between Thomas Jones, a Life Guardman, and John Smith, Late a Serjeant in the First Regiment of Foot Guards Just Returned from Flanders, (1749), BL.

[Egmont] *An Examination of the Principles, and an Enquiry into the Conduct of the Two B——rs, in Regard to the Establishment of their Power, and their Prosecution of the War, 'till the Signing of the Preliminaries* (1749), BodL.

[——?] *An Occasional Letter from a Gentleman in the Country to his Friend in Town, Concerning the Treaty Negociated at Hanau in the Year 1743* (1749), BodL.

[——?] *Constitutional Queries, Earnestly Recommended to the Serious Consideration of Every True Briton* (1751), BodL.

A Letter from a Person of Distinction to the Rt Hon J—— E—— of Eg——t (1749), BodL.

A Letter to the Author of an Examination of the Principles (1749), BodL.

Ministerial Artifice Detected, or, a Full Answer to a Pamphlet Lately Published, Intitled, the Interests of the Empress Queen, the Kings of France and Spain, and their Principal Allies (1749), BodL.

Miscellaneous Reflections upon the Peace (1749), BL.

National Expectations on the Late Change in the Ministry (1751), BL.

[Ralph, J.] *The Case of the Authors, by Profession or Trade, Stated with Regard to Booksellers, the State, and the Public* (1758), BodL.

A Second Series of Facts and Arguments, Tending to Prove that the Abilities of the Two B——rs, Are not More extraordinary than their Virtues (1749), BodL.

[Shebbeare, J.] *A Fifth Letter to the People of England on the Subversion of the Constitution, and the Necessity of its Being Restored* (1757), BodL.

[——] *A Sixth Letter to the People of England, on the Progress of National Ruin, in which it Is Shewn that the Present Grandeur of France, and the Calamities of this Nation, Are Owing to the Influence of Hanover on the Councils of England* (1757), BodL.

[Tucker, J.] *The Case for Going to War, for the Sake of Procuring, Enlarging, or Securing of Trade, Considered in a New Light* (1763), BodL.

Other Primary Sources in Print

Annals and Correspondence of the Viscount and the First and Second Earls of Stair, ed. J. M. Graham, 2 vols. (1875).

Collected Papers on the Jacobite Risings, ed. Rupert Jarvis, 2 vols. (Manchester, 1971–2).

Correspondence of John, Fourth Duke of Bedford, ed. Russell, Lord John, 3 vols. (1842–6).

The Correspondence of Philip Doddridge, 1702–1751, ed. G. F. Nuttall (Northants Record Soc., 29; 1979).

The Correspondence of the Dukes of Richmond and Newcastle, 1724–1750, ed. T. J. McCann (Sussex Record Soc., 73; 1982–3).

Coxe, W., *Memoirs of the Life and Administration of Sir Robert Walpole, Earl of Orford*, 3 vols. (1798).

—— *Memoirs of Horatio, Lord Walpole, Selected from his Correspondence and Papers and Connected with the History of the Times from 1678 to 1757* (1802).

—— *Memoirs of the Administration of the Right Honourable Henry Pelham*, 2 vols. (1827).

Davies, Thomas, *Memoirs of the Life of David Garrick* (1780).

Fielding, Henry, *The 'Jacobite's Journal' and Related Writings*, ed. W. B. Coley (Oxford, 1974).

—— *The 'True Patriot' and Related Writings*, ed. W. B. Coley (Oxford, 1987).

Glover, R., *Memoirs of a Celebrated Literary and Political Character from the Resignation of Sir Robert Walpole, in 1742, to the Establishment of Lord Chatham's Second Administration in 1757, Containing Strictures on Some of the Most Distinguished Men of that Time* (1873).

The Grenville Papers, ed. W. J. Smith, 4 vols. (1852)

Hardinge, G., *Biographical Memoirs of the Rev. Sneyd Davies, DD, Canon Residentiary of Lichfield* (1816).

Harwicke, Lord, *Walpoliana* (1781).

Henry Fox, First Lord Holland: His Family and Relations, ed. Earl of Ilchester (1920).

Historical Manuscripts Commission, Carlisle, Polwarth, Trevor, Stopford-Sackville, Onslow, and Buckinghamshire Papers; *Diary of Viscount Perceval, Afterwards First Earl of Egmont*, 3 vols. (1920–3).

Journals of the House of Commons.

Journals of the House of Lords.

King, W., *Political and Literary Anecdotes of his Times*, 2nd edn. (1879).

Le Blanc, L'Abbé, *Letters on the English and French Nations*, 2 vols. (1747).

A Ledger of Charles Ackers, Printer of the London Magazine, ed. D. F. McKenzie and J. C. Ross (Oxford, 1968).

The Letters of Philip Dormer Stanhope, Fourth Earl of Chesterfield, ed. B. Dobrée, 6 vols. (1932).

Letters to Henry Fox Lord Holland, with a Few Addressed to his Brother Stephen, Earl of Ilchester, ed. Earl of Ilchester (1915).

The Life and Correspondence of Philip Yorke, Earl of Hardwick, ed. Philip C. Yorke, 3 vols. (Cambridge, 1913).

Memoirs and Correspondence of George, Lord Lyttleton, ed. R. Phillimore, 2 vols. (1845).

The Memoirs and Speeches of James, 2nd Earl Waldegrave, 1742–1763, ed. J. C. D. Clark (Cambridge, 1988).

Memorials of the Public Life and Character of the Rt. Hon. James Oswald of Dunniker (Edinburgh, 1815).

The Orrery Papers, ed. E. C. Boyle, Countess of Cork and Orrery, 2 vols. (1903).

The Parliamentary History of England from the Earliest Period to the Year 1803, ed. William Cobbett, 36 vols. (1806–20).

A Selection of Papers of the Earls of Marchmont in the Possession of the Right Honourable Sir George Rose, ed. G. H. Rose, 3 vols. (1831).

A Series of Letters of the First Earl of Malmesbury, his Family and Friends from 1745 to 1820, ed. Earl of Malmesbury, 2 vols. (1820).

A Trip from St James's to the Royal Exchange, with Remarks Serious and Amusing on the Manners, Customs, and Amusements of the Inhabitants of London and Westminster (1744).

WALPOLE, HORACE, *Memoirs of the Reign of King George II*, ed. J. Brooke, 3 vols. (New Haven, Conn., 1985).

The Yale Edition of Horace Walpole's Correspondence, ed. W. S. Lewis *et al.*, 34 vols. (New Haven, Conn., 1937–70).

SECONDARY WORKS

ANDREWES, C. M., 'Anglo-French Commercial Rivalry, 1700–1750', *American Historical Review*, 20 (1914–15), 539–56, 761–88.

AYLING, S., *The Elder Pitt* (1976).

BALLANTYNE, A., *Lord Carteret* (1887).

BAUGH, D. A., 'Great Britain's "Blue-Water" Policy, 1689–1815', *International History Review*, 10 (1988), 33–58.

BAXTER, S. B., 'The Myth of the Grand Alliance in the Eighteenth Century', in P. R. Sellin and S. Baxter (eds.), *Anglo-Dutch Cross-Currents in the Seventeenth and Eighteenth Centuries* (Los Angeles, 1976), 42–59.

BLACK, J., 'A Genoese Gentleman', *Factotum*, 19 (1984), 16–17.

—— 'Falsely Attributed to Lord Bolingbroke', *Publishing History*, 17 (1985), 87–9.

BLACK, J., *British Foreign Policy in the Age of Walpole* (Edinburgh, 1985).

—— 'British Foreign Policy in the War of Austrian Succession, 1740–1748: A Research Priority', *Canadian Journal of History*, 21 (1986), 313–31.

—— *Natural and Necessary Enemies: Anglo-French Relations in the Eighteenth Century* (1986).

—— 'Whig Propaganda in the Early Eighteenth Century: A Yorkshire Example', *York Historian*, 7 (1986), 40–5.

—— *The English Press in the Eighteenth Century* (1987).

—— 'Parliamentary Reporting in England in the Early Eighteenth Century: An Abortive Attempt to Influence the Magazines in 1744', *Parliaments, Estates, and Representations*, 7 (1987), 61–9.

—— 'George II and the Juries Act: Royal Concern about the Control of the Press', *Bulletin of the Institute of Historical Research*, 61 (1988), 359–62.

—— (ed.), *Knights Errant and True Englishmen: British Foreign Policy, 1600–1800* (Edinburgh, 1989).

—— (ed.), *British Politics and Society from Walpole to Pitt, 1742–1789* (1990).

—— *Culloden and the '45* (Stroud, 1990).

BREWER, JOHN, *Party Ideology and Popular Politics at the Accession of George III* (Cambridge, 1976).

—— 'Commercialisation and Politics', in Neil McKendrick, John Brewer, J. H. Plumb (eds.), *The Birth of a Consumer Society: The Commercialisation of Eighteenth-Century England* (1982), 197–262.

—— *The Sinews of Power: War, Money and the English State, 1688–1783* (1989).

BROWNING, R., *The Duke of Newcastle* (New Haven, Conn., 1975).

—— *Political and Constitutional Ideas of the Court Whigs* (Baton Rouge, La., 1982).

BUTLER, ROHAN, *Choiseul: Father and Son, 1719–1754* (Oxford, 1980).

CARSTEN, F. L., *Essays on German History* (1985).

CANNON, J., *The Whig Ascendancy: Colloquies on Hanoverian England* (1981).

CHAPMAN, P., 'Jacobite Political Argument, 1714–1766', Ph.D. thesis (Cambridge, 1983).

CLARK, J. C. D., *The Dynamics of Change: The Crisis of the 1750s and English Party Systems* (Cambridge, 1982).

—— 'The Politics of the Excluded: Tories, Jacobites and Whig Patriots, 1715–1760', *Parliamentary History*, 2 (1983), 209–22.

—— *English Society, 1688–1832: Ideology, Social Structure and Political Practice during the Ancien Regime* (Cambridge, 1985).

COLLEY, L., 'Eighteenth-Century Radicalism before Wilkes', *Transactions of the Royal Historical Society*, 5th ser., 31 (1981), 1–19.

—— *In Defiance of Oligarchy: The Tory Party, 1714–60* (Cambridge, 1982).

—— 'Radical Patriotism in Eighteenth-Century England', in Raphael Samuel (ed.), *Patriotism: The Making and Unmaking of British National Identity* (1989), i. 168–88.

CRUICKSHANKS, E., *Political Untouchables: The Tories and the '45* (1979).

CUNNINGHAM, H., 'The Language of Patriotism, 1750–1914', *History Workshop*, 12 (1981), 8–33.

DANN, URIEL, *Hanover and Great Britain, 1740–60: Diplomacy and Survival* (Leicester, 1991).

DICKINSON, H. T., *Liberty and Property: Political Ideology in Eighteenth-Century Britain*, 2nd edn. (1979).

—— 'Popular Politics in the Age of Walpole', in J. Black (ed.), *Britain in the Age of Walpole* (1984), 45–68.

DICKSON, P. G. M., *The Financial Revolution in England: A Study in the Development of Public Credit, 1688–1756* (1967).

DOOLITTLE, I., 'A First-Hand Account of the Commons Debate on the Removal of Sir Robert Walpole, 13 Feb. 1741', *Bulletin of the Institute of Historical Research*, 53 (1980), 125–40.

DOWNIE, J. A., 'The Growth of Government Tolerance of the Press to 1790', in R. Myers and M. Harris (eds.), *Development of the English Book Trade, 1700–1899* (Oxford, 1981), 36–65.

FEATHER, J. P., 'From Censorship to Copyright: Aspects of the Government's Role in the English Book Trade, 1695–1775', in R. E. Carpenter (ed.), *Books and Society in History* (New York, 1983), 173–98.

FOORD, A., *His Majesty's Opposition, 1714–1830* (Oxford, 1964).

FRASER, E. J. S., 'The Pitt–Newcastle Ministry and the Conduct of the Seven Years War, 1757–1760', D.Phil. thesis (Oxford, 1976).

GIBBS, G. C., 'English Attitudes towards Hanover and the Hanoverian Succession in the First Half of the Eighteenth Century', in A. M. Birke and Kurt Kluxen (eds.), *England and Hanover* (Munich, 1986), 33–50.

GOLDSMITH, M. M., 'Faction Detected: Ideological Consequences of Robert Walpole's Decline and Fall', *History*, 64 (1979), 1–19.

GREEN, T. A., *Verdict According to Conscience: Perspectives on the English Criminal Trial Jury, 1200–1800* (Chicago, 1985).

GULICK, SIDNEY L., jun., 'A Chesterfield Bibliography to 1800', *Papers of the Bibliographical Society of America*, 39 (1985), 228–34.

GUNN, J. A. W., *Beyond Liberty and Property: The Process of Self-Recognition in Eighteenth-Century Political Thought* (Kingston and Montreal, 1983).

HAIG, R. L., *The Gazetteer, 1735–1797: A Study in the Eighteenth-Century English Newspaper* (Carbondale, Ill., 1960).

HANSON, L., *The Government and the Press, 1695–1763* (Oxford, 1967).

HARDING, R., 'Sir Robert Walpole's Ministry and the Conduct of the War with Spain, 1739–41', *Bulletin of the Institute of Historical Research*, 60 (1987), 299–320.

—— 'Sailors and Gentlemen of Parade: Some Professional and Technical Problems concerning the Conduct of Combined Operations in the Eighteenth Century', *Historical Journal*, 32 (1989), 35–55.

HARRIS, M., 'London Printers and Newspaper Production during the First

Half of the Eighteenth Century', *Journal of Printing Historical Society*, 12 (1977/8), 33–51.

HARRIS, M., *London Newspapers in the Age of Walpole: A Study in the Origins of the Modern English Press* (1987).

—— and LEE, A. (eds.), *The Press in English Society from the Seventeenth to the Nineteenth Centuries* (1986).

HAYDON, C. M., 'Anti-Catholicism in Eighteenth-Century England *c*.1714–*c*.1780', D.Phil. thesis (Oxford, 1985).

HOOVER, B. J., *Samuel Johnson's Parliamentary Reporting: Debates in the Senate of Lilliput* (Berkeley and Los Angeles, 1953).

JENKINS, P., *The Making of the Ruling Class: the Glamorgan Gentry, 1640–1790* (Cambridge, 1983).

—— 'Tory Industrialism and Town Politics: Swansea in the Eighteenth Century', *Historical Journal*, 28 (1985), 103–23.

JONES, CLYVE (ed.), *Party and Management in Parliament, 1660–1784* (New York, 1984).

—— *Britain in the First Age of Party, 1680–1750: Essays Presented to Geoffrey Holmes* (1987).

JORDAN, GERALD, and ROGERS, NICHOLAS, 'Admirals as Heroes: Patriotism and Liberty in Hanoverian England', *Journal of British Studies*, 28 (1989), 201–24.

LANGFORD, P., *The Excise Crisis: Society and Politics in the Age of Walpole* (Oxford, 1975).

—— *The Eighteenth Century, 1688–1815* (1976).

—— 'Tories and Jacobites, 1714–51', in L. S. Sutherland and L. G. Mitchell (eds.), *The History of the University of Oxford: The Eighteenth Century* (1986), 97–127.

—— *Walpole and the Robinocracy* (Cambridge, 1986).

—— *A Polite and Commercial People: England, 1727–1783* (Oxford, 1989).

LAWSON, PHILIP, *George Grenville: A Political Life* (Oxford, 1984).

LENNART, CARLSON C., *The First Magazine: A History of the 'Gentleman's Magazine'* (Providence, RI, 1938).

LODGE, R., 'The Hanau Controversy in 1744 and the Fall of Carteret', *English Historical Review*, 38 (1923), 509–31.

—— *Studies in Eighteenth-Century Diplomacy, 1740–1748* (1930).

LUFF, P. A., 'Henry Fox, the Duke of Cumberland, and Pelhamite Politics, 1748–1757', D.Phil. thesis (Oxford, 1981).

—— 'Matthews versus Lestock: Parliament, Politics, and the Navy in Mid-Eighteenth Century England' (unpublished paper).

MCLYNN, F. J., *France and the Jacobite Rising of 1745* (Edinburgh, 1981).

—— *The Jacobite Army in England: The Final Campaign* (Edinburgh, 1983).

MCNEILL, J. R., *Atlantic Empires of France and Spain: Louisbourg and Havanna, 1700–1763* (Chapel Hill, NC, 1985).

MASSIE, A. W., 'Great Britain and the Defence of the Low Countries, 1744–48', D.Phil. thesis (Oxford, 1987).

MIDDLETON, R., *The Bells of Victory: The Pitt–Newcastle Ministry and the Conduct of the Seven Years War, 1757–1762* (Cambridge, 1985).

MINCHINTON, W. E., *The Growth of English Overseas Trade in the Seventeenth and Eighteenth Centuries* (1969).

MONOD, P., *Jacobitism and the English People, 1688–1788* (Cambridge, 1989).

NEWMAN, A. (ed.), *Lucy Sutherland: Politics and Finance in the Eighteenth Century* (1984).

OWEN, J. B., *The Rise of the Pelhams* (1957).

PARES, R., 'American versus Continental Warfare, 1739–1763', *English Historical Review*, 51 (1936), 429–65.

—— *War and Trade in the West Indies, 1739–1763* (Oxford, 1936).

PERRY, T. W., *Public Opinion, Propaganda and Politics in Eighteenth-Century England* (Cambridge, Mass., 1962).

PETERS, M., 'The "Monitor" on the Constitution, 1755–65: New Light on the Ideological Origins of English Radicalism', *English Historical Review*, 86 (1971), 706–25.

—— *Pitt and Popularity: The Patriot Minister and London Opinion during the Seven Years War* (Oxford, 1980).

—— ' "Names and Cant": Party Labels in English Political Propaganda *c.*1753–1763', *Parliamentary History*, 7 (1984), 103–27.

—— 'Historians and the Eighteenth-Century Press: A Review of Possibilities and Problems', *Australian Journal of Politics and History*, 24 (1988), 37–50.

RICHMOND, SIR HERBERT, *The Navy in the War of 1739–1748*, 3 vols. (Cambridge, 1920).

ROGERS, N., 'London Politics from Walpole to Pitt: Patriotism and Independency in an Era of Commercial Imperialism, 1738–63', Ph.D. thesis (Toronto, 1975).

—— 'Popular Disaffection in London during the Forty-Five', *London Journal*, 1 (1975), 5–27.

—— 'Resistance to Oligarchy: The City Opposition to Walpole and his Successors, 1725–47', in J. Stevenson (ed.), *London in the Age of Reform* (Oxford, 1977), 1–29.

—— *Whigs and Cities: Popular Politics in the Age of Walpole and Pitt* (Oxford, 1989).

SCHWEIZER, K., and BLACK, J. (eds.), *Politics and the Press in Hanoverian Britain* (Lewiston, NY, 1990).

SHELTON, G., *Dean Tucker: Eighteenth-Century Economic and Political Thought* (1981).

SHIPLEY, J. B., 'James Ralph: Pretender to Genius', Ph.D. thesis (Columbia, NY, 1963).

SPECK, W. A., *The Butcher: The Duke of Cumberland and the Suppression of the '45* (Oxford, 1981).

THOMAS, P. D. G., 'Party Politics in Eighteenth-Century Britain: Some Myths and a Touch of Reality', *British Journal for Eighteenth-Century Studies,* 10 (1987), 201–11.

TREADWELL, MICHAEL, 'London Trade Publishers, 1675–1750', *The Library,* 6th ser., 4 (1982), 91–134.

VAREY, S. R., 'Printers as Rivals: The "Craftsman", 1739–40', *The Library,* 6th ser., 2 (1980), 220–2.

—— (ed.), *Lord Bolingbroke: Contributions to the 'Craftsman'* (Oxford, 1982).

WHITWORTH, R., *Field Marshal Ligonier* (Oxford, 1981).

WILKES, J. W., *A Whig in Power: The Political Career of Henry Pelham* (Chicago, 1964).

WILLIAMS, B., *The Life of William Pitt, Earl of Chatham,* 2 vols. (1913).

—— *Carteret and Newcastle* (Cambridge, 1943).

WILSON, KATHLEEN, 'Empire, Trade and Popular Politics in Mid-Hanoverian Britain: The Case of Admiral Vernon', *Past and Present,* 121 (1988), 74–109.

—— 'Inventing Revolution: 1688 and Eighteenth-Century Popular Politics', *Journal of British Studies,* 28 (1989), 349–86.

WINKLER, K. T., 'The Forces of the Market and the London Newspaper in the First Half of the Eighteenth Century', *Journal of Newspaper and Periodical History,* 4 (1988), 22–35.

WOODFINE, PHILIP, 'Ideas of Naval Power and the Conflict with Spain, 1737–1742', in Jeremy Black and Philip Woodfine (eds.), *The British Navy and the Use of Naval Power in the Eighteenth Century* (Leicester, 1989), 71–90.

INDEX

Only those pamphlets named in the text have been indexed